Akira Segami

TRANSLATED BY
Satsuki Yamashita

ADAPTED BY
Nunzio DeFilippis & Christina Weir

LETTERED BY
North Market Street Graphics

BALLANTINE BOOKS · NEW YORK

Kagetora, volume 10 is a work of fiction. Names, characters, places, and incidents are the products of the author's imagination or are used fictitiously. Any resemblance to actual events, locales, or persons, living or dead, is entirely coincidental.

A Del Rey Manga/Kodansha Trade Paperback Original

Published in the United States by Del Rey Books, an imprint of The Random House Publishing Group, a division of Random House, Inc., New York.

Publication rights arranged through Kodansha Ltd.

First published in Japan in 2006 by Kodansha Ltd., Tokyo.

ISBN 978-0-345-49897-7

Printed in the United States of America

www.delreymanga.com

9 8 7 6 5 4 3 2 1

Translator—Satsuki Yamashita
Adapters—Nunzio DeFilippis and Christina Weir
Lettering and retouch—North Market Street Graphics

Contents

Featured in Magazine Special 2006 No. 2 – 2006 No. 7 except for No. 3

KAGETORA

A Note from the Author

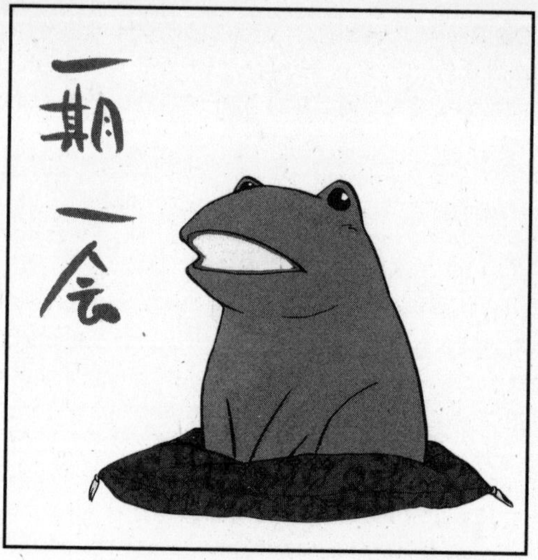
一期一会

**Treasure every encounter,
for it will never recur.**
They say that even a
chance meeting is due to karma
in a previous life.
I've met many people and
was able to come this far with
this manga.
Now there's only one volume left!
To all the readers who
helped me make it happen, thank
you and please stick with me
till the end!

Honorifics Explained

Throughout the Del Rey Manga books, you will find Japanese honorifics left intact in the translations. For those not familiar with how the Japanese use honorifics and, more important, how they differ from American honorifics, we present this brief overview.

Politeness has always been a critical facet of Japanese culture. Ever since the feudal era, when Japan was a highly stratified society, use of honorifics—which can be defined as polite speech that indicates relationship or status—has played an essential role in the Japanese language. When you address someone in Japanese, an honorific usually takes the form of a suffix attached to one's name (example: "Asuna-san"), is used as a title at the end of one's name, or appears in place of the name itself (example: "Negi-sensei," or simply "Sensei!").

Honorifics can be expressions of respect or endearment. In the context of manga and anime, honorifics give insight into the nature of the relationship between characters. Many English translations leave out these important honorifics, and therefore distort the feel of the original Japanese. Because Japanese honorifics contain nuances that English honorifics lack, it is our policy at Del Rey not to translate them. Here, instead, is a guide to some of the honorifics you may encounter in Del Rey Manga.

-san: This is the most common honorific and is equivalent to Mr., Miss, Ms., or Mrs. It is the all-purpose honorific and can be used in any situation where politeness is required.

-sama: This is one level higher than "-san," and is used to confer great respect.

-dono: This comes from the word "tono," which means "lord." It is an even higher level than "-sama" and confers utmost respect.

-kun: This suffix is used at the end of boys' names to express familiarity or endearment. It is also sometimes used by men among friends, or when addressing someone younger or of a lower station.

-chan: This is used to express endearment, mostly toward girls. It is also used for little boys, pets, and even among lovers. It gives a sense of childish cuteness.

Bozu: This is an informal way to refer to a boy, similar to the English terms "kid" and "squirt."

Sempai/
Senpai: This title suggests that the addressee is one's senior in a group or organization. It is most often used in a school setting, where underclassmen refer to their upperclassmen as "sempai." It can also be used in the workplace, such as when a newer employee addresses an employee who has seniority in the company.

Kohai: This is the opposite of "sempai" and is used toward underclassmen in school or newcomers in the workplace. It connotes that the addressee is of a lower station.

Sensei: Literally meaning "one who has come before," this title is used for teachers, doctors, or masters of any profession or art.

-[blank]: This is usually forgotten in these lists, but it is perhaps the most significant difference between Japanese and English. The lack of honorific means that the speaker has permission to address the person in a very intimate way. Usually, only family, spouses, or very close friends have this kind of permission. Known as *yobisute,* it can be gratifying when someone who has earned the intimacy starts to call one by one's name without an honorific. But when that intimacy hasn't been earned, it can be very insulting.

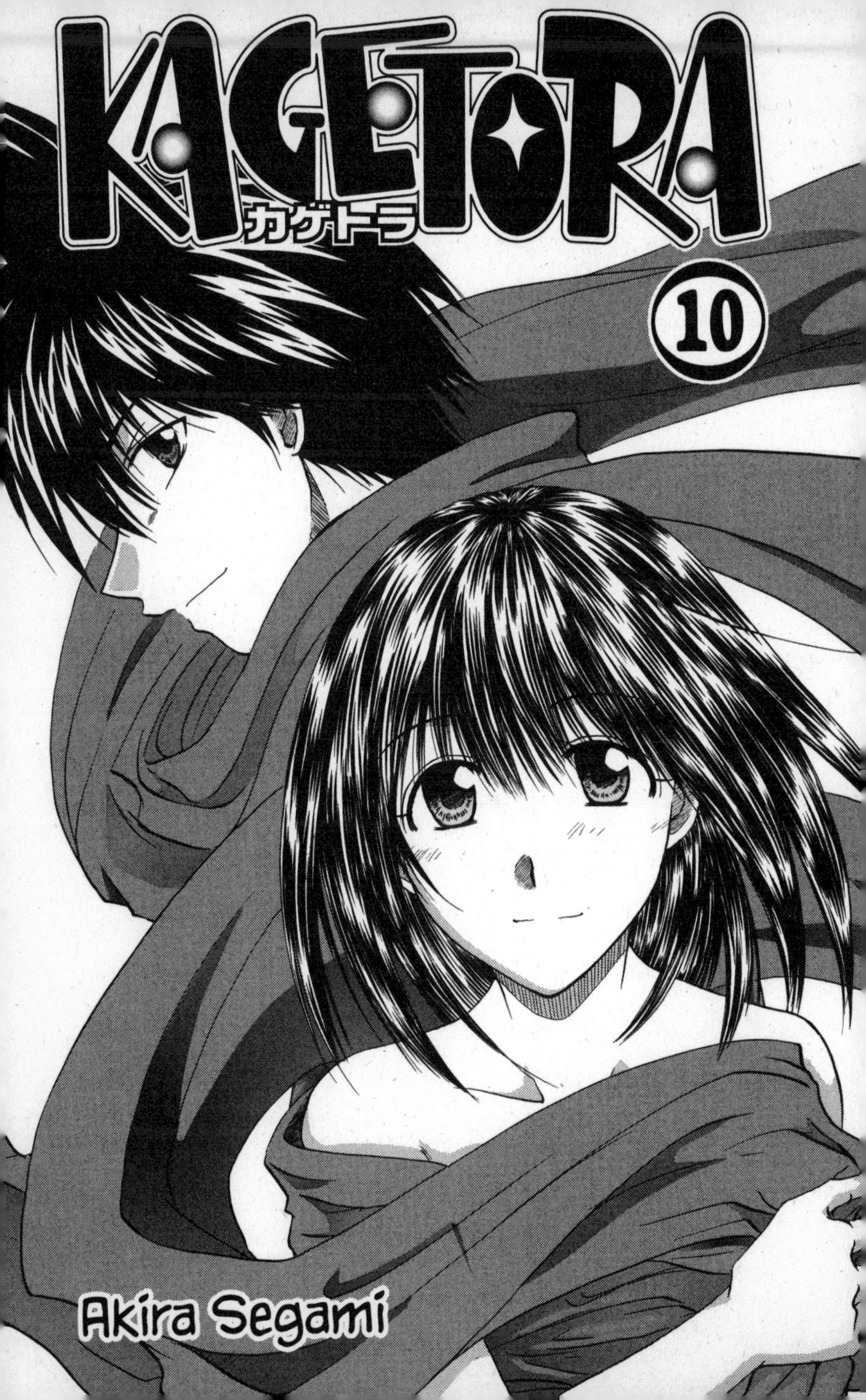
KAGETORA
カゲトラ
10
Akira Segami

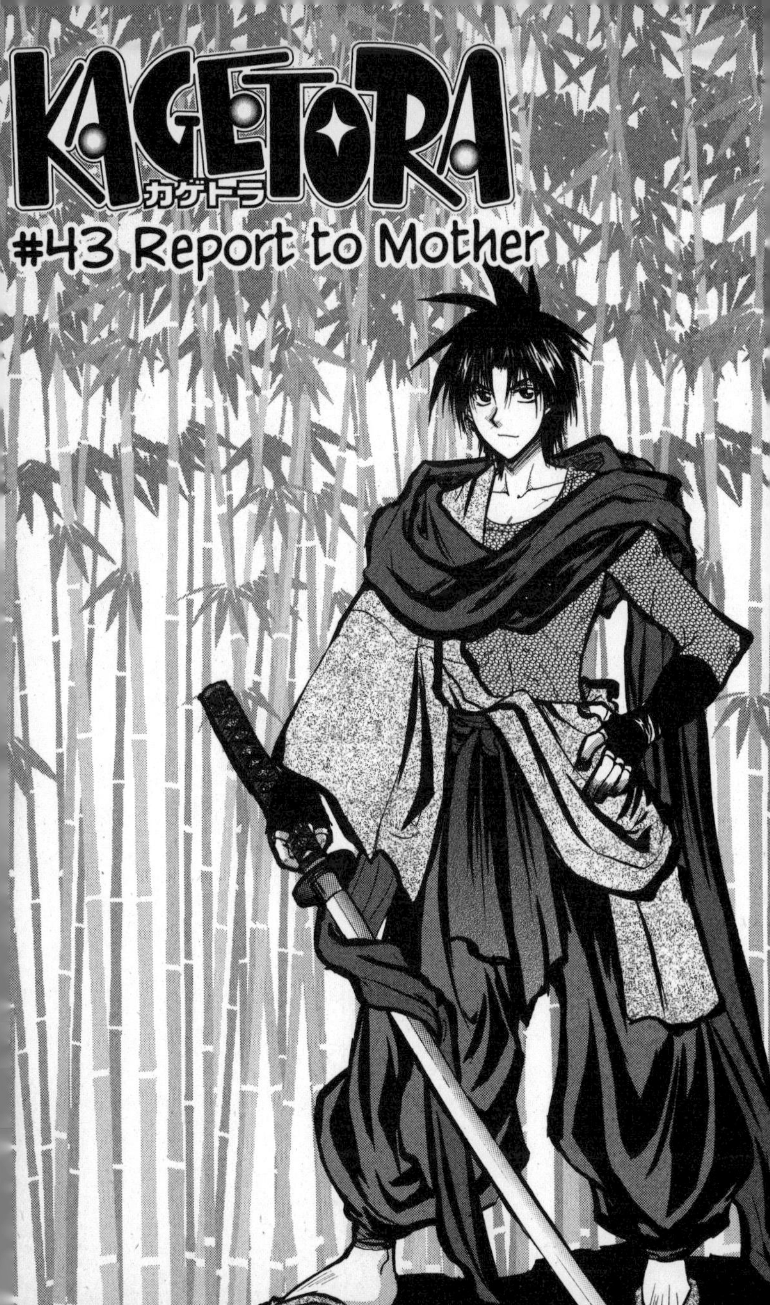
KAGETORA
カゲトラ
#43 Report to Mother

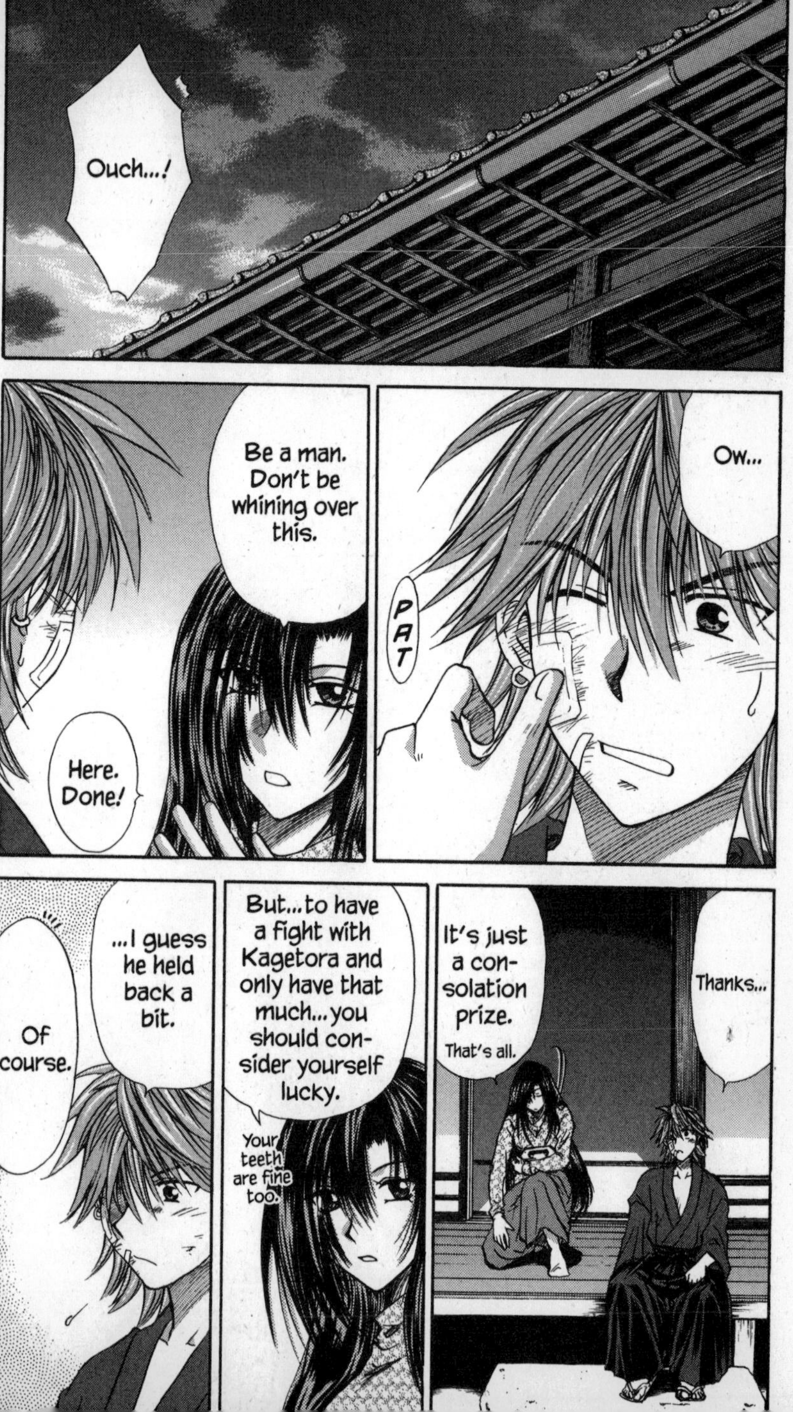
Ouch...!
Ow...
PAT
Be a man. Don't be whining over this.
Here. Done!
Thanks...
It's just a con-solation prize.
That's all.
But...to have a fight with Kagetora and only have that much...you should con-sider yourself lucky.
Your teeth are fine too.
...I guess he held back a bit.
Of course.

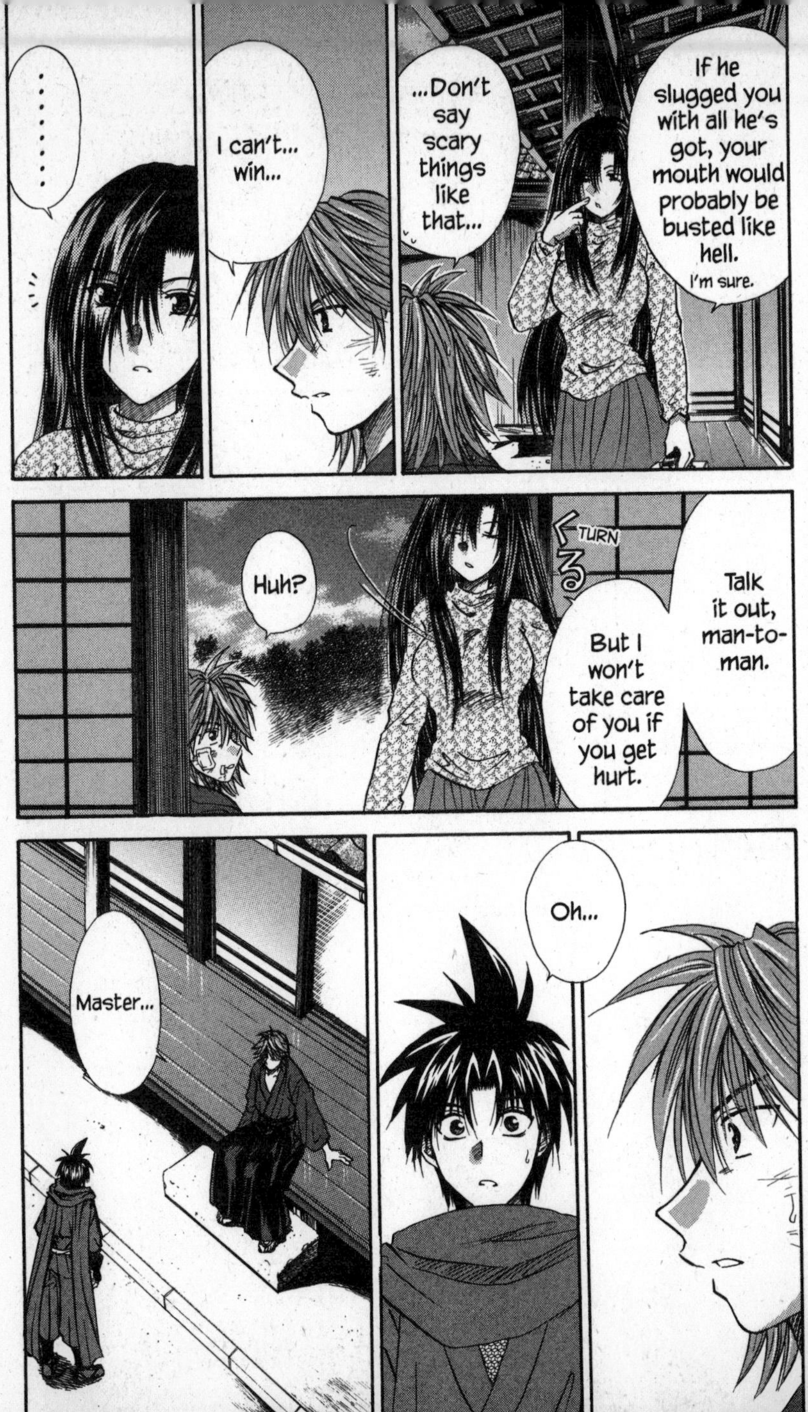
If he slugged you with all he's got, your mouth would probably be busted like hell.
I'm sure.
...Don't say scary things like that...
I can't... win...
......
TURN
Talk it out, man-to-man.
But I won't take care of you if you get hurt.
Huh?
Oh...
Master...

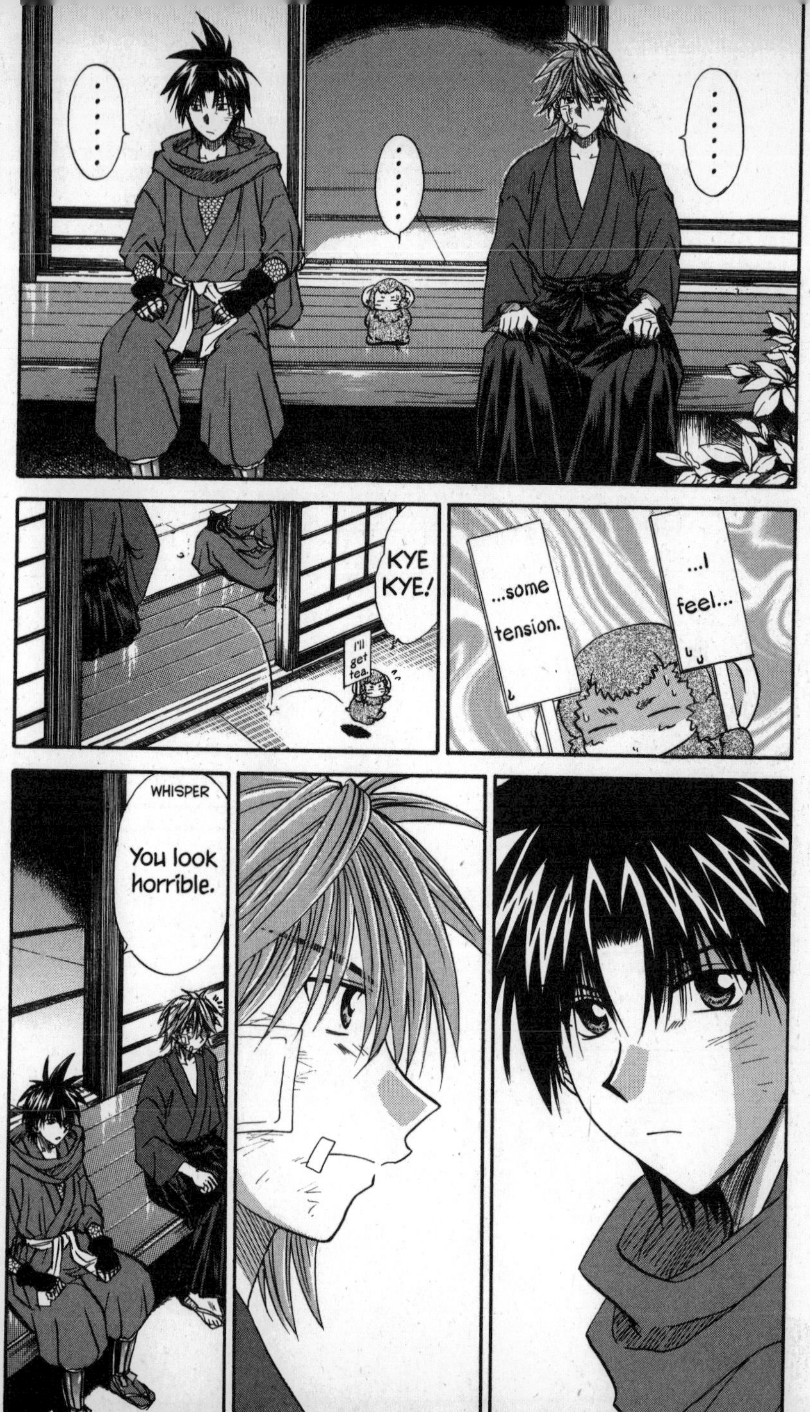
......
......
......
...I feel...
...some tension.
KYE KYE!
I'll get tea.
WHISPER
You look horrible.

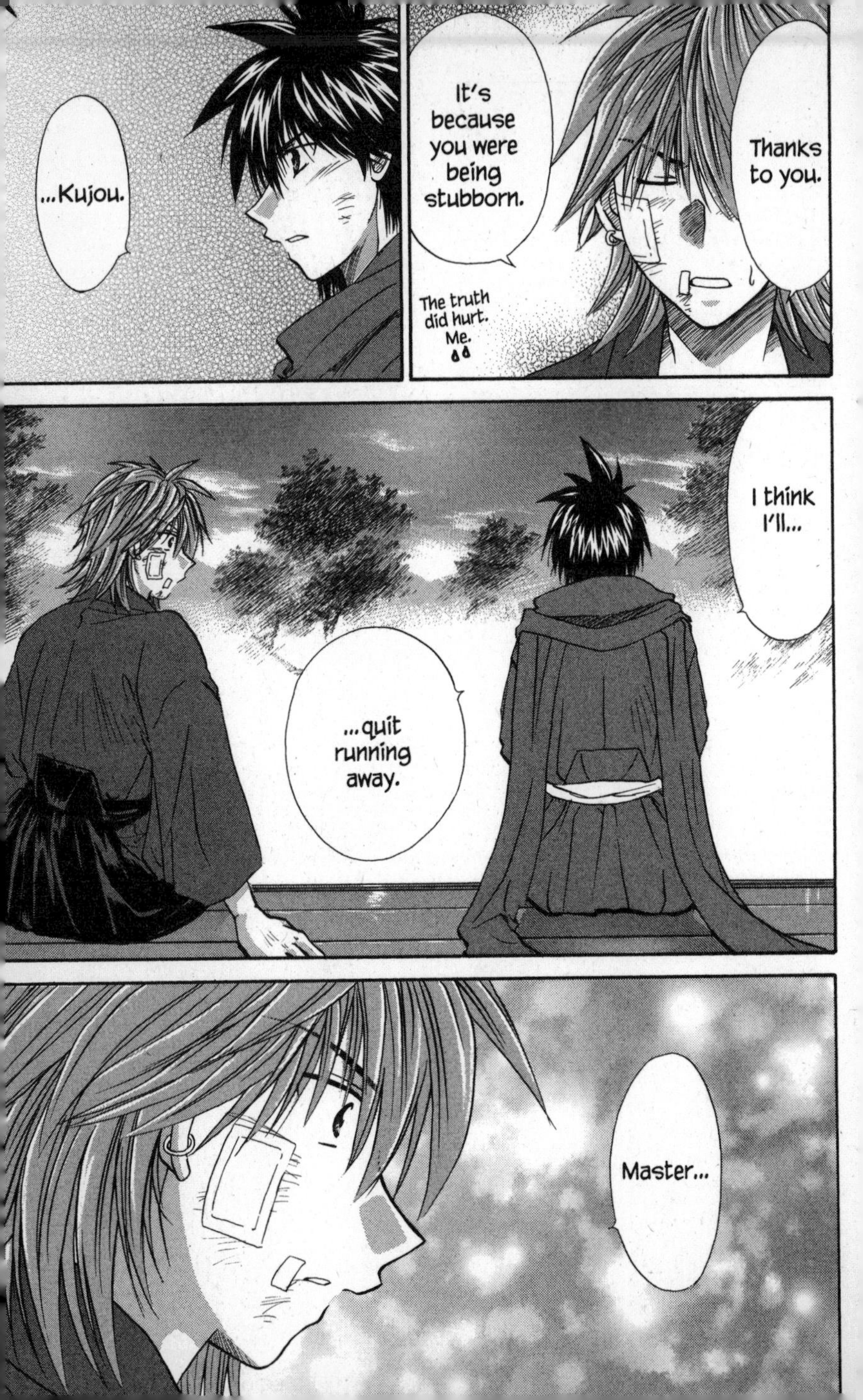
Thanks to you.
It's because you were being stubborn.
The truth did hurt. Me.
...Kujou.
I think I'll...
...quit running away.
Master...

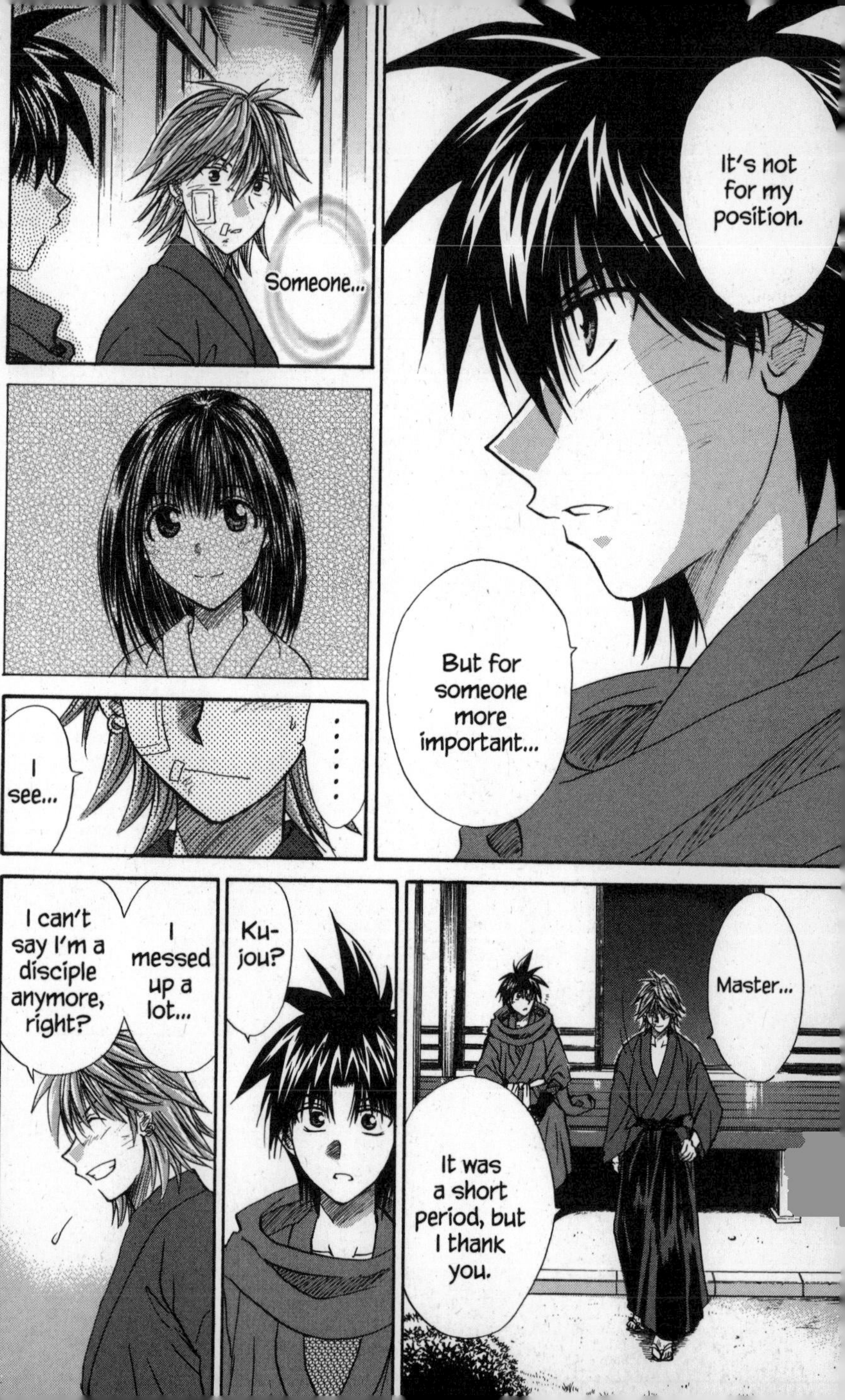

It's not for my position.
But for someone more important...
Someone...
......
I see...
Master...
It was a short period, but I thank you.
Ku-jou?
I messed up a lot...
I can't say I'm a disciple anymore, right?

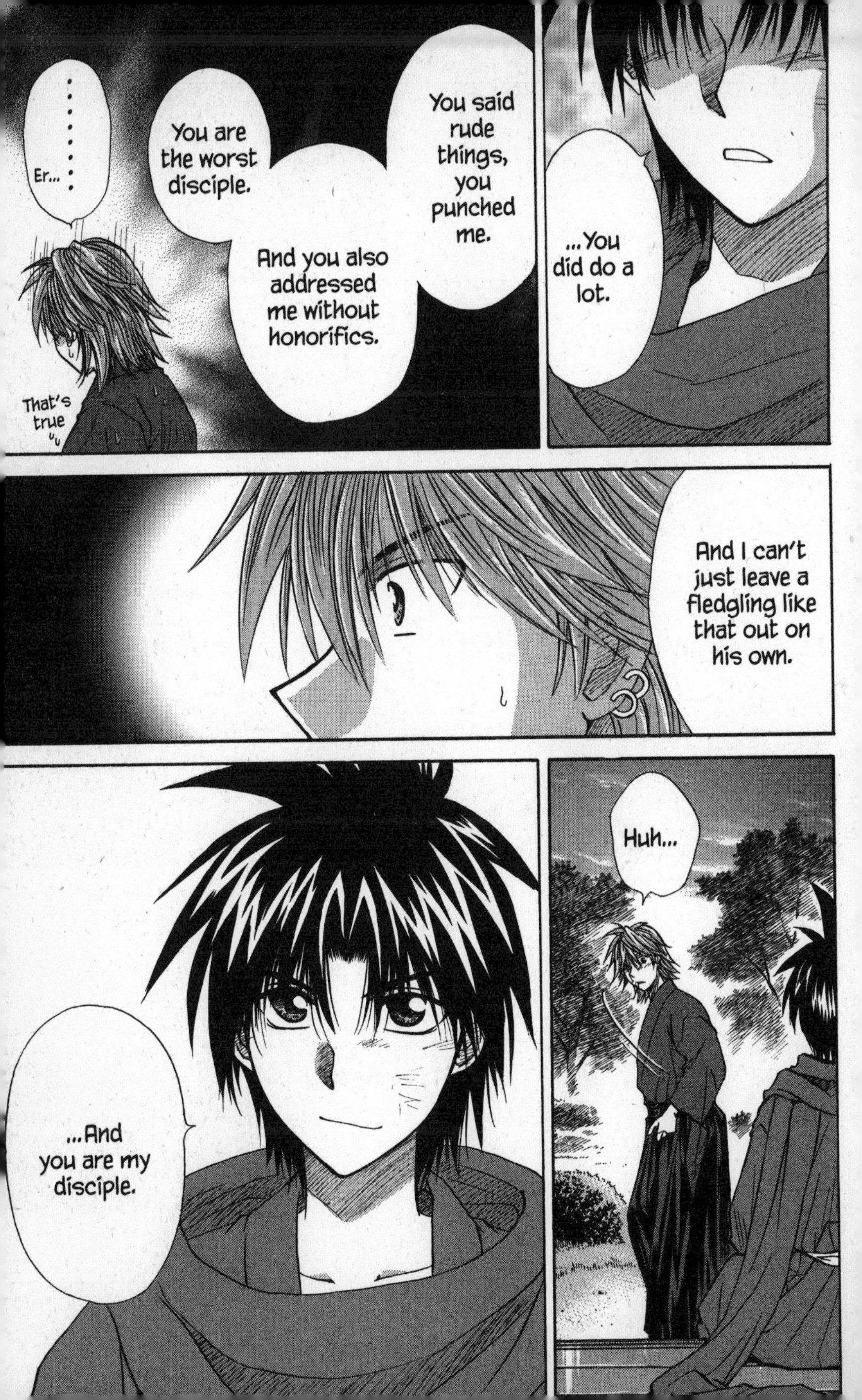
...You did do a lot.
You said rude things, you punched me.
And you also addressed me without honorifics.
You are the worst disciple.
Er......
That's true
And I can't just leave a fledgling like that out on his own.
Huh...
...And you are my disciple.

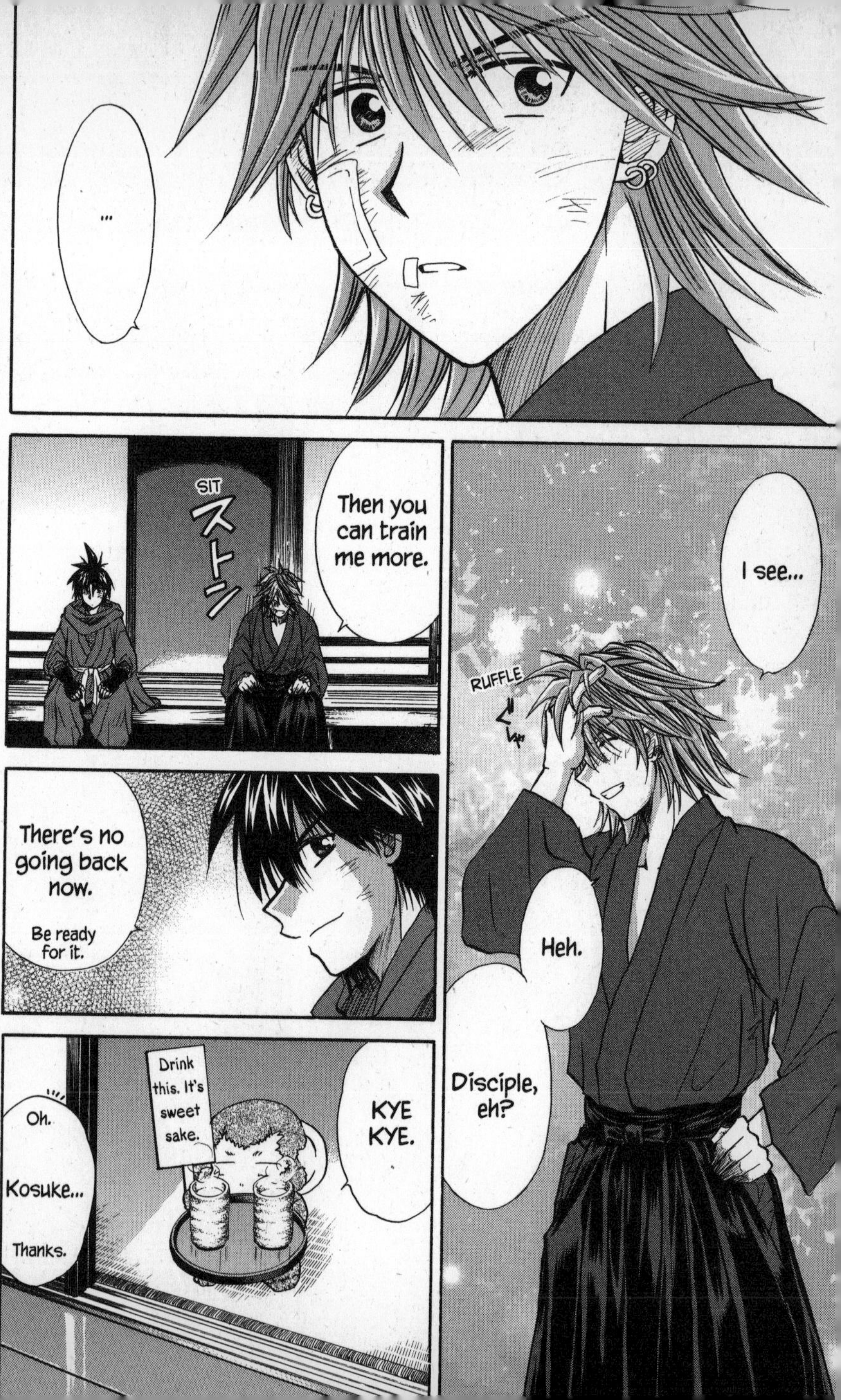
...
I see...
RUFFLE
Heh.
Disciple, eh?
Then you can train me more.
SIT
ストン
There's no going back now.
Be ready for it.
KYE KYE.
Drink this. It's sweet sake.
Oh.
Kosuke...
Thanks.

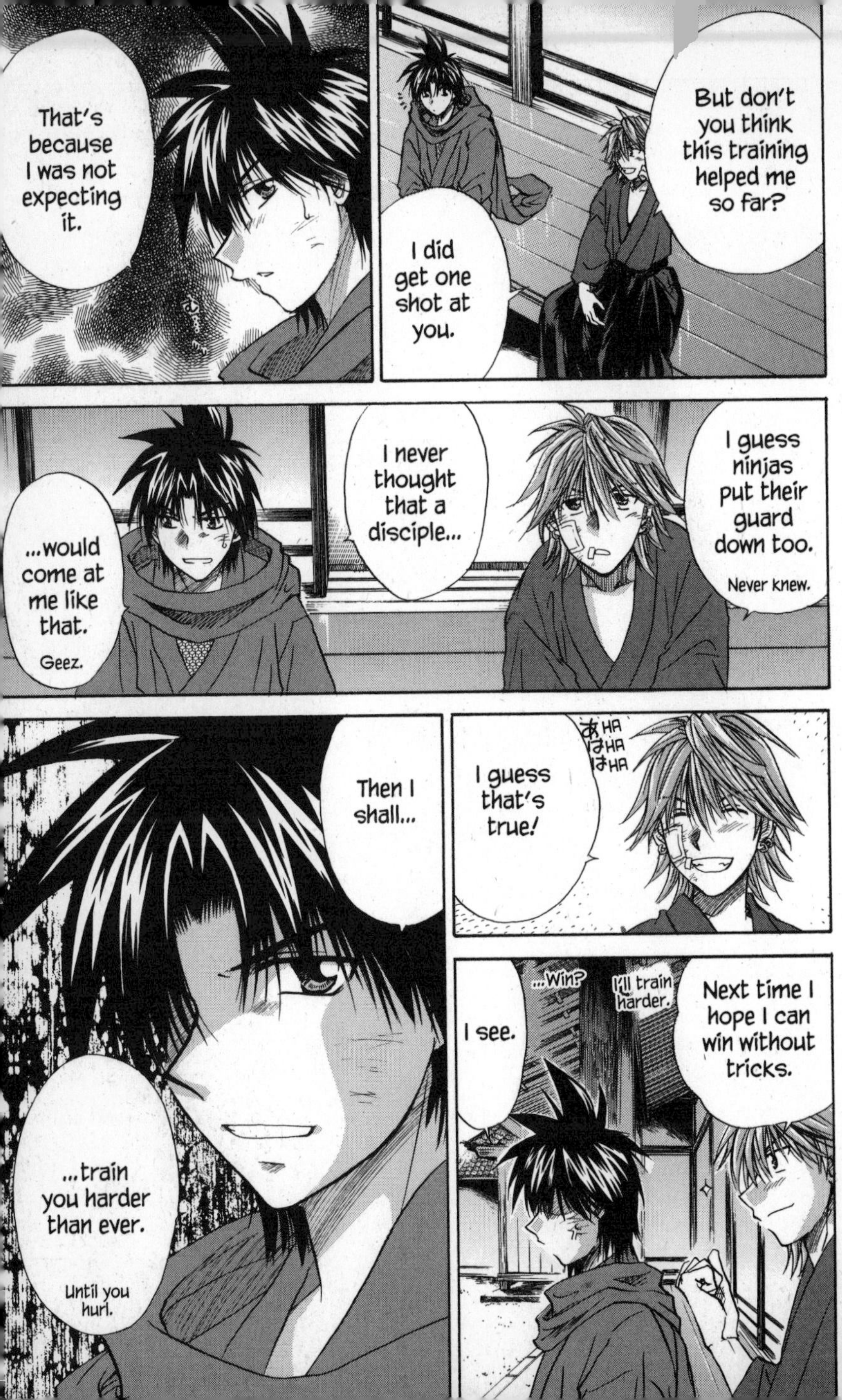
But don't you think this training helped me so far?
I did get one shot at you.
That's because I was not expecting it.
I guess ninjas put their guard down too.
Never knew.
I never thought that a disciple...
...would come at me like that.
Geez.
あはは
HA HA HA
I guess that's true!
Next time I hope I can win without tricks.
I'll train harder.
...Win?
I see.
Then I shall...
...train you harder than ever.
Until you hurl.

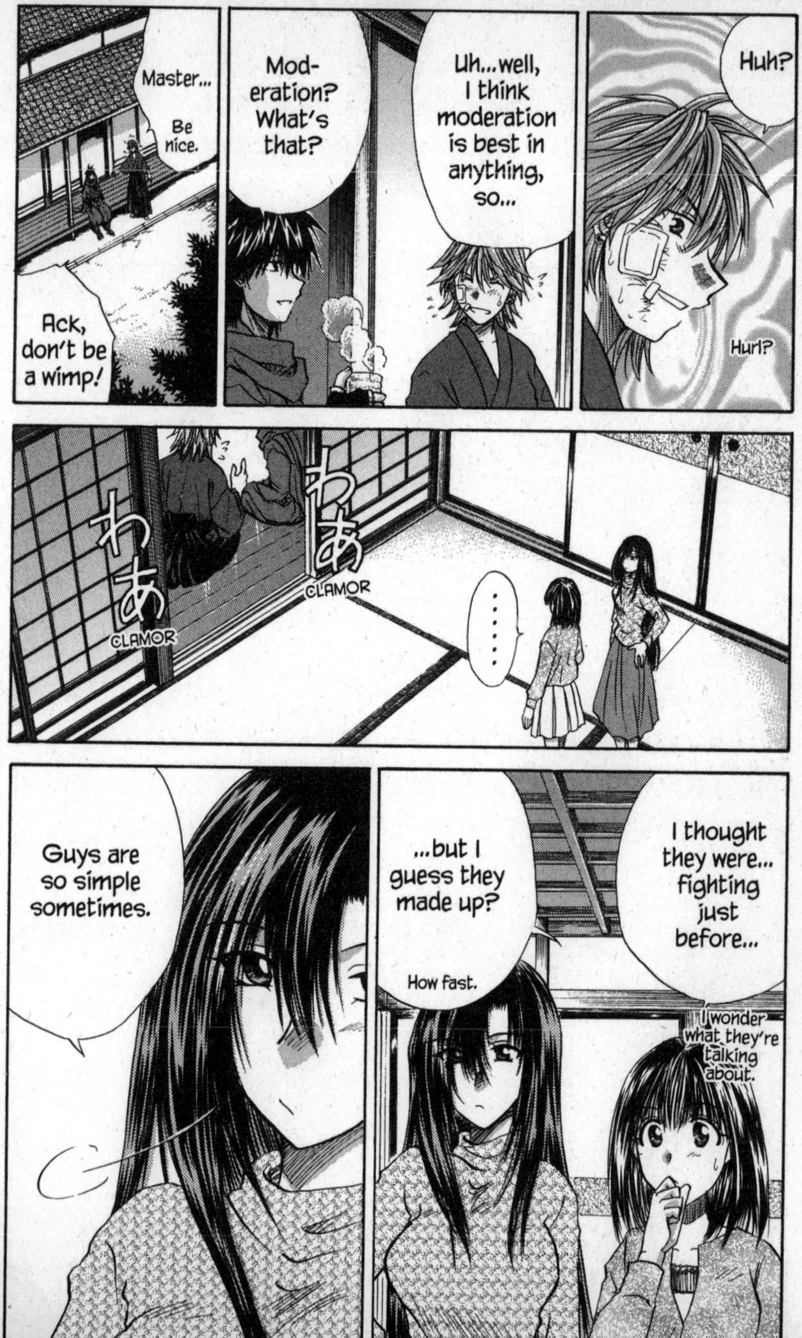
Huh?
Hurl?
Uh...well, I think moderation is best in anything, so...
Mod-eration? What's that?
Master...
Be nice.
Ack, don't be a wimp!
わあ
CLAMOR
わあ
CLAMOR
......
I thought they were... fighting just before...
...but I guess they made up?
How fast.
I wonder what they're talking about.
Guys are so simple sometimes.

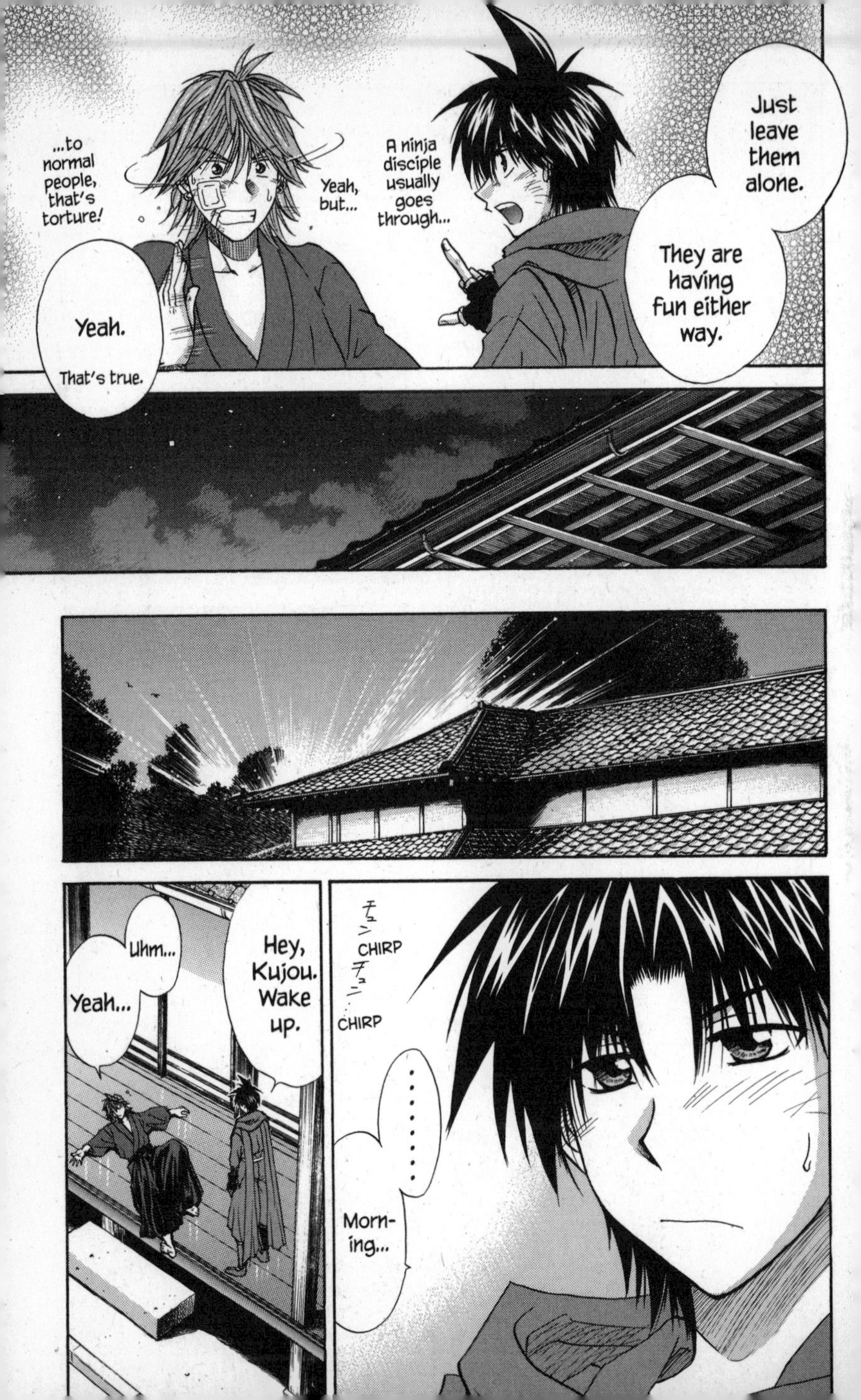
Just leave them alone.
They are having fun either way.
A ninja disciple usually goes through...
Yeah, but...
...to normal people, that's torture!
Yeah.
That's true.
チュン
CHIRP
チュン
CHIRP
......
Morn-ing...
Hey, Kujou. Wake up.
Uhm...
Yeah...

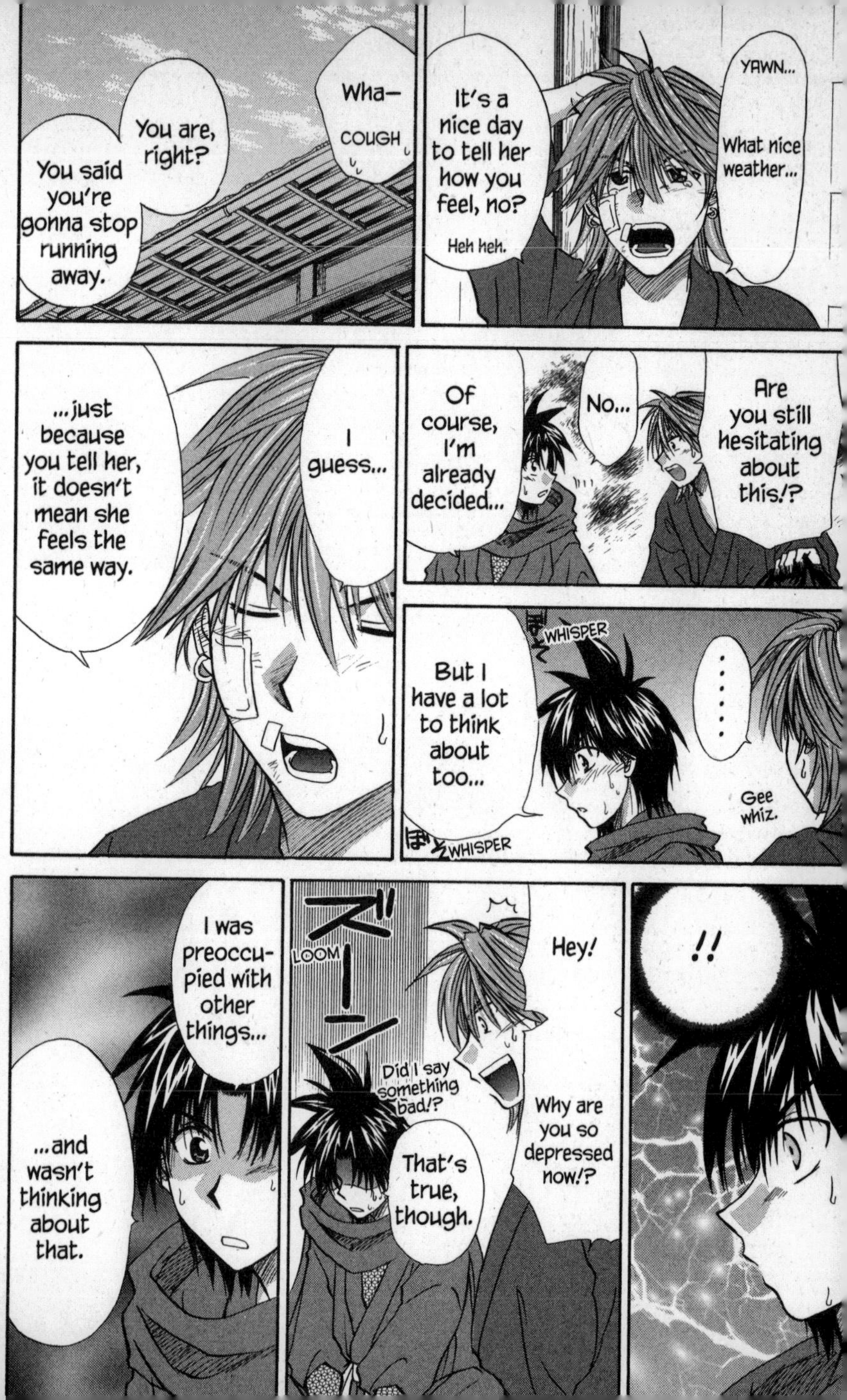

YAWN...
What nice weather...
It's a nice day to tell her how you feel, no?
Heh heh.
Wha—
COUGH
You are, right?
You said you're gonna stop running away.
Are you still hesitating about this!?
No...
Of course, I'm already decided...
WHISPER
......
Gee whiz.
But I have a lot to think about too...
WHISPER
I guess...
...just because you tell her, it doesn't mean she feels the same way.
!!
Hey!
Why are you so depressed now!?
Did I say something bad!?
LOOM
That's true, though.
I was preoccupied with other things...
...and wasn't thinking about that.

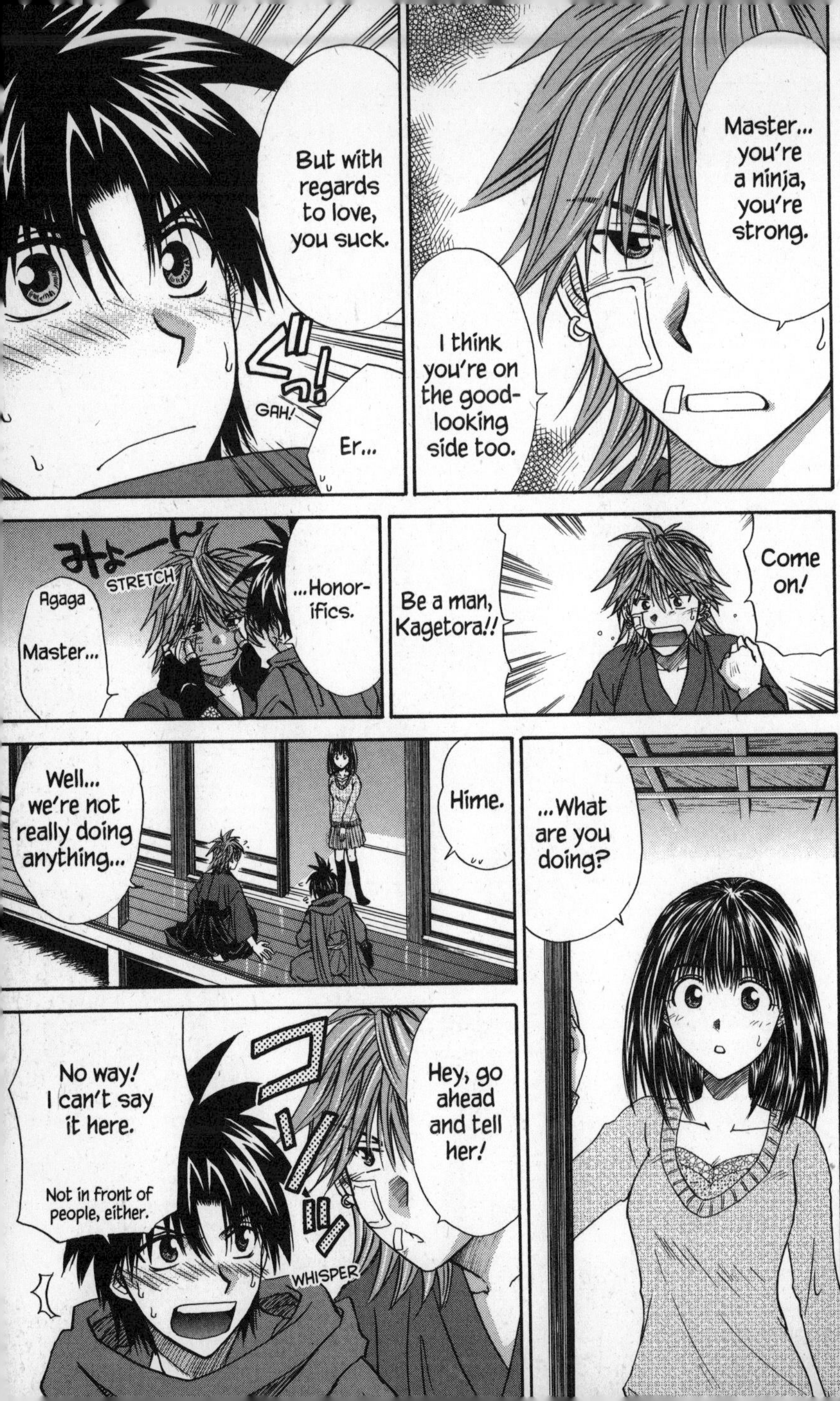
Master... you're a ninja, you're strong.
I think you're on the good-looking side too.
But with regards to love, you suck.
GAH!
Er...
Come on!
Be a man, Kagetora!!
...Honorifics.
STRETCH
Agaga
Master...
...What are you doing?
Hime.
Well... we're not really doing anything...
Hey, go ahead and tell her!
WHISPER
No way! I can't say it here.
Not in front of people, either.

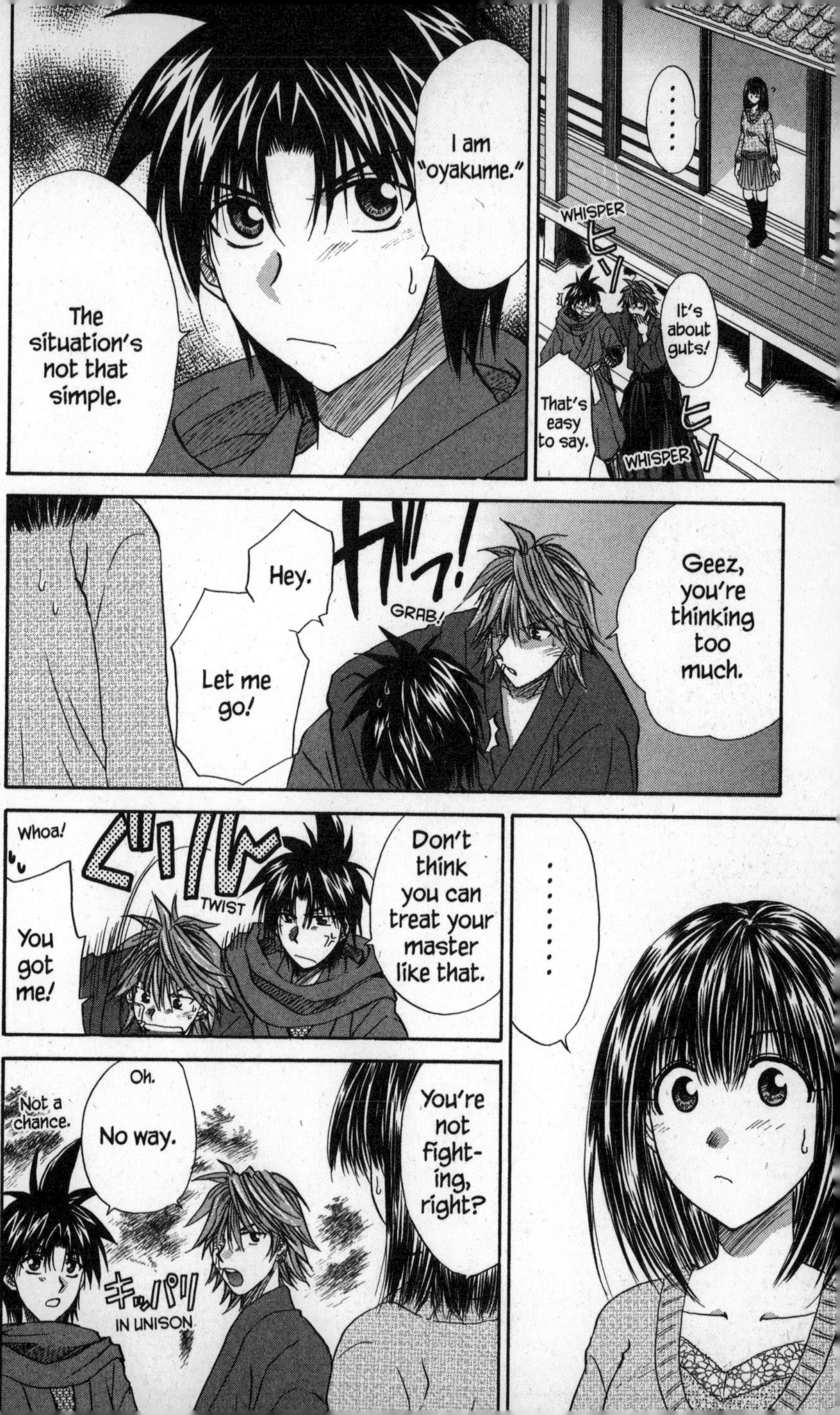
......
WHISPER
It's about guts!
That's easy to say.
WHISPER
I am "oyakume."
The situation's not that simple.
Geez, you're thinking too much.
GRAB!
Hey.
Let me go!
......
Don't think you can treat your master like that.
TWIST
Whoa!
You got me!
You're not fighting, right?
Oh.
No way.
Not a chance.
IN UNISON

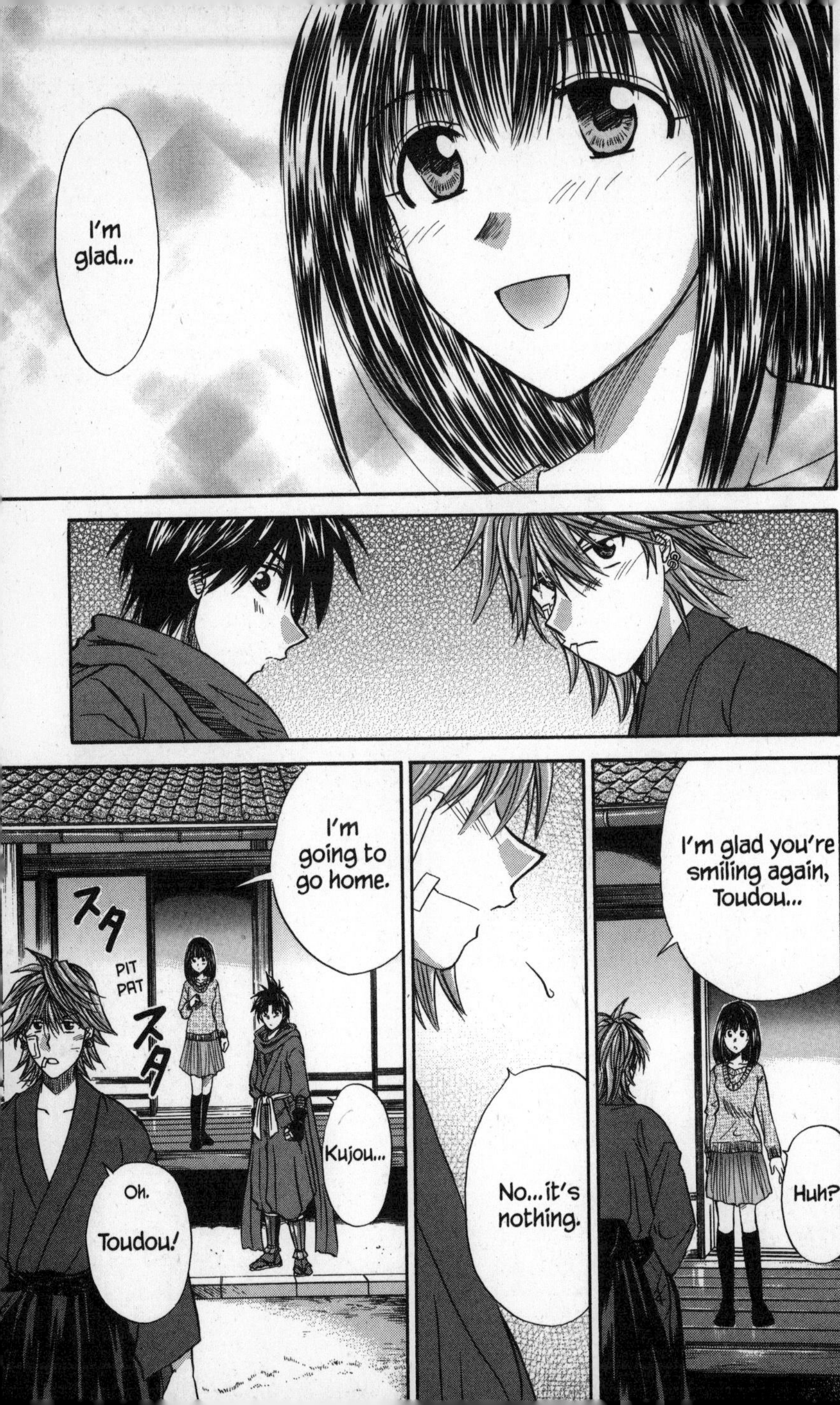
I'm glad...
I'm glad you're smiling again, Toudou...
Huh?
No...it's nothing.
I'm going to go home.
スタ
PIT PAT
スタ
Kujou...
Oh.
Toudou!

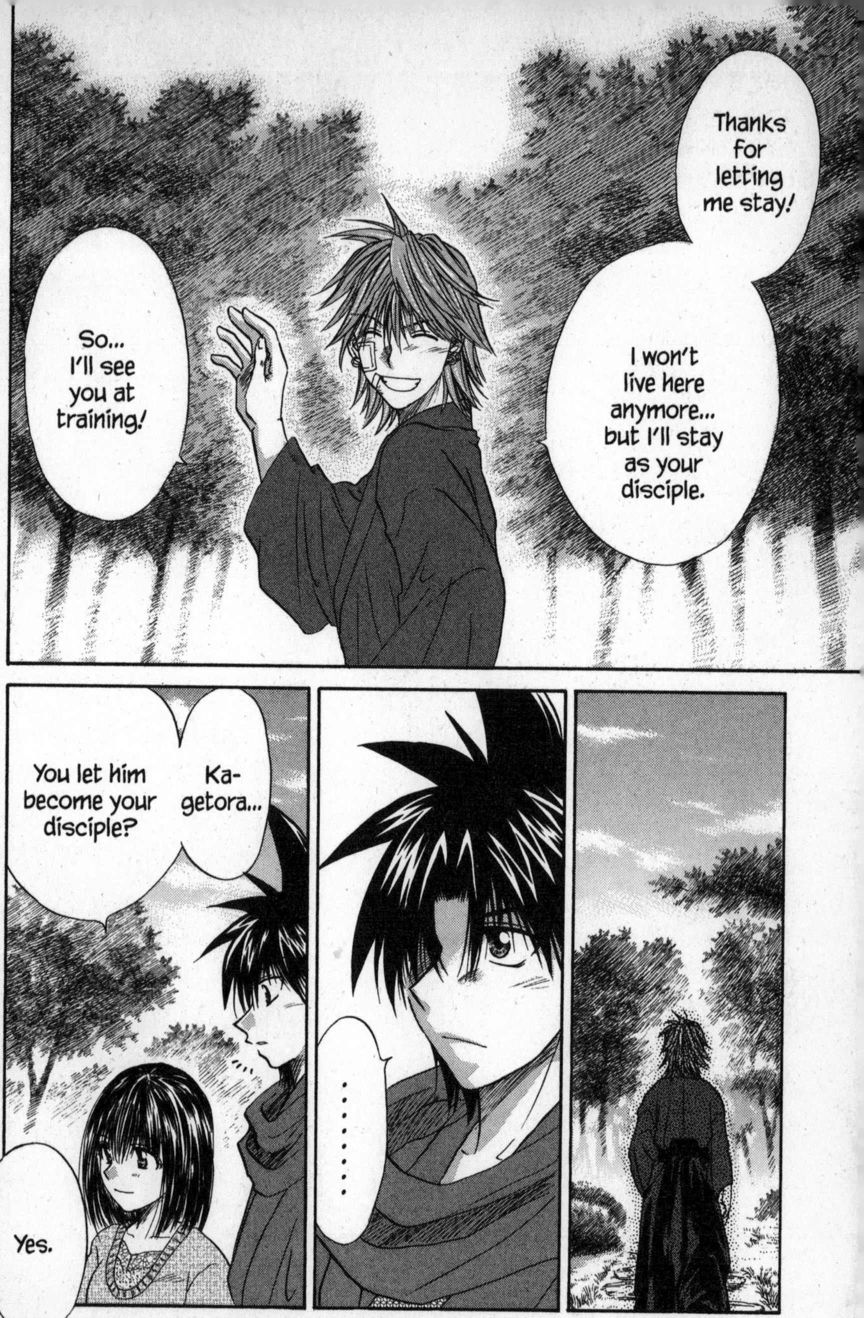

Thanks for letting me stay!
I won't live here anymore... but I'll stay as your disciple.
So... I'll see you at training!
......
Ka-getora...
You let him become your disciple?
...
Yes.

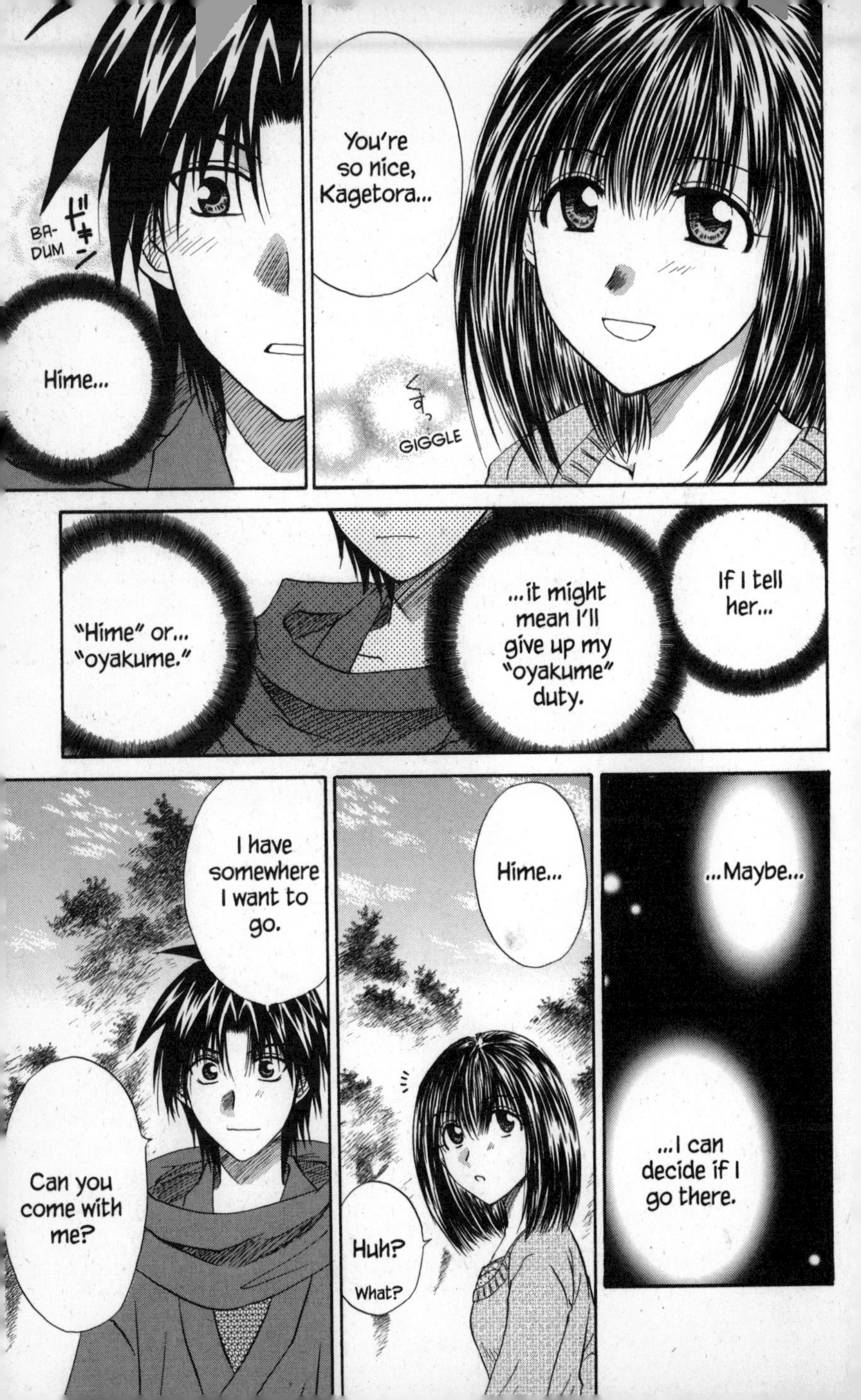
You're so nice, Kagetora...
くすっ
GIGGLE
ドキン
BA-DUM
Hime...
If I tell her...
...it might mean I'll give up my "oyakume" duty.
"Hime" or... "oyakume."
...Maybe...
...I can decide if I go there.
Hime...
Huh?
What?
I have somewhere I want to go.
Can you come with me?

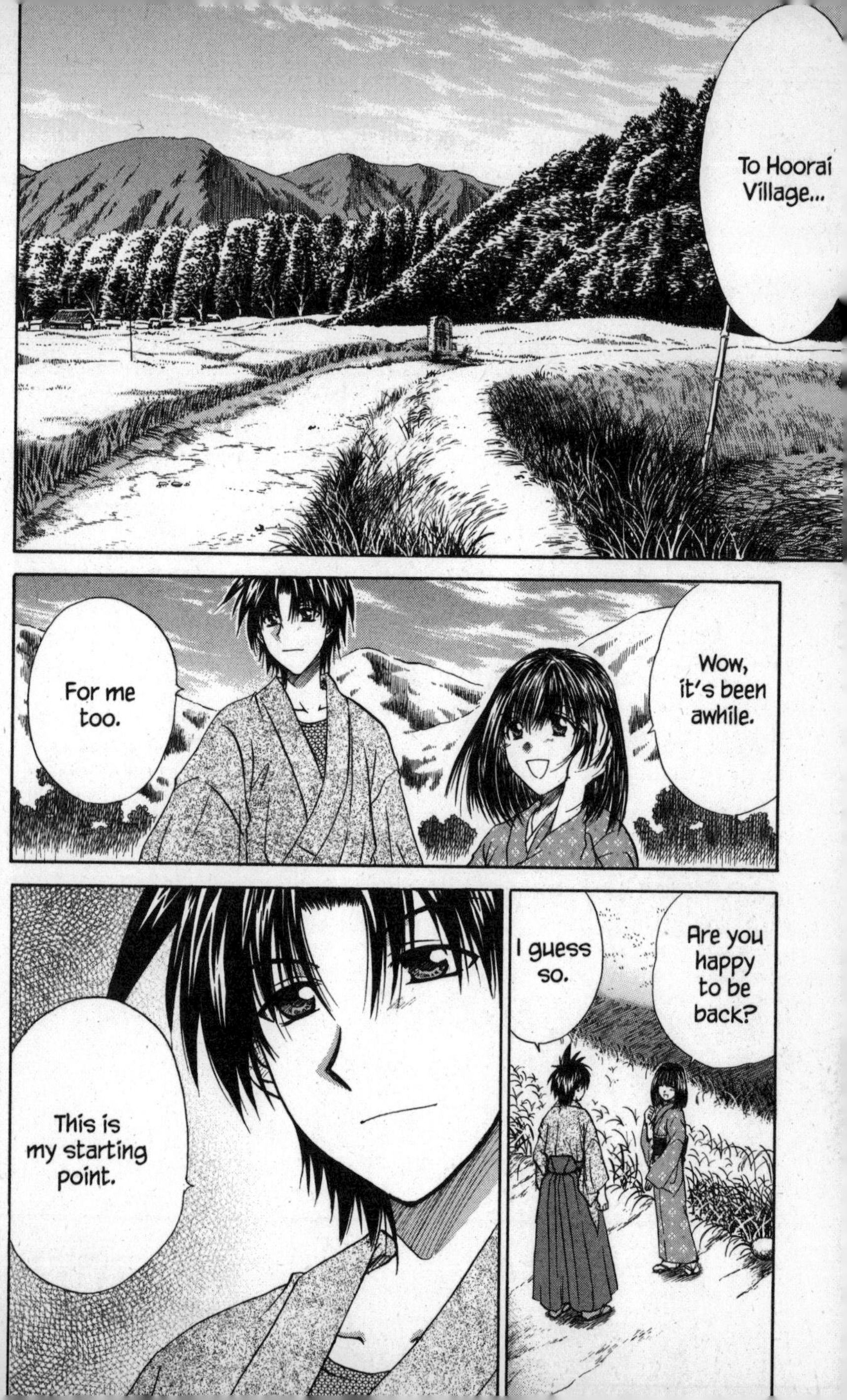
To Hoorai Village...
Wow, it's been awhile.
For me too.
Are you happy to be back?
I guess so.
This is my starting point.

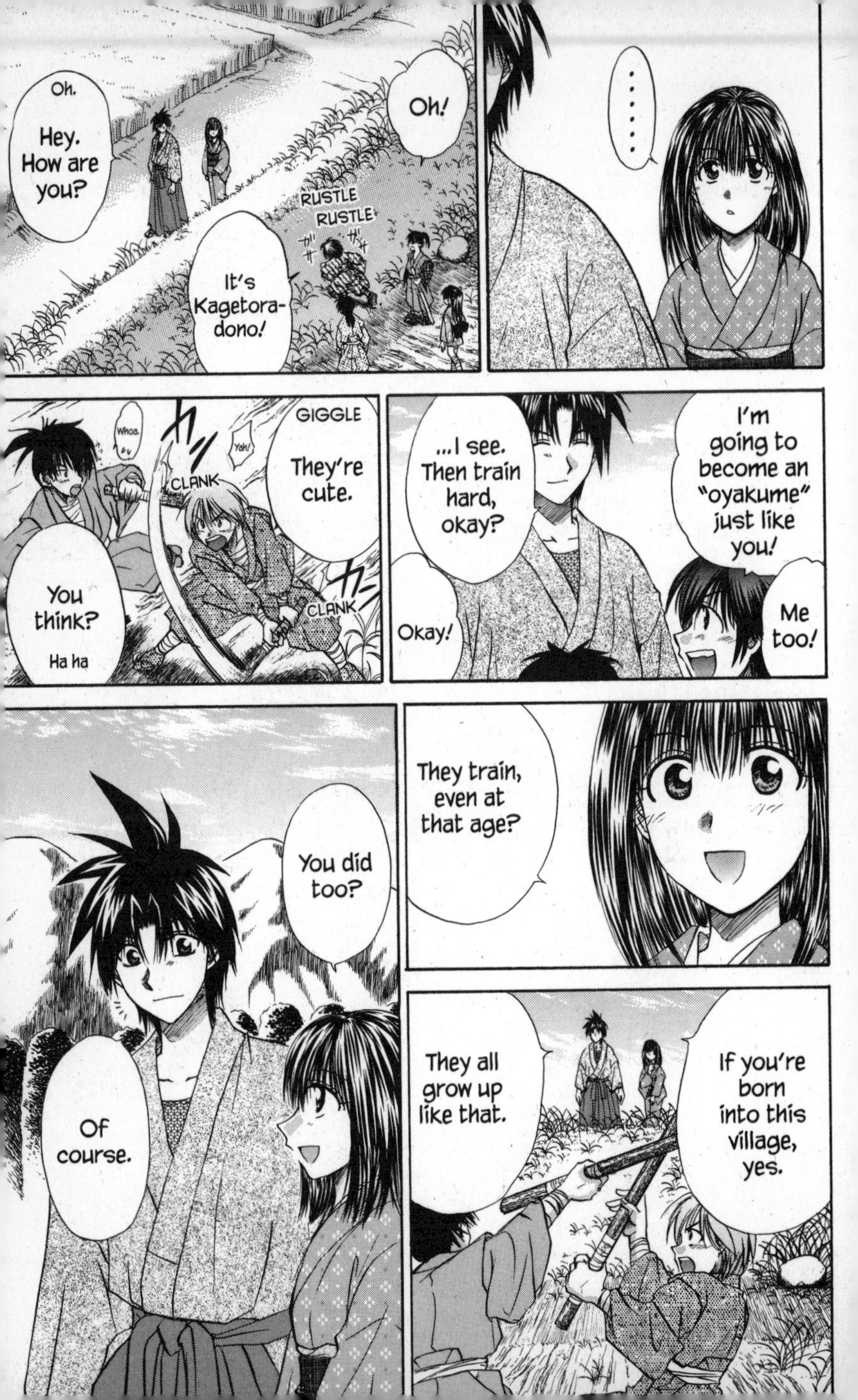
.....
Oh!
RUSTLE RUSTLE
It's Kagetora-dono!
Oh. Hey. How are you?
I'm going to become an "oyakume" just like you!
Me too!
...I see. Then train hard, okay?
Okay!
GIGGLE
They're cute.
Yah!
CLANK
Whoa.
You think?
Ha ha
CLANK
They train, even at that age?
If you're born into this village, yes.
They all grow up like that.
You did too?
Of course.

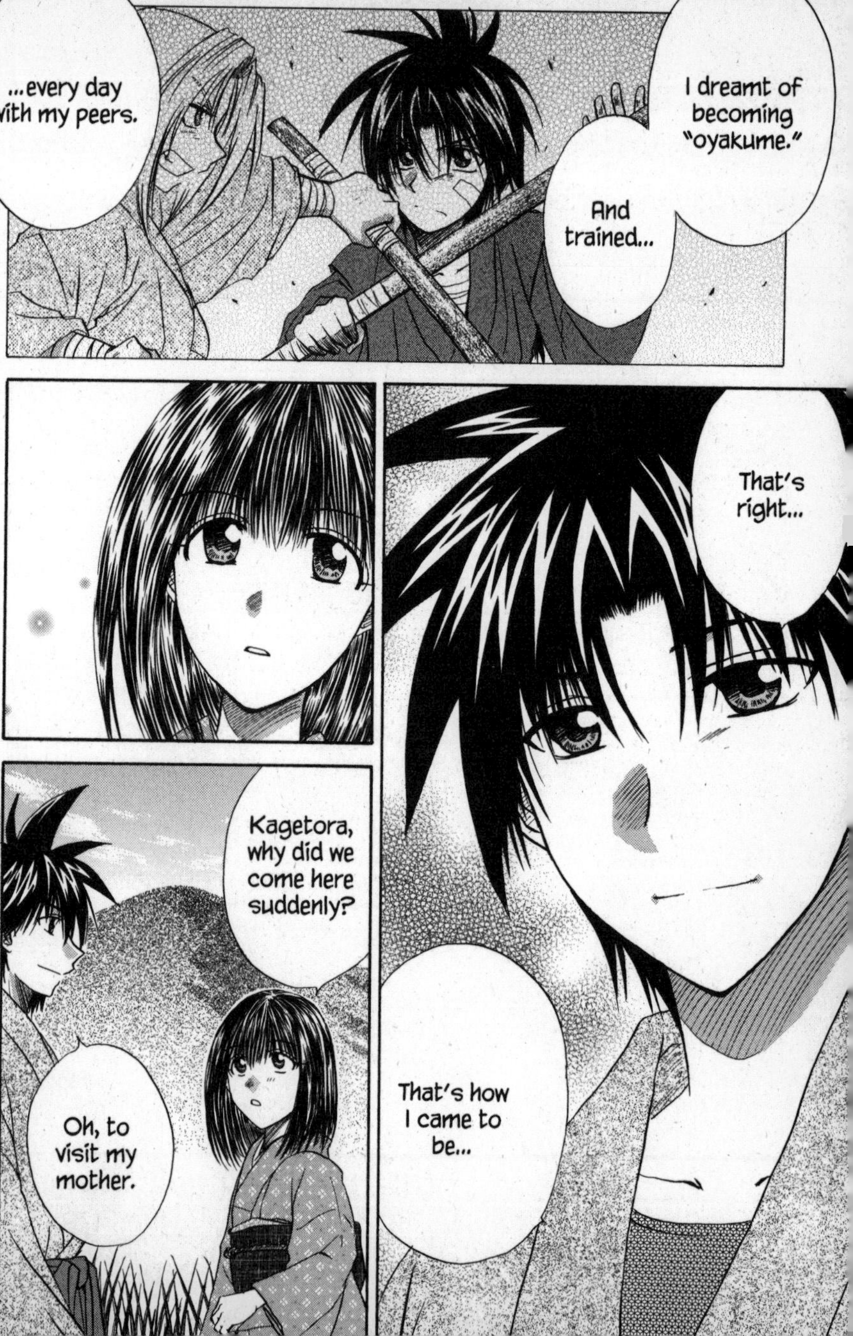
I dreamt of becoming "oyakume."
And trained...
...every day with my peers.
That's right...
That's how I came to be...
Kagetora, why did we come here suddenly?
Oh, to visit my mother.

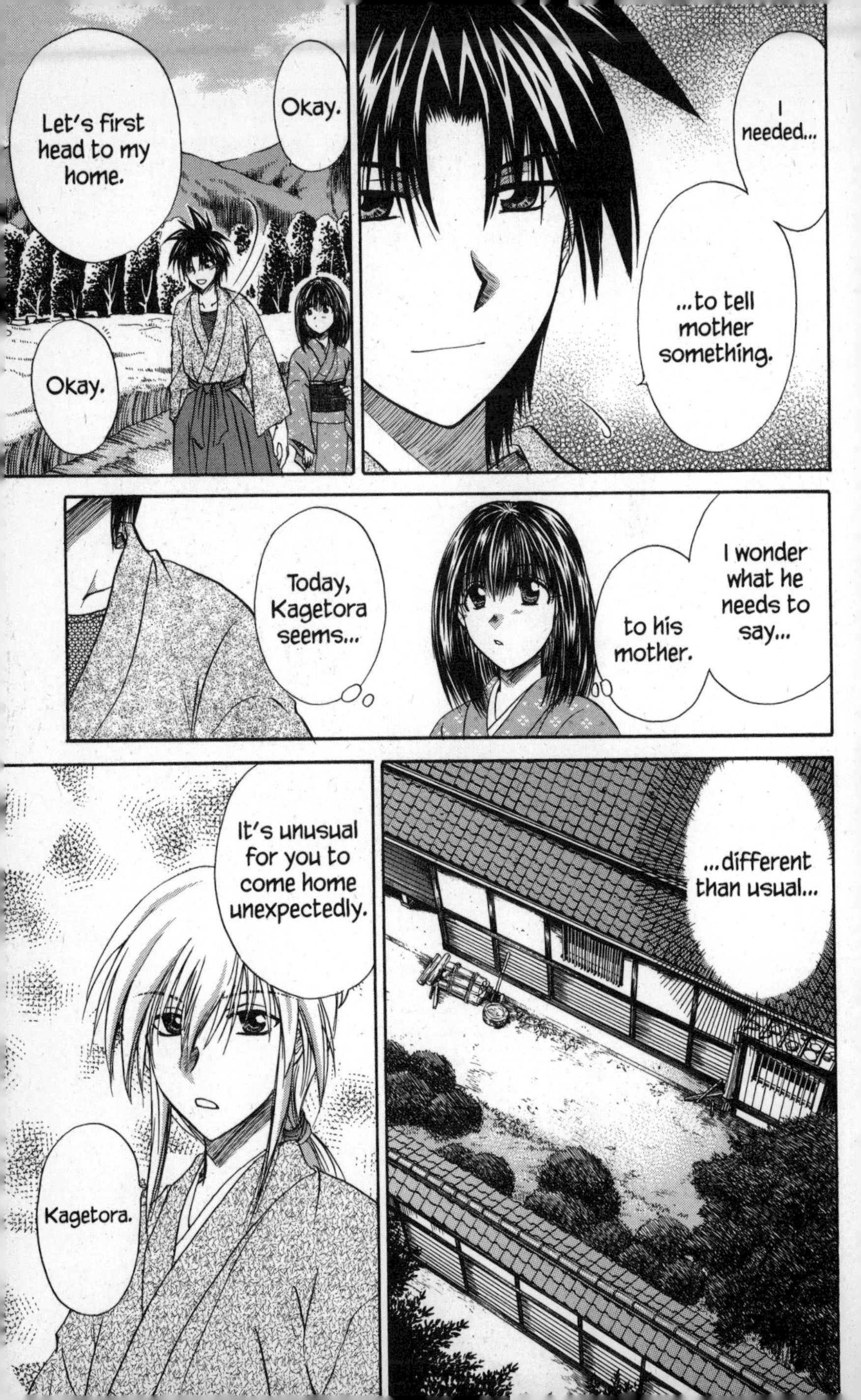
I needed...
...to tell mother something.
Okay.
Let's first head to my home.
Okay.
I wonder what he needs to say...
to his mother.
Today, Kagetora seems...
...different than usual...
It's unusual for you to come home unexpectedly.
Kagetora.

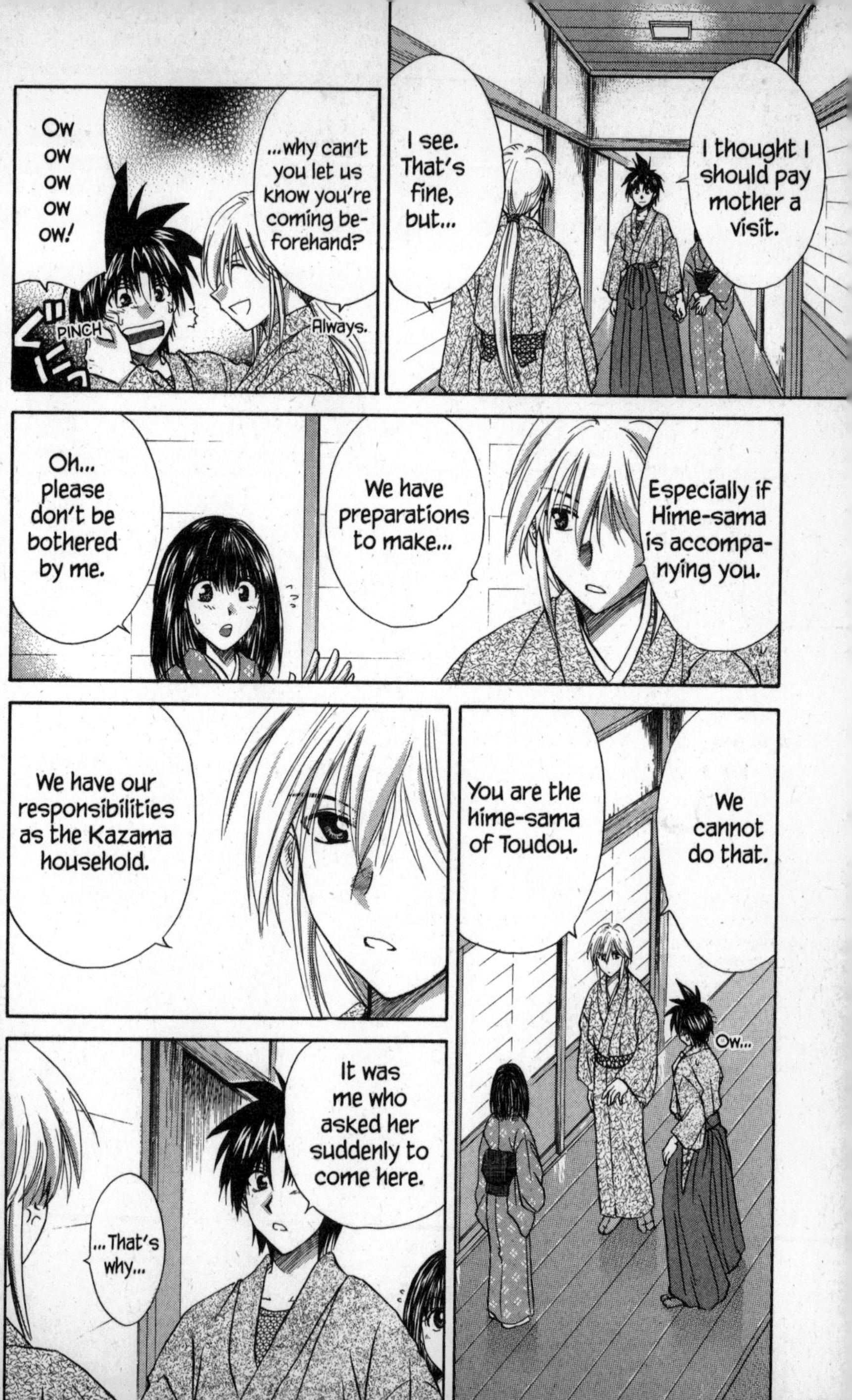
I thought I should pay mother a visit.
I see. That's fine, but...
...why can't you let us know you're coming beforehand?
Always.
Ow ow ow ow ow!
PINCH
Especially if Hime-sama is accompanying you.
We have preparations to make...
Oh... please don't be bothered by me.
We cannot do that.
You are the hime-sama of Toudou.
Ow...
We have our responsibilities as the Kazama household.
It was me who asked her suddenly to come here.
...That's why...

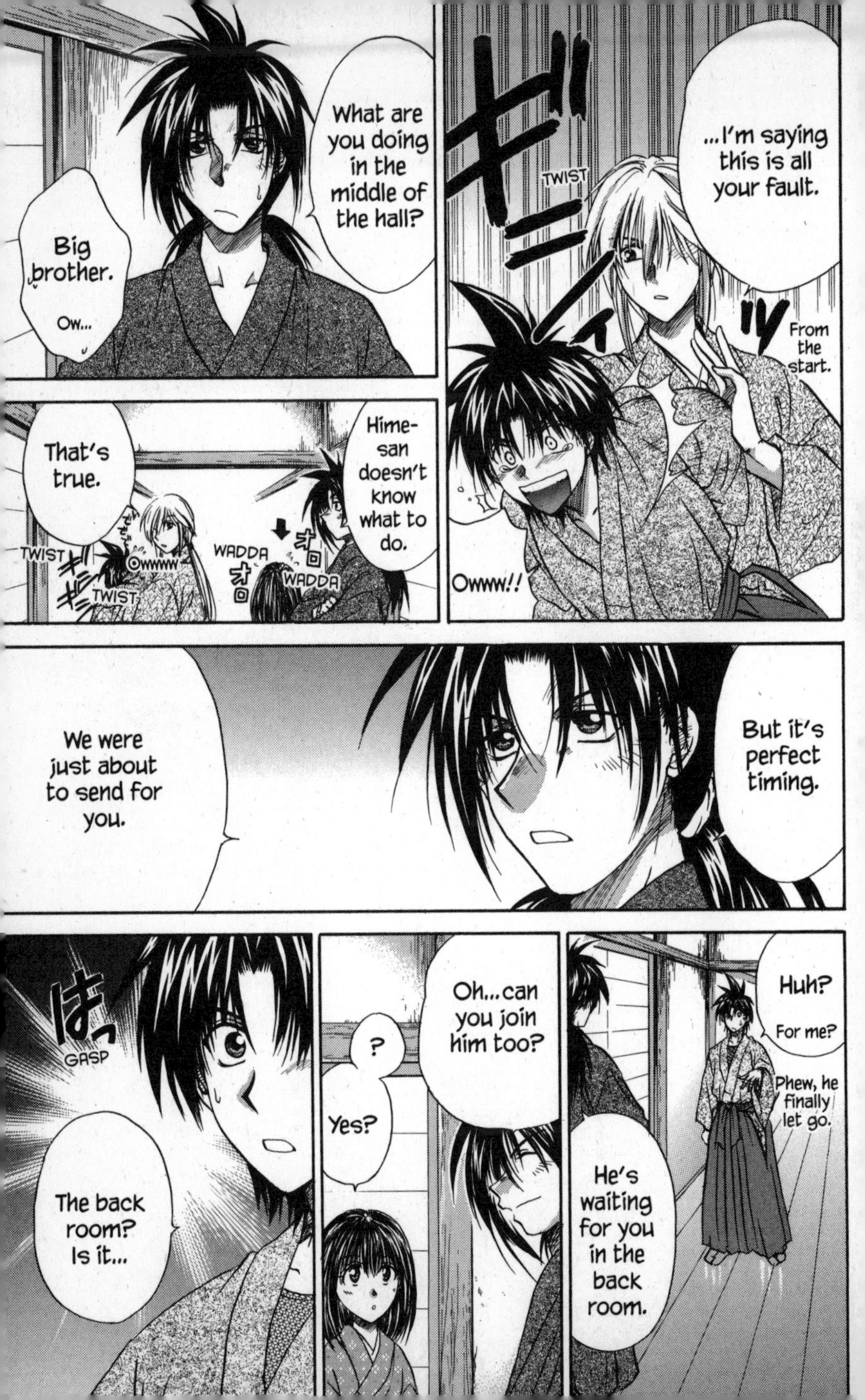
...I'm saying this is all your fault.
TWIST
From the start.
Owww!!
What are you doing in the middle of the hall?
Big brother.
Ow...
Hime-san doesn't know what to do.
WADDA
WADDA
That's true.
Owwww
TWIST
TWIST
But it's perfect timing.
We were just about to send for you.
Huh?
For me?
Phew, he finally let go.
He's waiting for you in the back room.
Oh...can you join him too?
?
Yes?
GASP
The back room? Is it...

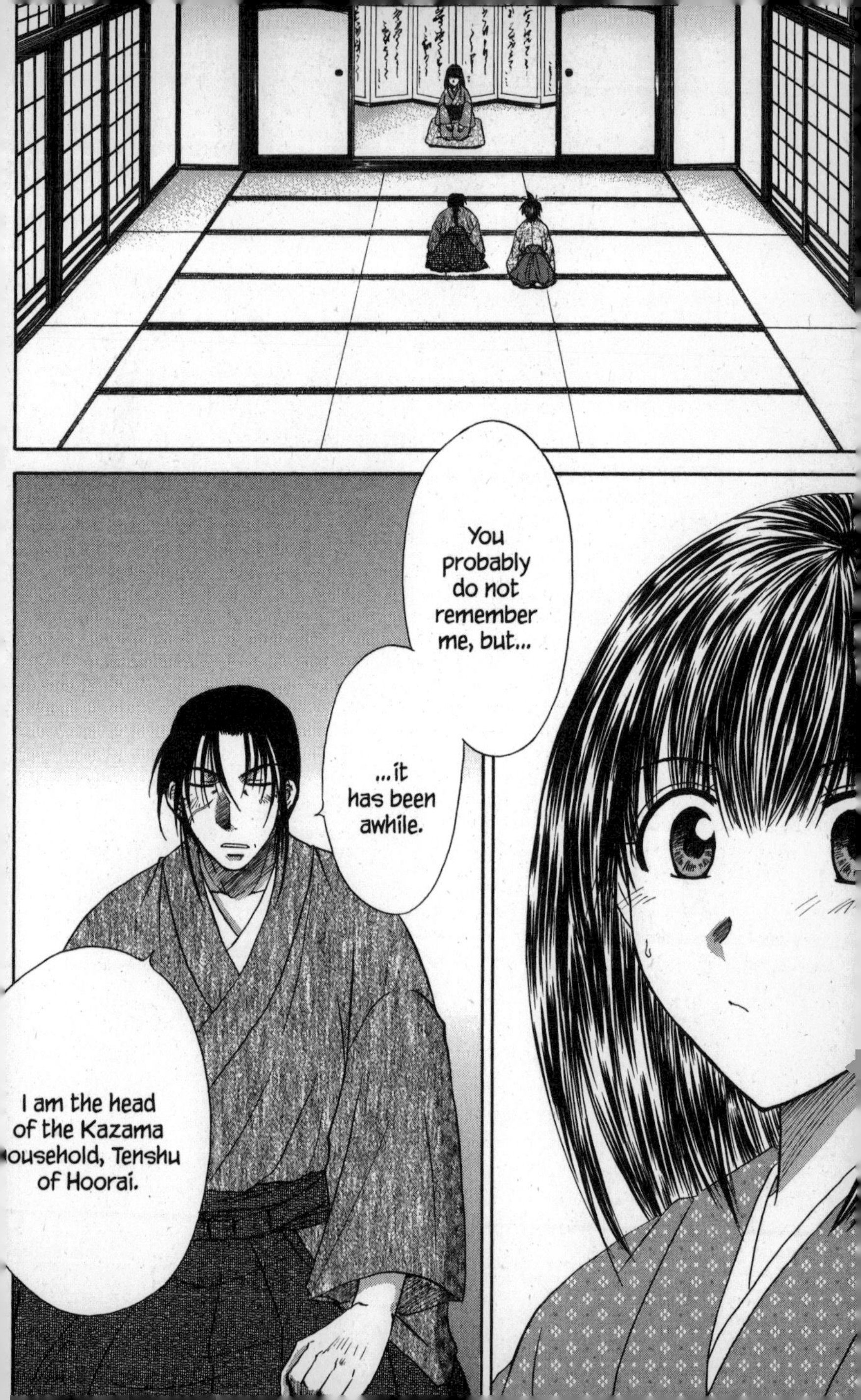
You probably do not remember me, but...
...it has been awhile.
I am the head of the Kazama ousehold, Tenshu of Hoorai.

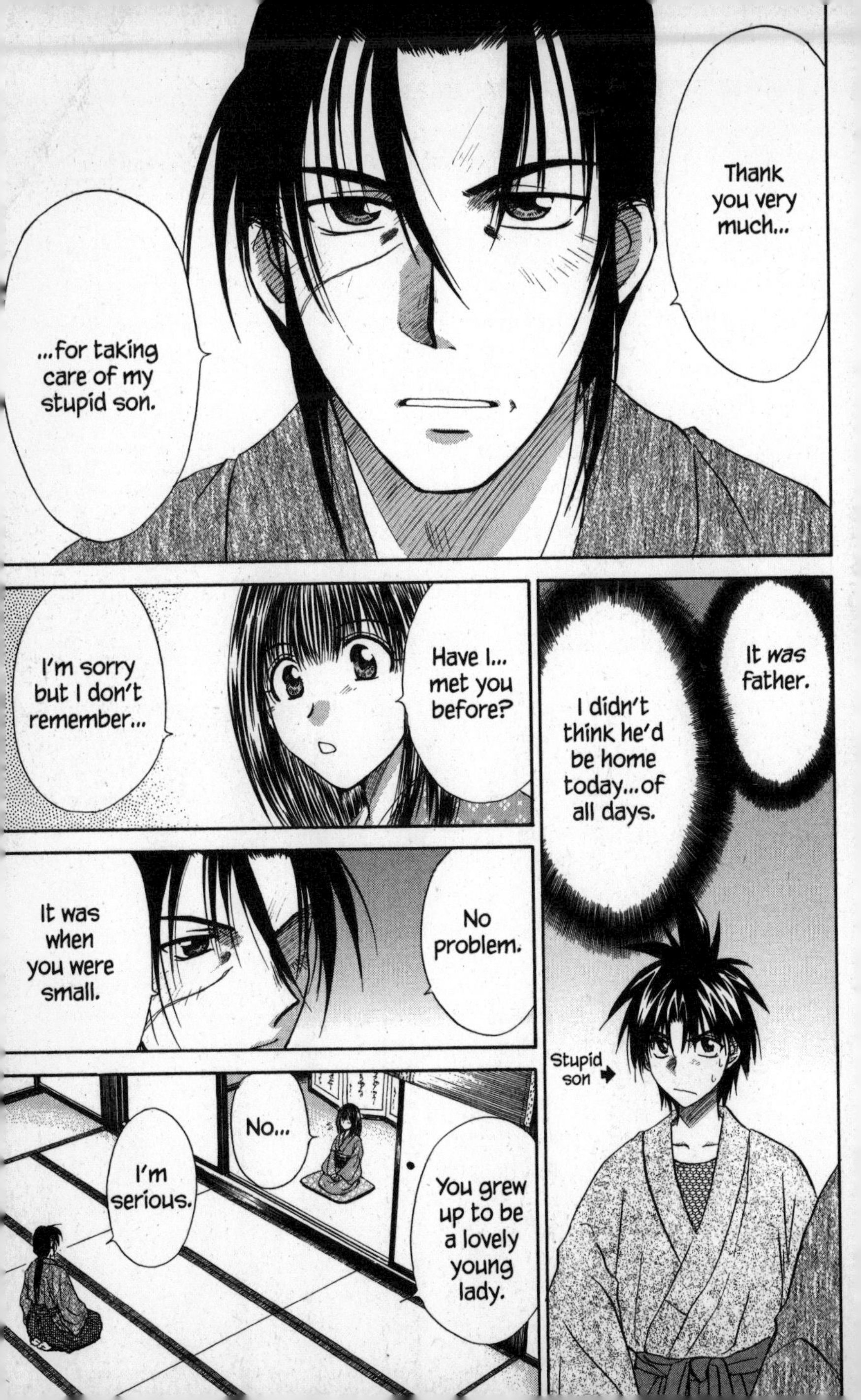
Thank you very much...
...for taking care of my stupid son.
It *was* father.
I didn't think he'd be home today...of all days.
Stupid son ➔
Have I... met you before?
I'm sorry but I don't remember...
No problem.
It was when you were small.
You grew up to be a lovely young lady.
No...
I'm serious.

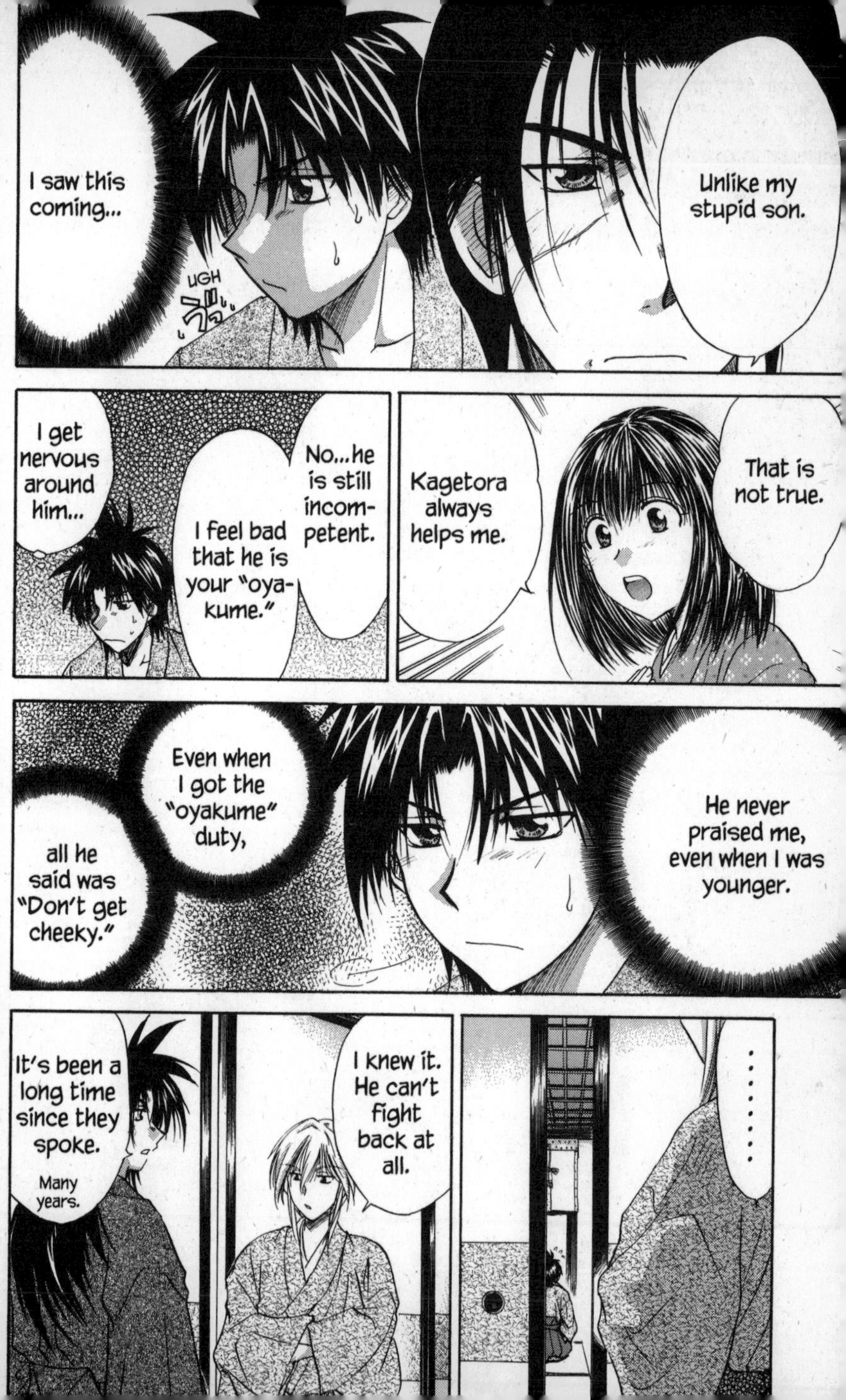
Unlike my stupid son.
I saw this coming...
UGH
That is not true.
Kagetora always helps me.
No...he is still incompetent.
I feel bad that he is your "oya-kume."
I get nervous around him...
He never praised me, even when I was younger.
Even when I got the "oyakume" duty,
all he said was "Don't get cheeky."
......
I knew it. He can't fight back at all.
It's been a long time since they spoke.
Many years.

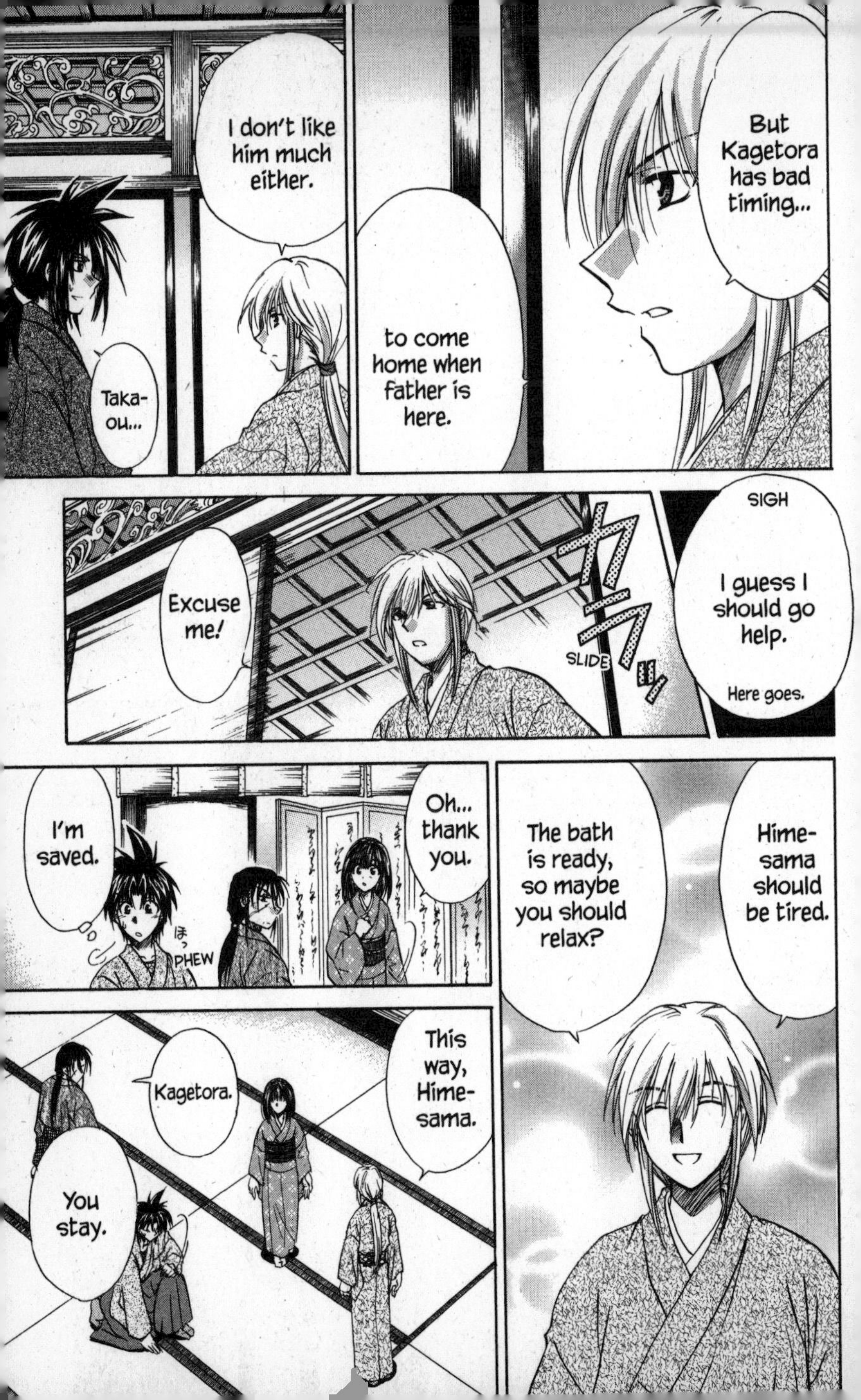

But Kagetora has bad timing...
to come home when father is here.
I don't like him much either.
Taka-ou...
SIGH
I guess I should go help.
Here goes.
SLIDE
Excuse me!
Hime-sama should be tired.
The bath is ready, so maybe you should relax?
Oh... thank you.
I'm saved.
PHEW
This way, Hime-sama.
Kagetora.
You stay.

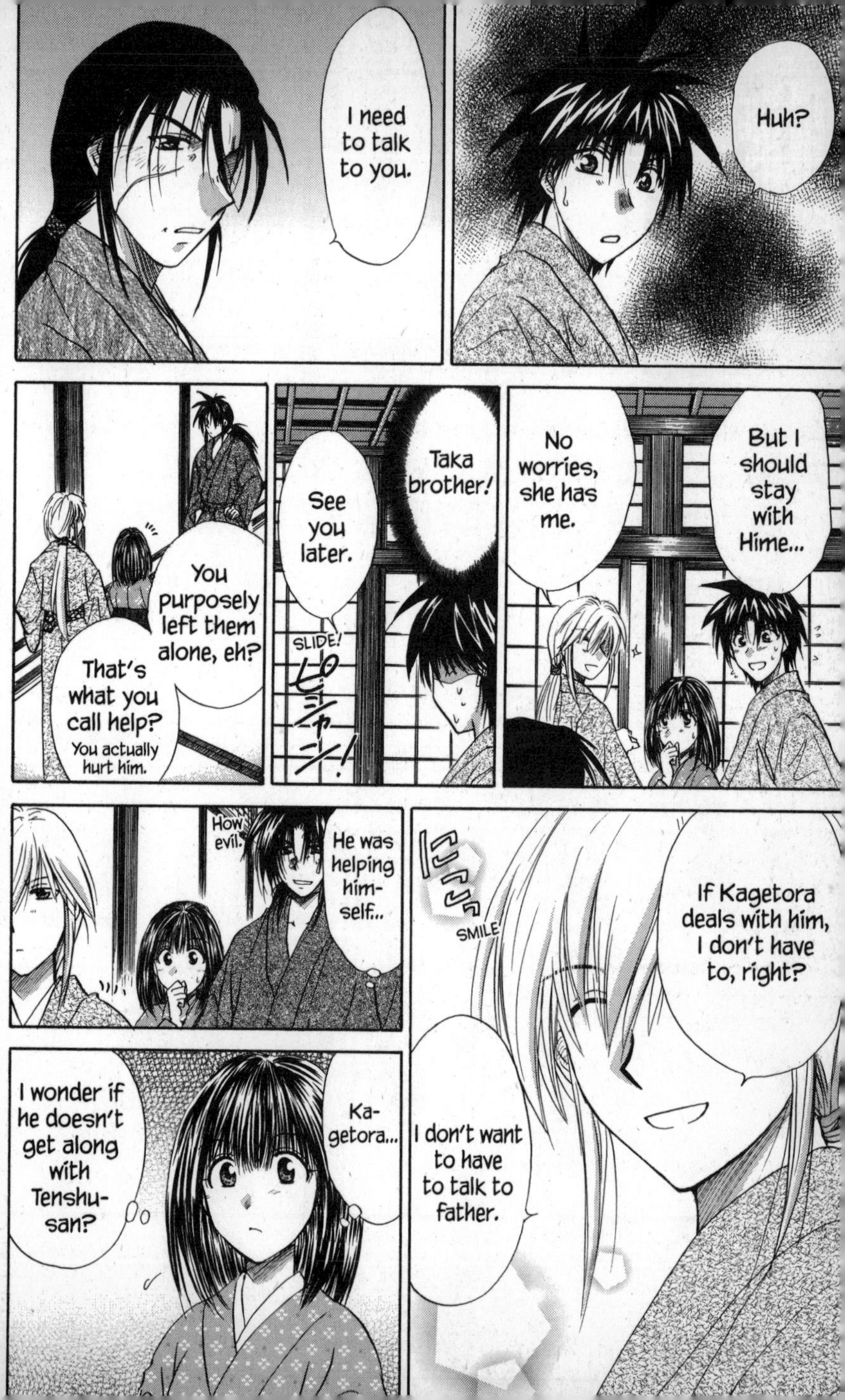
Huh?
I need to talk to you.
But I should stay with Hime...
No worries, she has me.
Taka brother!
See you later.
SLIDE!
You purposely left them alone, eh?
That's what you call help?
You actually hurt him.
If Kagetora deals with him, I don't have to, right?
SMILE
I don't want to have to talk to father.
He was helping him-self...
How evil.
Ka-getora...
I wonder if he doesn't get along with Tenshu-san?

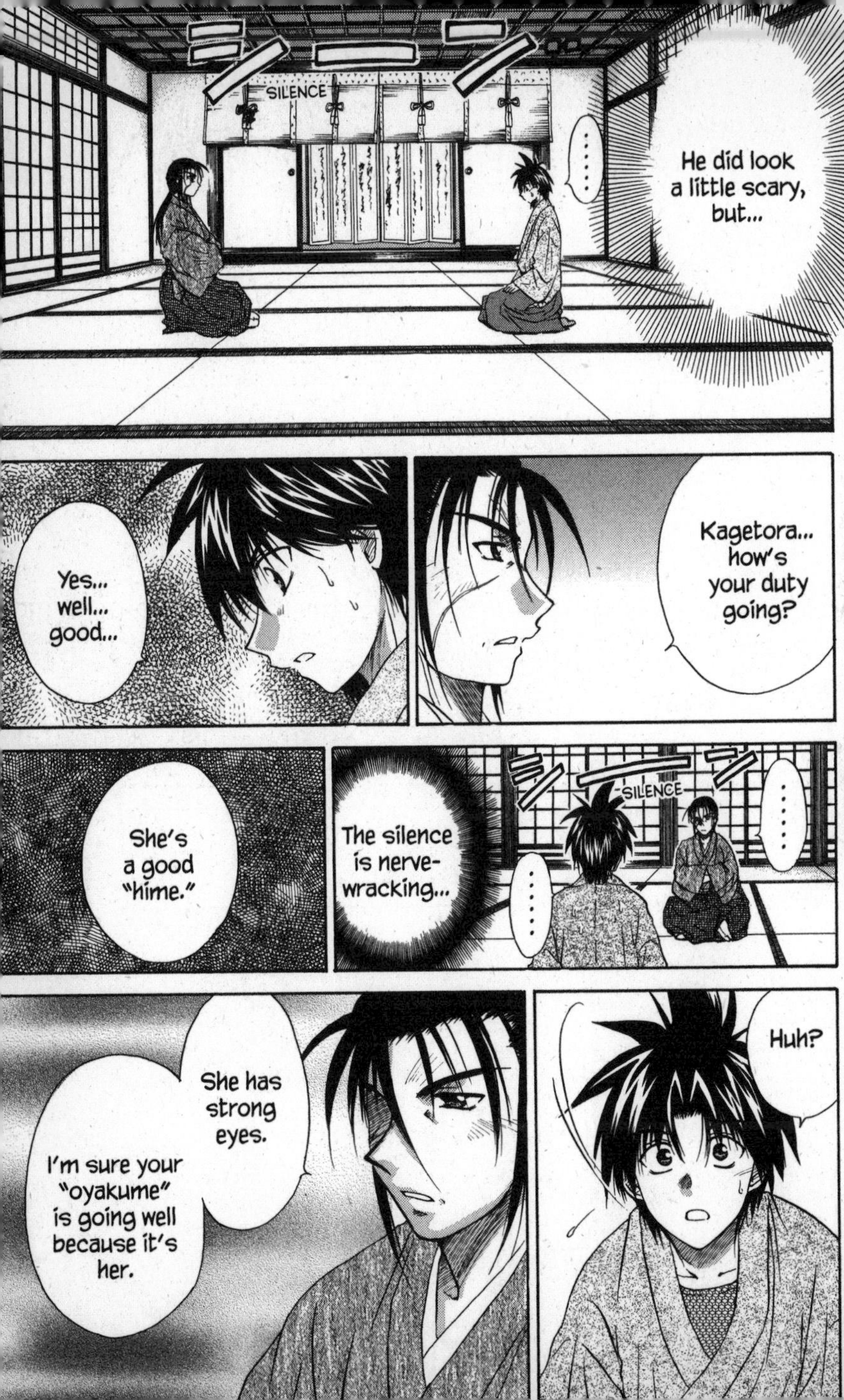
He did look a little scary, but...
......
SILENCE
Kagetora... how's your duty going?
Yes... well... good...
SILENCE
......
......
The silence is nerve-wracking...
She's a good "hime."
Huh?
She has strong eyes.
I'm sure your "oyakume" is going well because it's her.

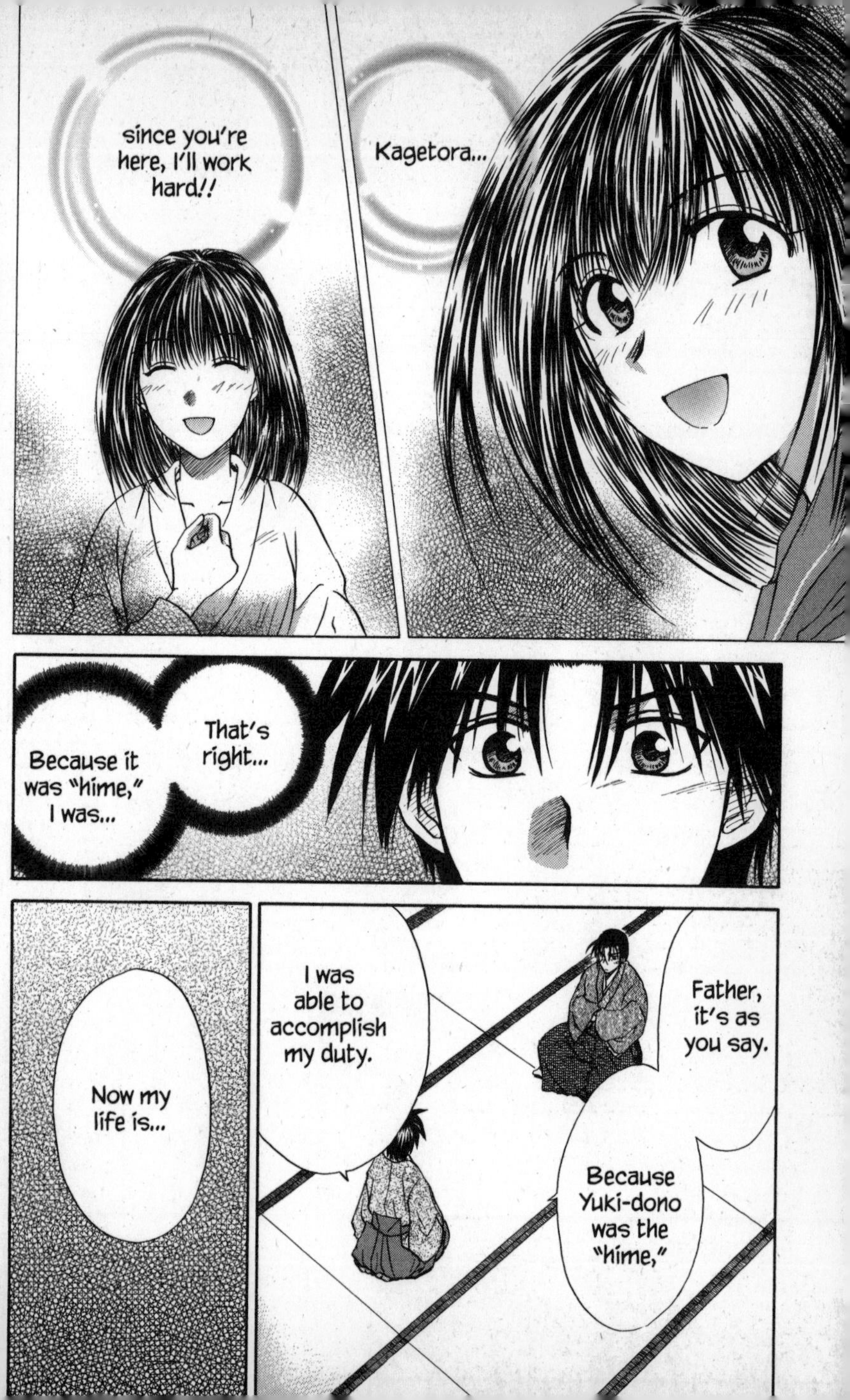
Kagetora...
since you're here, I'll work hard!!
That's right...
Because it was "hime," I was...
Father, it's as you say.
Because Yuki-dono was the "hime,"
I was able to accomplish my duty.
Now my life is...

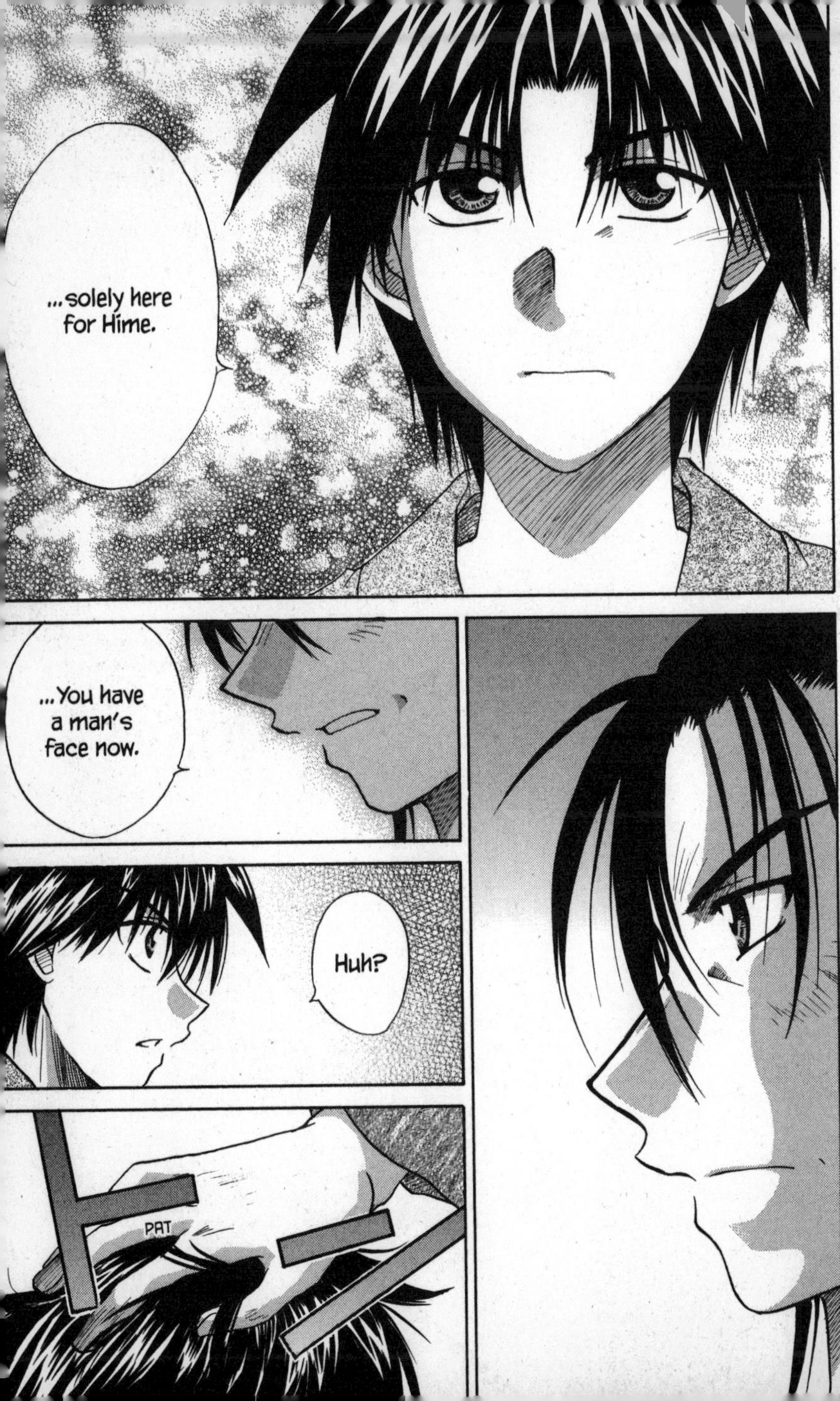
...solely here for Hime.
...You have a man's face now.
Huh?
PAT

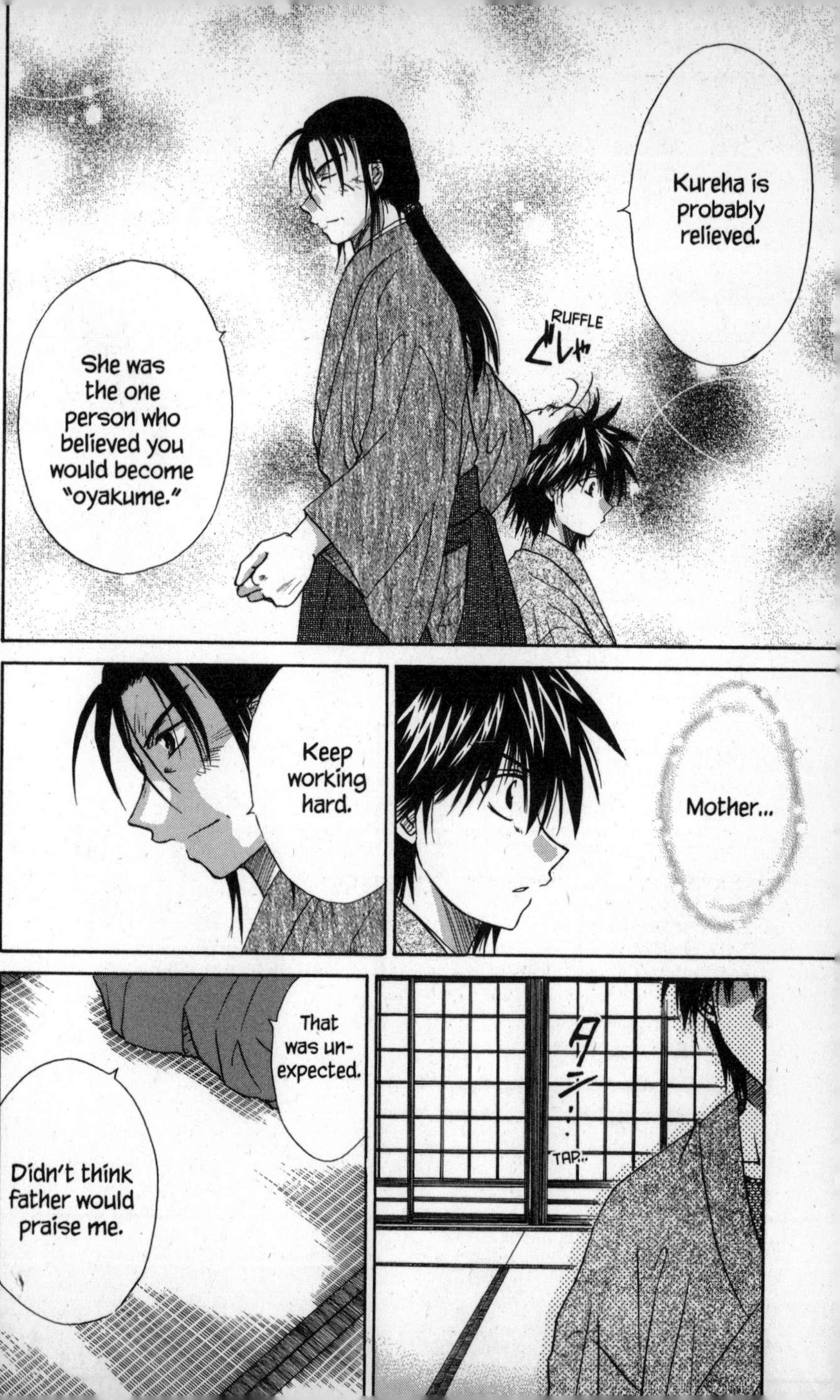
Kureha is probably relieved.
RUFFLE
She was the one person who believed you would become "oyakume."
Mother...
Keep working hard.
TAP...
That was un-expected.
Didn't think father would praise me.

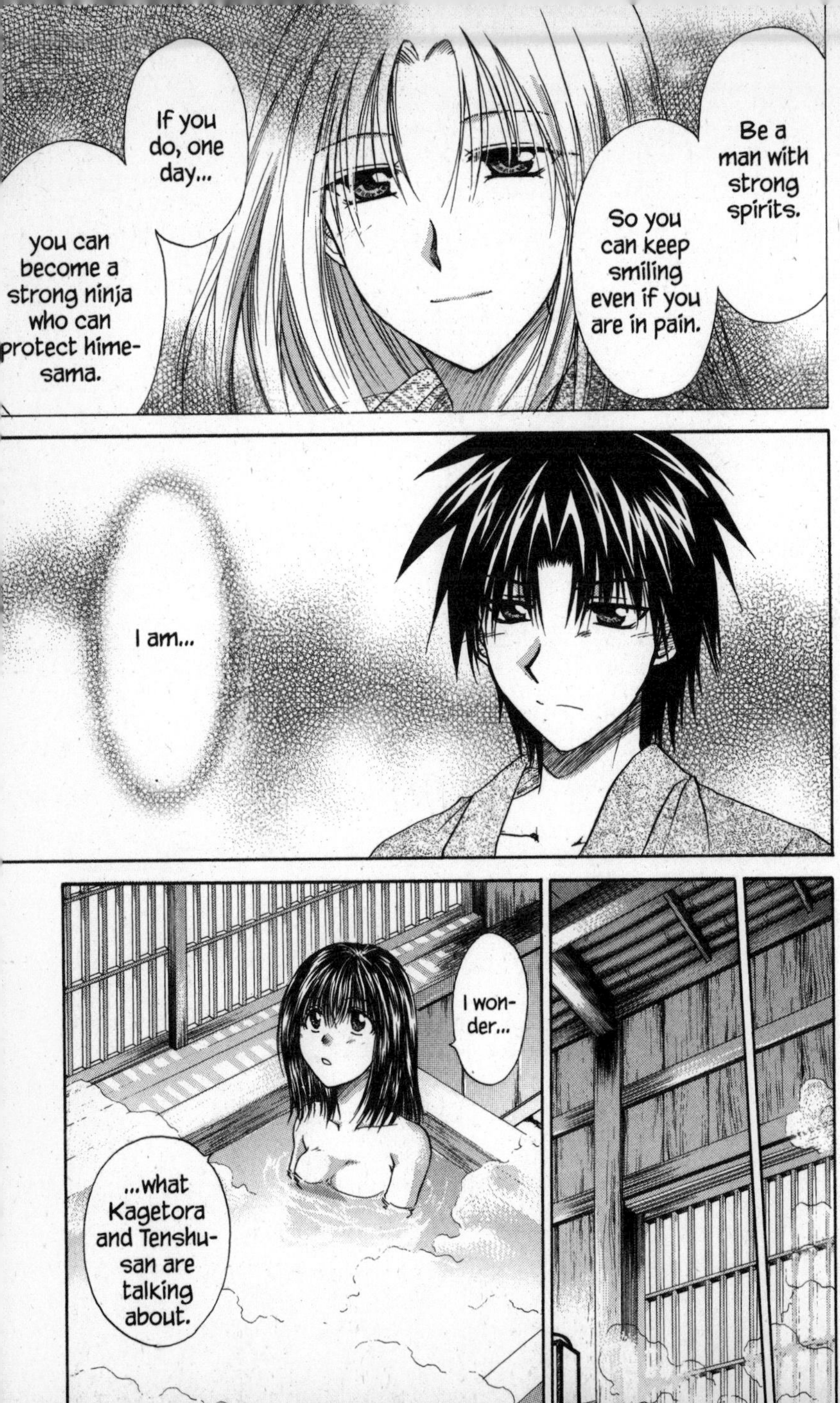
Be a man with strong spirits.
So you can keep smiling even if you are in pain.
If you do, one day...
you can become a strong ninja who can protect hime-sama.
I am...
I wonder...
...what Kagetora and Tenshu-san are talking about.

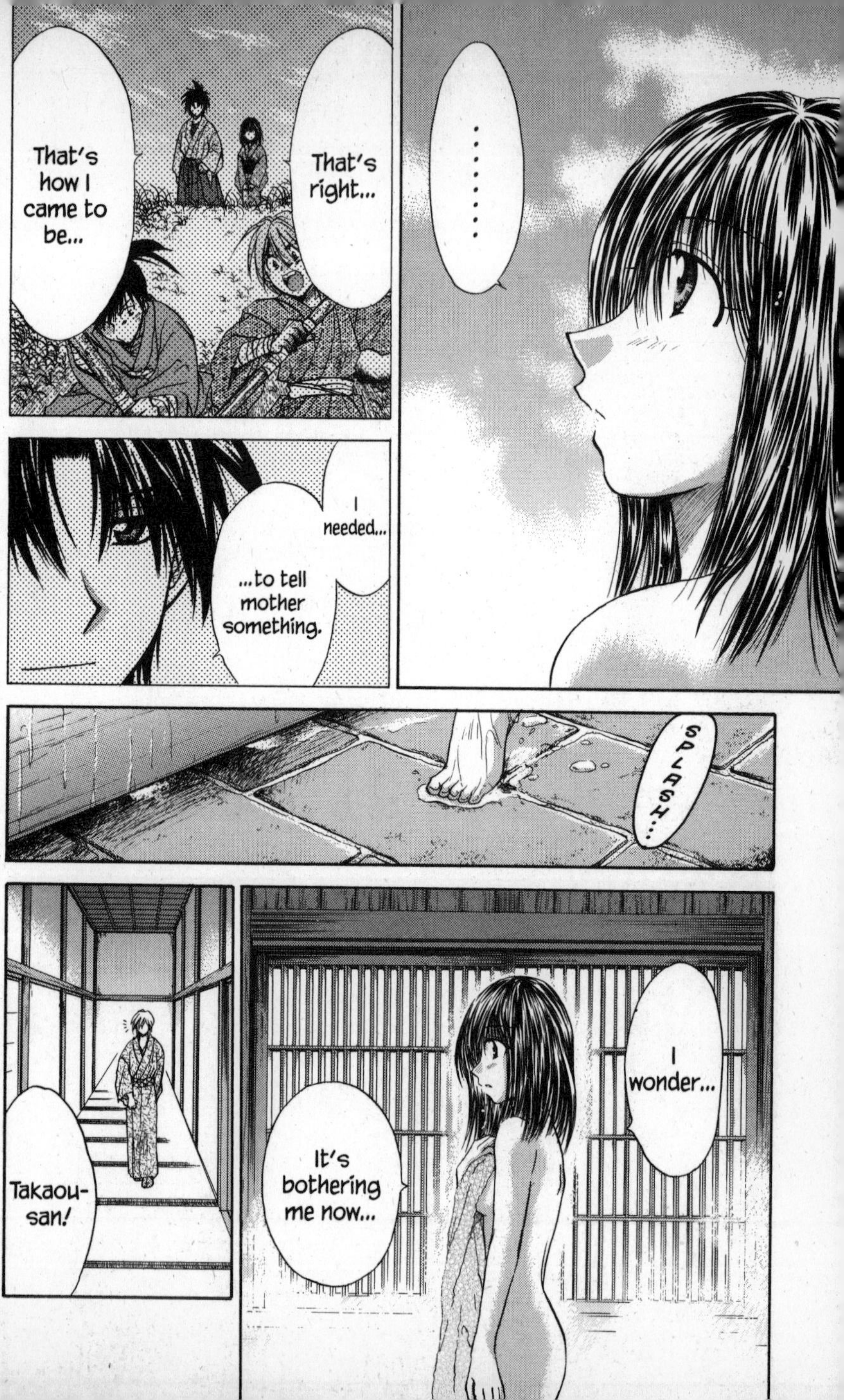

....
That's right...
That's how I came to be...
I needed...
...to tell mother something.
SPLASH...
I wonder...
It's bothering me now...
Takaou-san!

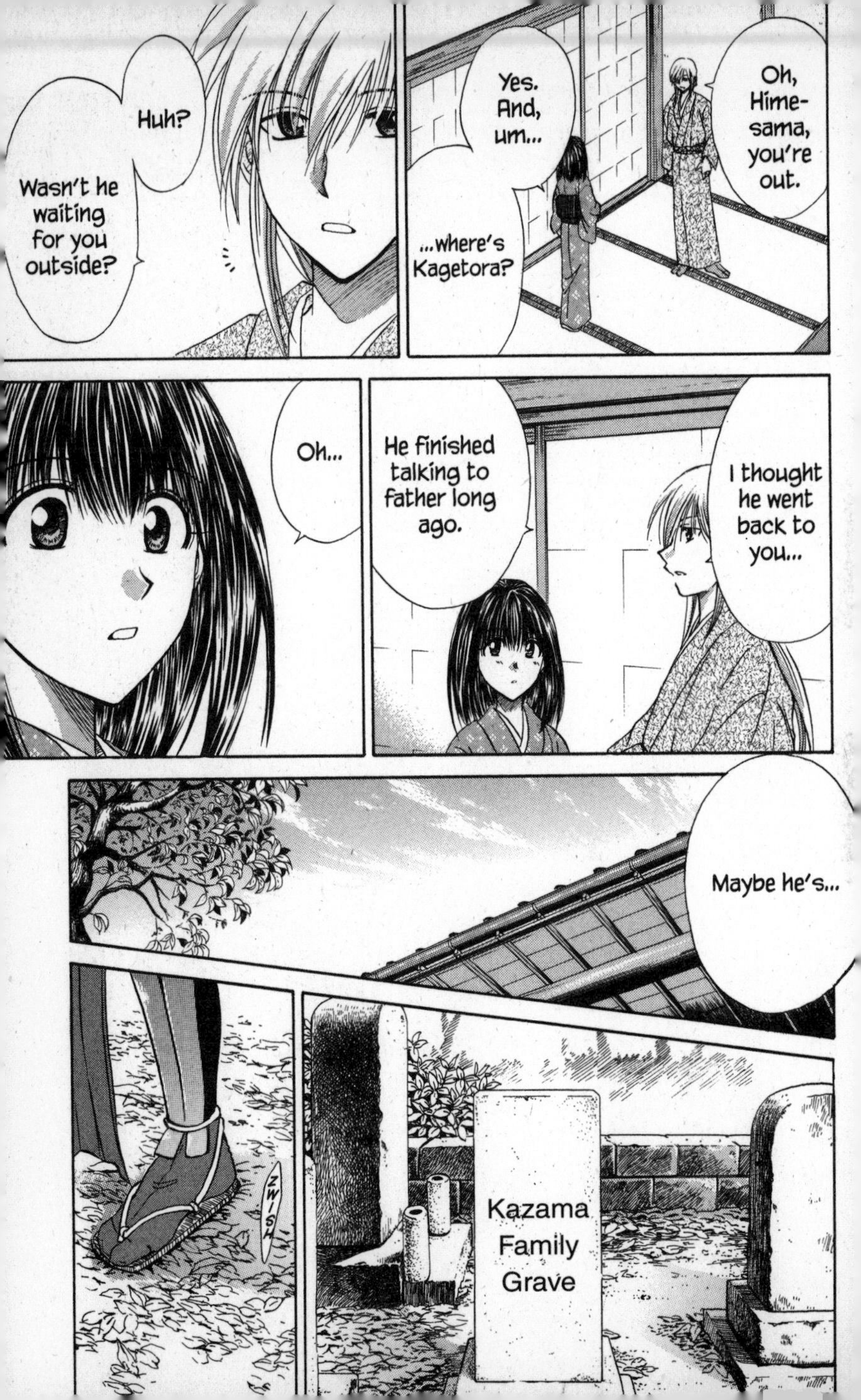
Oh, Hime-sama, you're out.
Yes. And, um...
...where's Kagetora?
Huh?
Wasn't he waiting for you outside?
I thought he went back to you...
He finished talking to father long ago.
Oh...
Maybe he's...
Kazama Family Grave
ZWISH

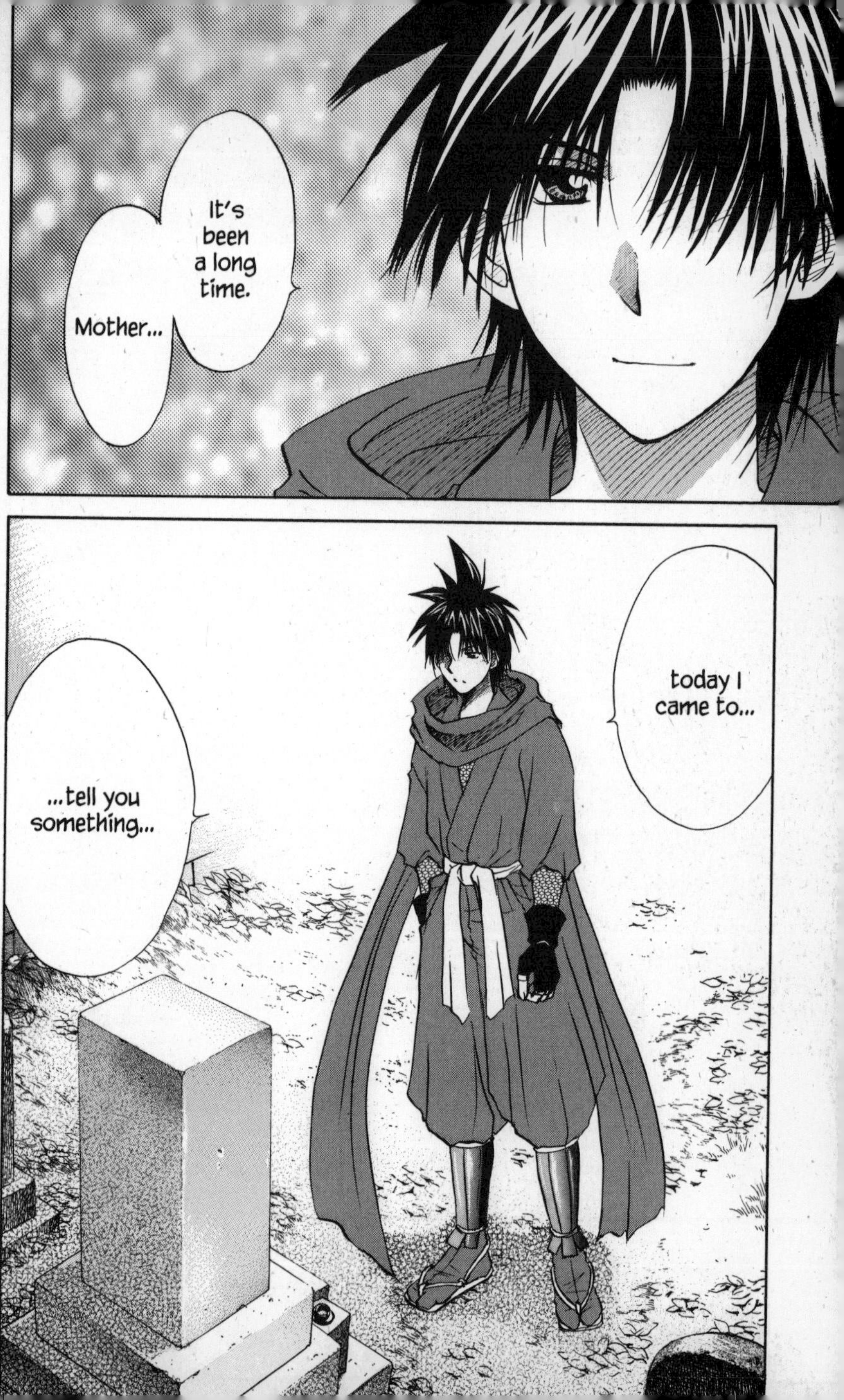
It's been a long time.
Mother...
today I came to...
...tell you something...

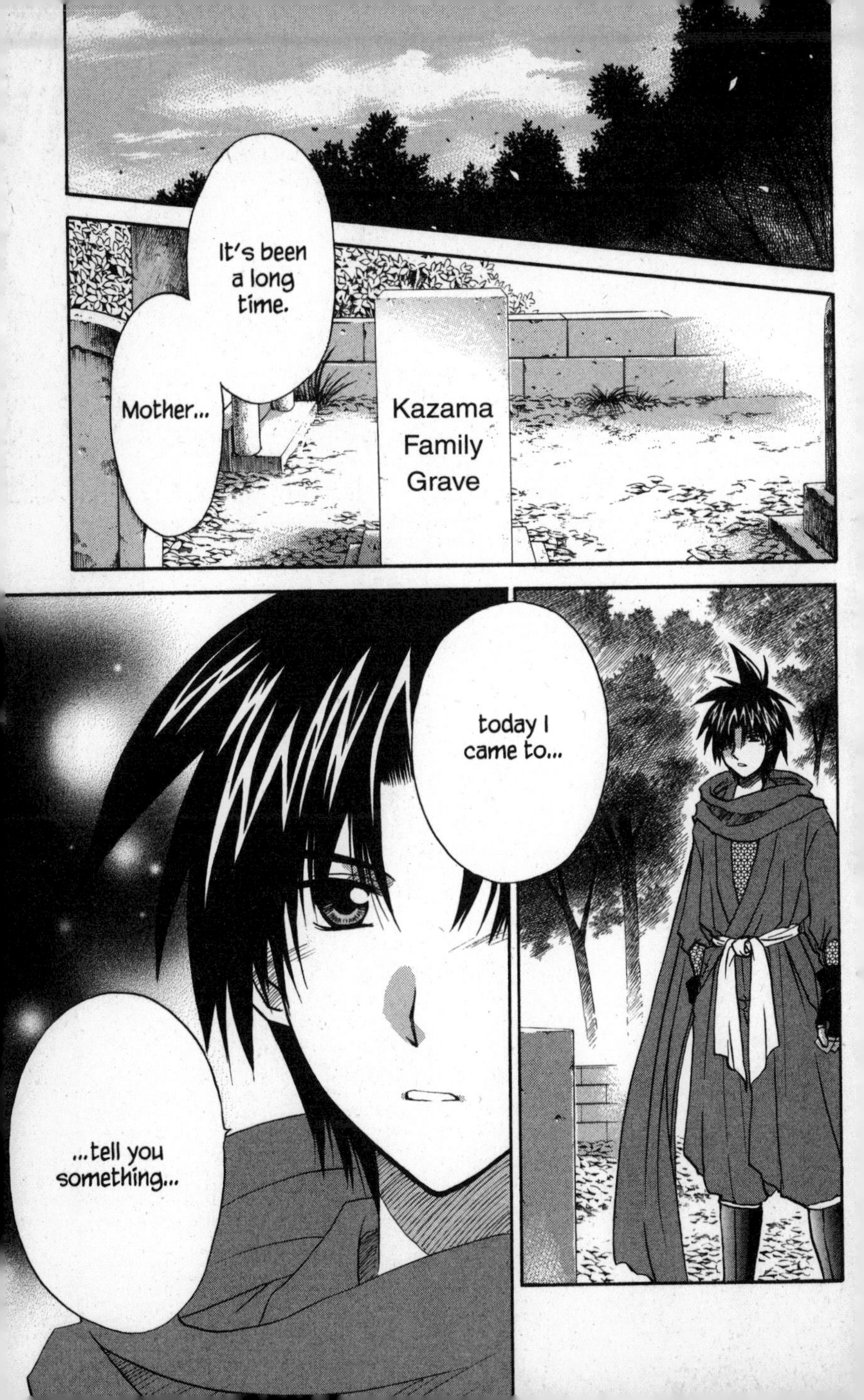
Kazama Family Grave
It's been a long time.
Mother...
today I came to...
...tell you something...

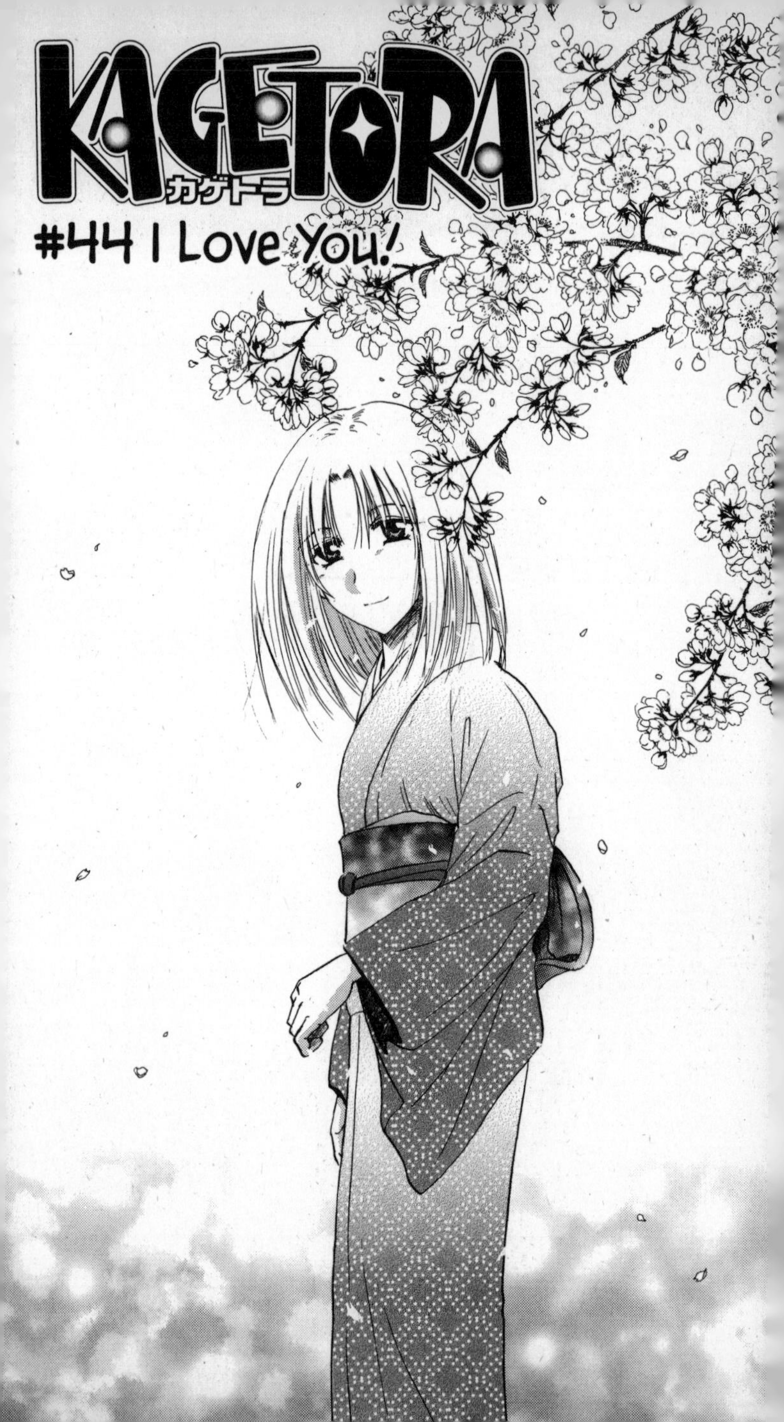
KAGETORA
カゲトラ
#44 I Love You!

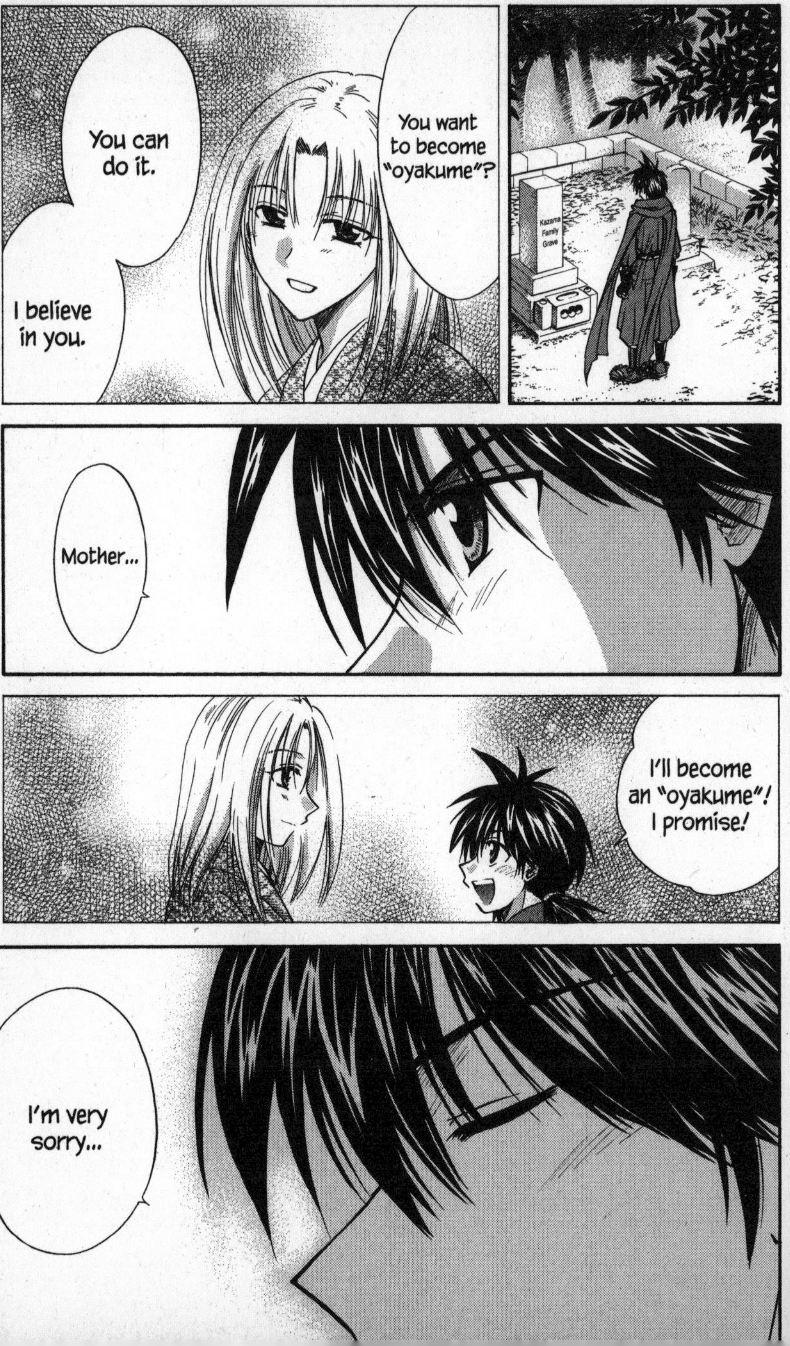
Kazama Family Grave
You want to become "oyakume"?
You can do it.
I believe in you.
Mother...
I'll become an "oyakume"! I promise!
I'm very sorry...

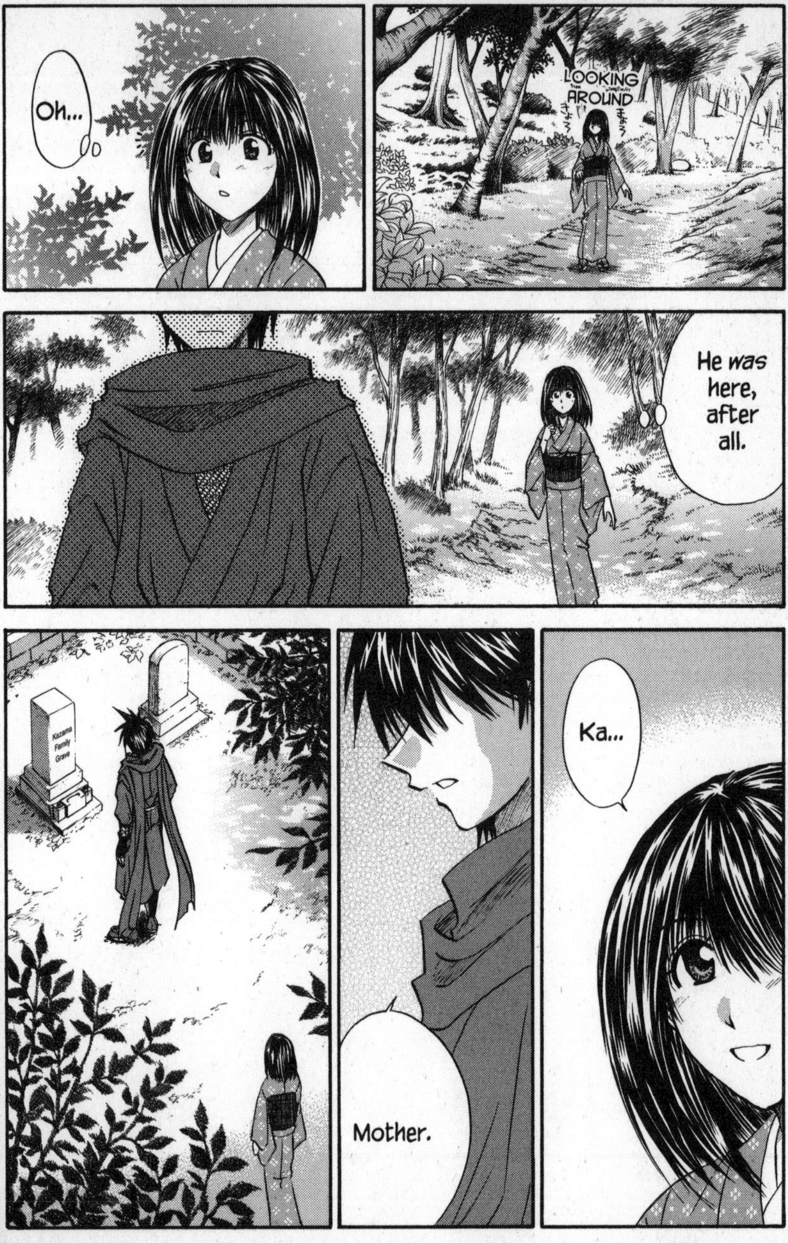
LOOKING AROUND
きょろ きょろ
Oh...
He was here, after all.
Ka...
Mother.
Kazama Family Grave

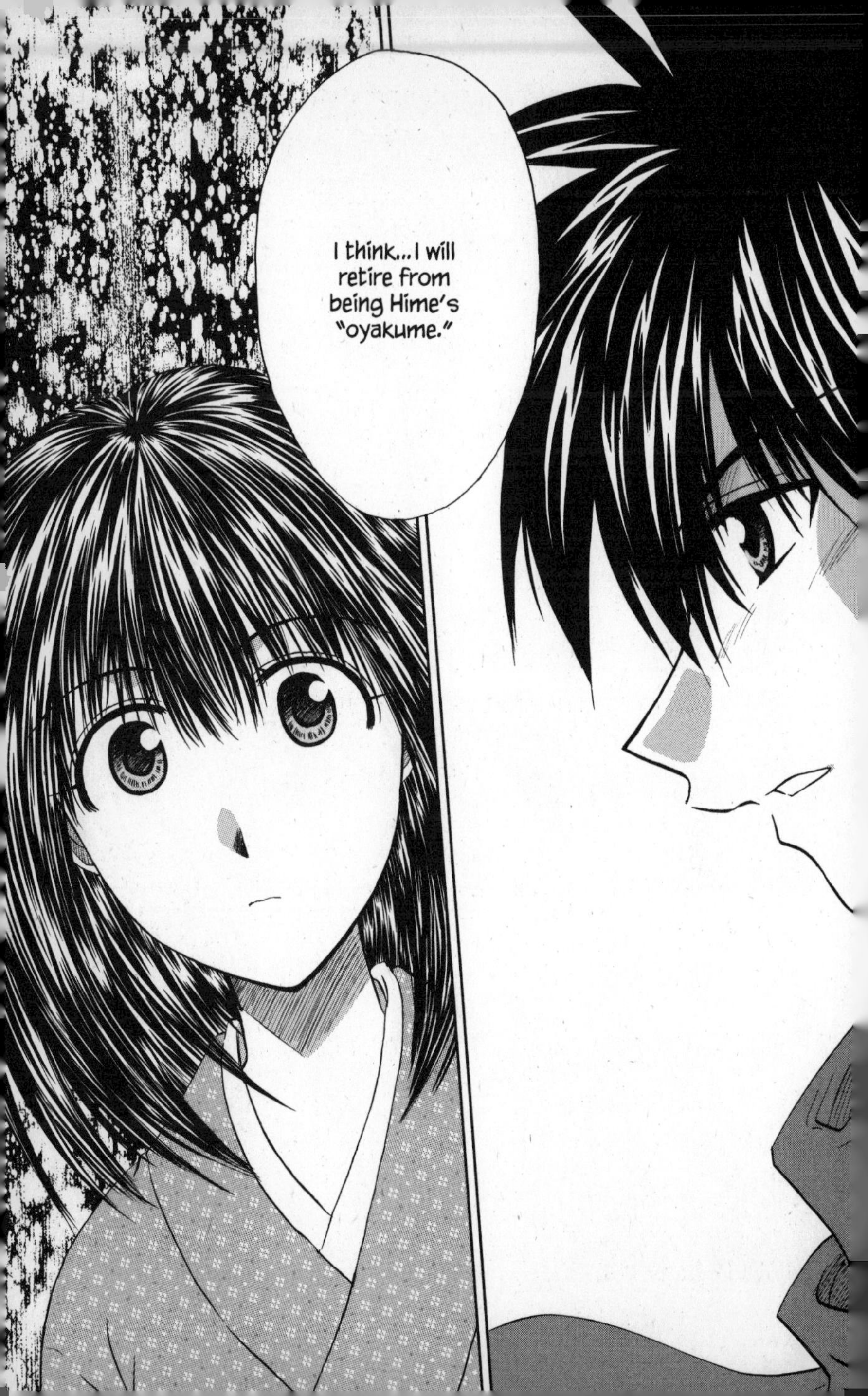
I think...I will retire from being Hime's "oyakume."

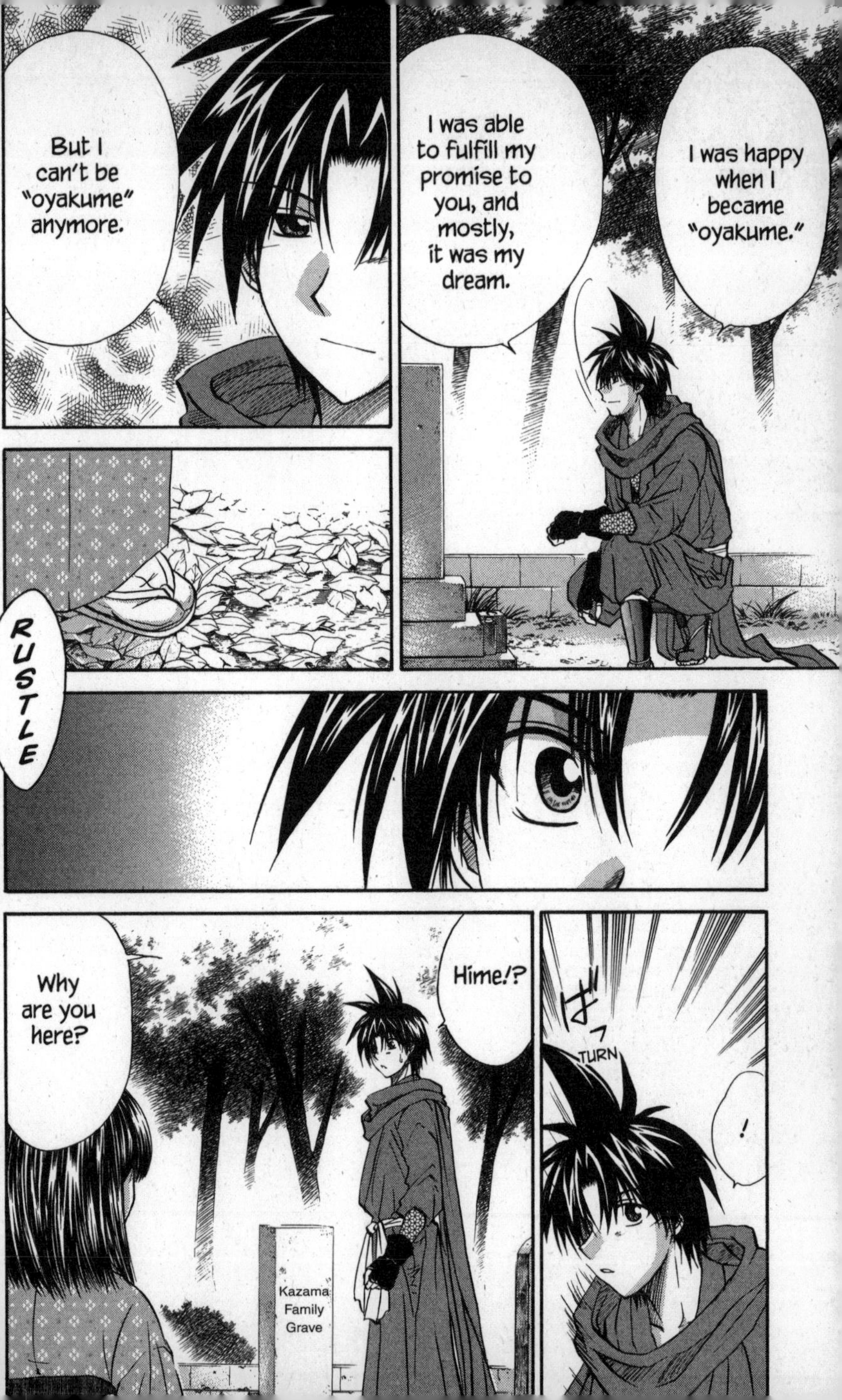
I was happy when I became "oyakume."
I was able to fulfill my promise to you, and mostly, it was my dream.
But I can't be "oyakume" anymore.
RUSTLE
ばっ
TURN
!
Hime!?
Why are you here?
Kazama Family Grave

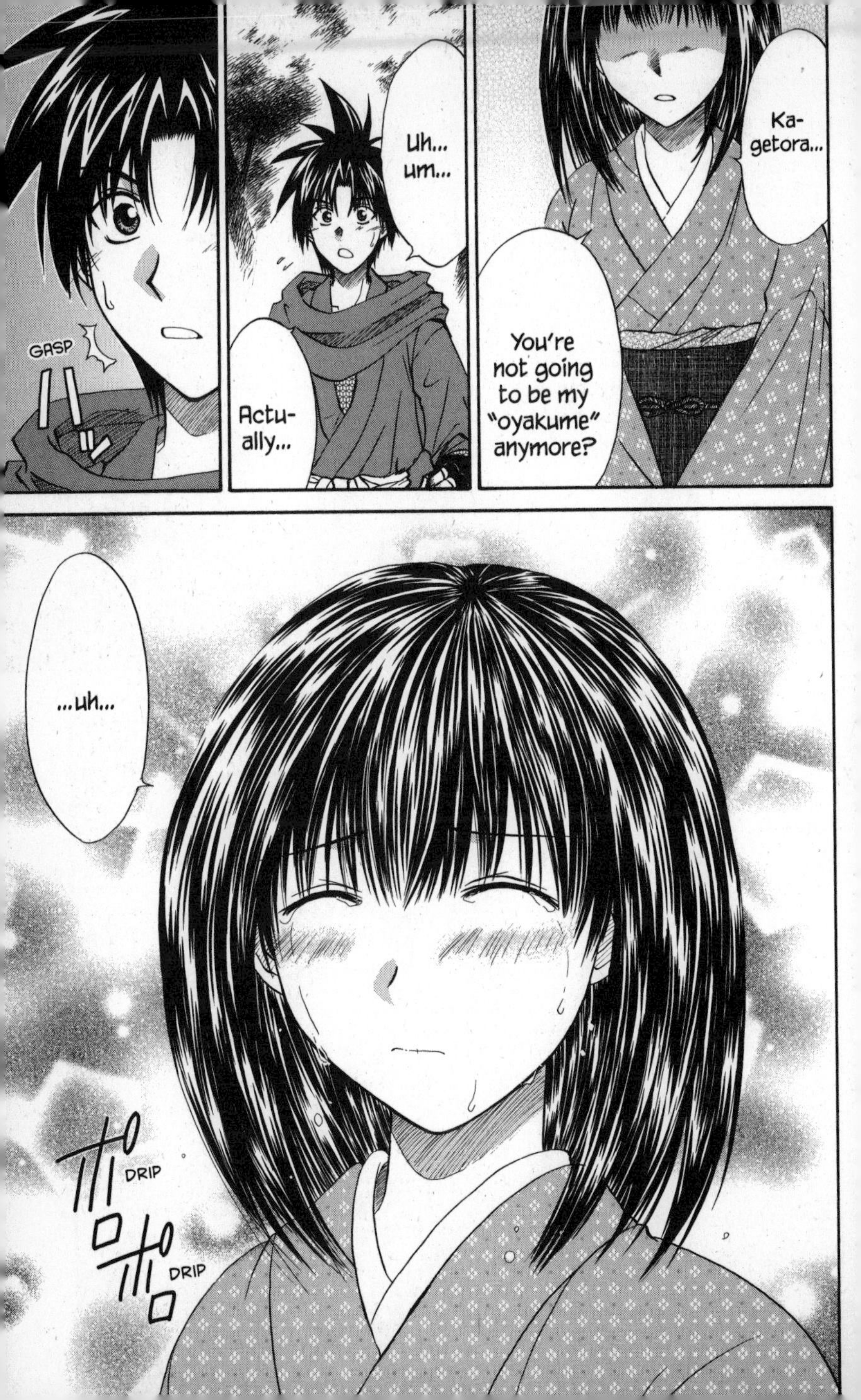
Ka-getora...
You're not going to be my "oyakume" anymore?
Uh... um...
Actu-ally...
GASP
...uh...
DRIP
DRIP

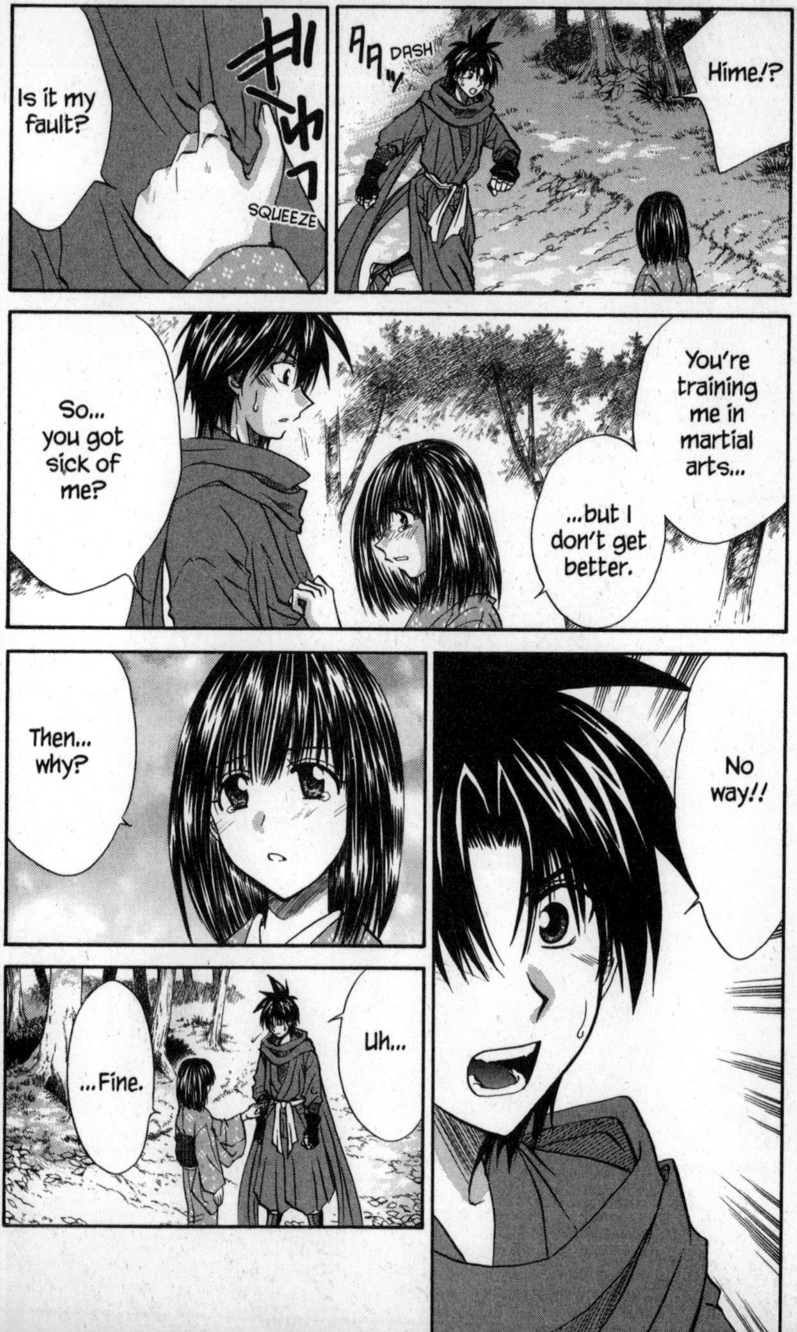
Hime!?
DASH
SQUEEZE
Is it my fault?
You're training me in martial arts...
...but I don't get better.
So... you got sick of me?
No way!!
Then... why?
Uh...
...Fine.

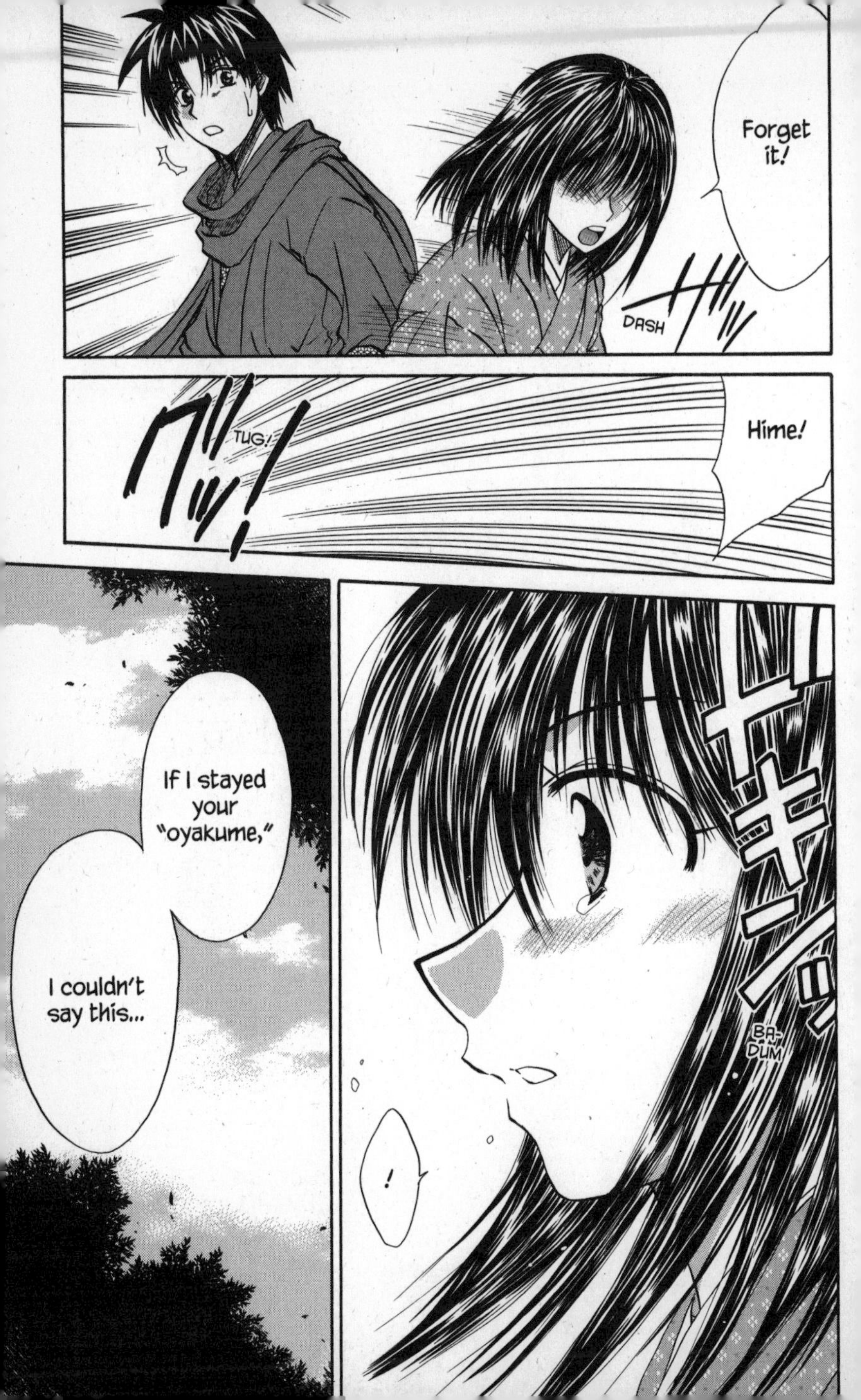
Forget it!
DASH
Hime!
TUG!
BA-DUM
!
If I stayed your "oyakume,"
I couldn't say this...

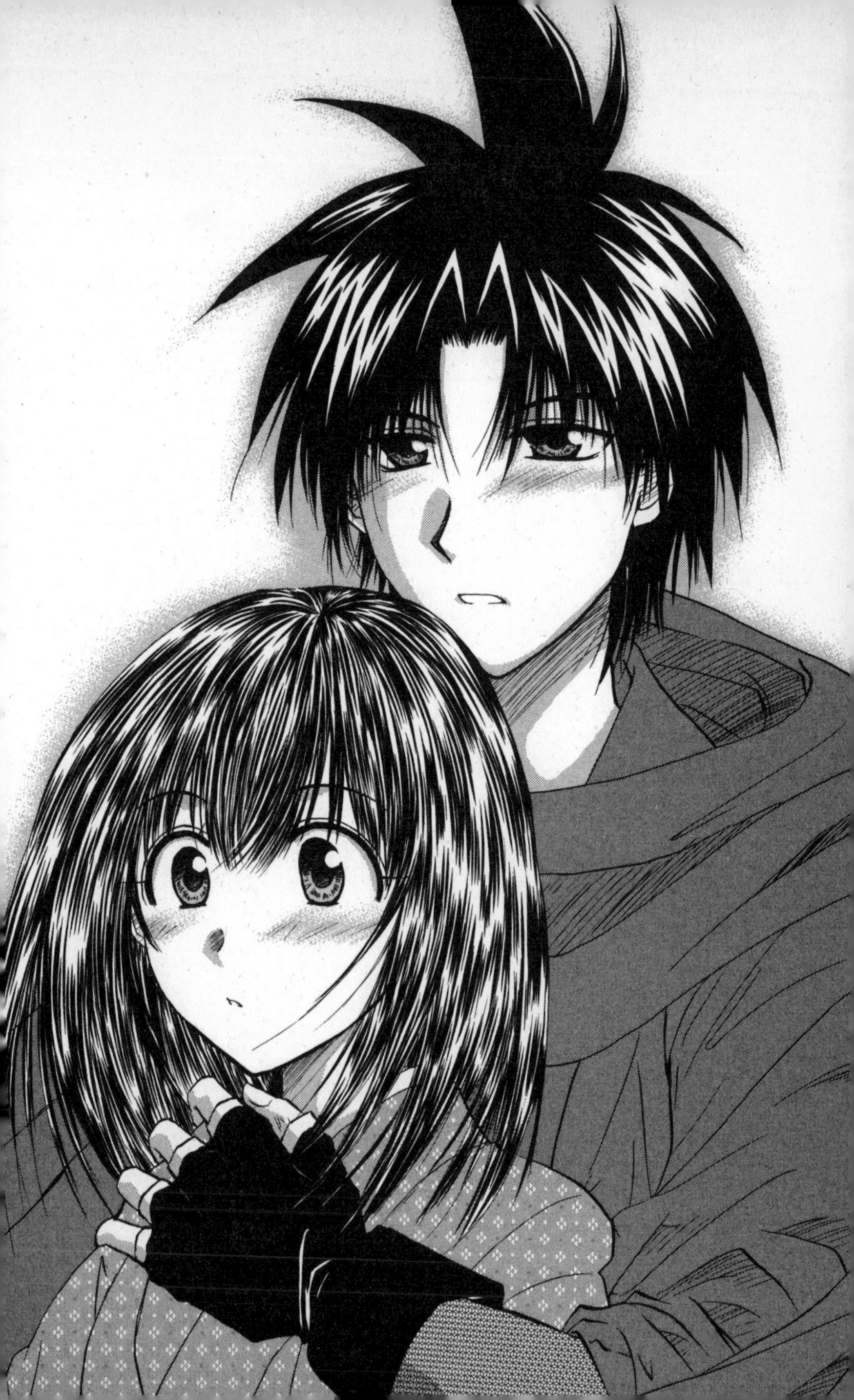

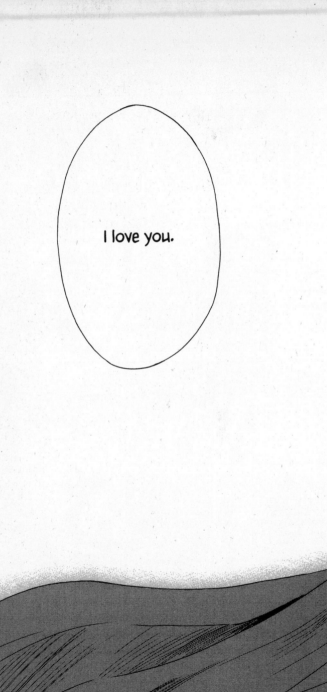

I love you.

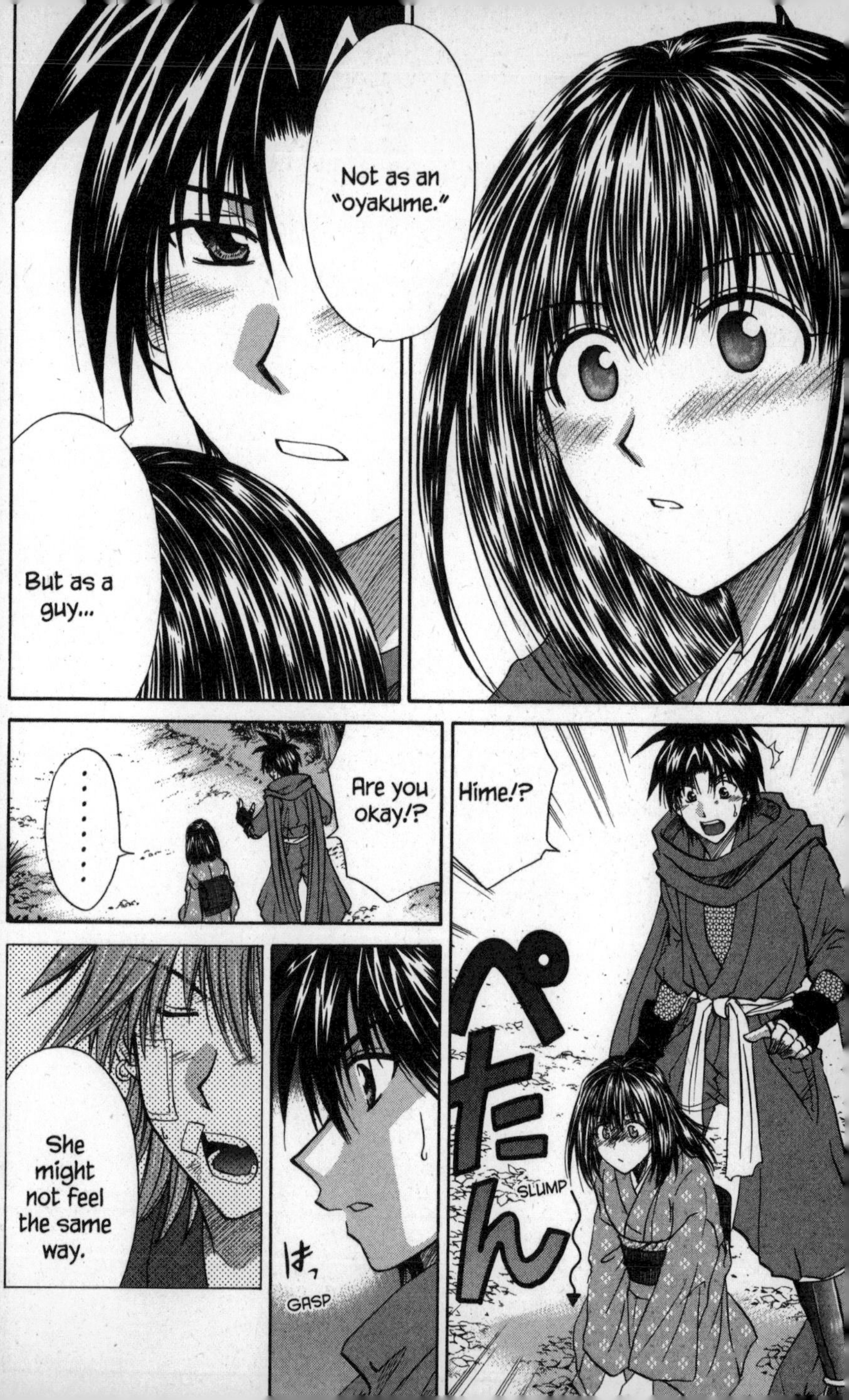
Not as an "oyakume."
But as a guy...
Hime!?
ぺたん
SLUMP
Are you okay!?
......
はっ
GASP
She might not feel the same way.

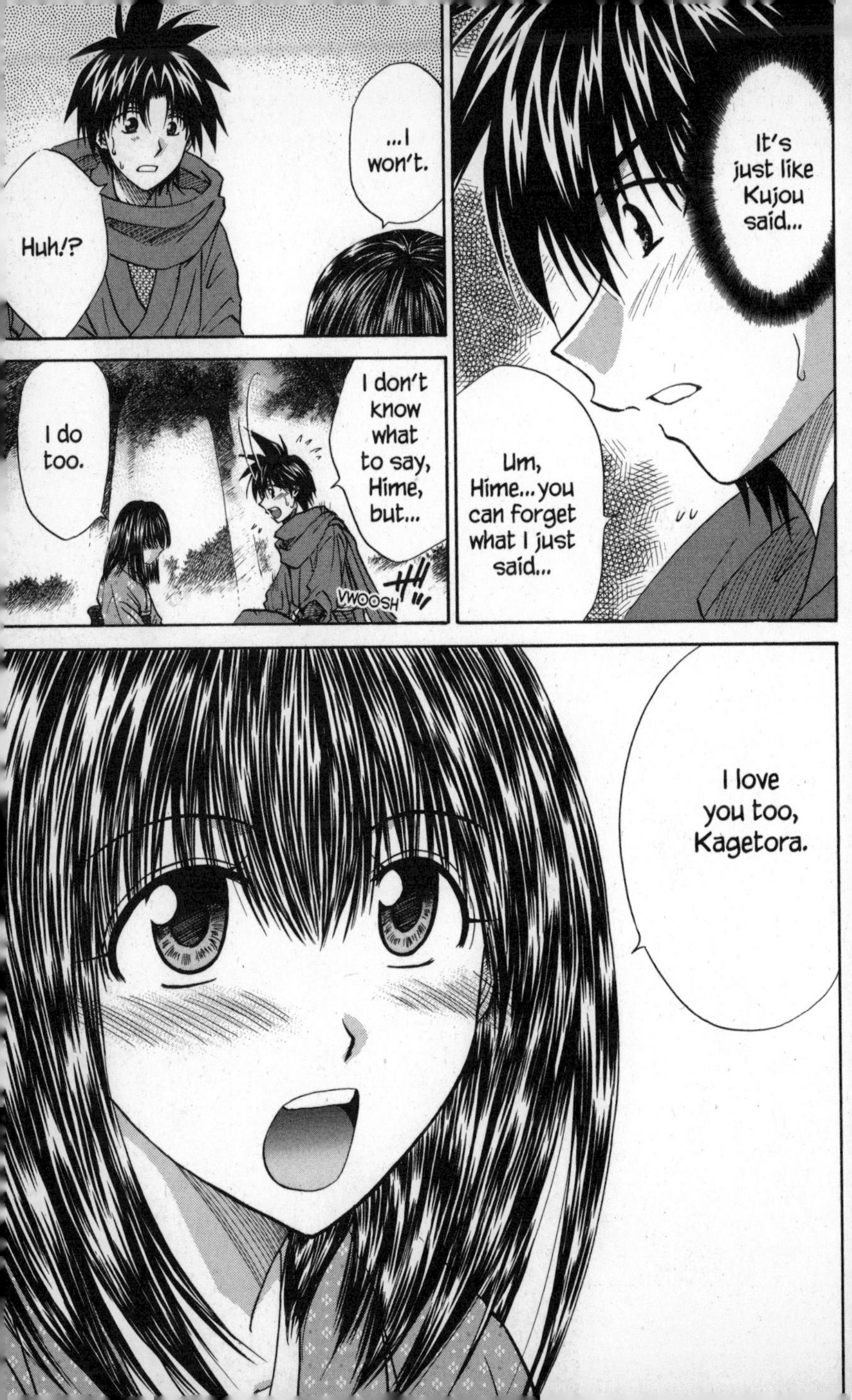
It's just like Kujou said...
Um, Hime...you can forget what I just said...
...I won't.
Huh!?
I don't know what to say, Hime, but...
VWOOSH
I do too.
I love you too, Kagetora.

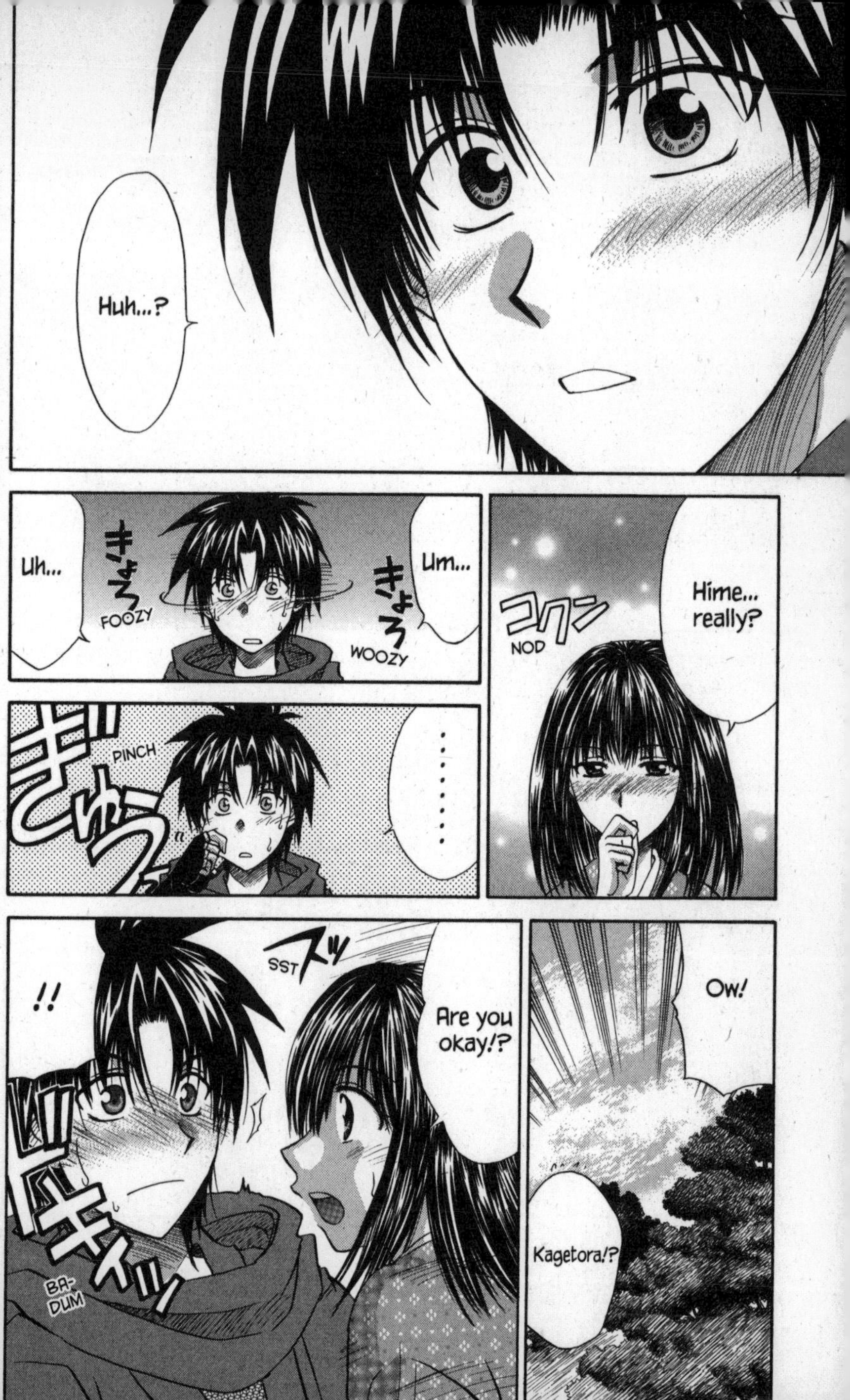
Huh...?
Hime... really?
コクン
NOD
Um...
きょろ
WOOZY
きょろ
FOOZY
Uh...
......
ぎゅう
PINCH
Ow!
Kagetora!?
Are you okay!?
スッ
SST
!!
ドキッ
BA-DUM

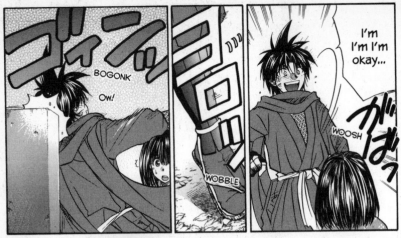

BOGONK

Ow!

WOBBLE

I'm I'm I'm okay...

WOOSH

I guess it wasn't a dream...

STING
STING

Ouch.

er...

GOOONG

Ka-getora!

. . . .

I see...

It's real...

GIGGLE

It's real...

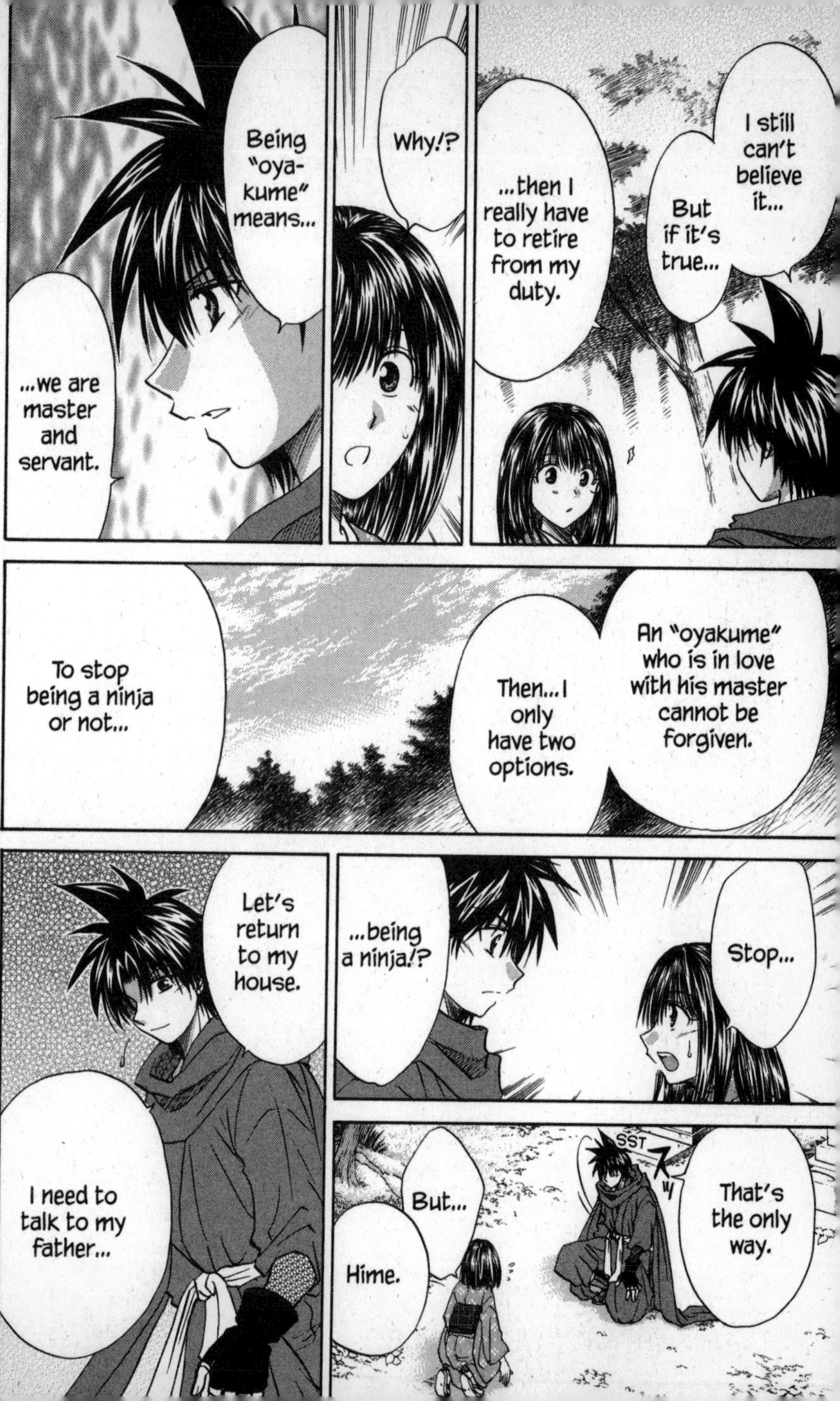
I still can't believe it...
But if it's true...
...then I really have to retire from my duty.
Why!?
Being "oya-kume" means...
...we are master and servant.
An "oyakume" who is in love with his master cannot be forgiven.
Then...I only have two options.
To stop being a ninja or not...
Stop...
...being a ninja!?
SST
That's the only way.
But...
Hime.
Let's return to my house.
I need to talk to my father...

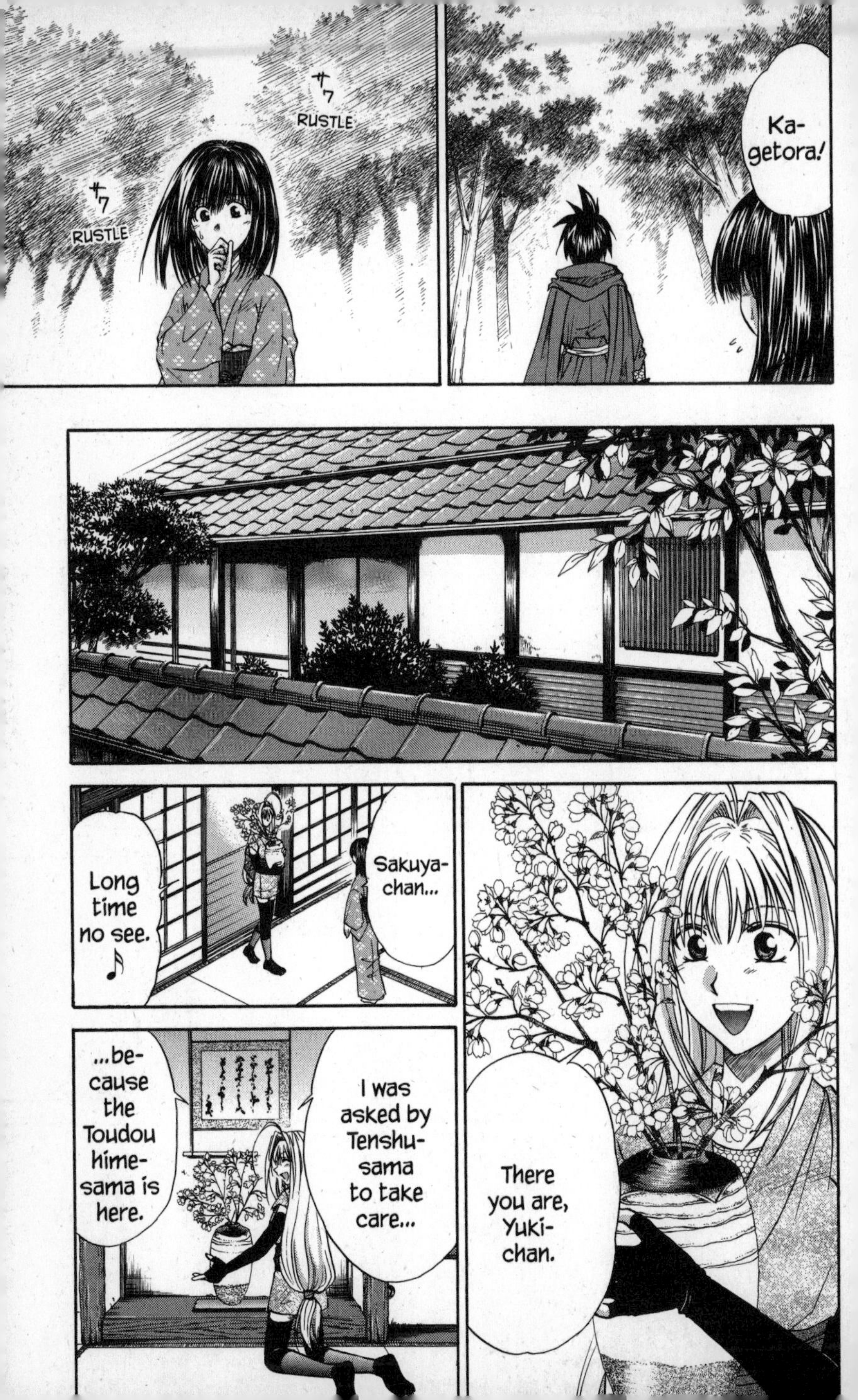
Ka-getora!
RUSTLE
RUSTLE
There you are, Yuki-chan.
Sakuya-chan...
Long time no see. ♪
I was asked by Tenshu-sama to take care...
...because the Toudou hime-sama is here.

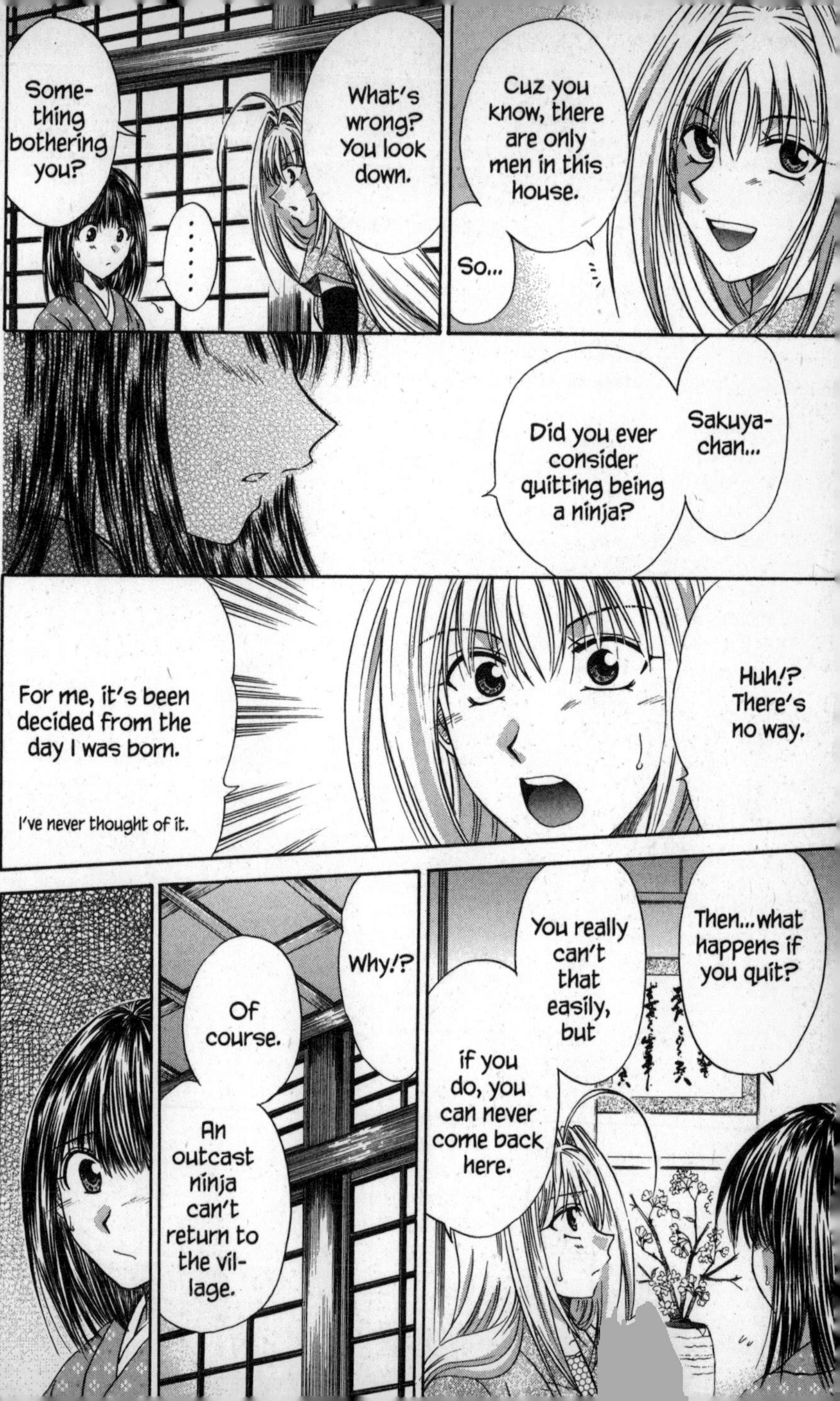
Cuz you know, there are only men in this house.
So...
What's wrong? You look down.
Some-thing bothering you?
......
Sakuya-chan...
Did you ever consider quitting being a ninja?
Huh!? There's no way.
For me, it's been decided from the day I was born.
I've never thought of it.
Then...what happens if you quit?
You really can't that easily, but
if you do, you can never come back here.
Why!?
Of course.
An outcast ninja can't return to the vil-lage.

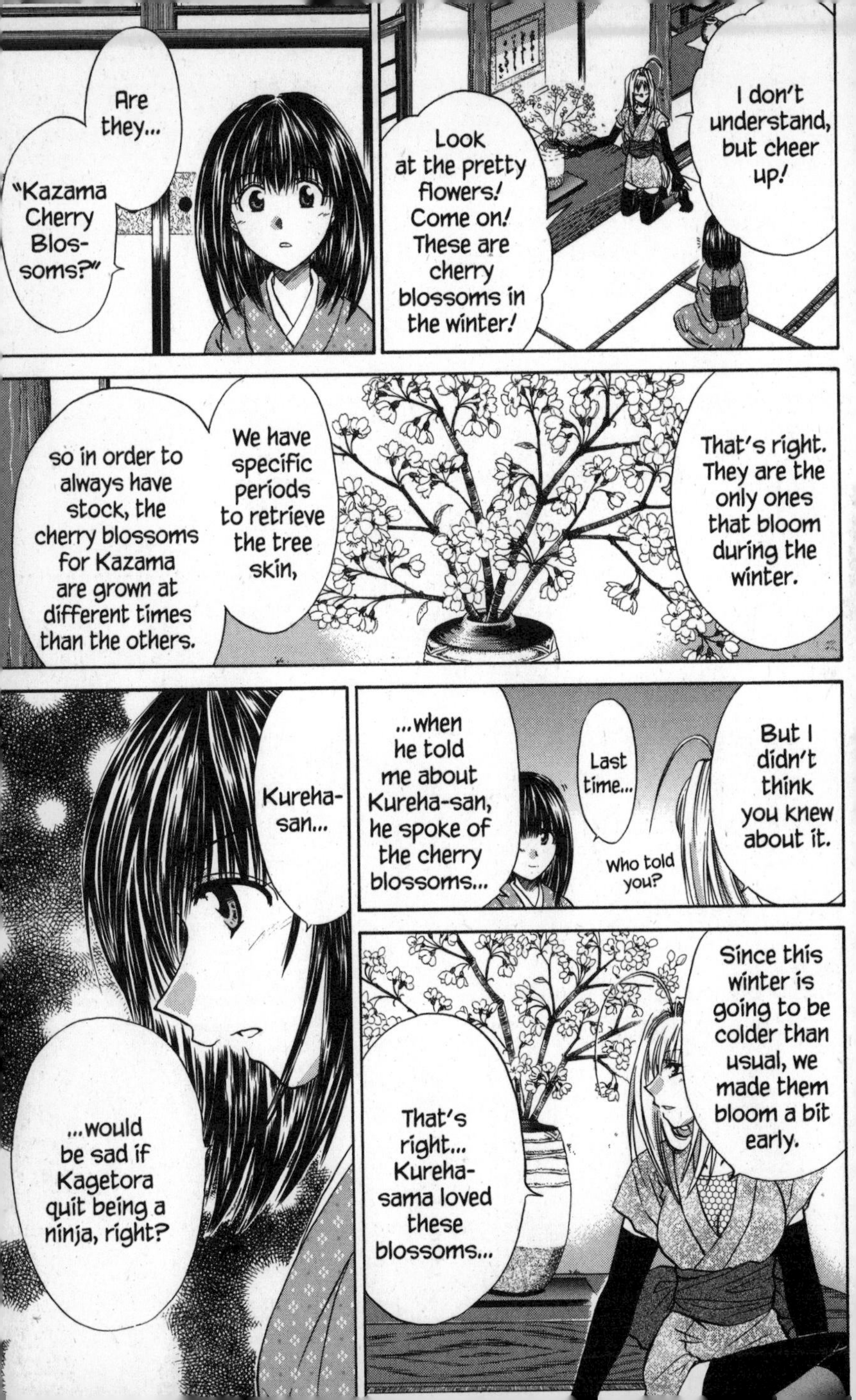
I don't understand, but cheer up!
Look at the pretty flowers! Come on! These are cherry blossoms in the winter!
Are they...
"Kazama Cherry Blossoms?"
That's right. They are the only ones that bloom during the winter.
We have specific periods to retrieve the tree skin,
so in order to always have stock, the cherry blossoms for Kazama are grown at different times than the others.
But I didn't think you knew about it.
Who told you?
Last time...
...when he told me about Kureha-san, he spoke of the cherry blossoms...
Since this winter is going to be colder than usual, we made them bloom a bit early.
That's right... Kureha-sama loved these blossoms...
Kureha-san...
...would be sad if Kagetora quit being a ninja, right?

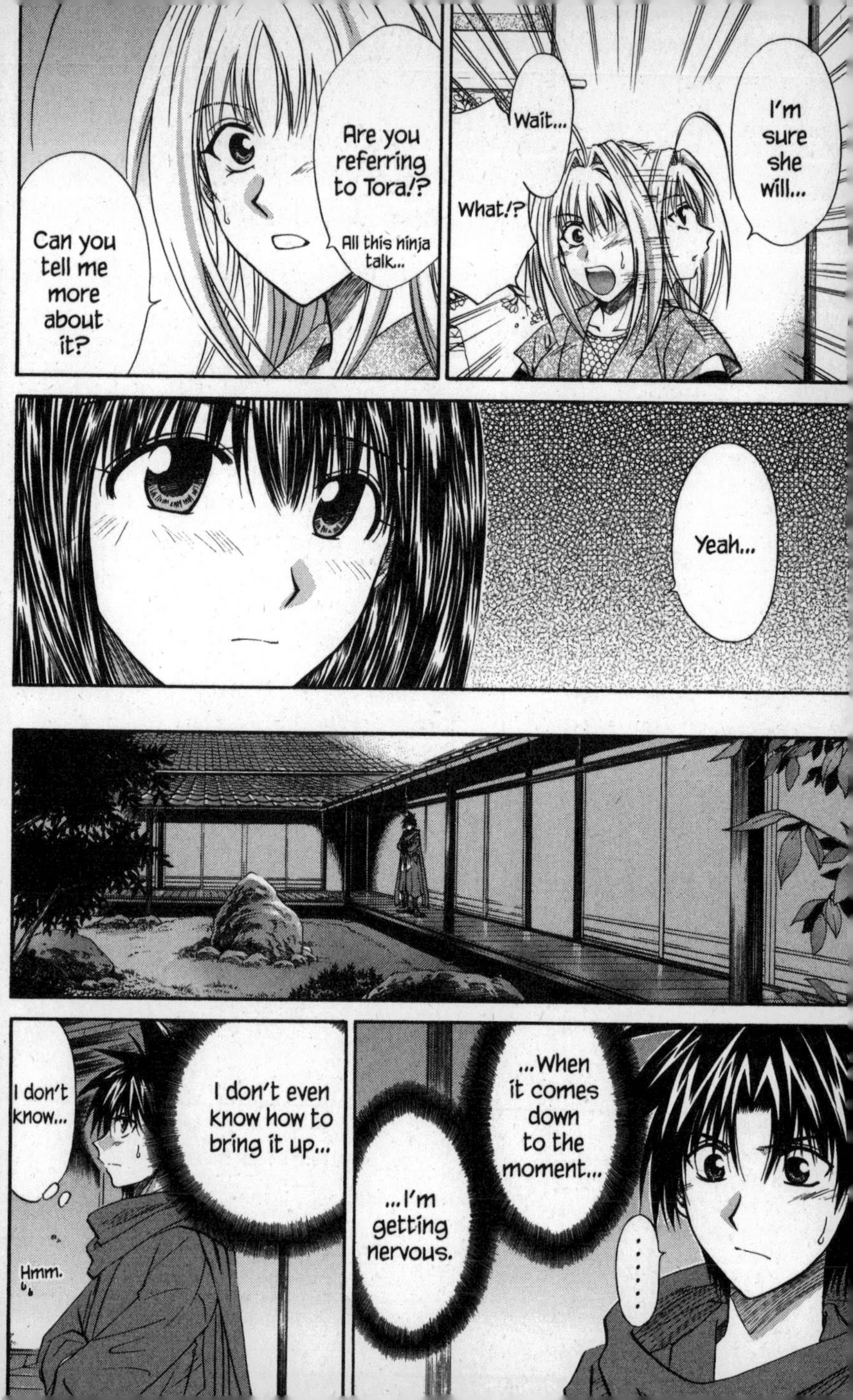
I'm sure she will...
Wait...
What!?
Are you referring to Tora!?
All this ninja talk...
Can you tell me more about it?
Yeah...
...When it comes down to the moment...
...I'm getting nervous.
......
I don't even know how to bring it up...
I don't know...
Hmm.

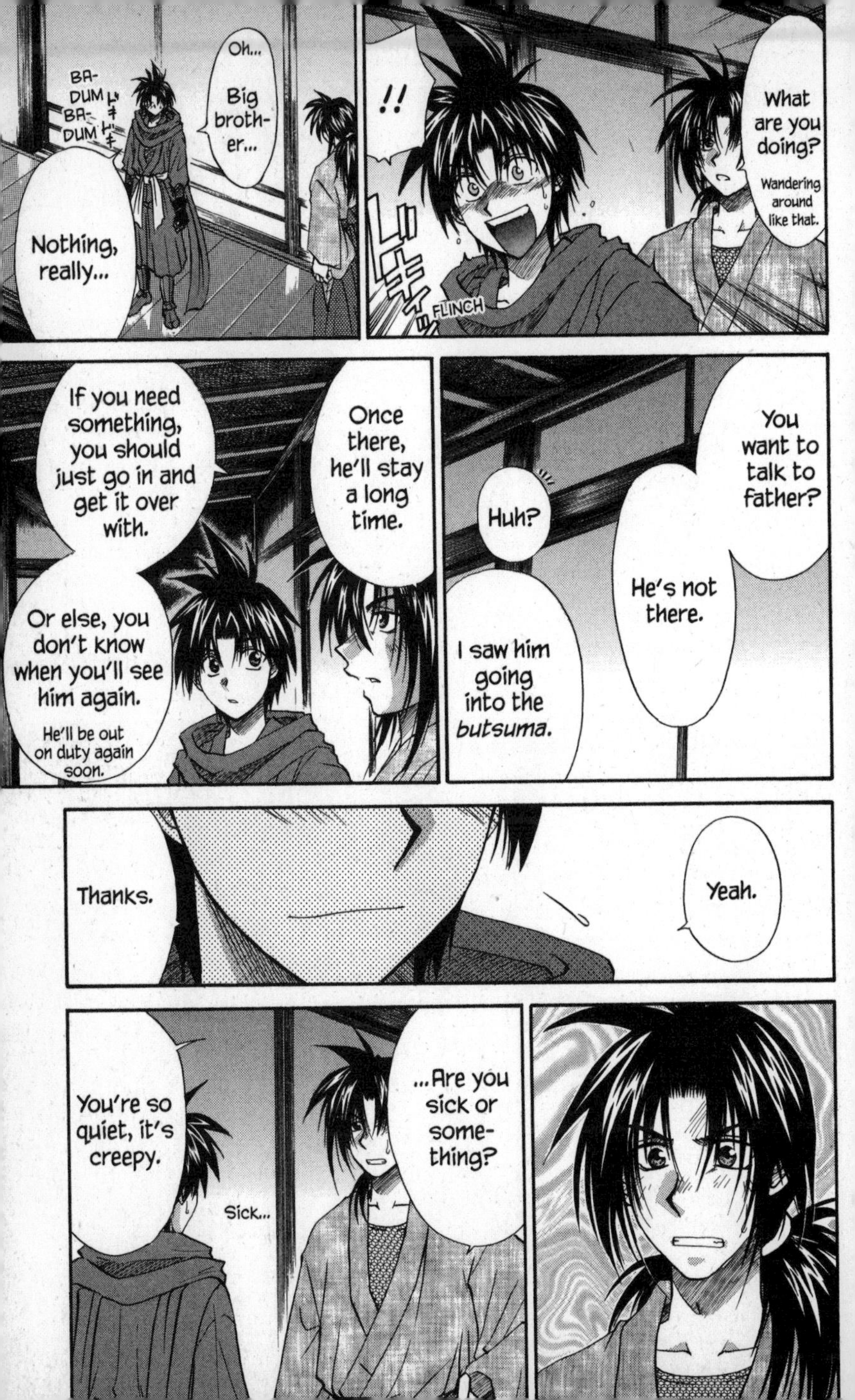
What are you doing?
Wandering around like that.
!!
FLINCH
Oh... Big brother...
BA-DUM BA-DUM
Nothing, really...
You want to talk to father?
He's not there.
Huh?
I saw him going into the *butsuma*.
Once there, he'll stay a long time.
If you need something, you should just go in and get it over with.
Or else, you don't know when you'll see him again.
He'll be out on duty again soon.
Yeah.
Thanks.
...Are you sick or something?
You're so quiet, it's creepy.
Sick...

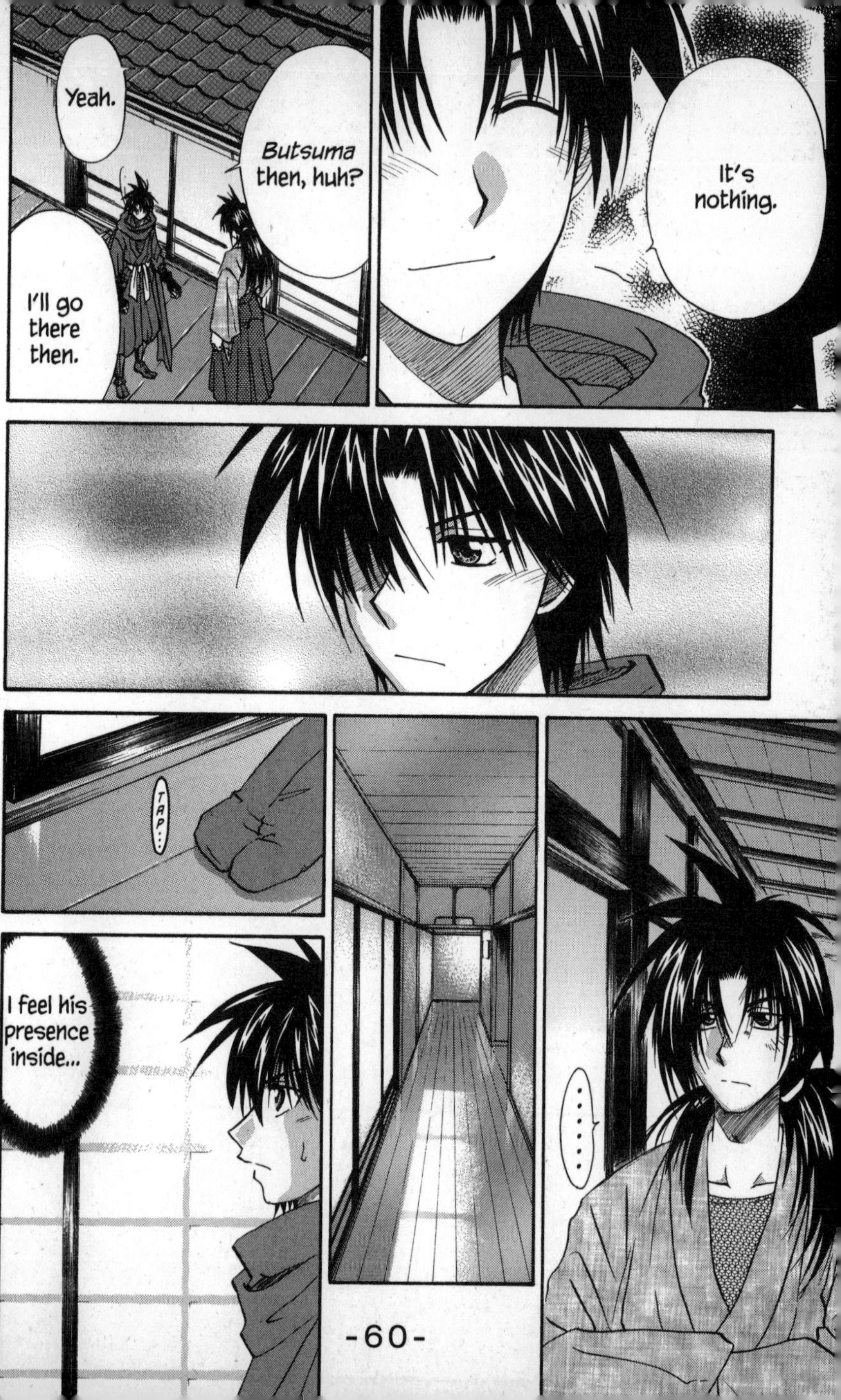
It's nothing.
Butsuma then, huh?
Yeah.
I'll go there then.
......
TAP...
I feel his presence inside...

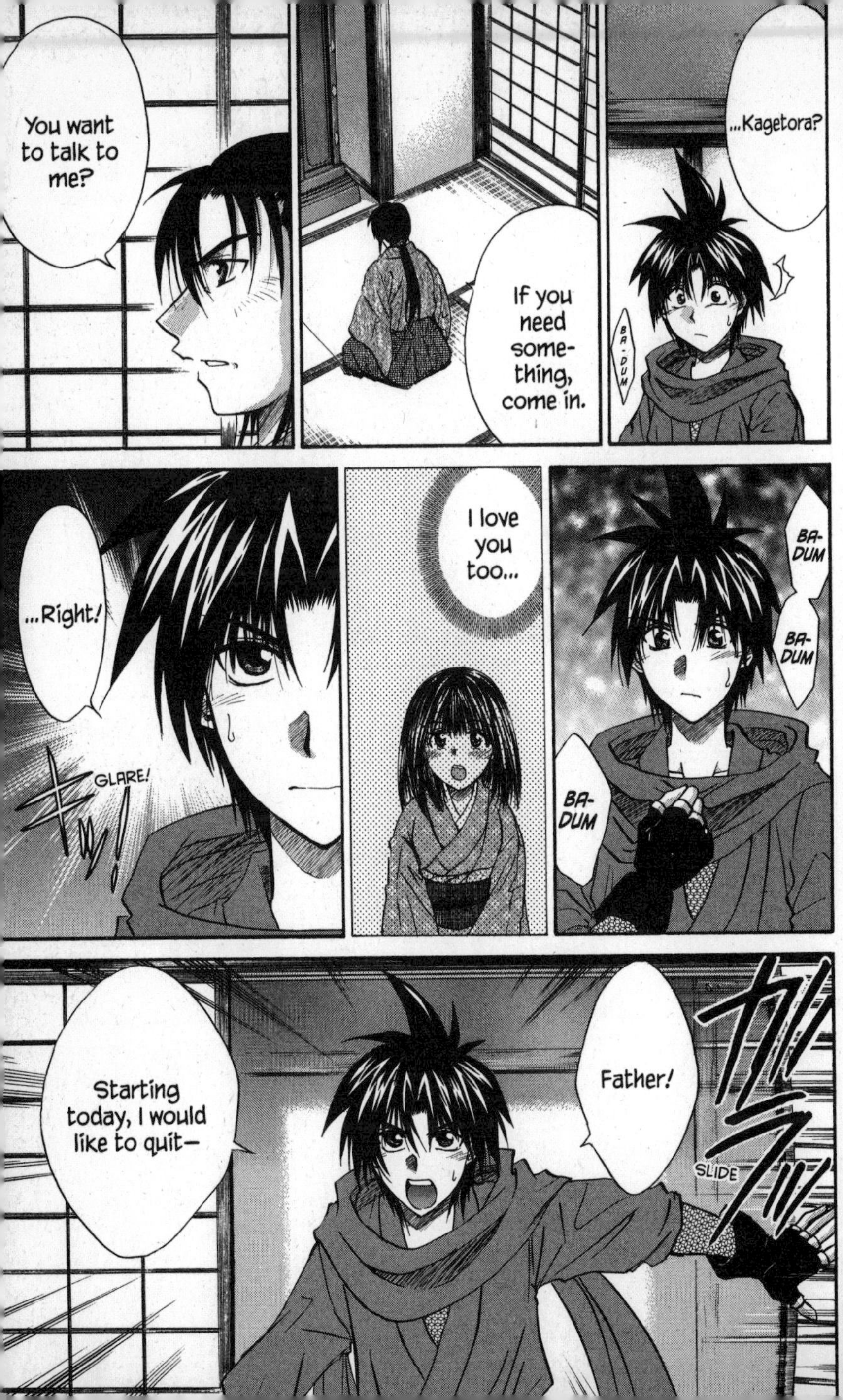
...Kagetora?
BA-DUM
If you need some-thing, come in.
You want to talk to me?
BA-DUM
BA-DUM
BA-DUM
I love you too...
...Right!
GLARE!
SLIDE
Father!
Starting today, I would like to quit—

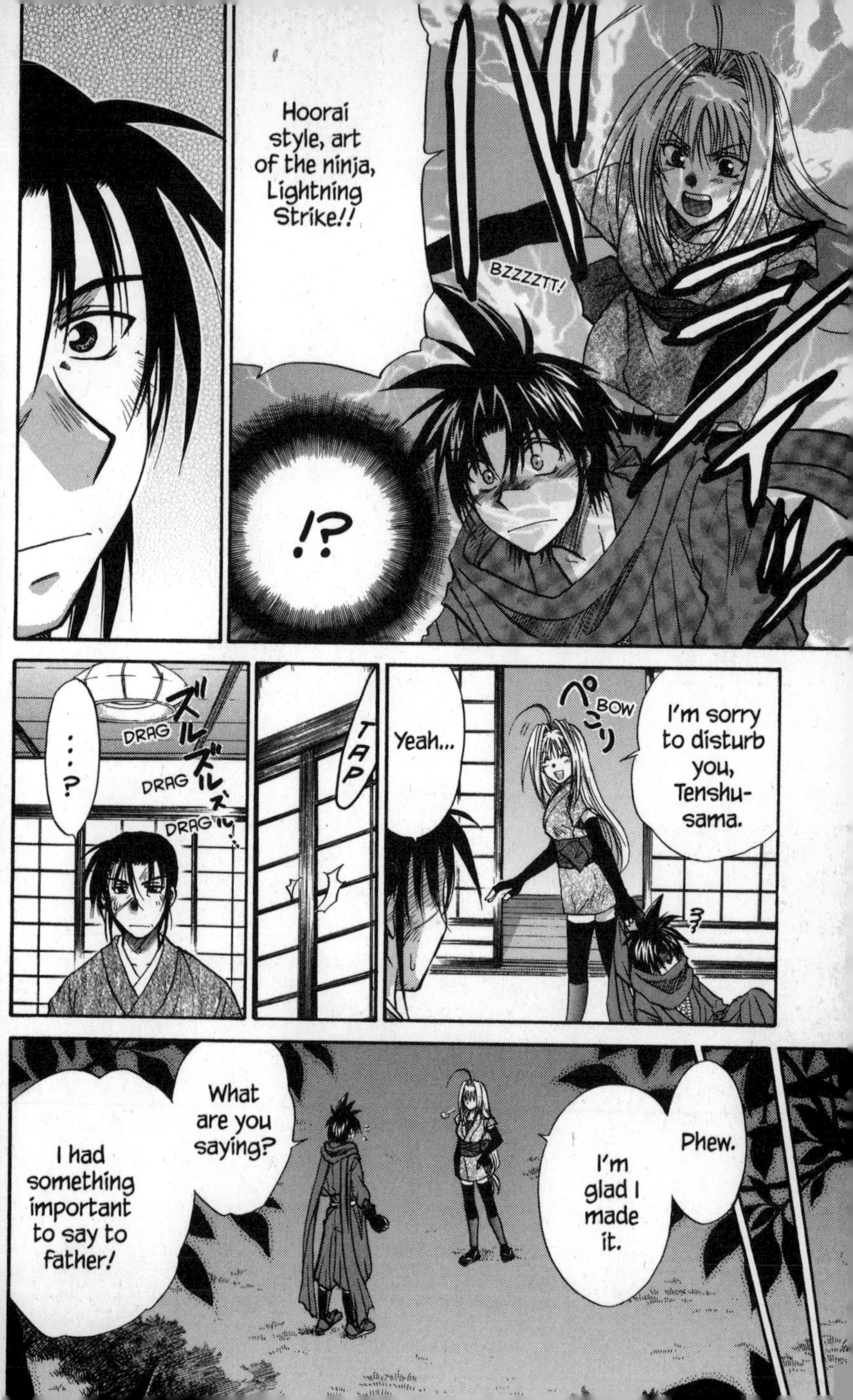
Hoorai style, art of the ninja, Lightning Strike!!
BZZZZTT!
!?
I'm sorry to disturb you, Tenshu-sama.
ぺこり
BOW
Yeah...
TAP
...?
ズルズルズル...
DRAG
DRAG
DRAG
Phew.
I'm glad I made it.
What are you saying?
I had something important to say to father!

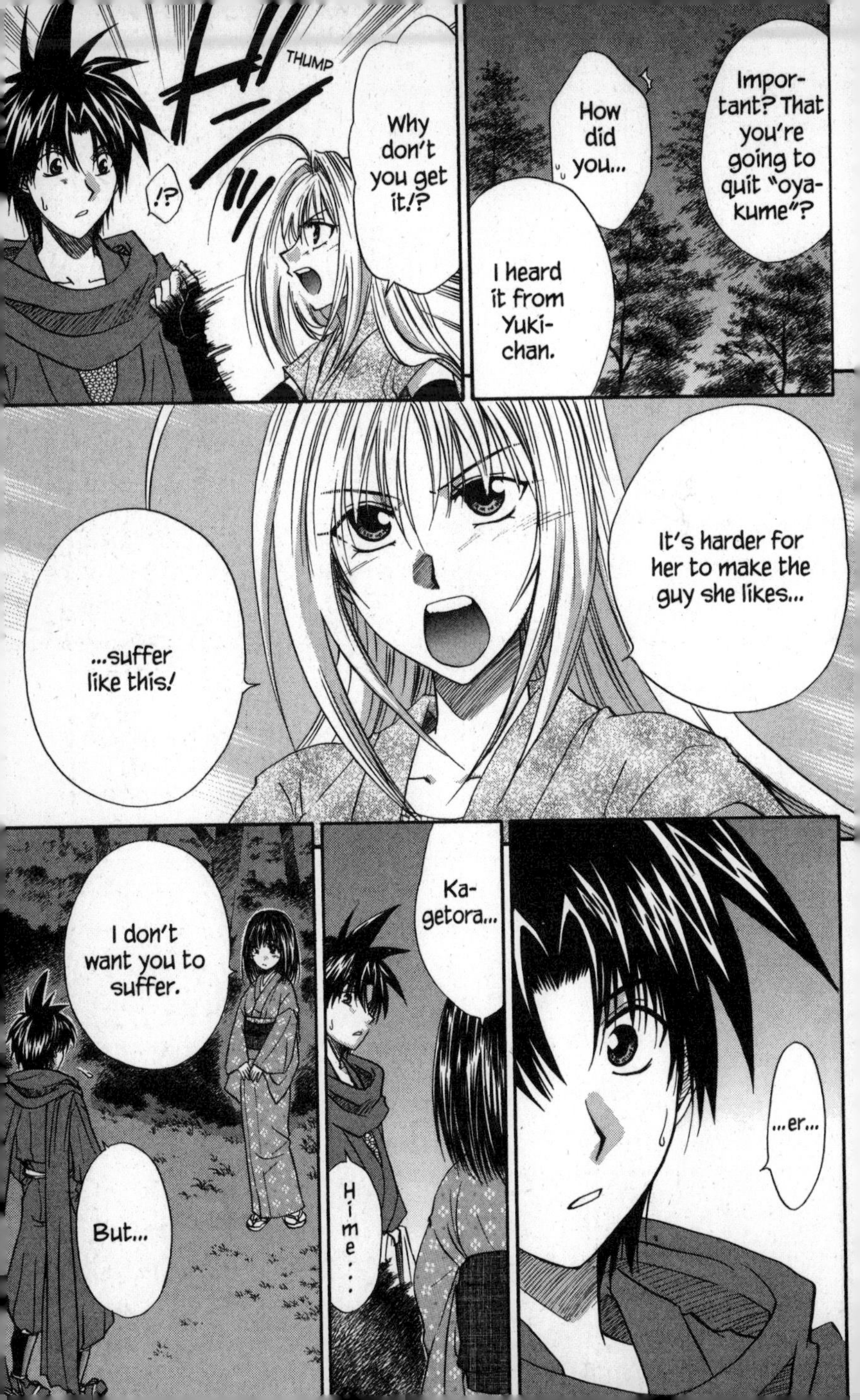
Impor-tant? That you're going to quit "oya-kume"?
How did you...
I heard it from Yuki-chan.
THUMP
Why don't you get it!?
!?
It's harder for her to make the guy she likes...
...suffer like this!
Ka-getora...
...er...
Hime...
I don't want you to suffer.
But...

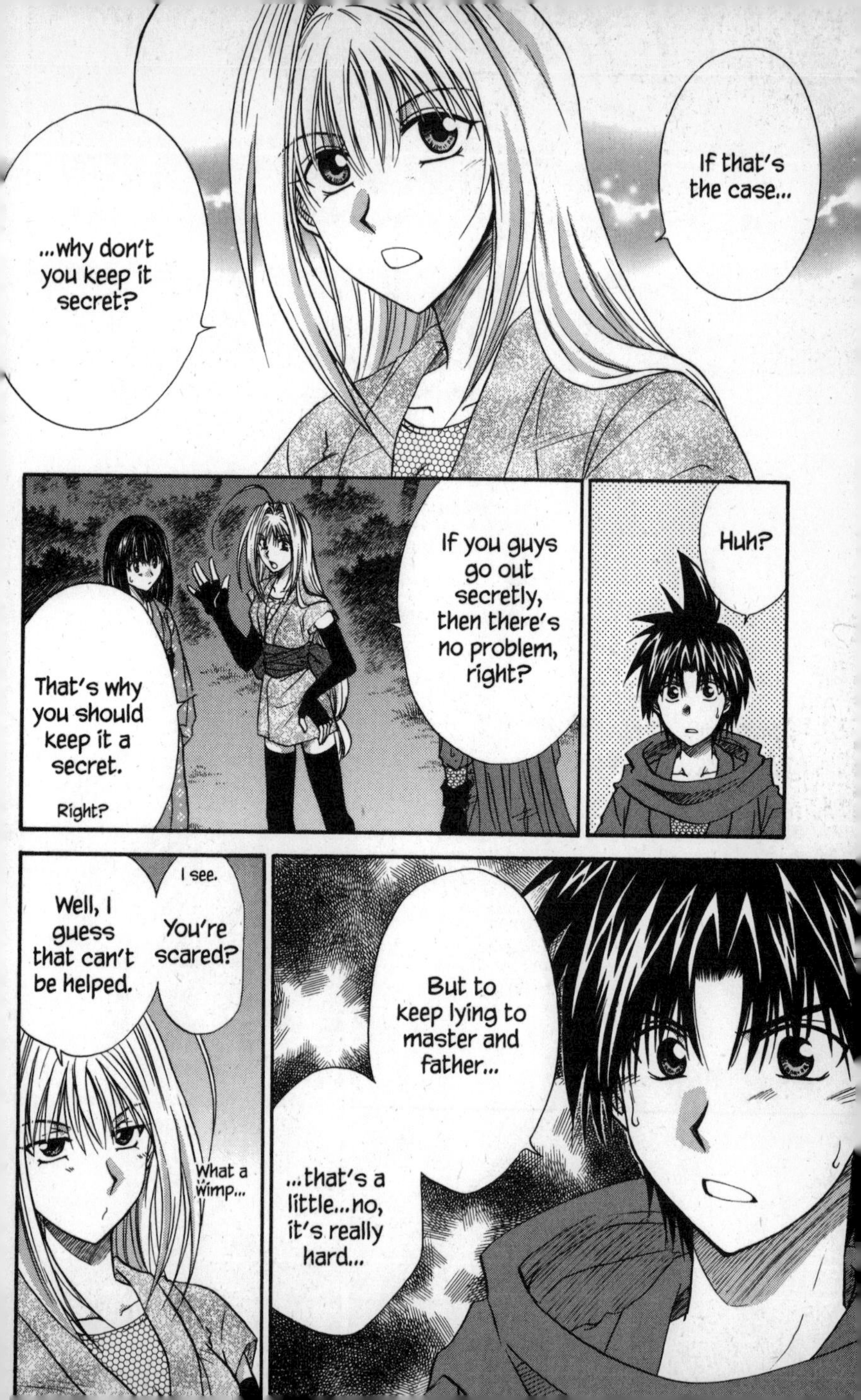
If that's the case...
...why don't you keep it secret?
Huh?
If you guys go out secretly, then there's no problem, right?
That's why you should keep it a secret.
Right?
But to keep lying to master and father...
...that's a little...no, it's really hard...
I see.
You're scared?
Well, I guess that can't be helped.
What a wimp...

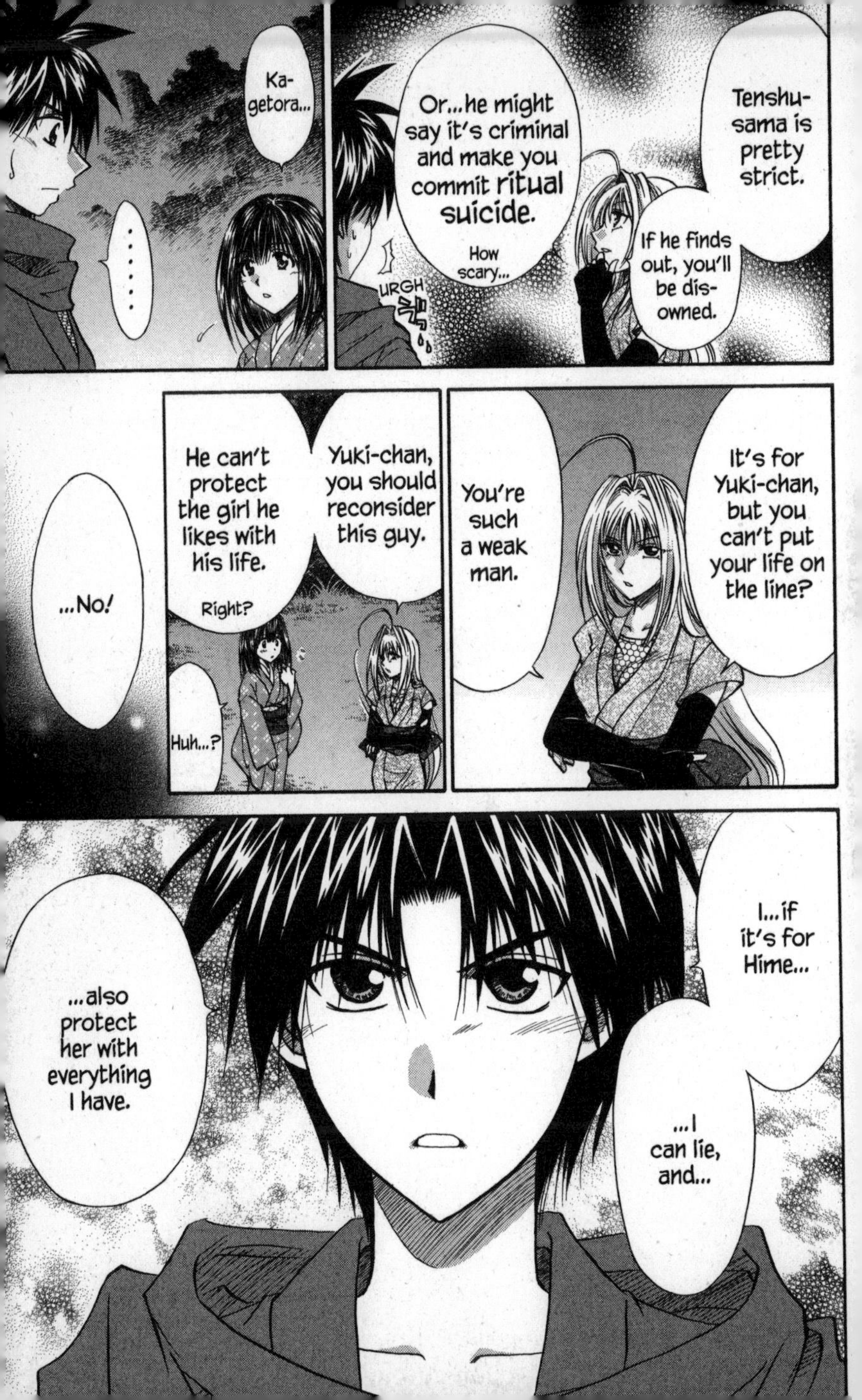
Tenshu-sama is pretty strict.
If he finds out, you'll be dis-owned.
Or...he might say it's criminal and make you commit ritual suicide.
How scary...
URGH
Ka-getora...
......
It's for Yuki-chan, but you can't put your life on the line?
You're such a weak man.
Yuki-chan, you should reconsider this guy.
He can't protect the girl he likes with his life.
Right?
Huh...?
...No!
I...if it's for Hime...
...I can lie, and...
...also protect her with everything I have.

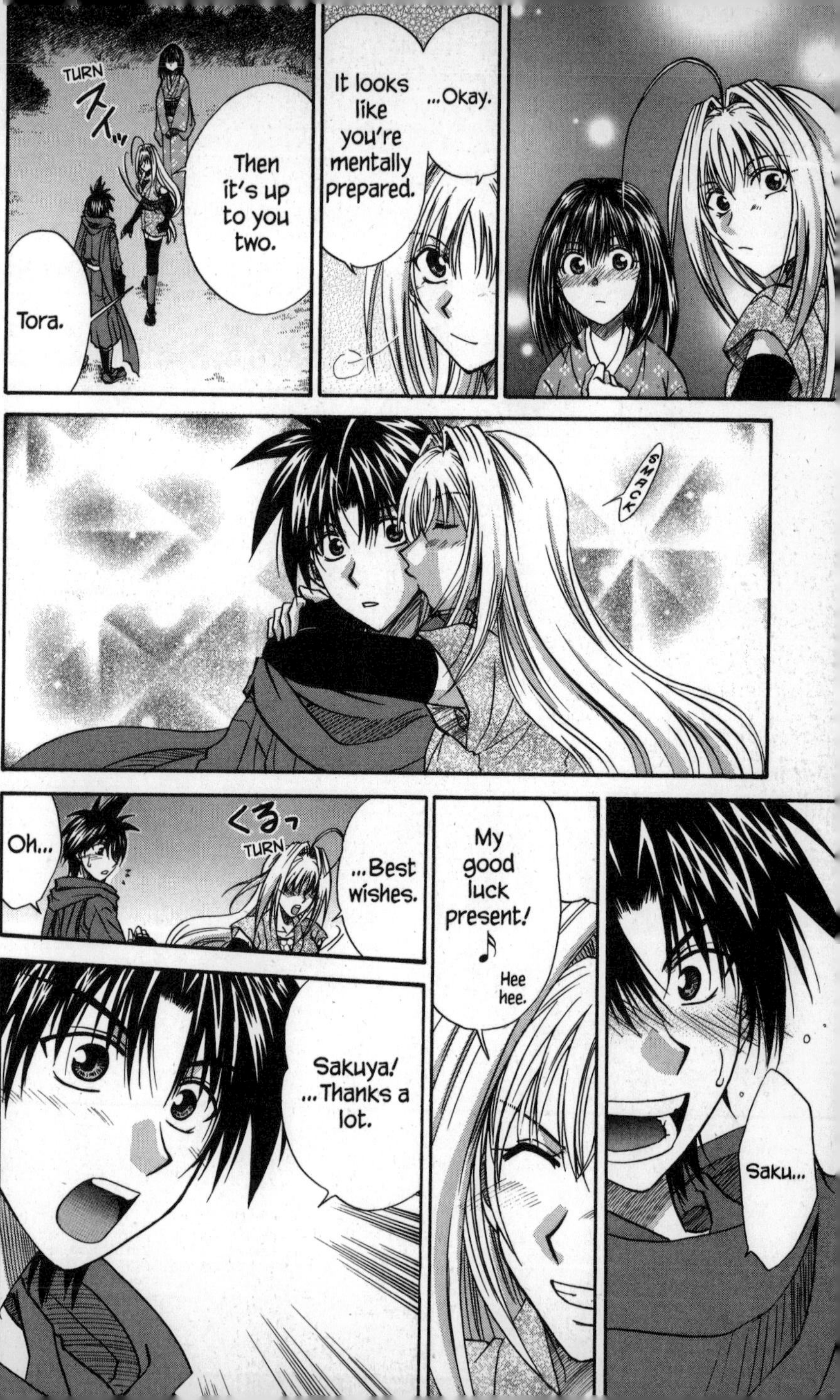
It looks like you're mentally prepared.
...Okay.
TURN
スイッ
Then it's up to you two.
Tora.
SMACK
Saku...
My good luck present! ♪
Hee hee.
くるっ
TURN
...Best wishes.
Oh...
Sakuya! ...Thanks a lot.

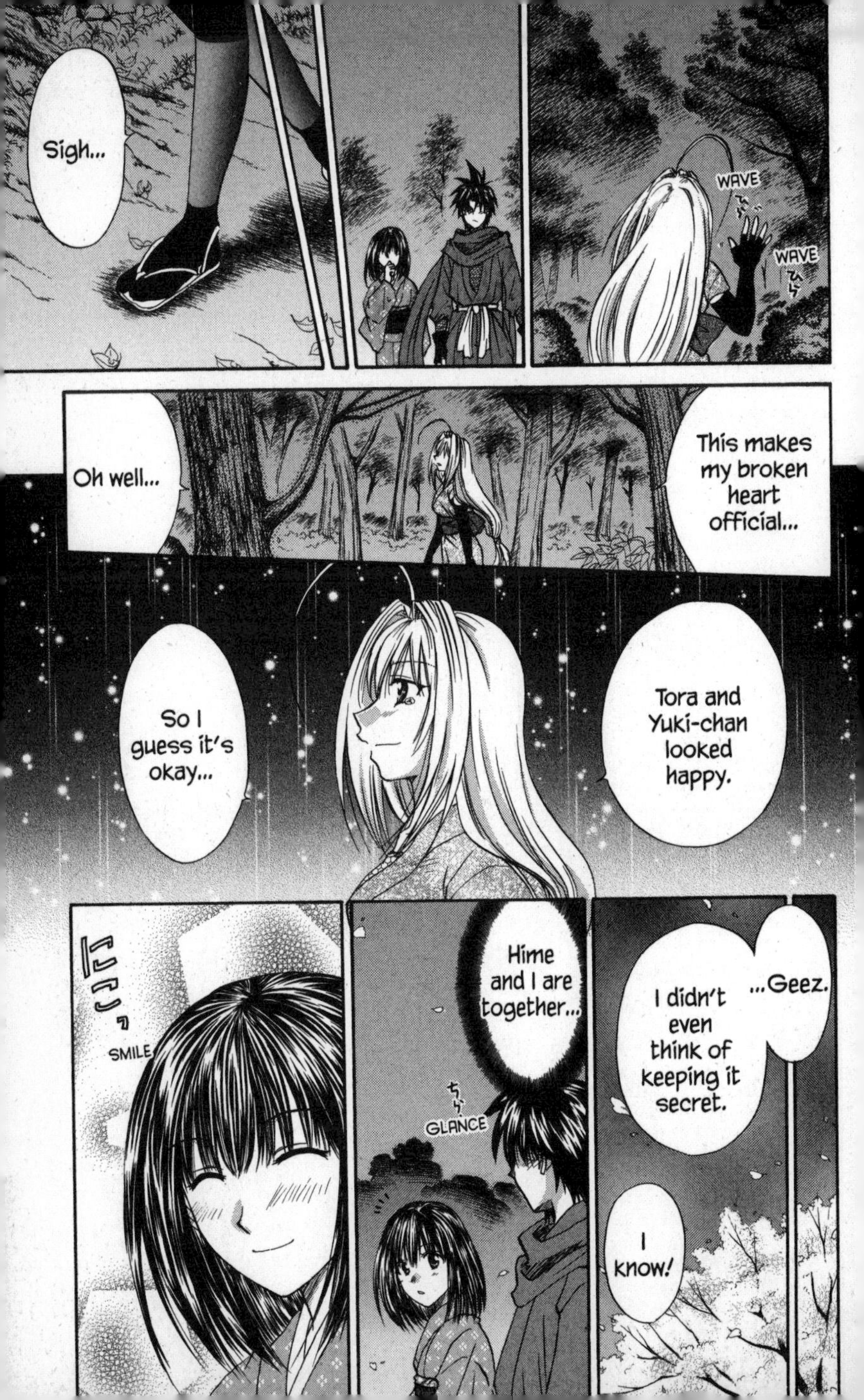
WAVE
WAVE
Sigh...
This makes my broken heart official...
Oh well...
Tora and Yuki-chan looked happy.
So I guess it's okay...
...Geez.
I didn't even think of keeping it secret.
I know!
Hime and I are together...
GLANCE
SMILE

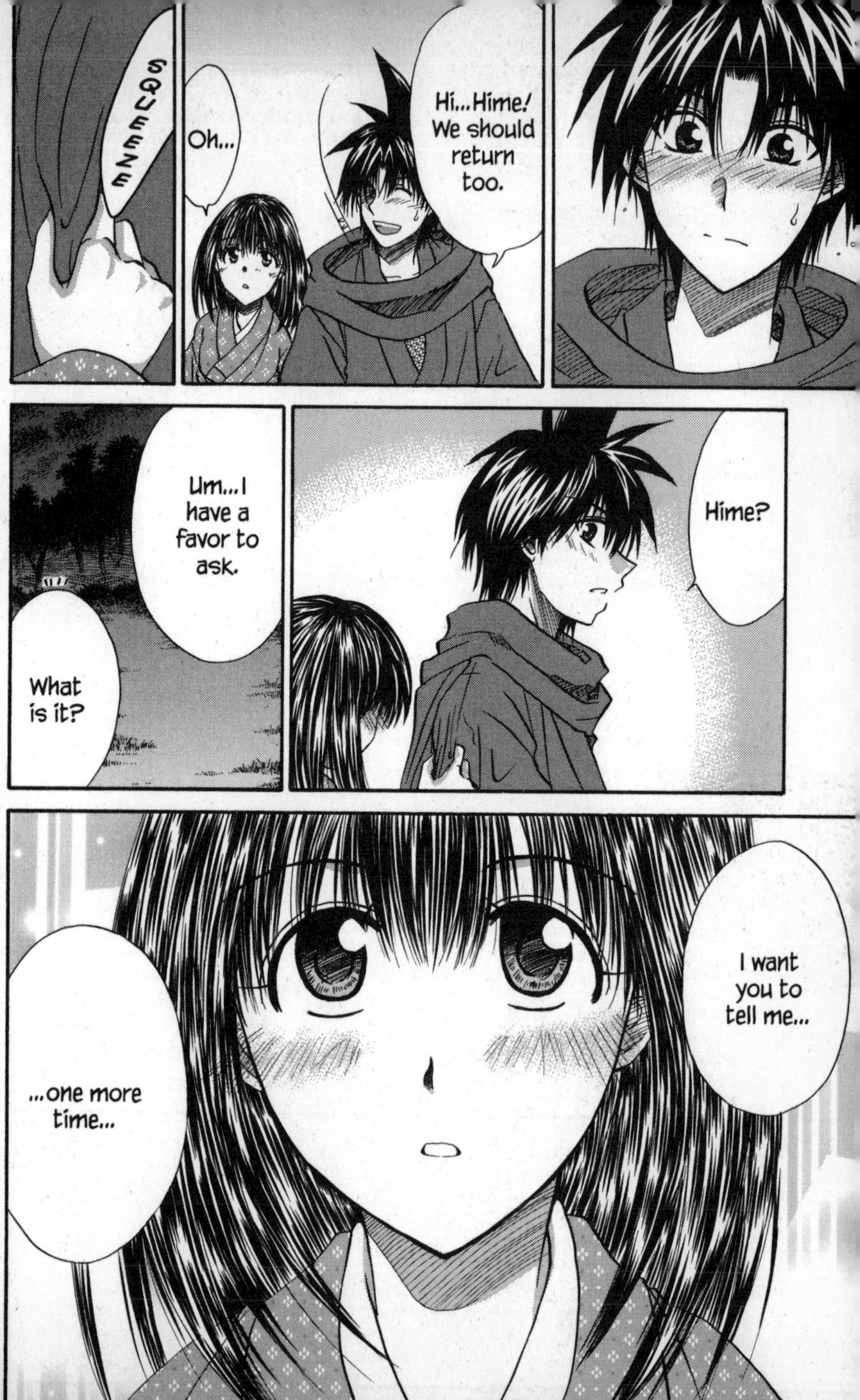
Hi...Hime! We should return too.
Oh...
SQUEEZE
Hime?
Um...I have a favor to ask.
What is it?
I want you to tell me...
...one more time...

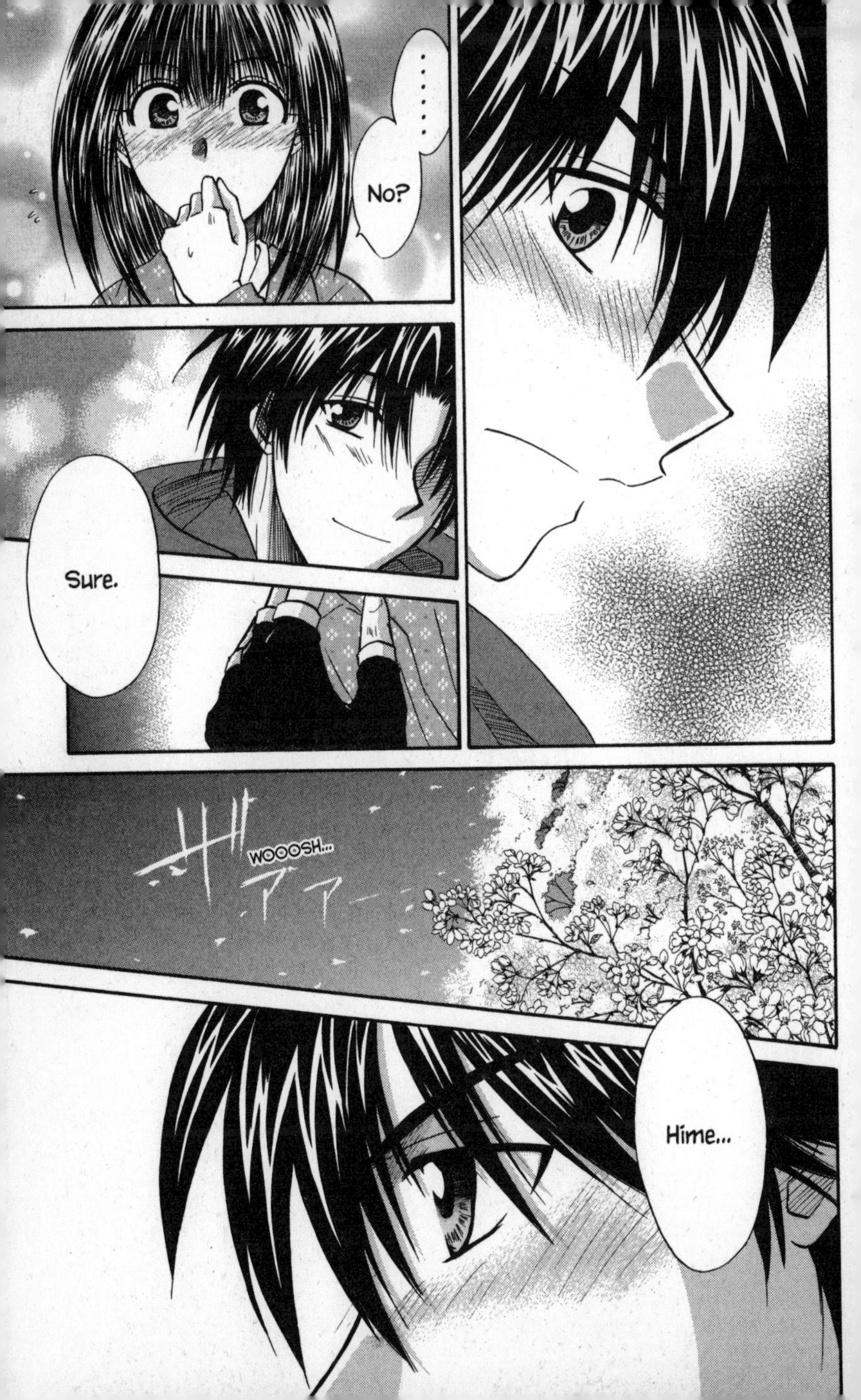
......
No?
Sure.
WOOOSH...
Hime...

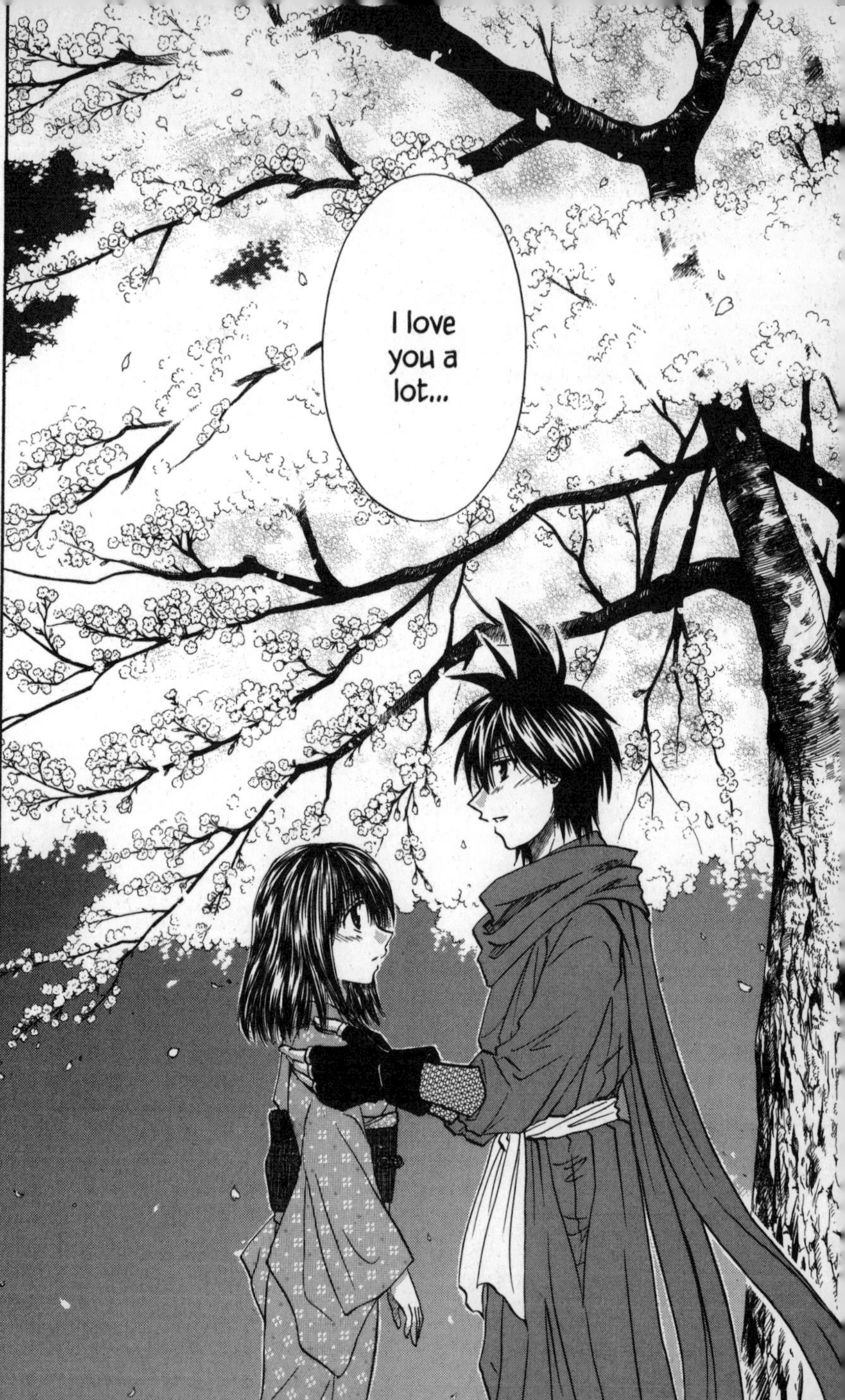
I love you a lot...

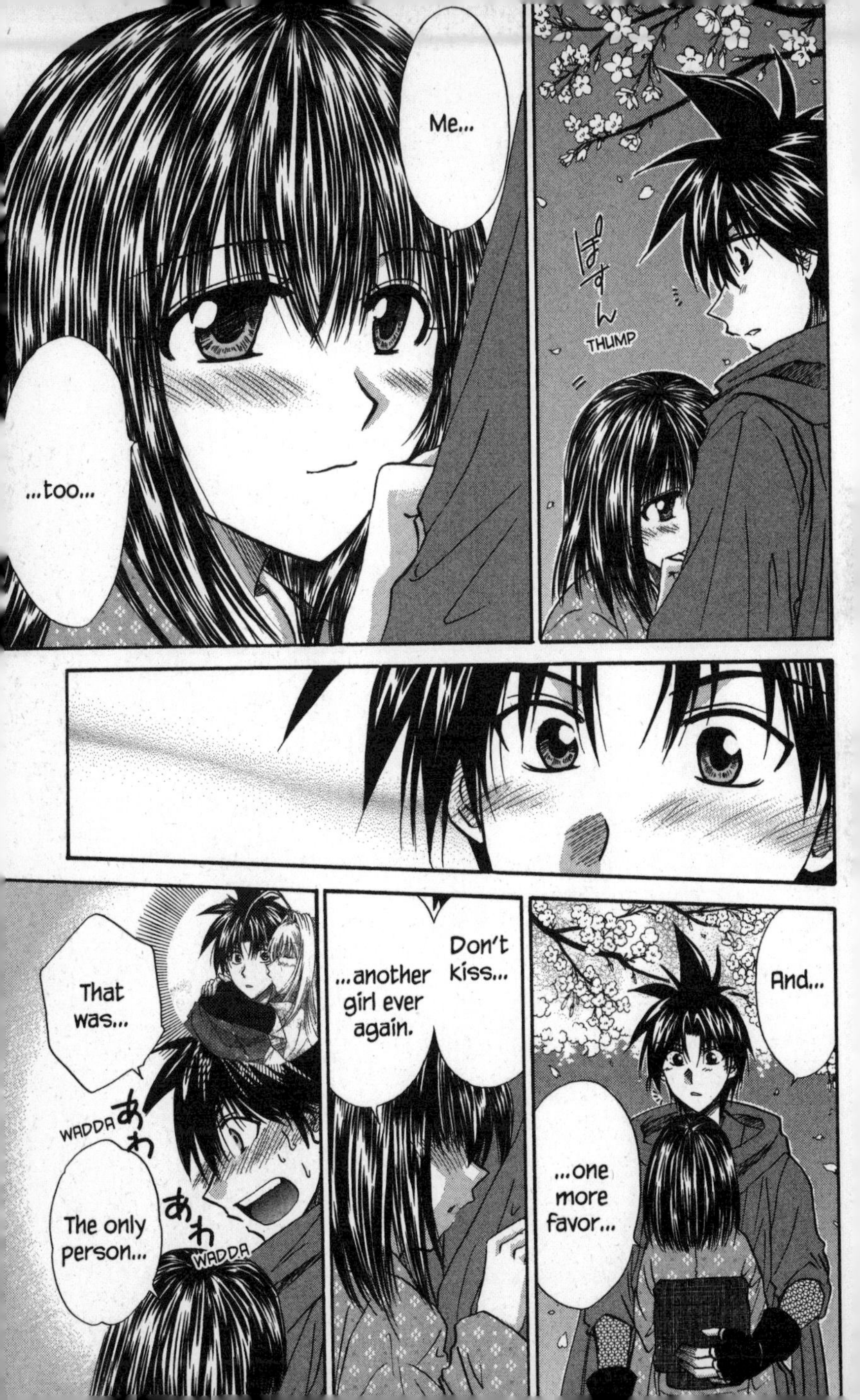
ぽすん
THUMP
Me...
...too...
And...
...one more favor...
Don't kiss...
...another girl ever again.
That was...
あわ
WADDA
The only person...
あわ
WADDA

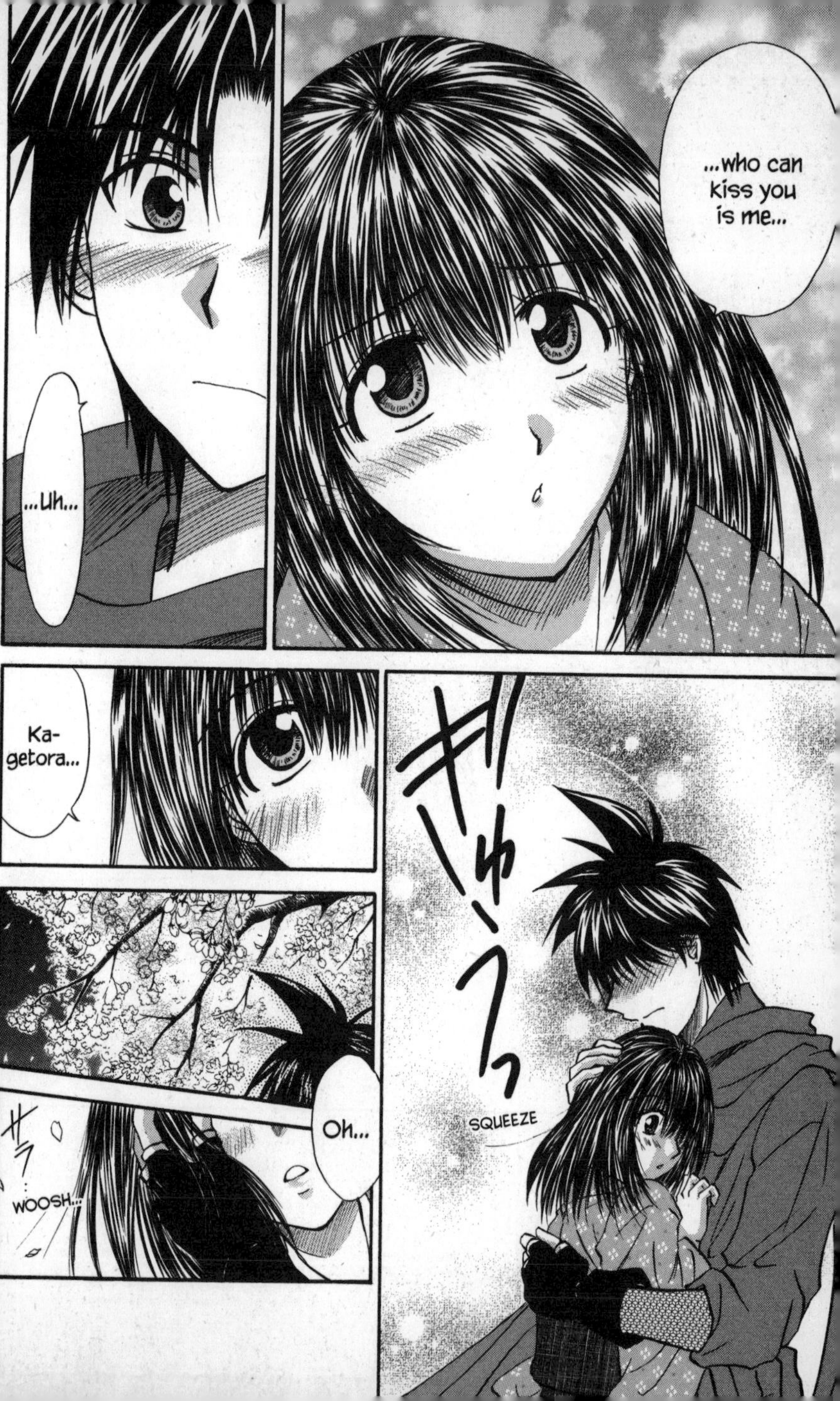
...who can kiss you is me...
...uh...
ぎゅうっ
SQUEEZE
Ka-getora...
Oh...
サラ
WOOSH...

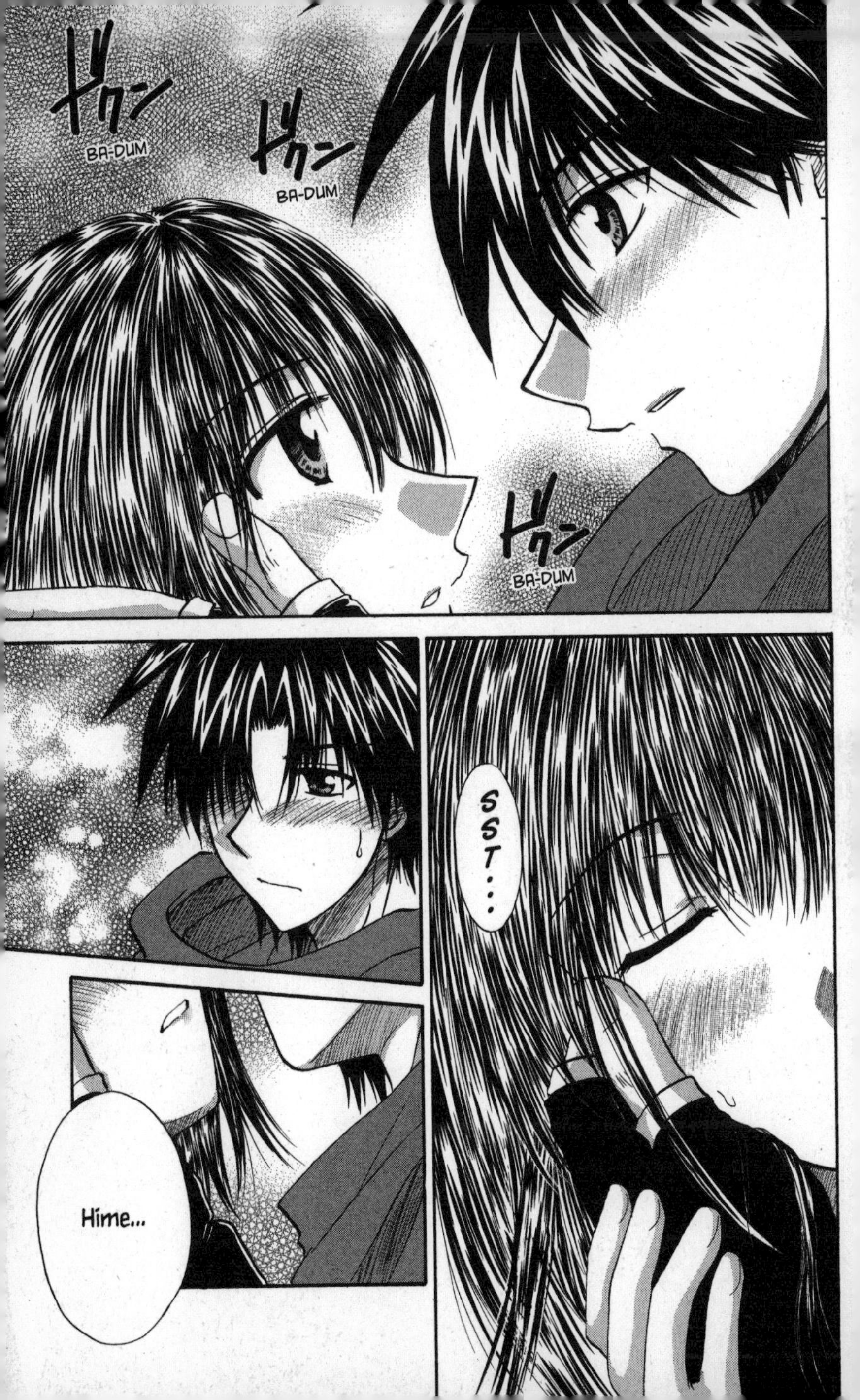
ドクン
BA-DUM
ドクン
BA-DUM
ドクン
BA-DUM
SST...
Hime...

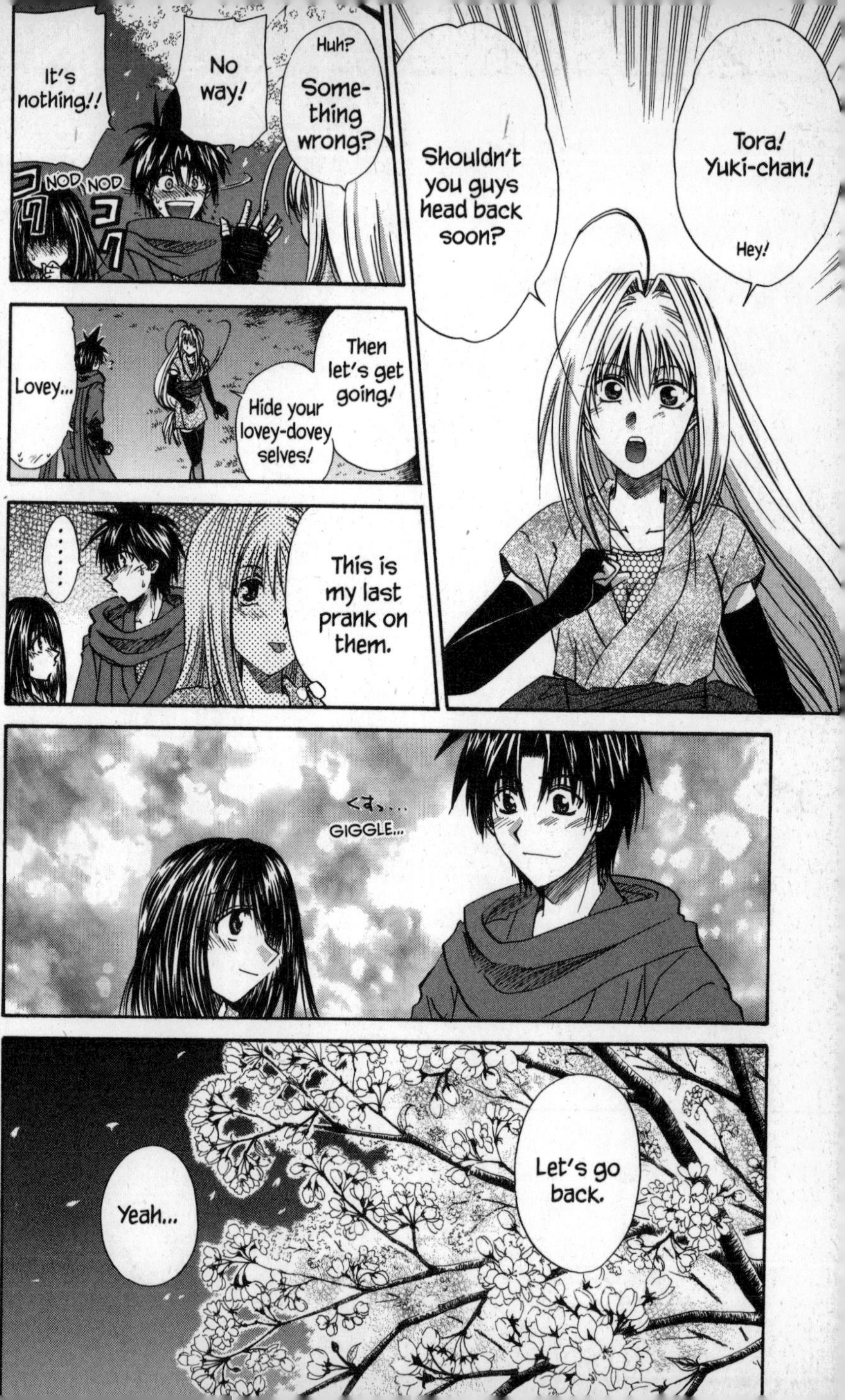
Tora! Yuki-chan!
Hey!
Shouldn't you guys head back soon?
Huh? Some-thing wrong?
No way!
It's nothing!!
NOD NOD
Then let's get going!
Hide your lovey-dovey selves!
Lovey...
This is my last prank on them.
......
くすっ...
GIGGLE...
Let's go back.
Yeah...

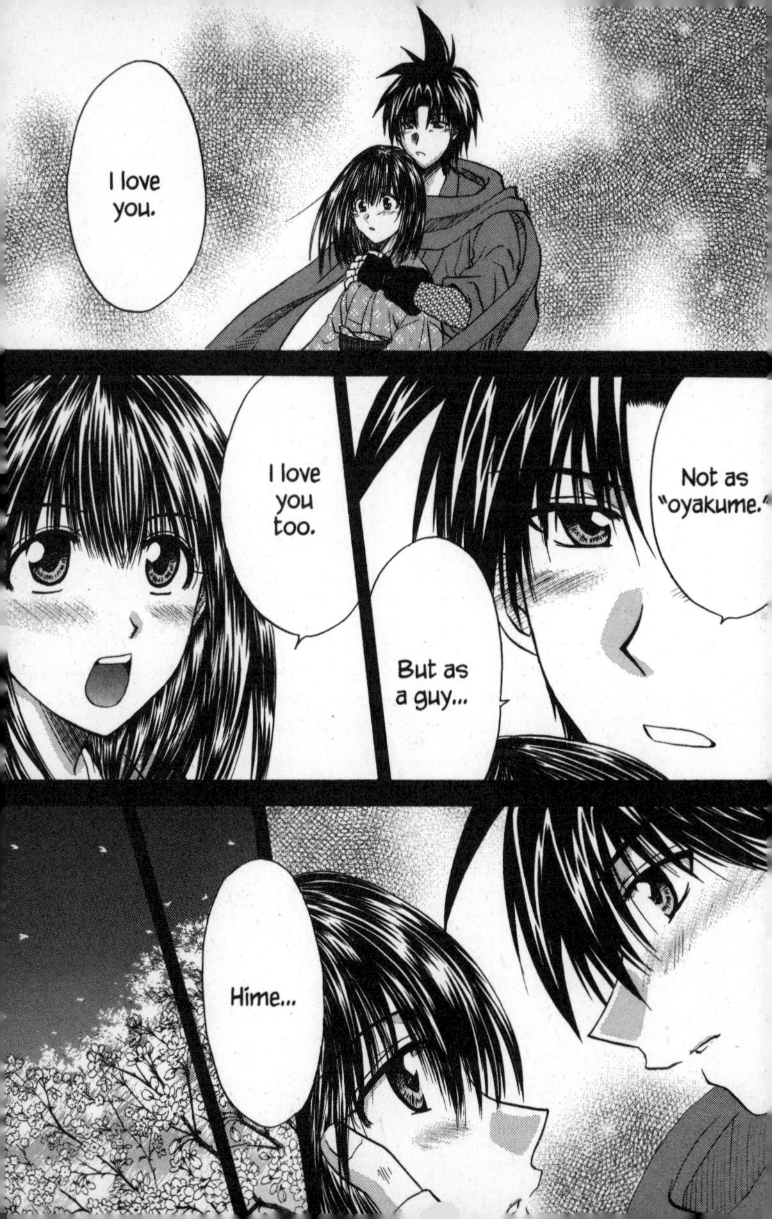
I love you.
Not as "oyakume."
But as a guy...
I love you too.
Hime...

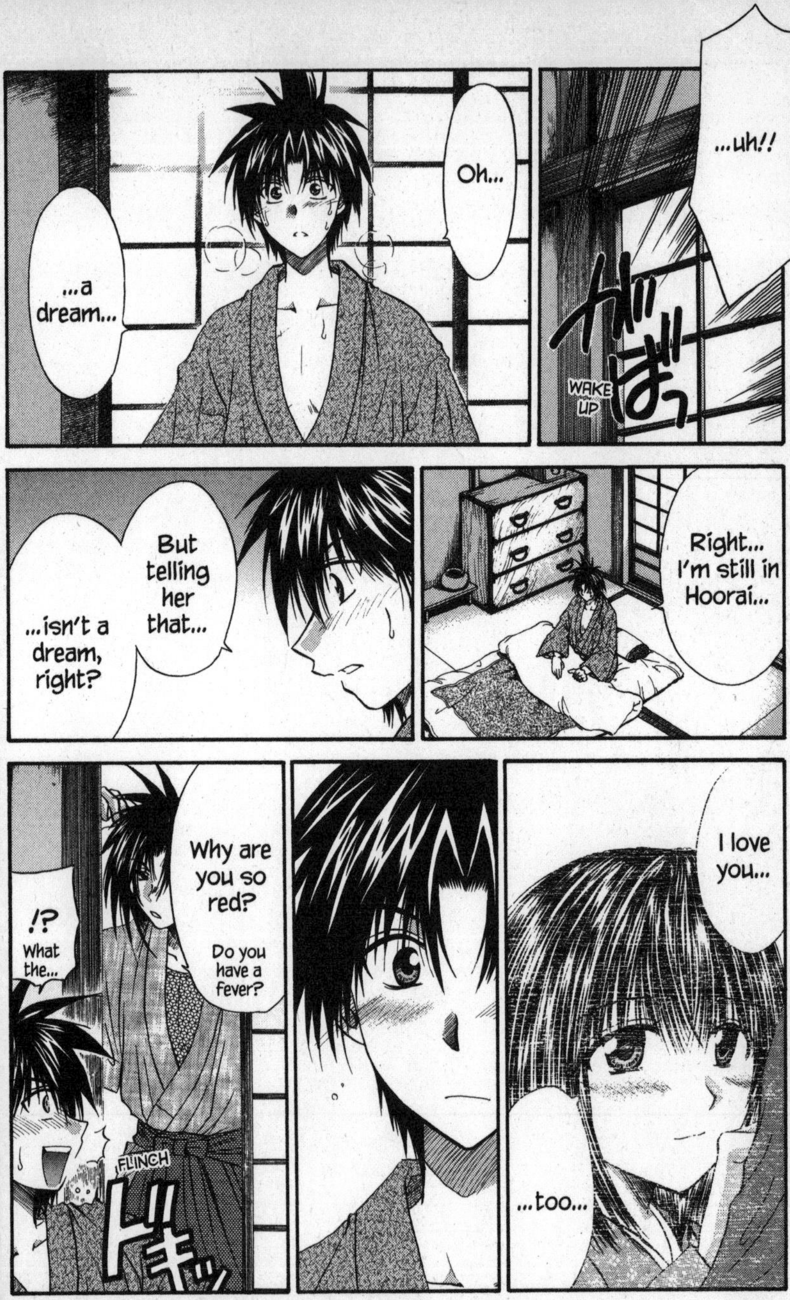

...uh!!
がばっ
WAKE UP
Oh...
...a dream...
Right... I'm still in Hoorai...
But telling her that...
...isn't a dream, right?
I love you...
...too...
Why are you so red?
Do you have a fever?
!? What the...
FLINCH
ドキッ

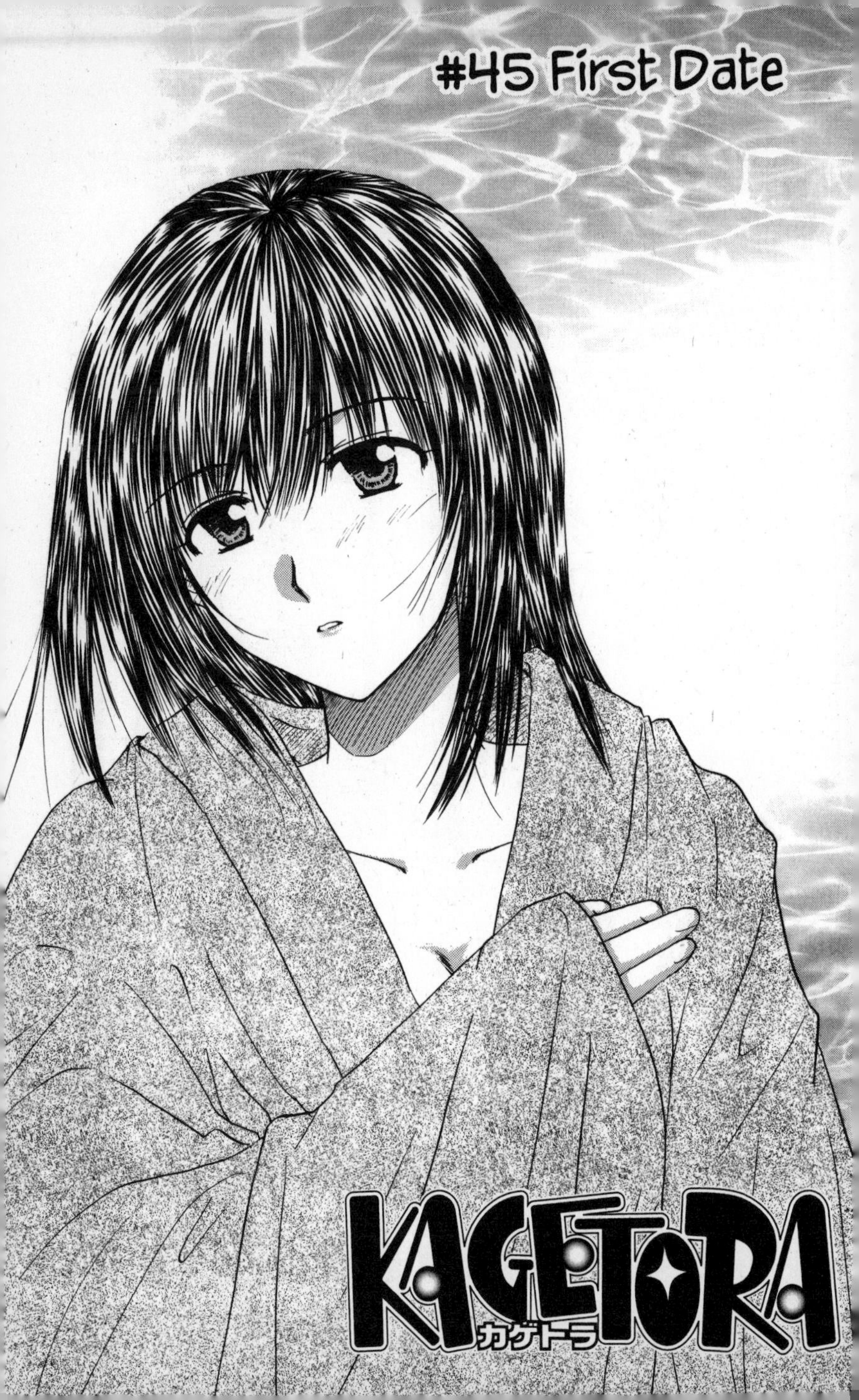
#45 First Date
KAGETORA
カゲトラ

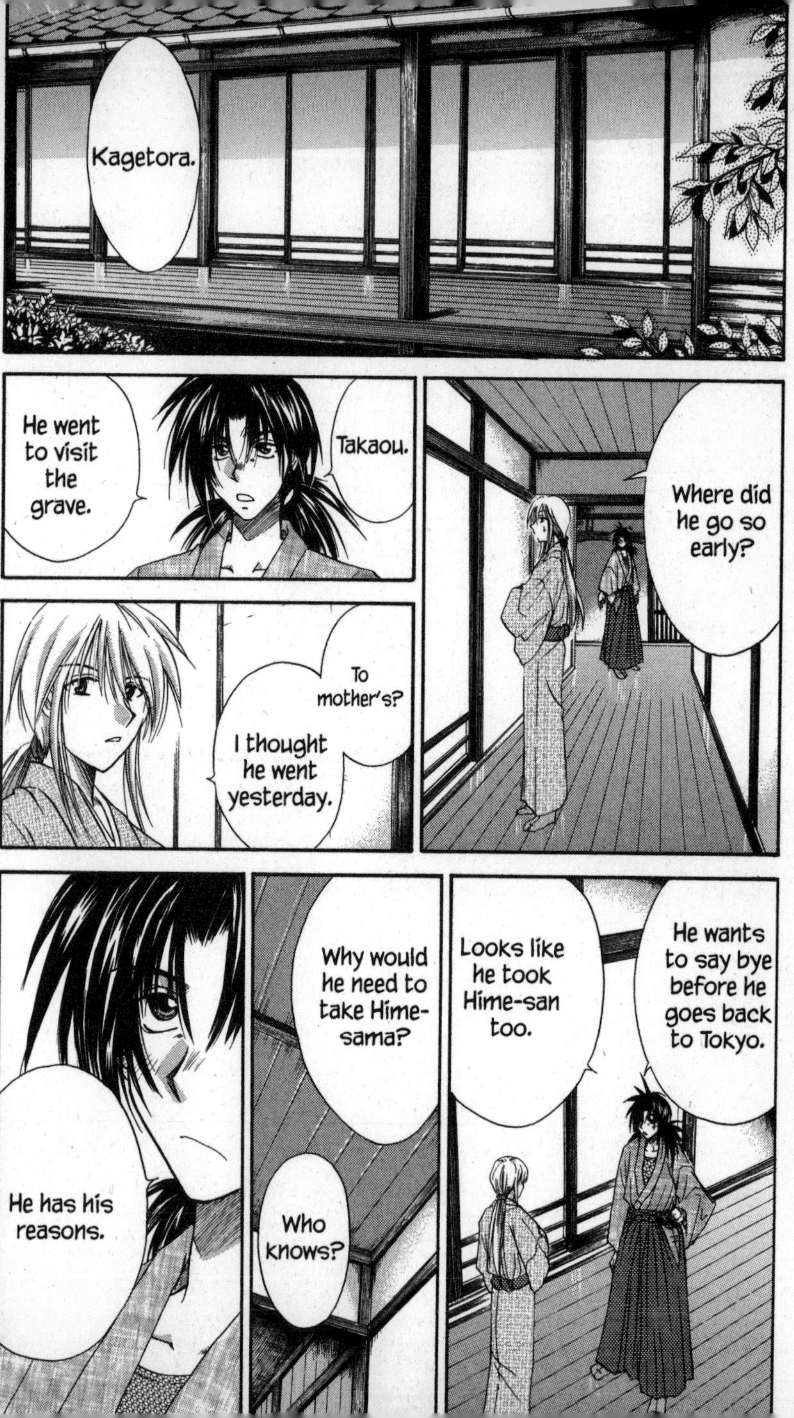
Kagetora.
Where did he go so early?
Takaou.
He went to visit the grave.
To mother's?
I thought he went yesterday.
He wants to say bye before he goes back to Tokyo.
Looks like he took Hime-san too.
Why would he need to take Hime-sama?
Who knows?
He has his reasons.

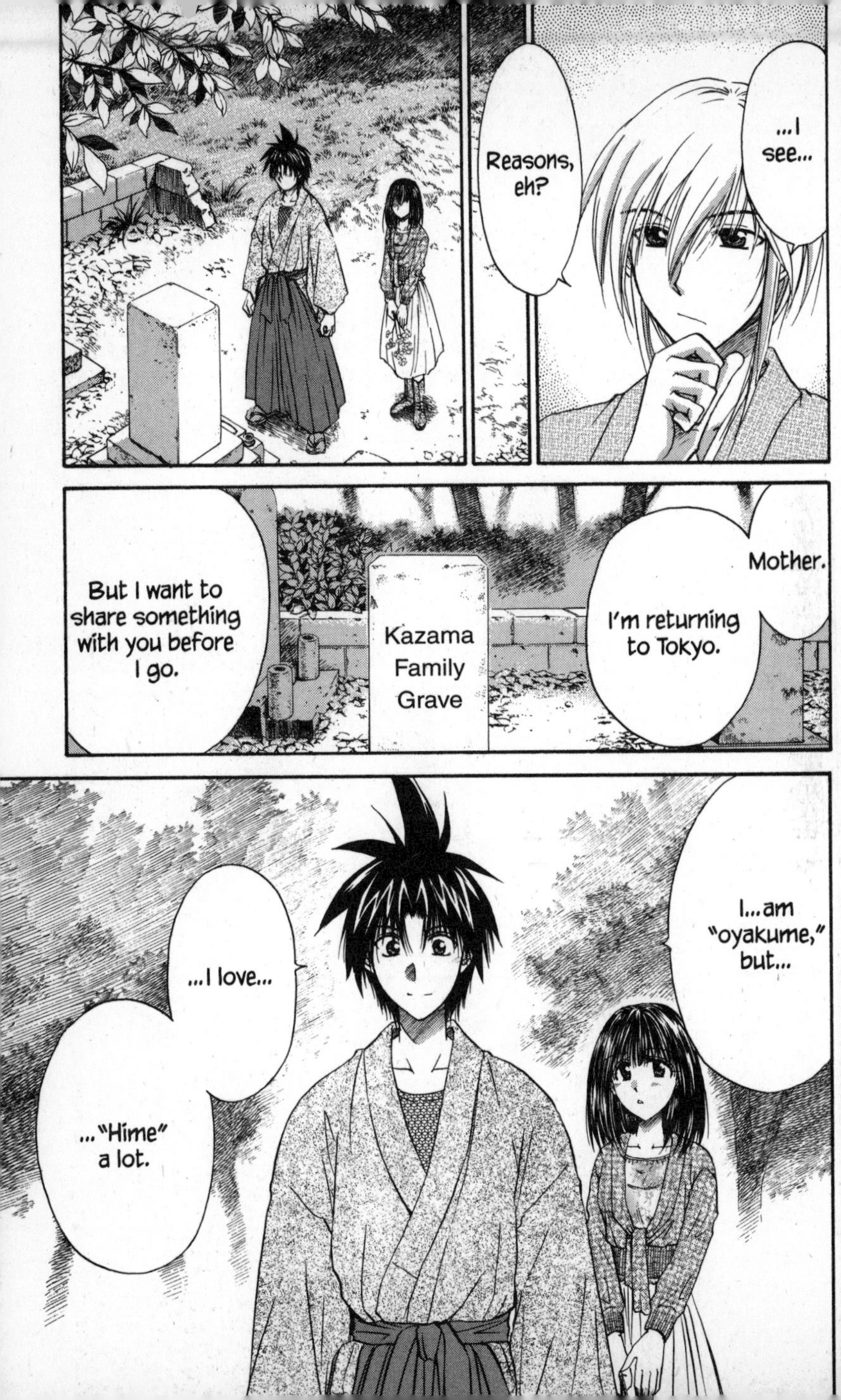
...I see...
Reasons, eh?
Mother.
I'm returning to Tokyo.
Kazama Family Grave
But I want to share something with you before I go.
I...am "oyakume," but...
...I love...
..."Hime" a lot.

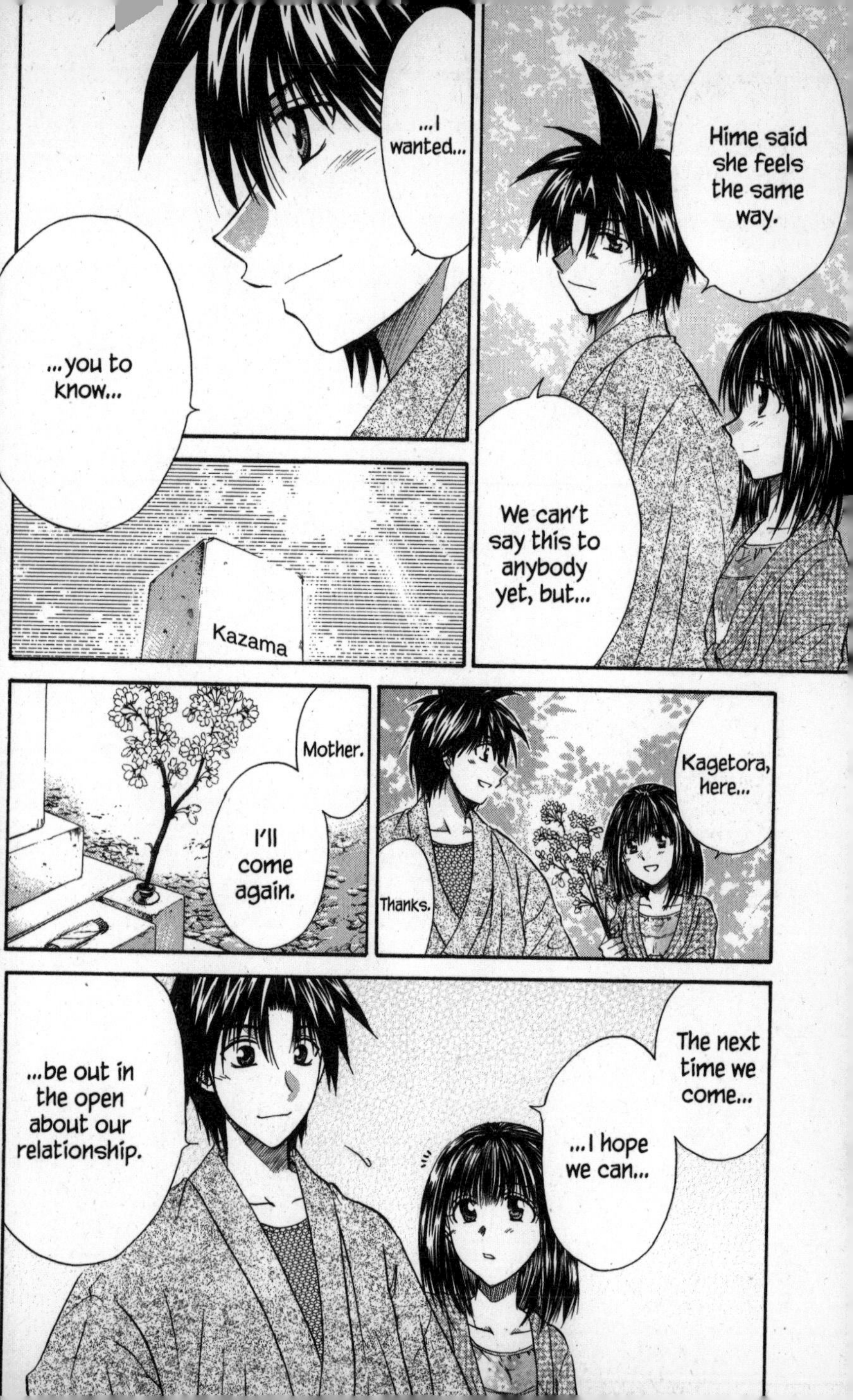
Hime said she feels the same way.
We can't say this to anybody yet, but...
...I wanted...
...you to know...
Kazama
Kagetora, here...
Thanks.
Mother.
I'll come again.
The next time we come...
...I hope we can...
...be out in the open about our relationship.

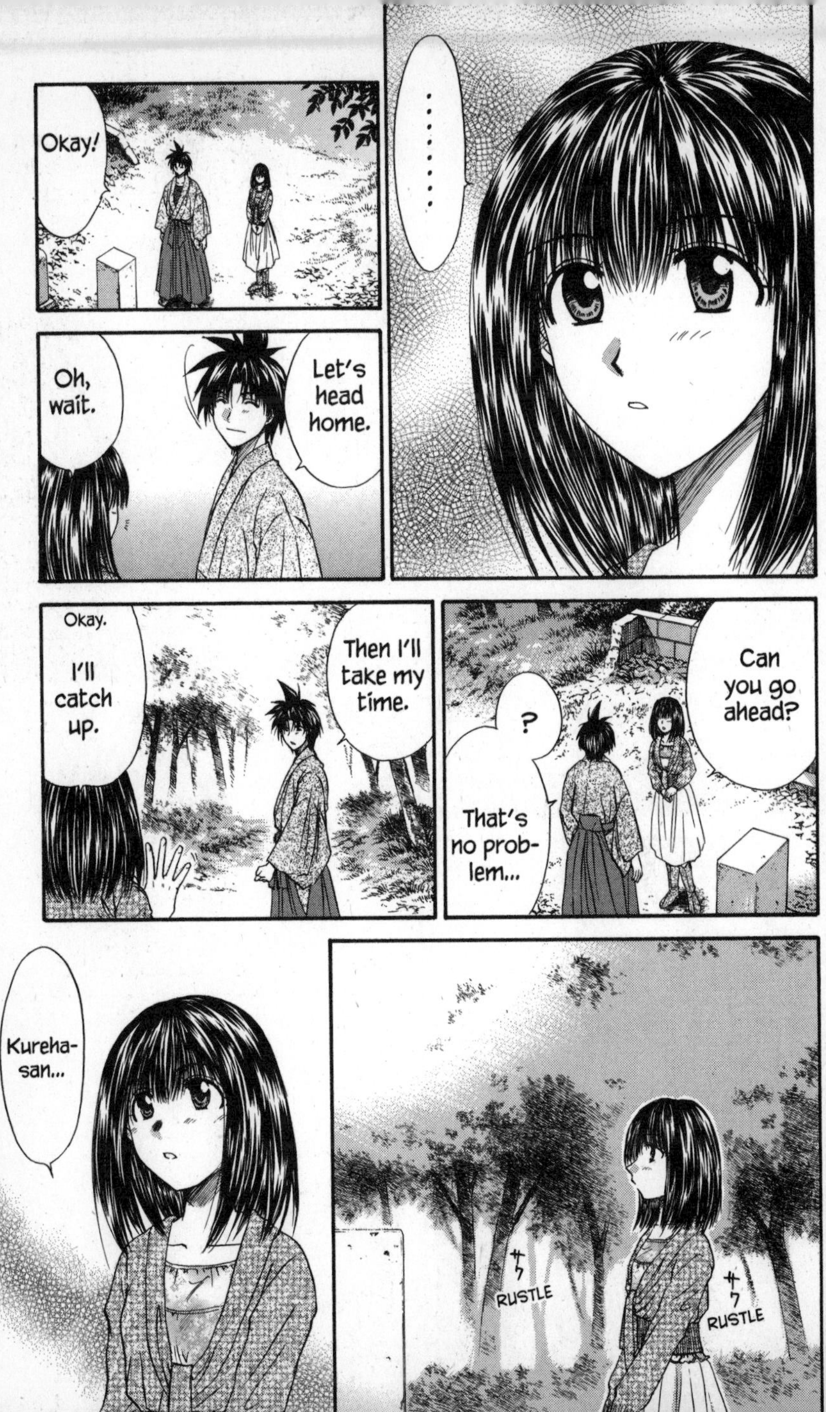
......
Okay!
Let's head home.
Oh, wait.
Can you go ahead?
?
That's no problem...
Then I'll take my time.
Okay.
I'll catch up.
サク
RUSTLE
サク
RUSTLE
Kureha-san...

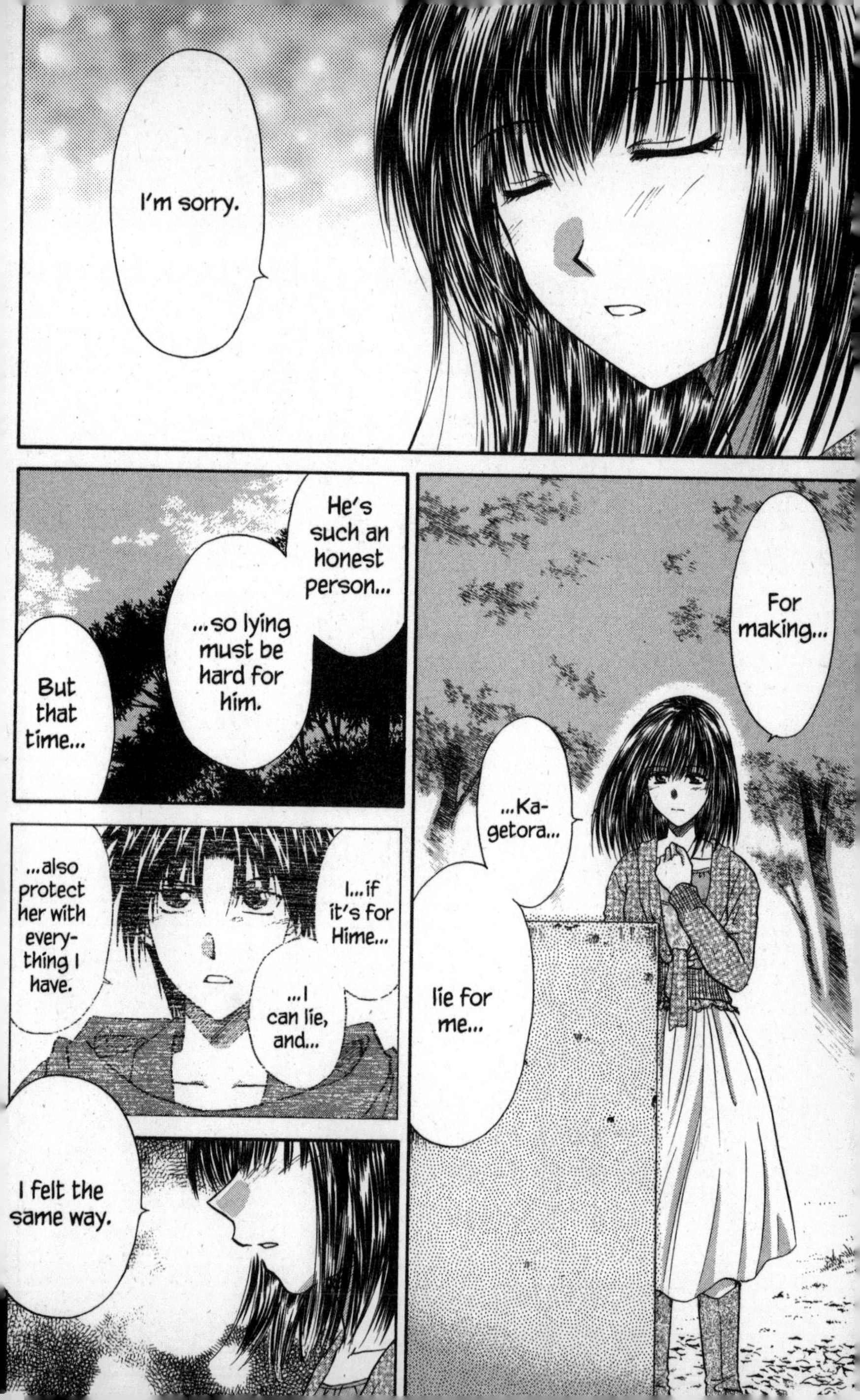
I'm sorry.
For making...
...Kagetora...
lie for me...
He's such an honest person...
...so lying must be hard for him.
But that time...
I...if it's for Hime...
...I can lie, and...
...also protect her with everything I have.
I felt the same way.

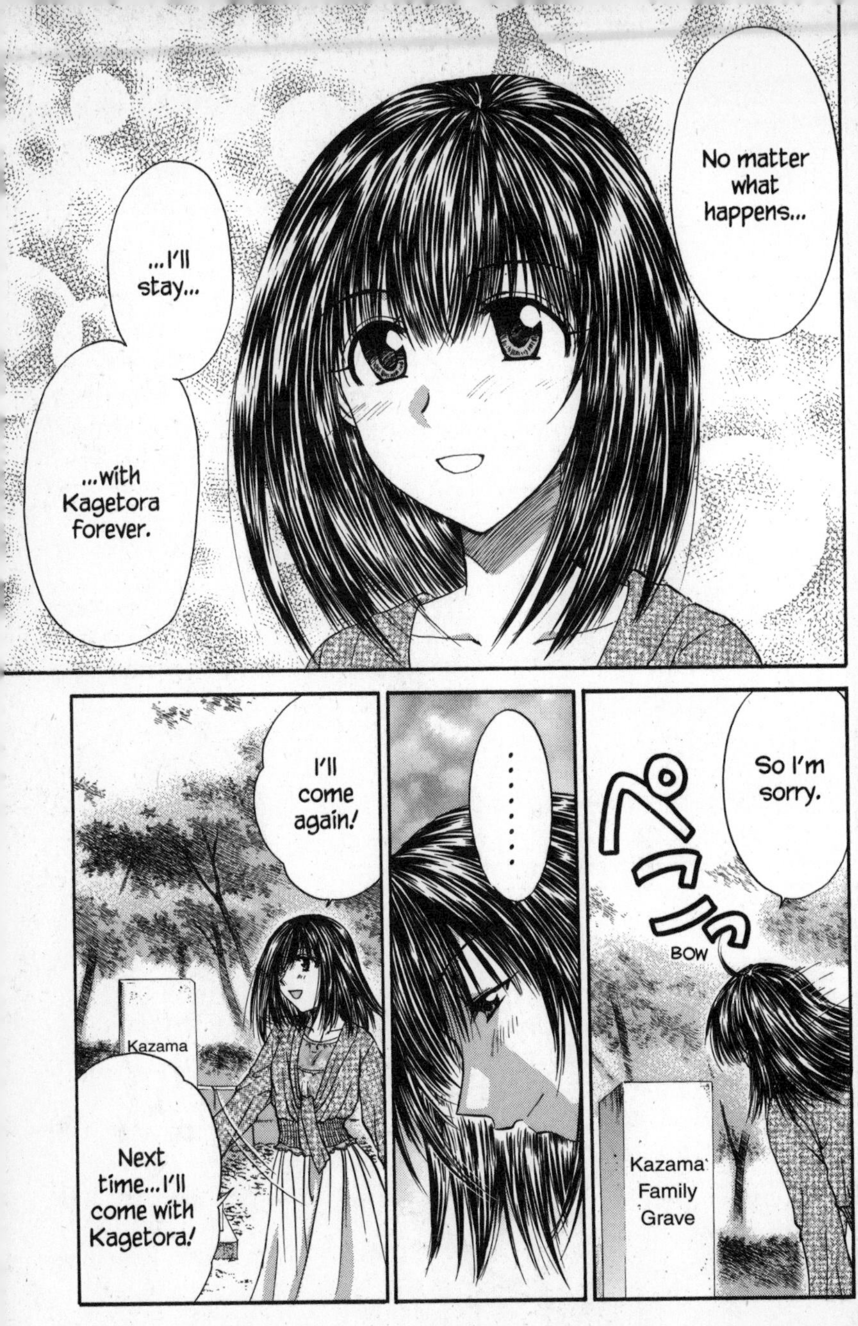
No matter what happens...
...I'll stay...
...with Kagetora forever.
So I'm sorry.
BOW
Kazama Family Grave
......
I'll come again!
Kazama
Next time...I'll come with Kagetora!

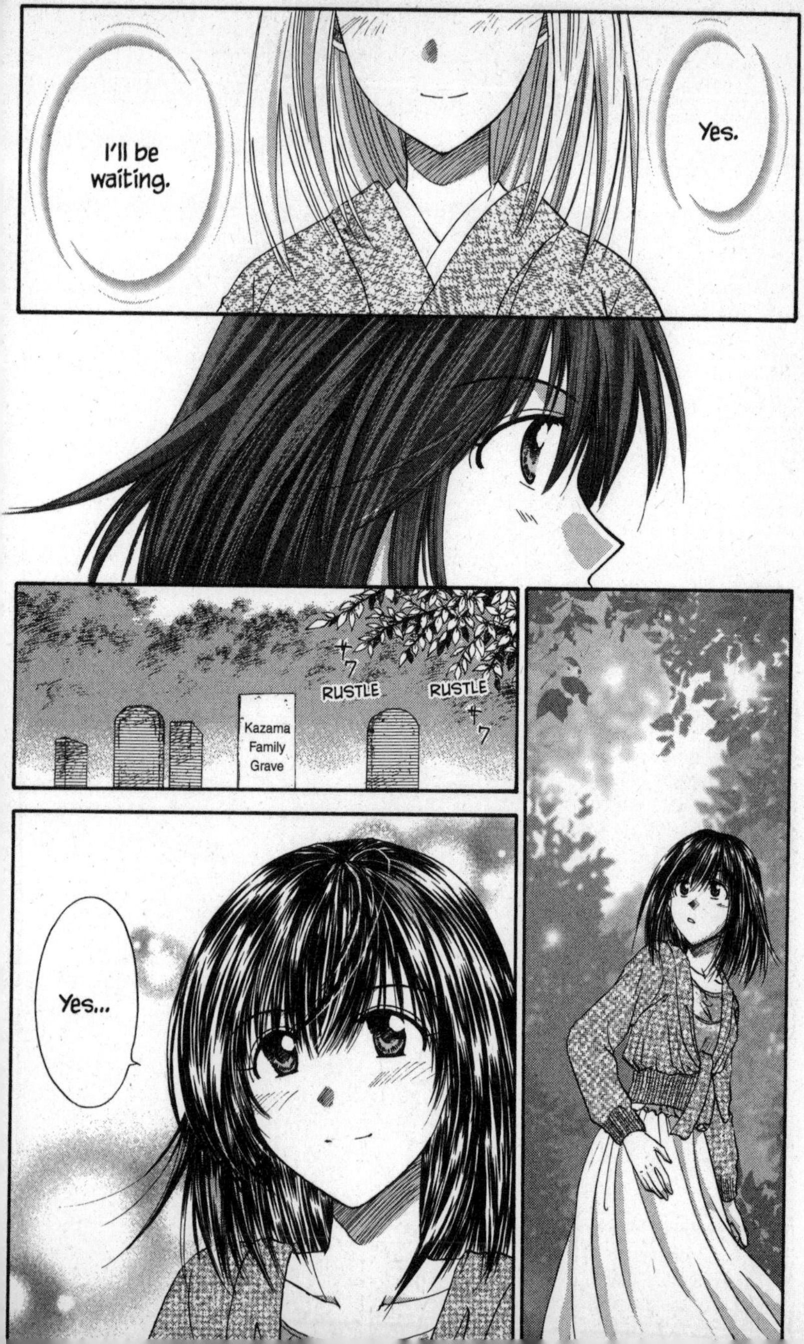
Yes.
I'll be waiting.
サク
RUSTLE
RUSTLE
サク
Kazama Family Grave
Yes...

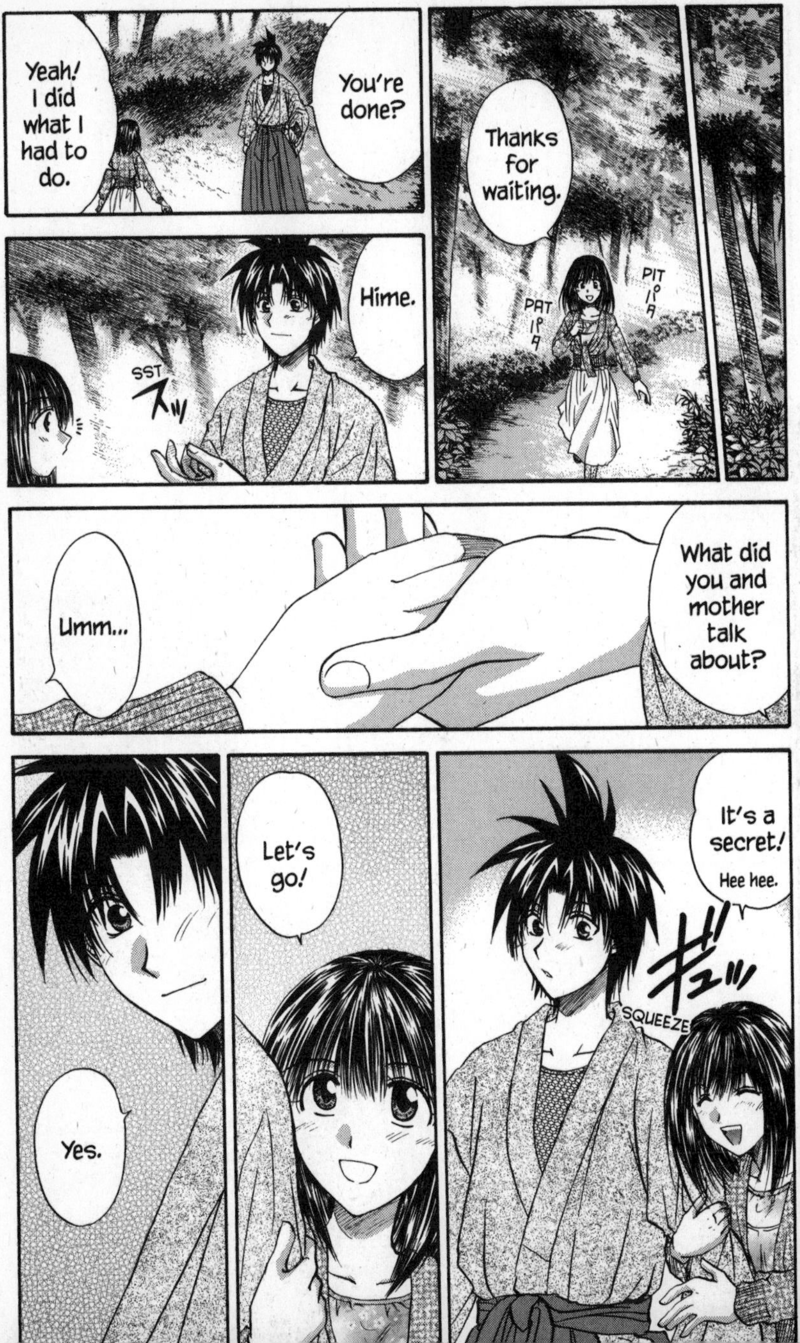
Thanks for waiting.
PIT
PAT
You're done?
Yeah! I did what I had to do.
Hime.
SST
What did you and mother talk about?
Umm...
It's a secret!
Hee hee.
SQUEEZE
Let's go!
Yes.

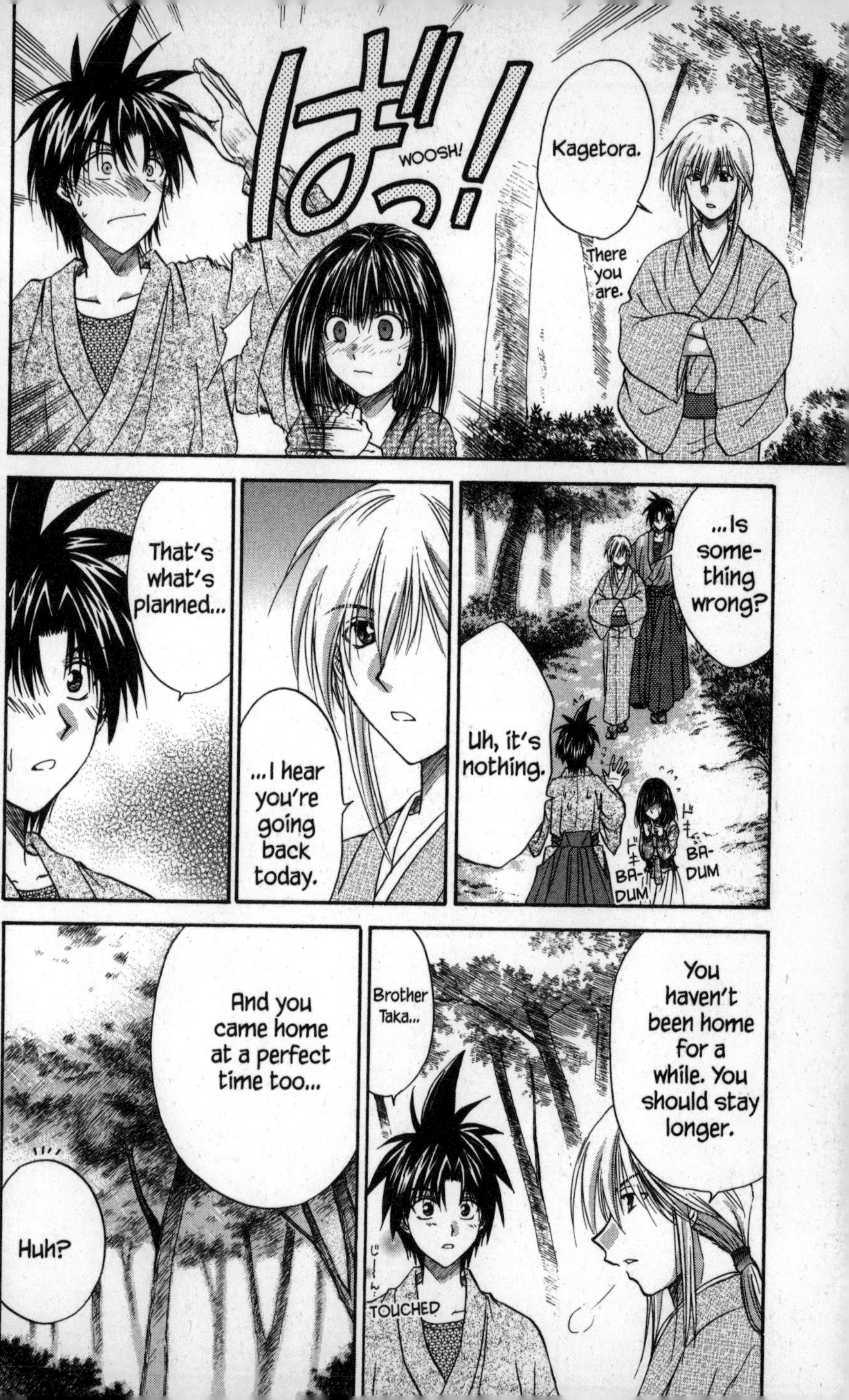
ばっ!
WOOSH!
Kagetora.
There you are.
...Is something wrong?
Uh, it's nothing.
BA-DUM
BA-DUM
...I hear you're going back today.
That's what's planned...
You haven't been home for a while. You should stay longer.
Brother Taka...
TOUCHED
And you came home at a perfect time too...
Huh?

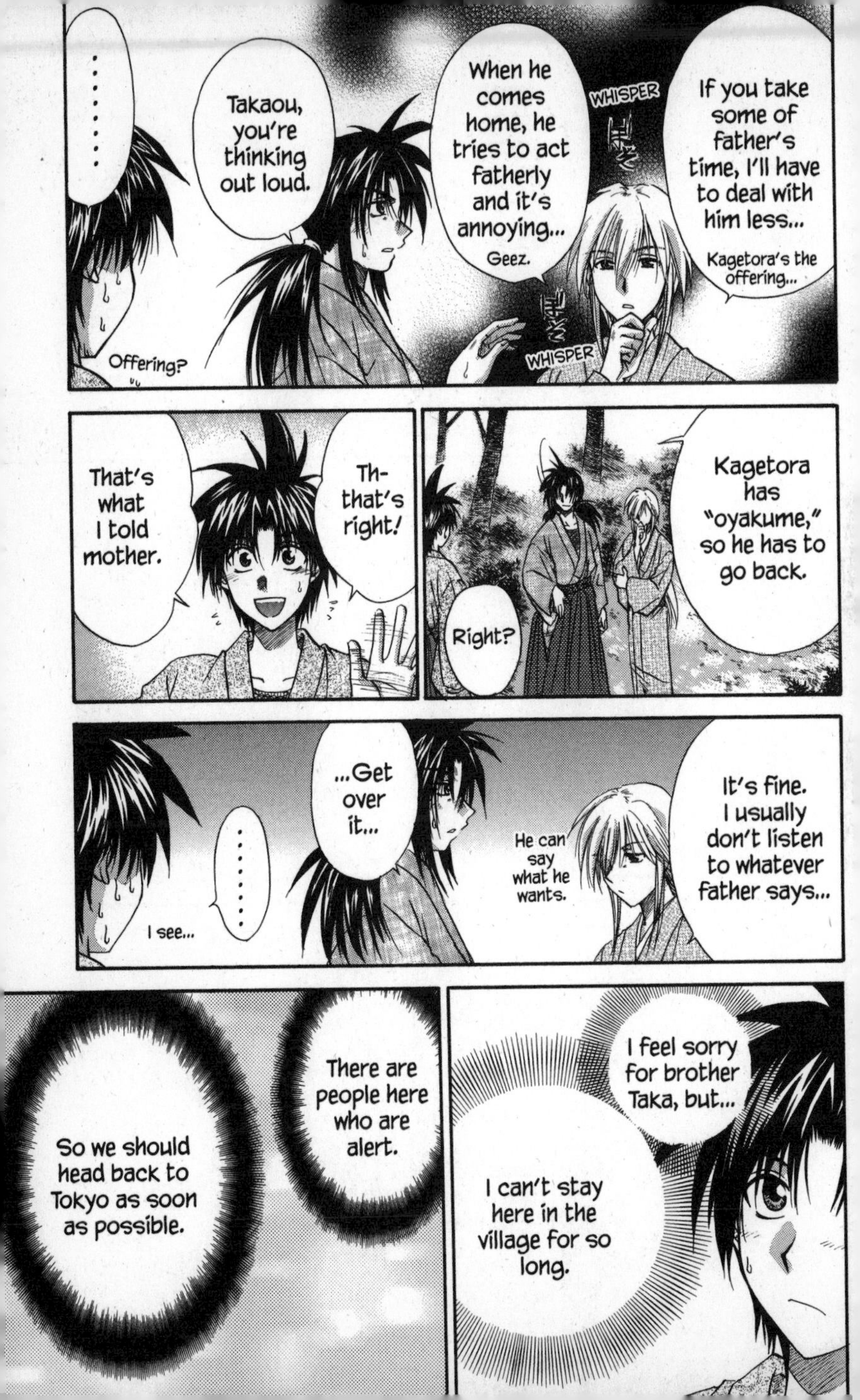
If you take some of father's time, I'll have to deal with him less...
Kagetora's the offering...
WHISPER
When he comes home, he tries to act fatherly and it's annoying...
Geez.
WHISPER
Takaou, you're thinking out loud.
......
Offering?
Kagetora has "oyakume," so he has to go back.
Right?
Th-that's right!
That's what I told mother.
It's fine. I usually don't listen to whatever father says...
He can say what he wants.
...Get over it...
......
I see...
I feel sorry for brother Taka, but...
I can't stay here in the village for so long.
There are people here who are alert.
So we should head back to Tokyo as soon as possible.

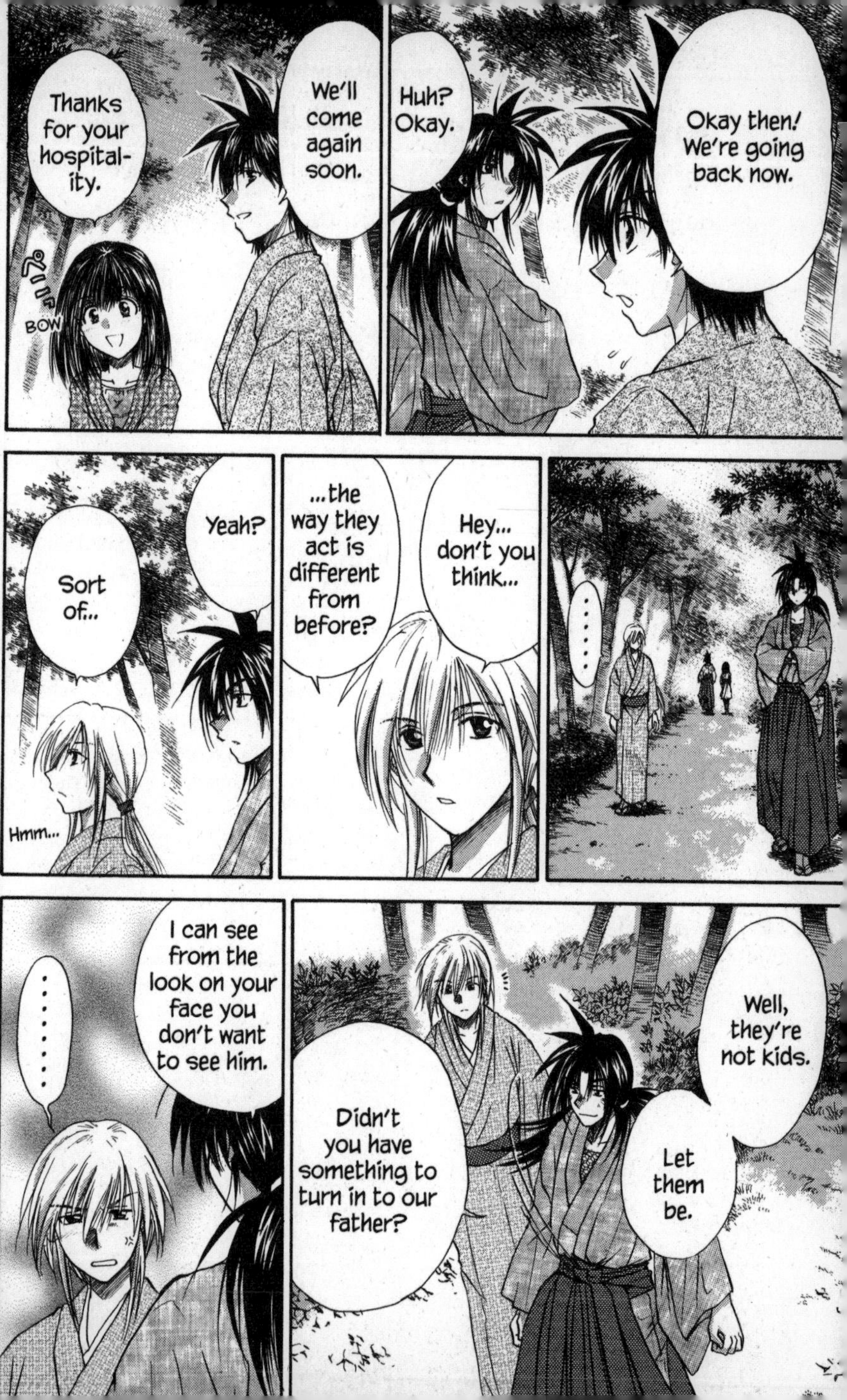
Okay then! We're going back now.
Huh? Okay.
We'll come again soon.
Thanks for your hospital-ity.
BOW
......
Hey... don't you think...
...the way they act is different from before?
Yeah?
Sort of...
Hmm...
Well, they're not kids.
Let them be.
Didn't you have something to turn in to our father?
I can see from the look on your face you don't want to see him.
......

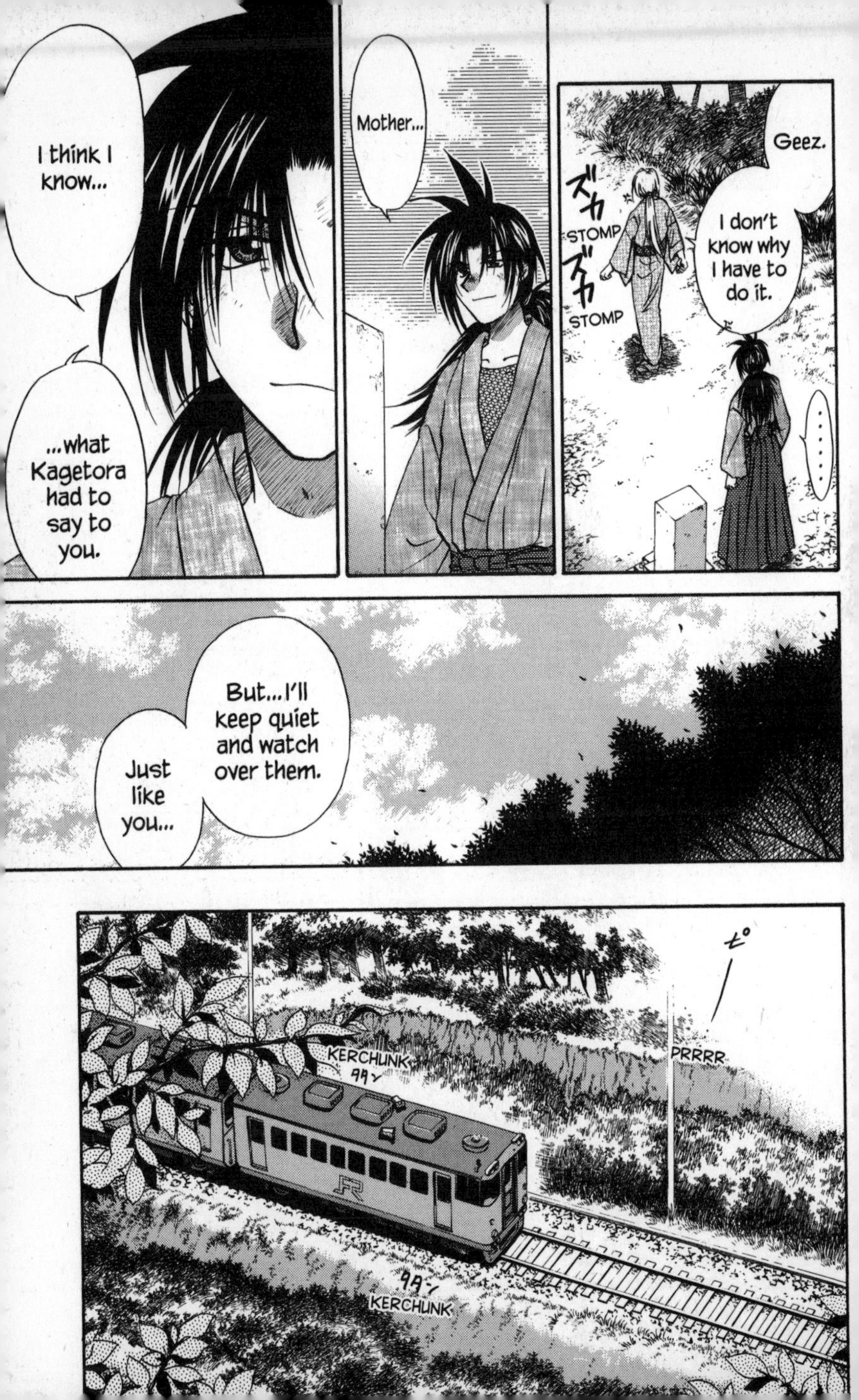
Geez.
I don't know why I have to do it.
STOMP
STOMP
......
Mother...
I think I know...
...what Kagetora had to say to you.
But...I'll keep quiet and watch over them.
Just like you...
PRRRR
KERCHUNK
KERCHUNK

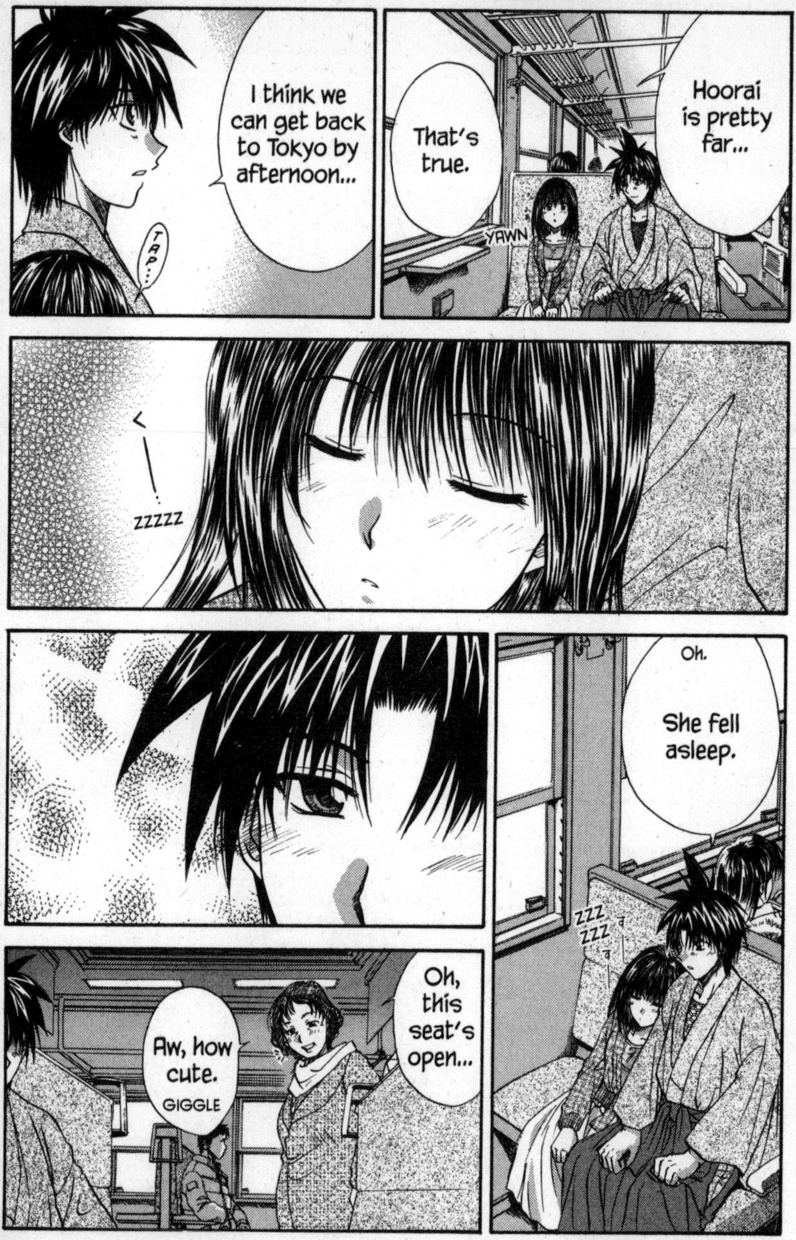
Hoorai is pretty far...
That's true.
YAWN
I think we can get back to Tokyo by afternoon...
TAP...
ZZZZZ
Oh.
She fell asleep.
ZZZ ZZZ
Oh, this seat's open...
Aw, how cute.
GIGGLE

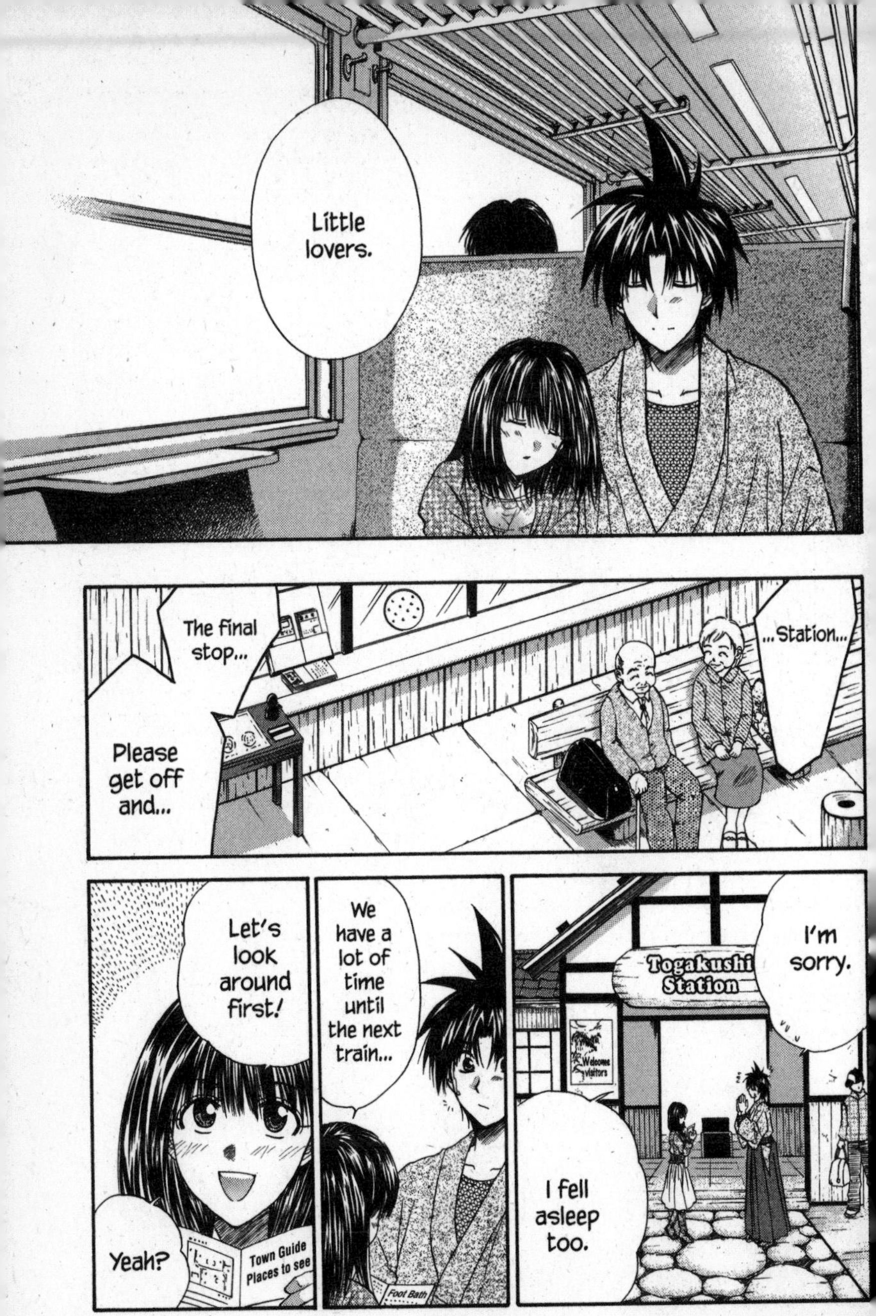
Little lovers.
...Station...
The final stop...
Please get off and...
I'm sorry.
Togakushi Station
Welcome visitors
I fell asleep too.
We have a lot of time until the next train...
Foot Bath
Let's look around first!
Town Guide Places to see
Yeah?

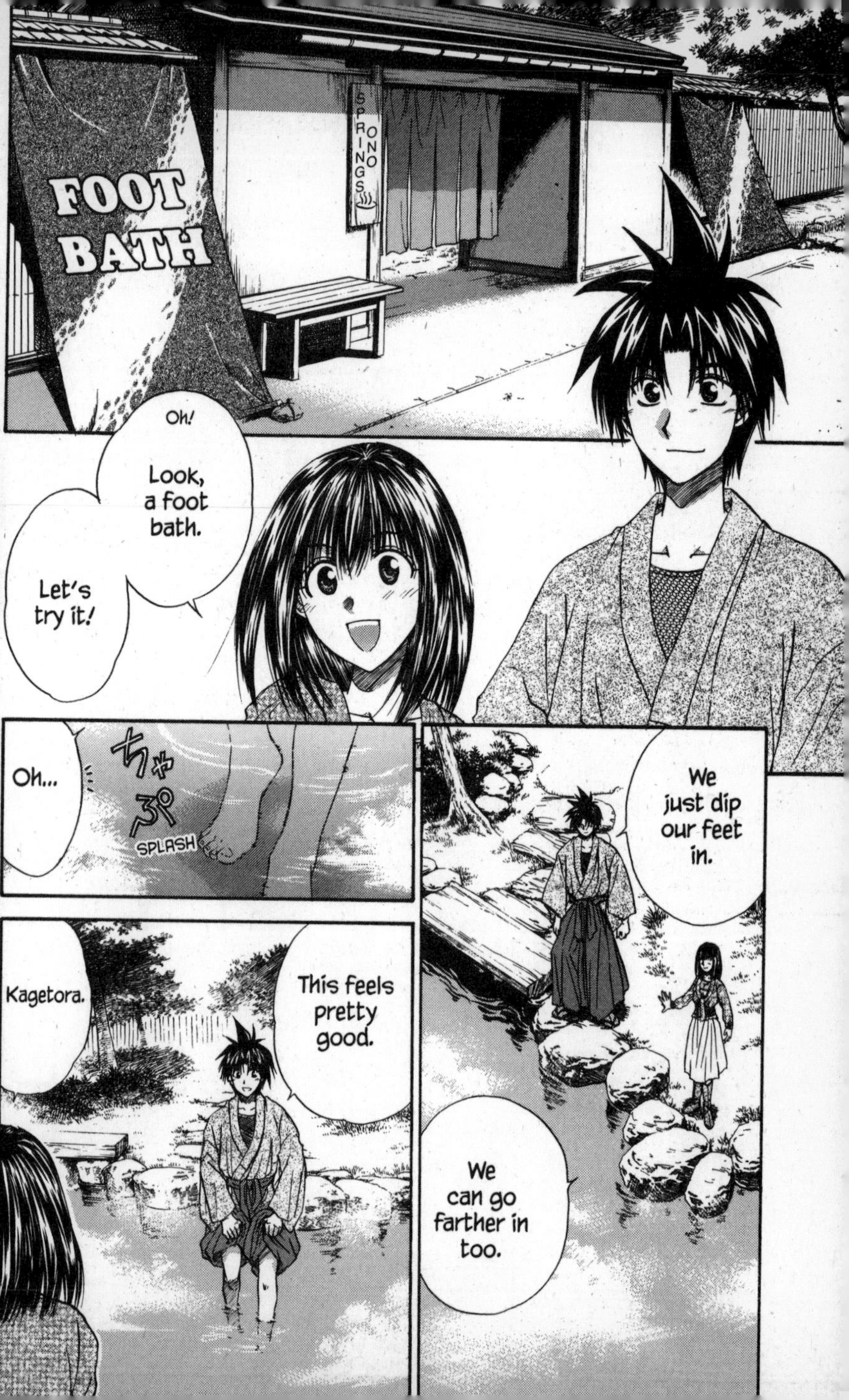
ONO SPRINGS
FOOT BATH
Oh!
Look, a foot bath.
Let's try it!
We just dip our feet in.
We can go farther in too.
Oh...
ちゃぷ
SPLASH
This feels pretty good.
Kagetora.

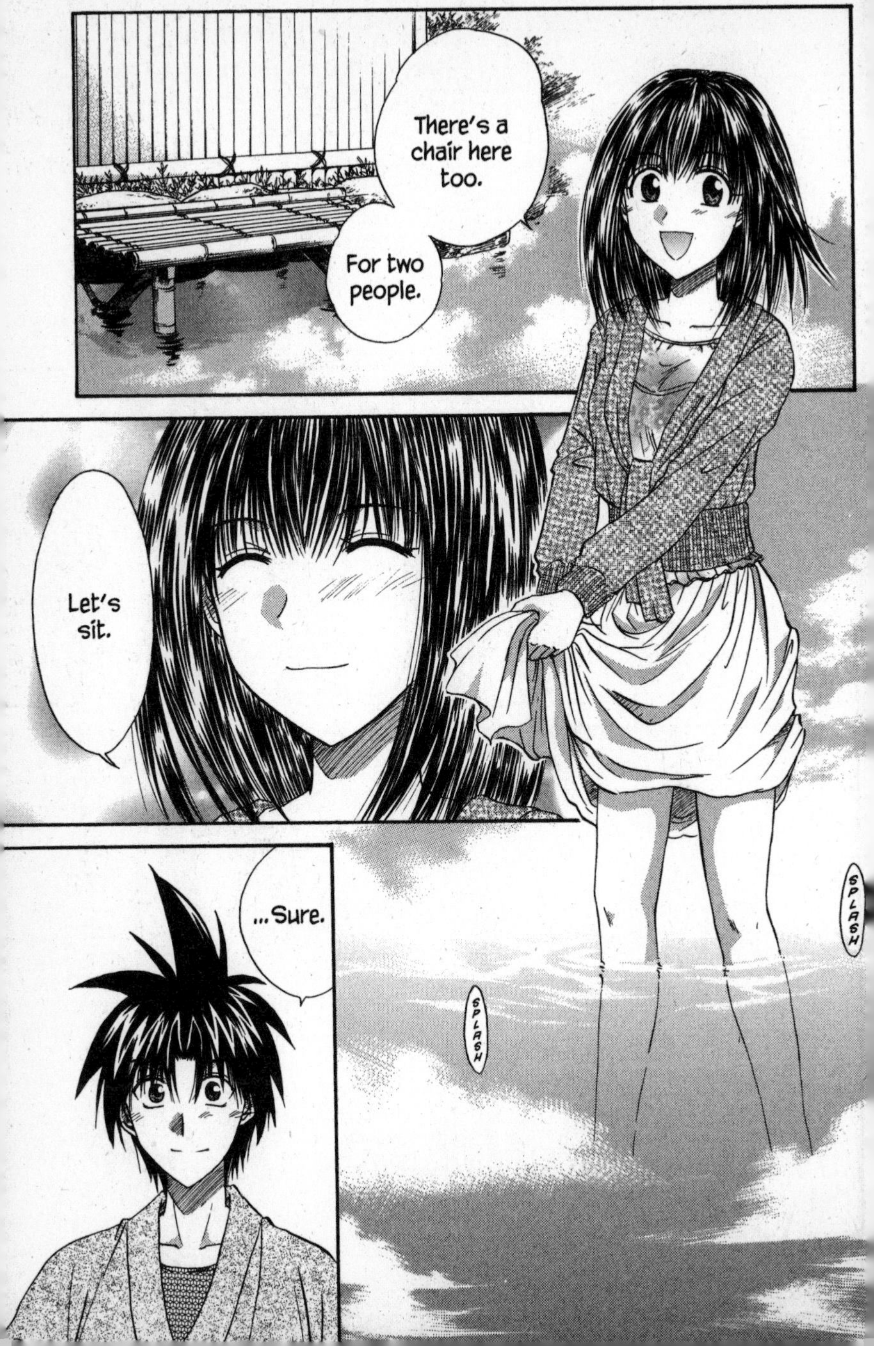

There's a chair here too.
For two people.
Let's sit.
SPLASH
SPLASH
...Sure.

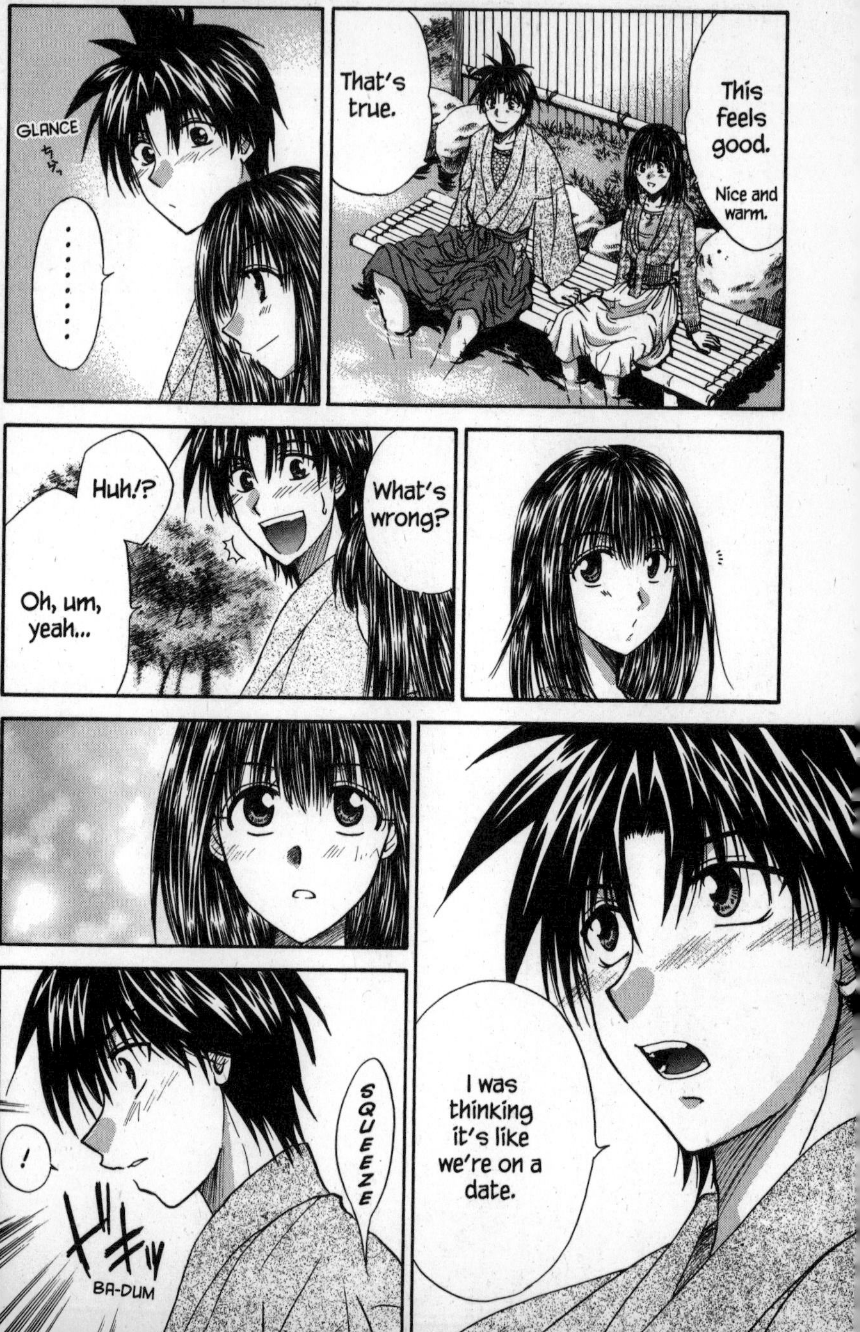
This feels good.
Nice and warm.
That's true.
GLANCE
......
What's wrong?
Huh!?
Oh, um, yeah...
I was thinking it's like we're on a date.
SQUEEZE
!
BA-DUM

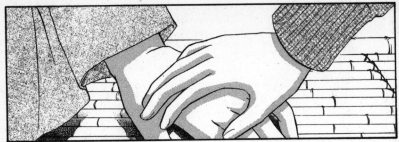

It is.

Because I'm out with someone I like.

Ka-getora.

I have one more place I want to see.

One more?

にこ、
SMILE

Hime...

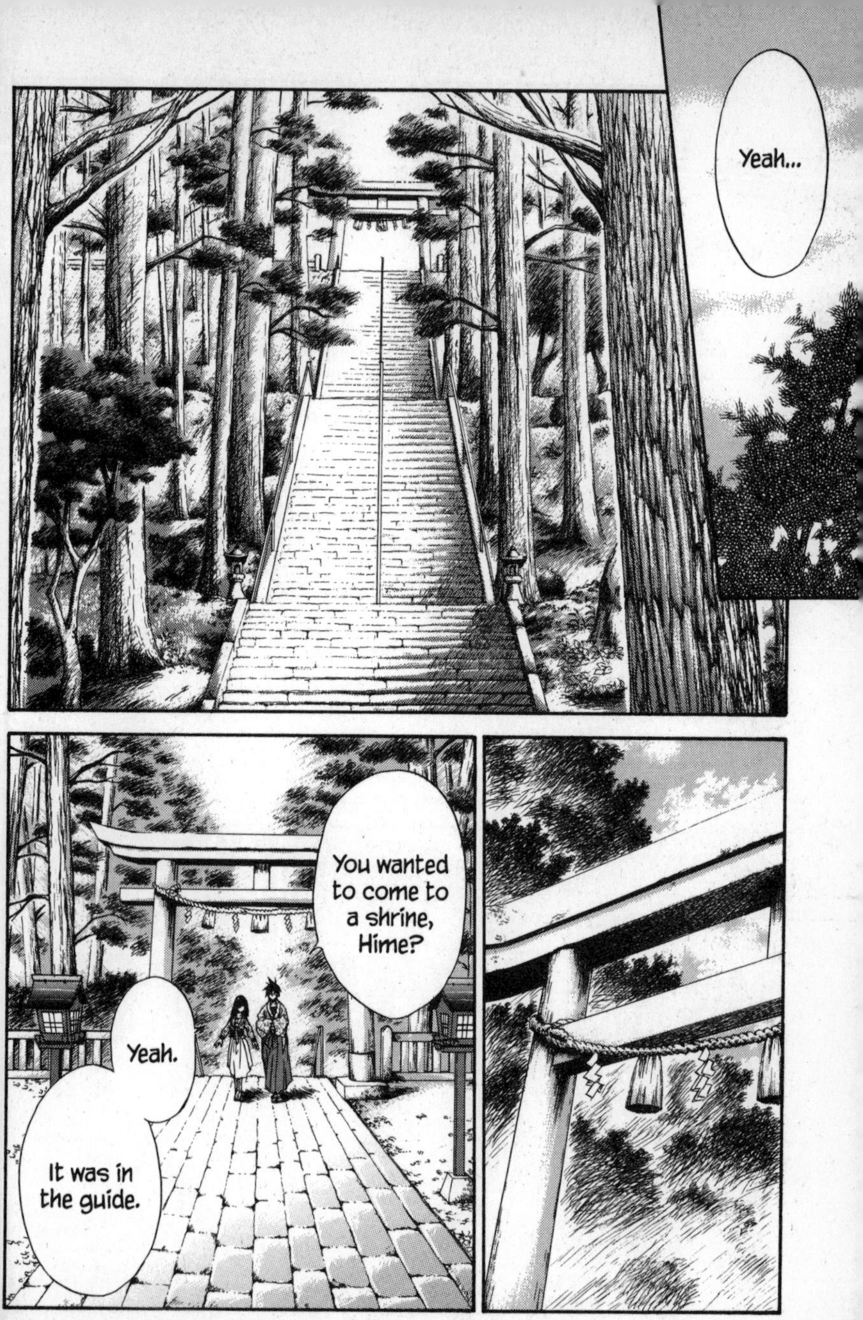
Yeah...
You wanted to come to a shrine, Hime?
Yeah.
It was in the guide.

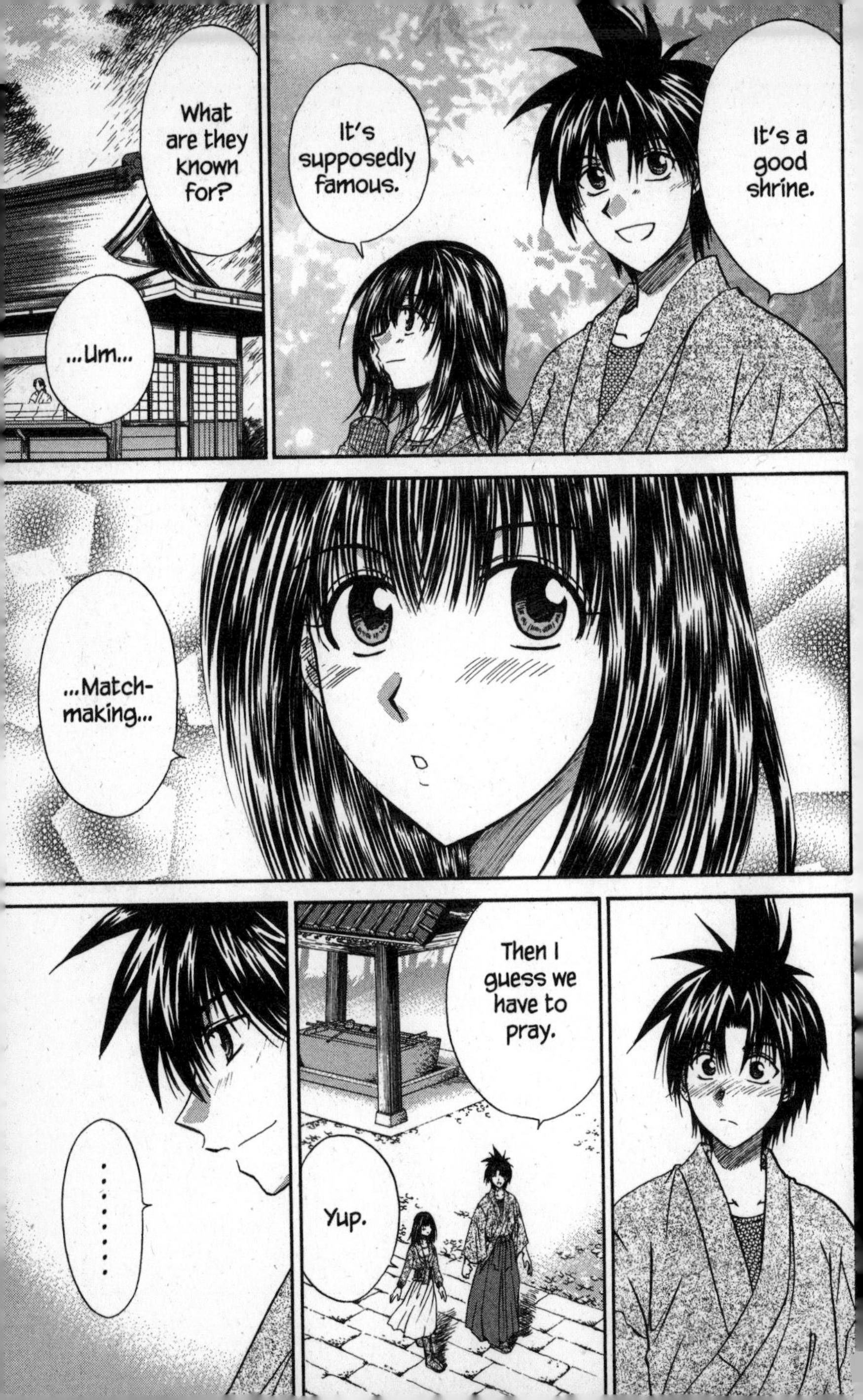

It's a good shrine.
It's supposedly famous.
What are they known for?
...Um...
...Match-making...
Then I guess we have to pray.
Yup.
....

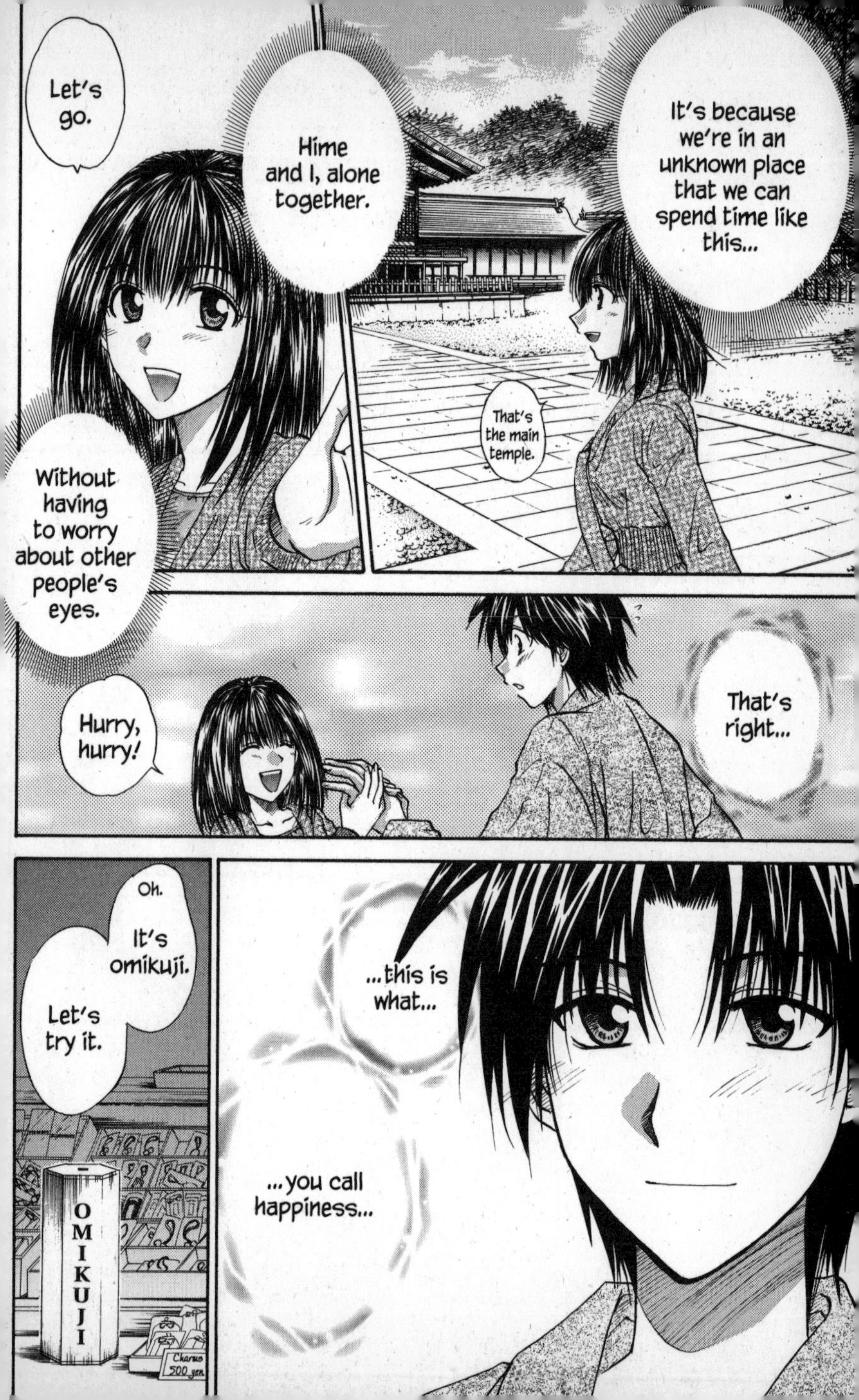
It's because we're in an unknown place that we can spend time like this...
That's the main temple.
Hime and I, alone together.
Let's go.
Without having to worry about other people's eyes.
That's right...
Hurry, hurry!
...this is what...
...you call happiness...
Oh.
It's omikuji.
Let's try it.
OMIKUJI
Charms 500 yen

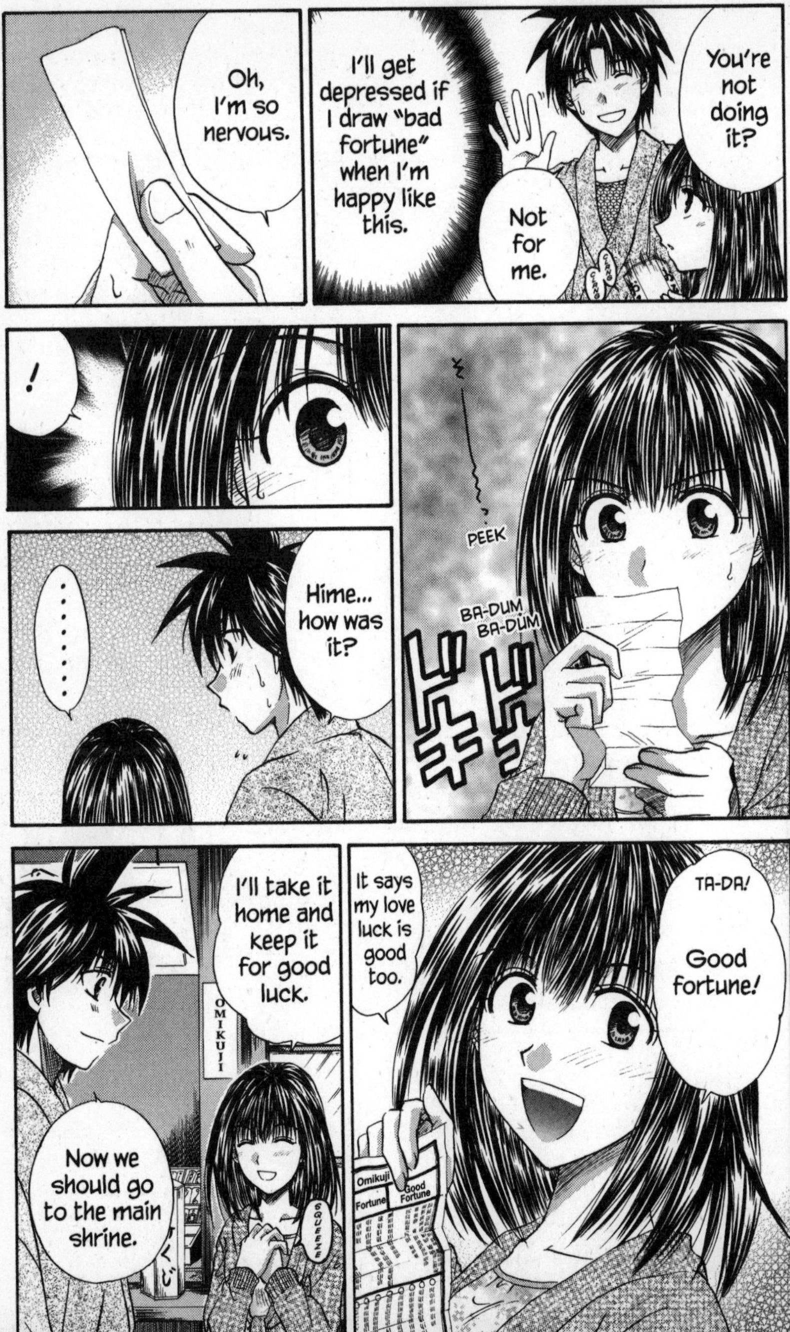
You're not doing it?
Not for me.
I'll get depressed if I draw "bad fortune" when I'm happy like this.
Oh, I'm so nervous.
PEEK
BA-DUM BA-DUM
!
Hime... how was it?
....
TA-DA!
Good fortune!
It says my love luck is good too.
Omikuji
Fortune
Good Fortune
I'll take it home and keep it for good luck.
OMIKUJI
Now we should go to the main shrine.
SQUEEZE

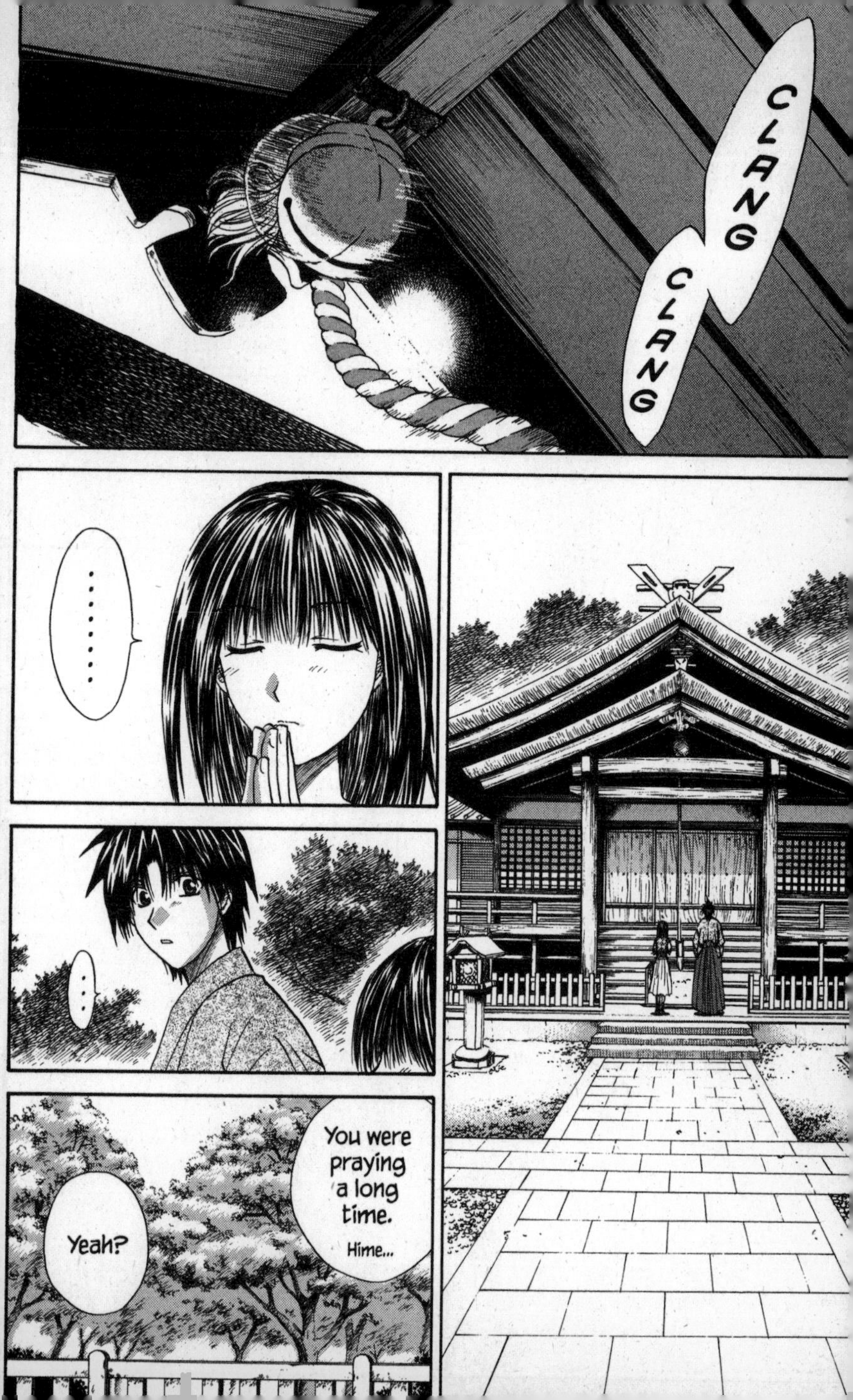
CLANG
CLANG
....
...
You were praying a long time.
Hime...
Yeah?

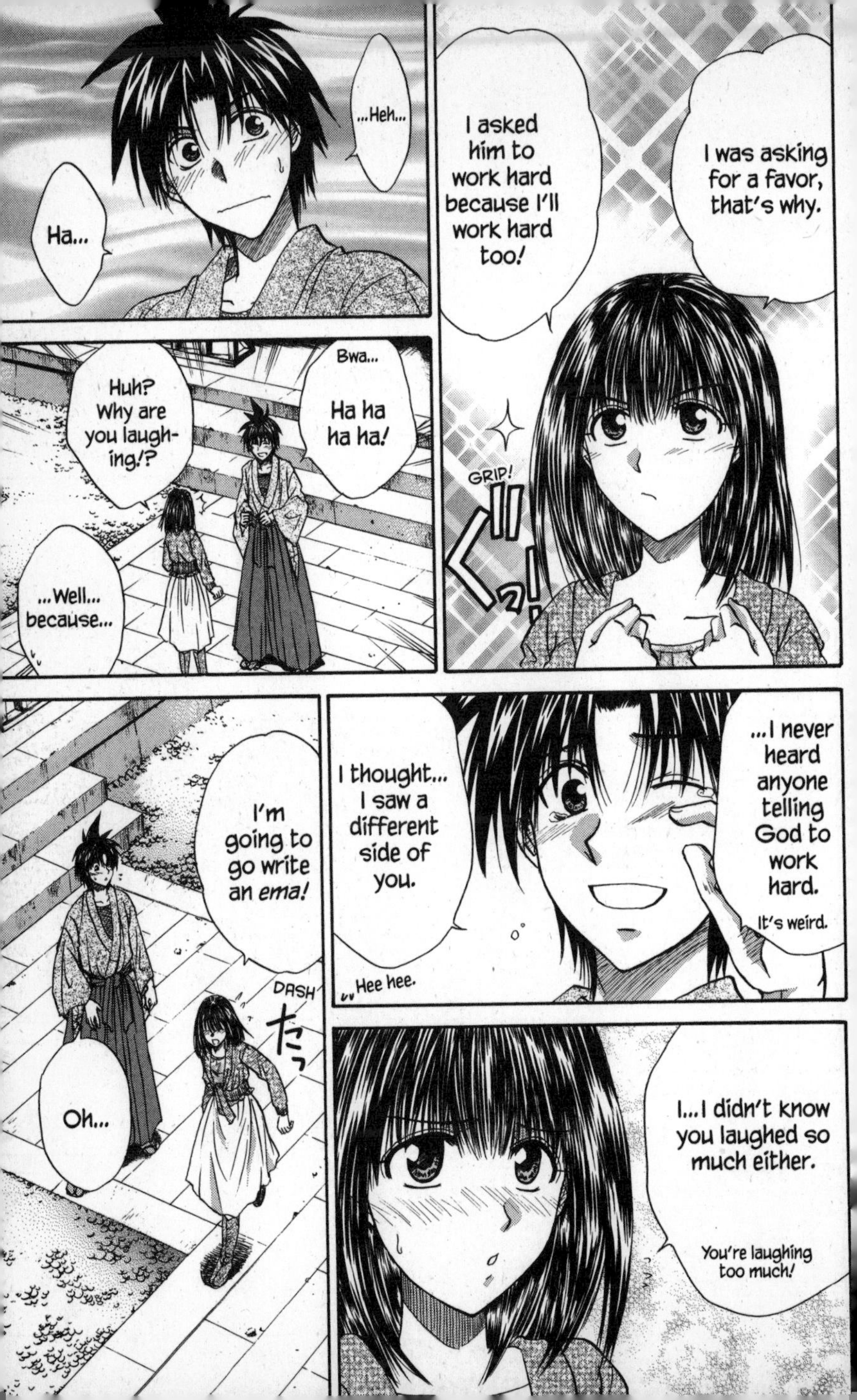
I was asking for a favor, that's why.
I asked him to work hard because I'll work hard too!
GRIP!
...Heh...
Ha...
Bwa...
Ha ha ha ha!
Huh? Why are you laughing!?
...Well... because...
...I never heard anyone telling God to work hard.
It's weird.
I thought... I saw a different side of you.
Hee hee.
I...I didn't know you laughed so much either.
You're laughing too much!
I'm going to go write an *ema*!
DASH
Oh...

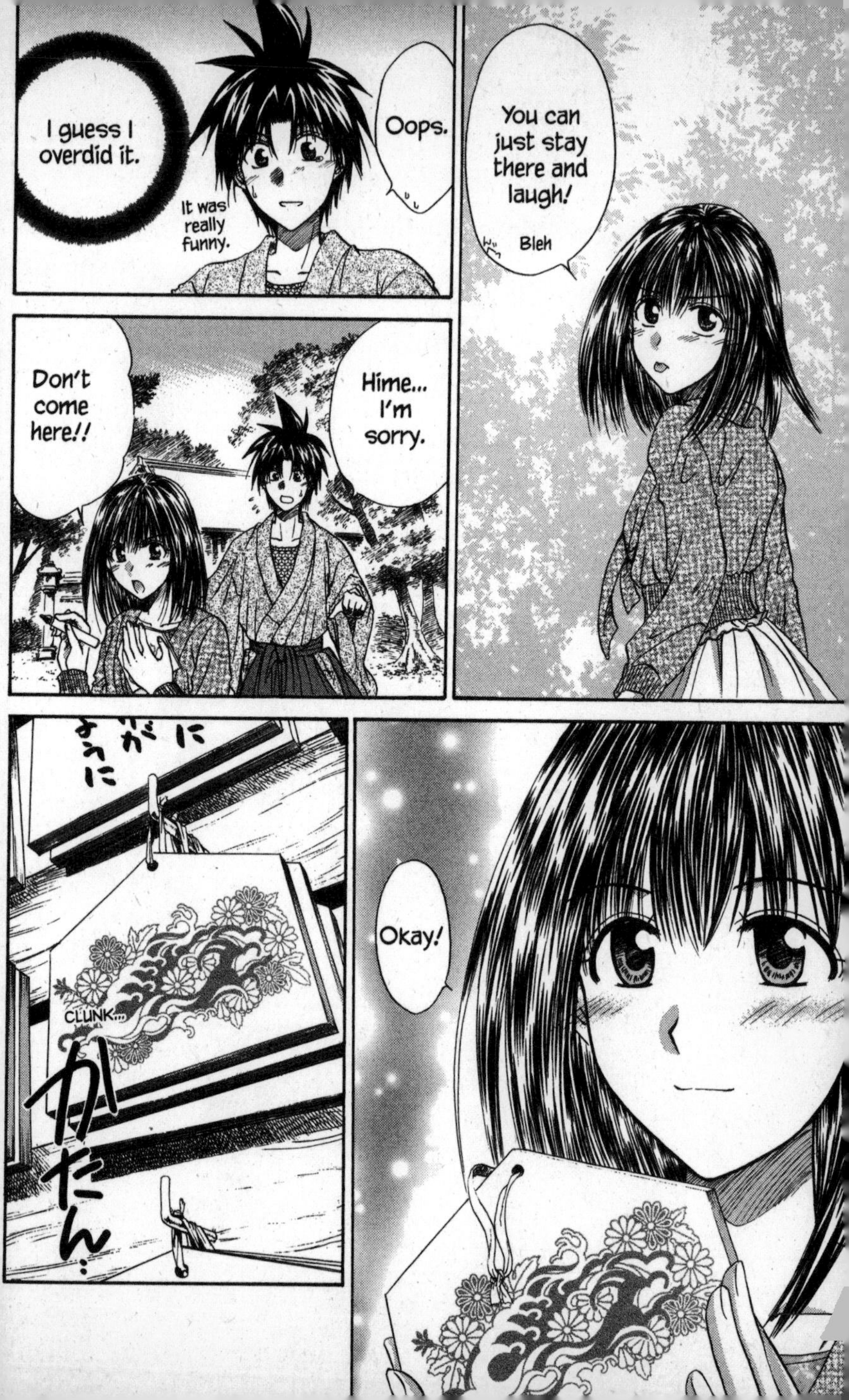

Oops.
I guess I overdid it.
It was really funny.
Hime... I'm sorry.
Don't come here!!
You can just stay there and laugh!
Bleh
Okay!
ように
がに
CLUNK...
かたん

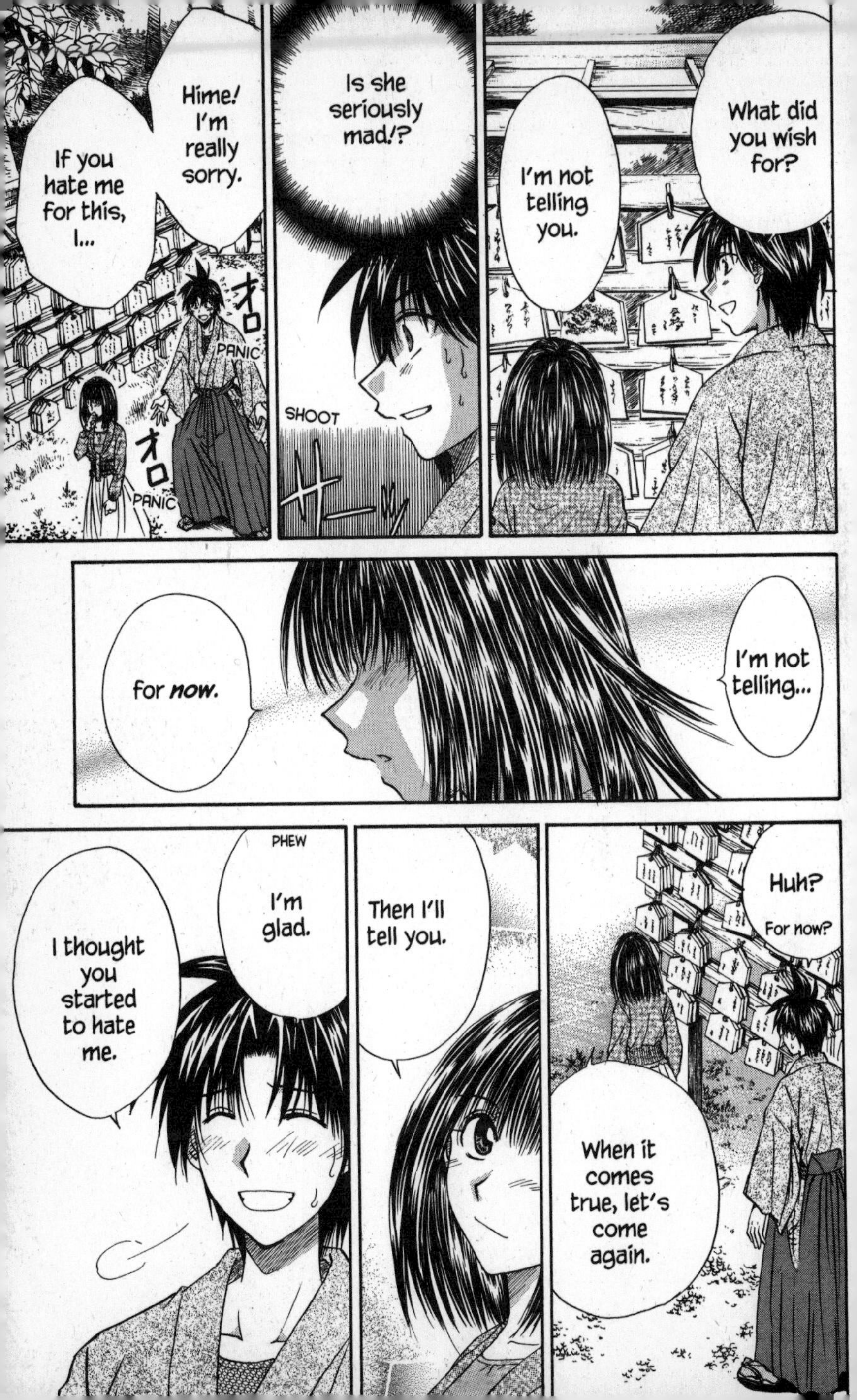
What did you wish for?
I'm not telling you.
Is she seriously mad!?
SHOOT
Hime! I'm really sorry.
If you hate me for this, I...
オロ
PANIC
オロ
PANIC
I'm not telling...
for *now*.
Huh?
For now?
When it comes true, let's come again.
Then I'll tell you.
PHEW
I'm glad.
I thought you started to hate me.

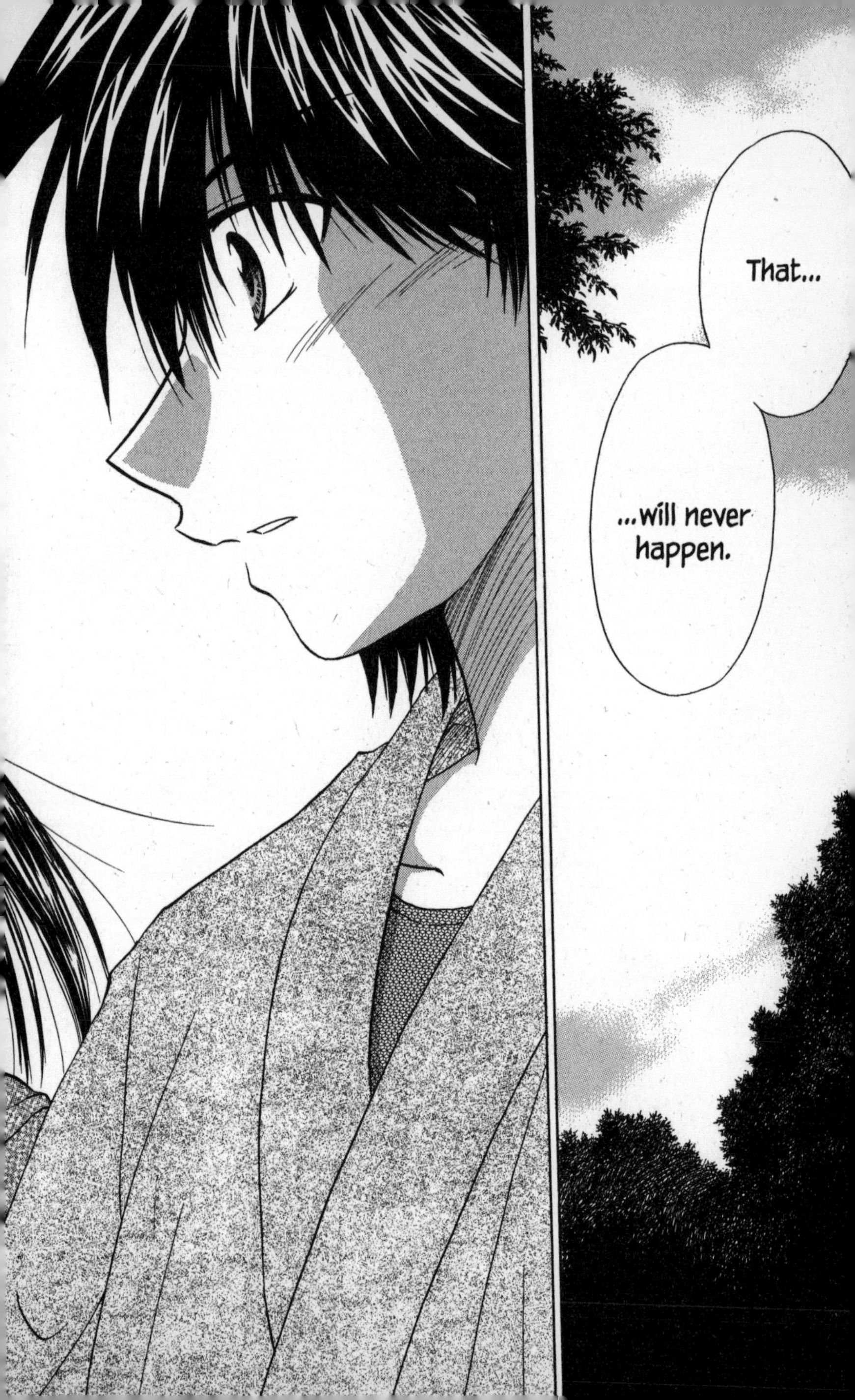
That...
...will never happen.

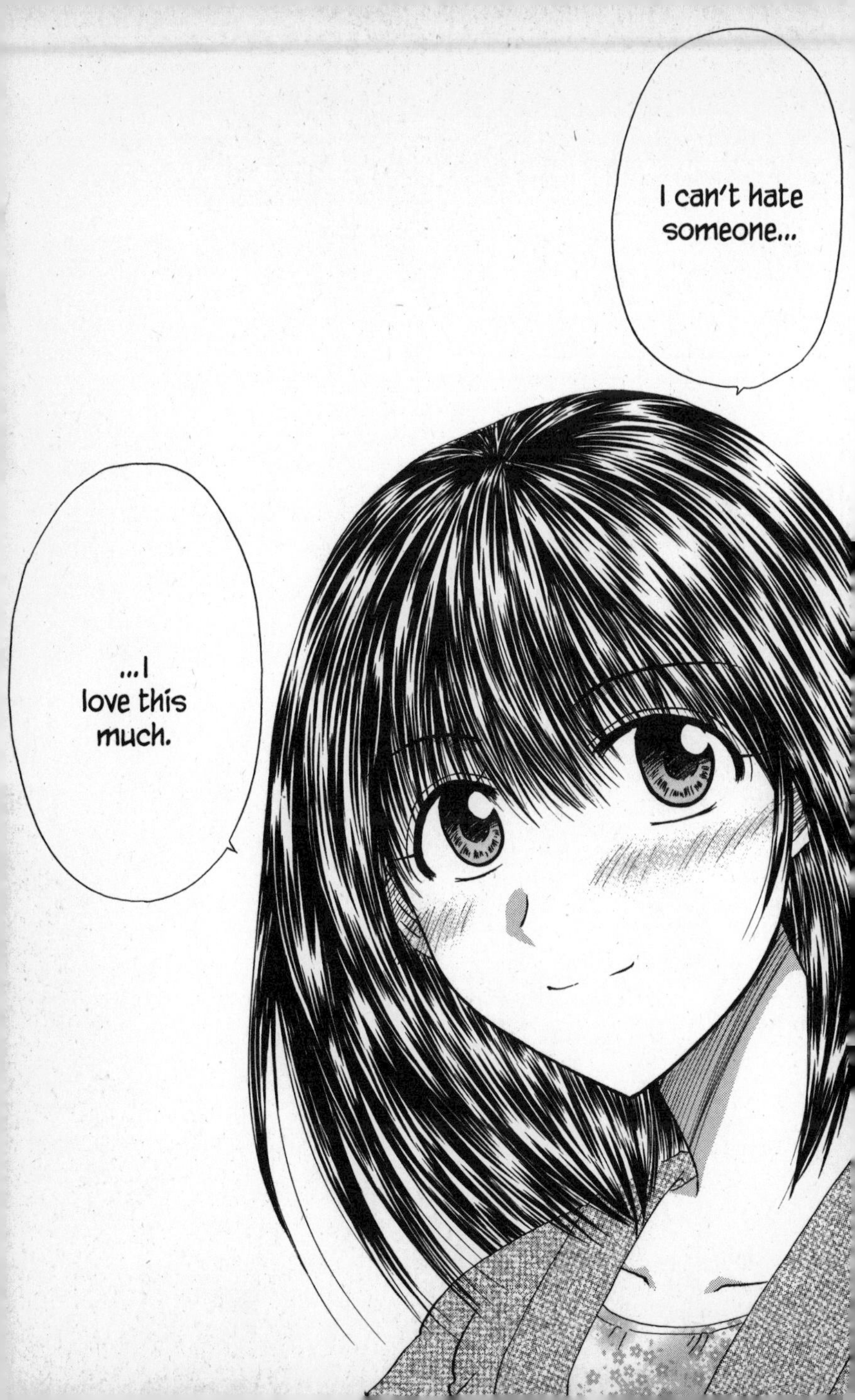
I can't hate someone...
...I love this much.

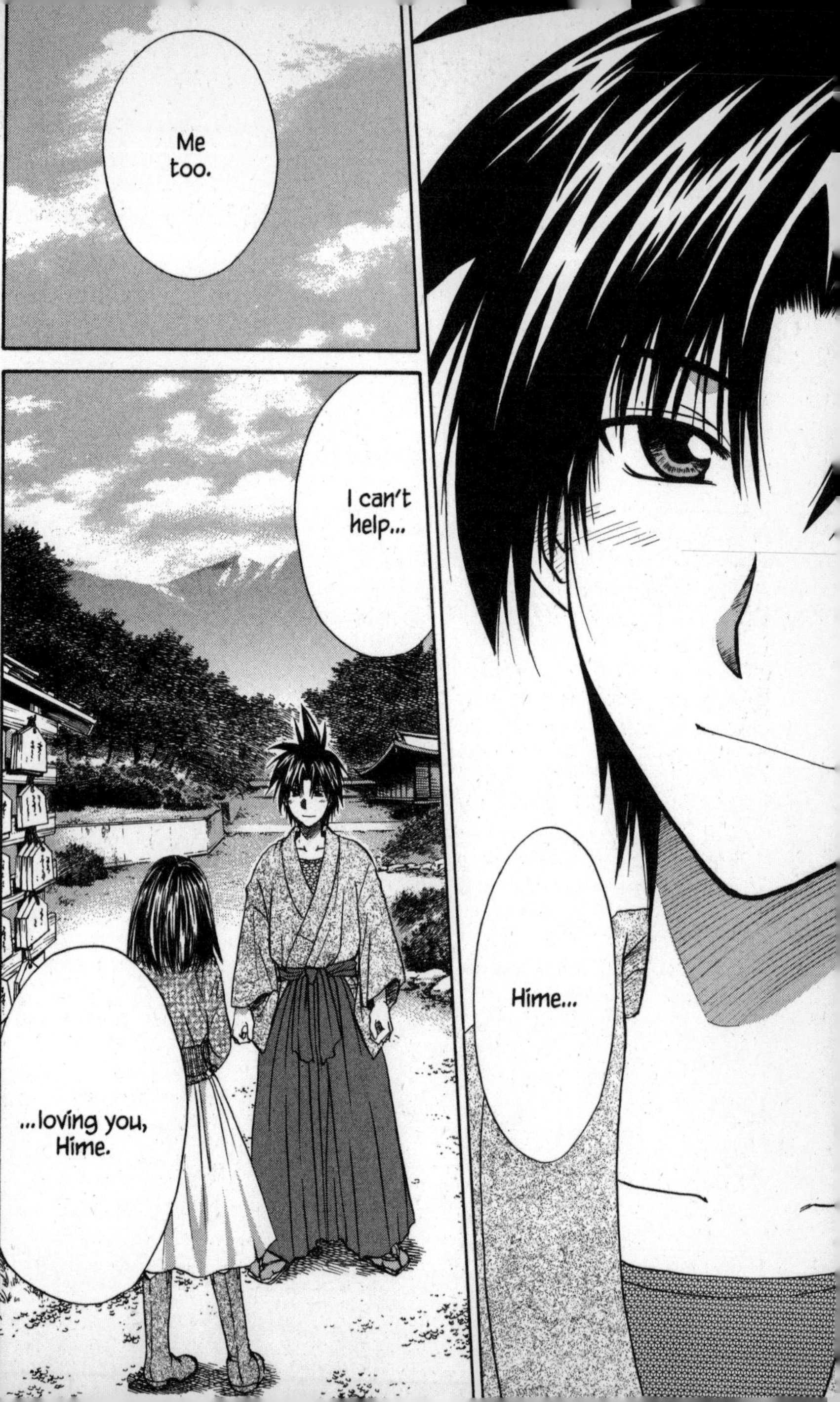
Hime...
Me too.
I can't help...
...loving you, Hime.

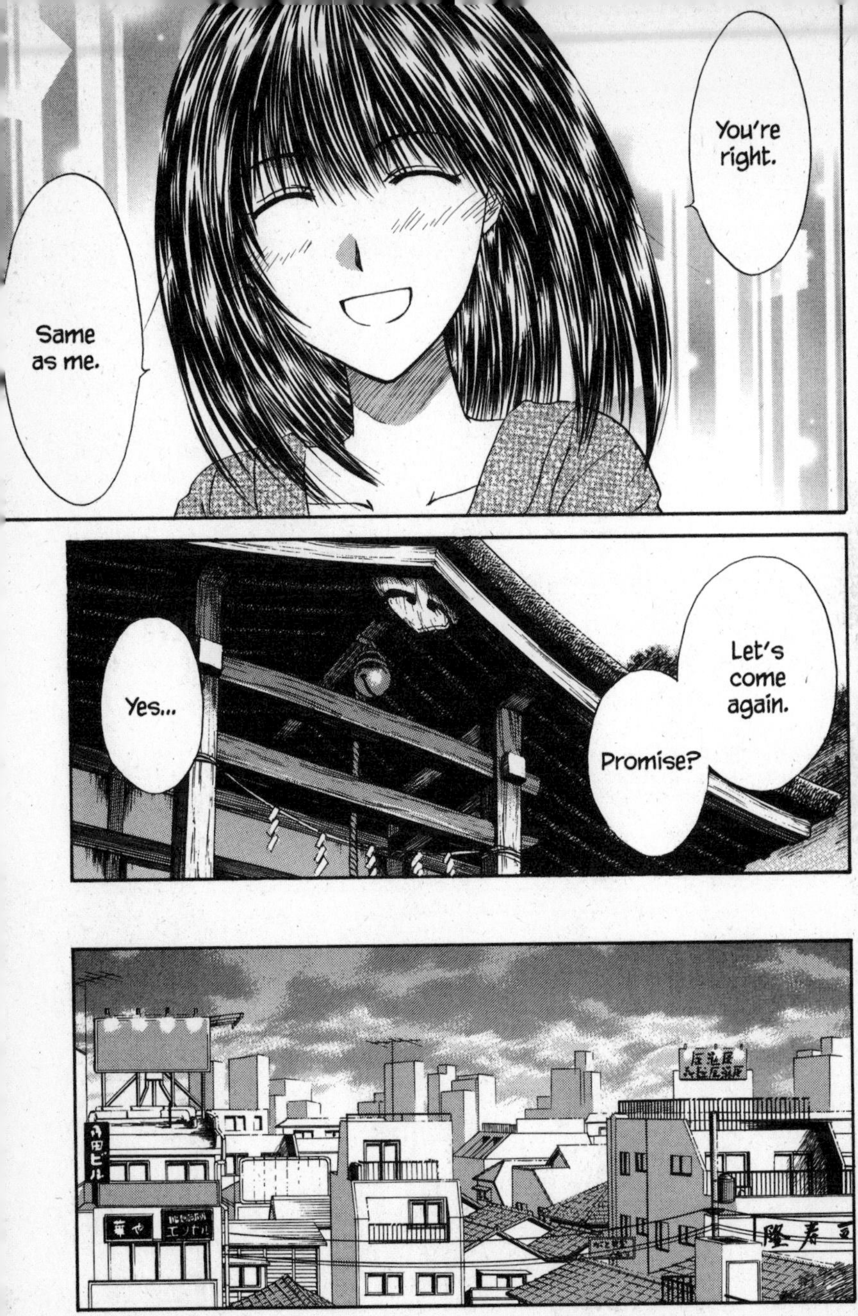
You're right.
Same as me.
Let's come again.
Promise?
Yes...

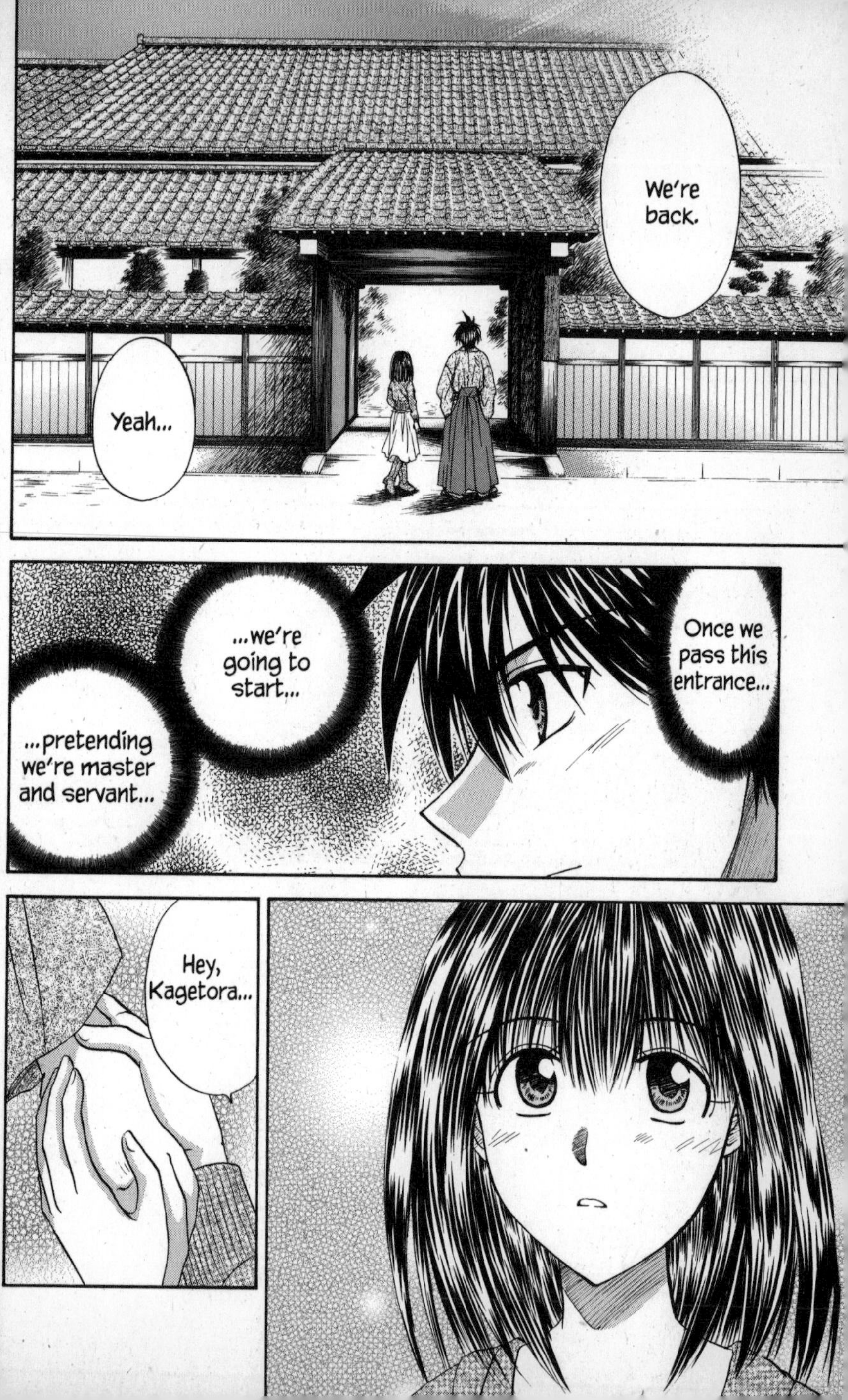
We're back.
Yeah...
Once we pass this entrance...
...we're going to start...
...pretending we're master and servant...
Hey, Kagetora...

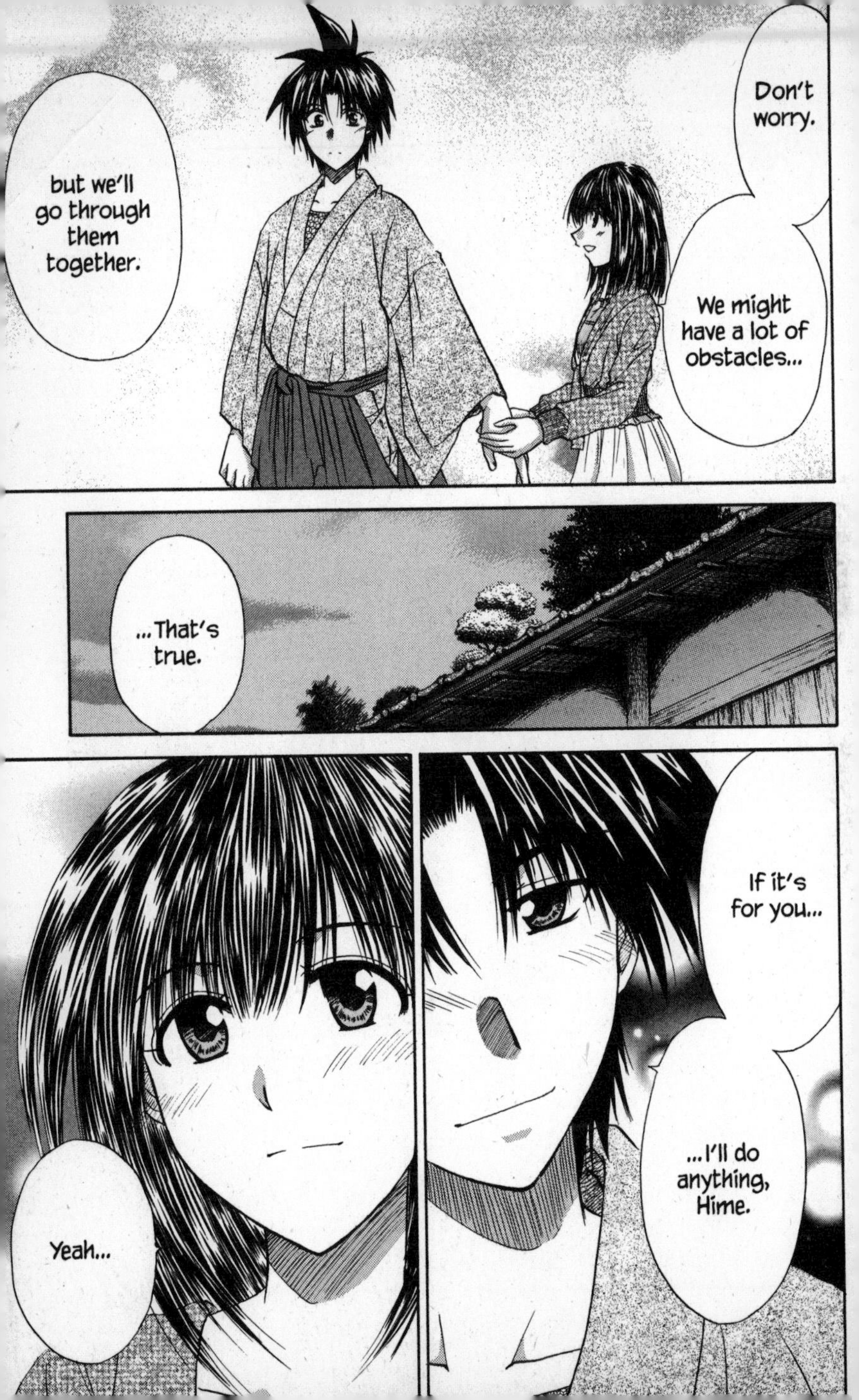
Don't worry.
We might have a lot of obstacles...
but we'll go through them together.
...That's true.
If it's for you...
...I'll do anything, Hime.
Yeah...

[redacted]

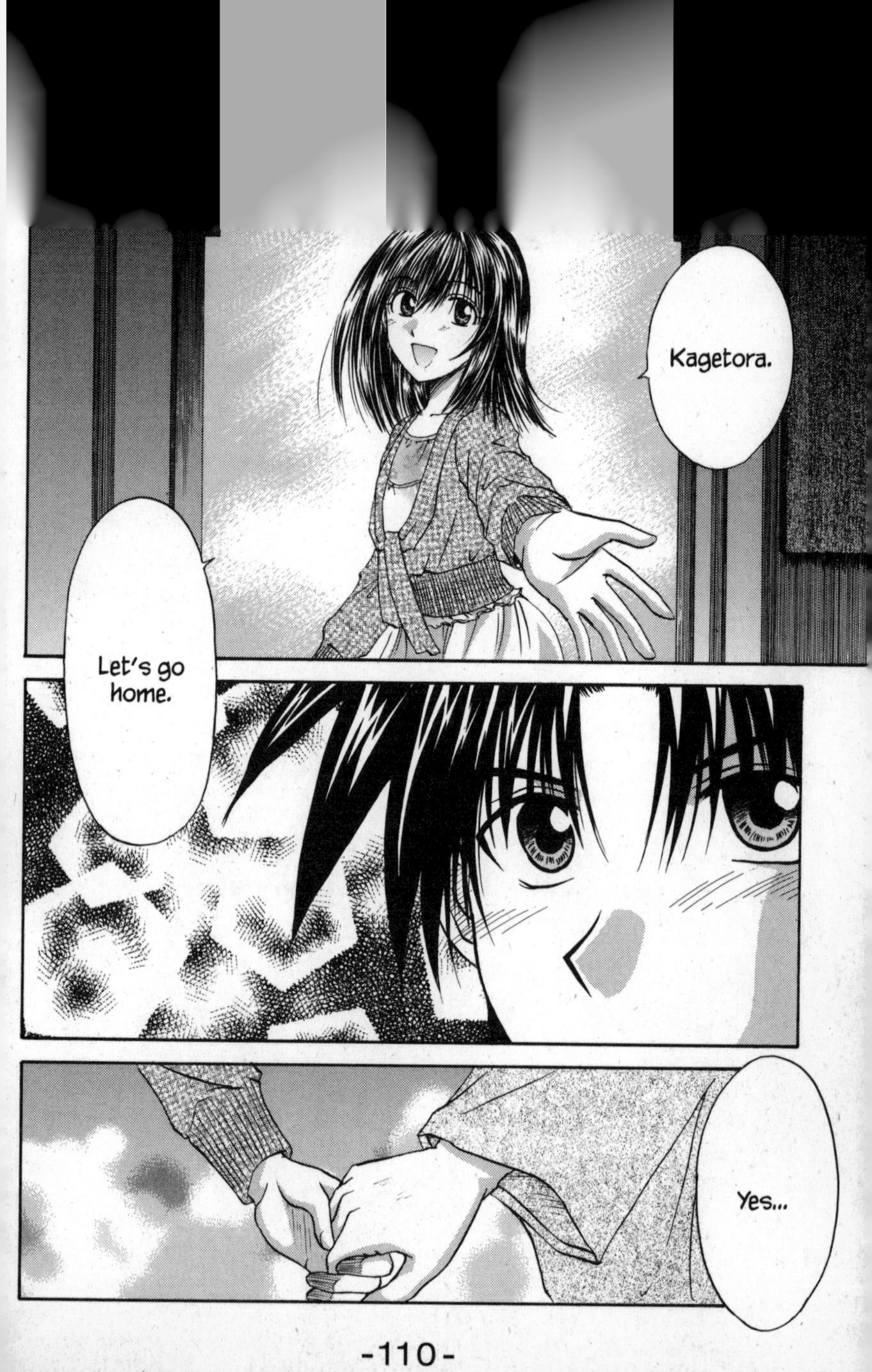
Kagetora.
Let's go home.
Yes...

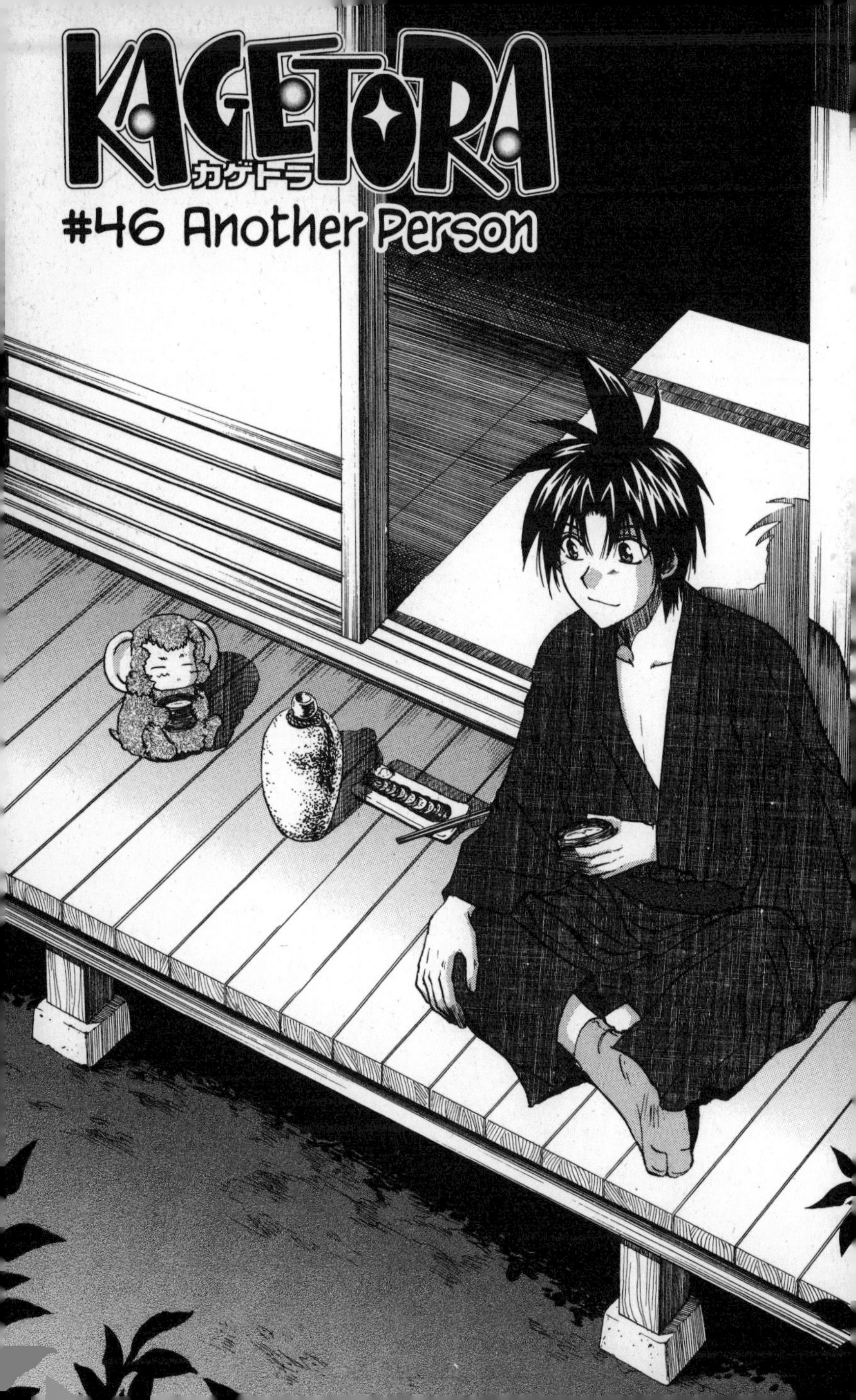
KAGETORA
カゲトラ
#46 Another Person

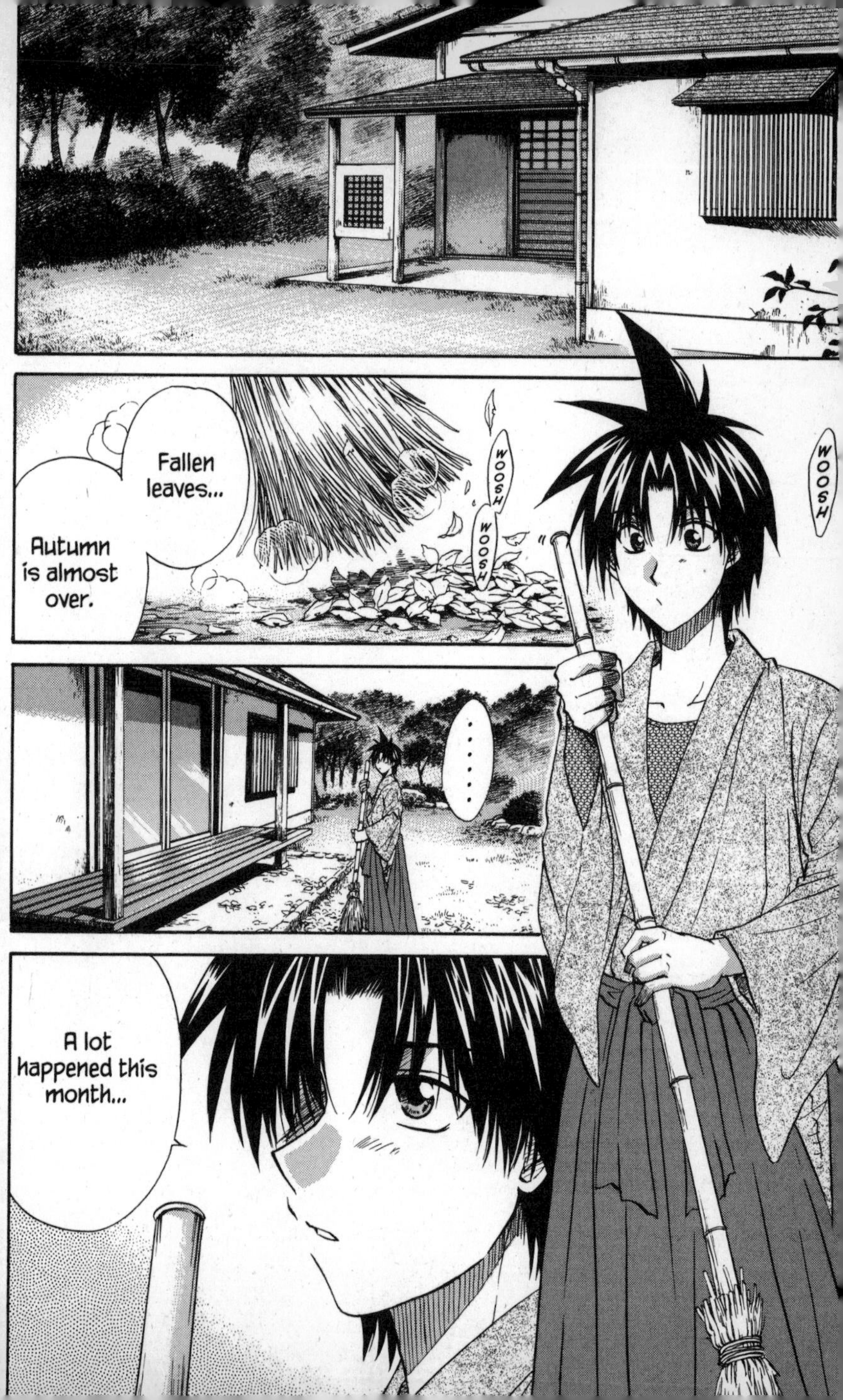
WOOSH
WOOSH
WOOSH
Fallen leaves...
Autumn is almost over.
......
A lot happened this month...

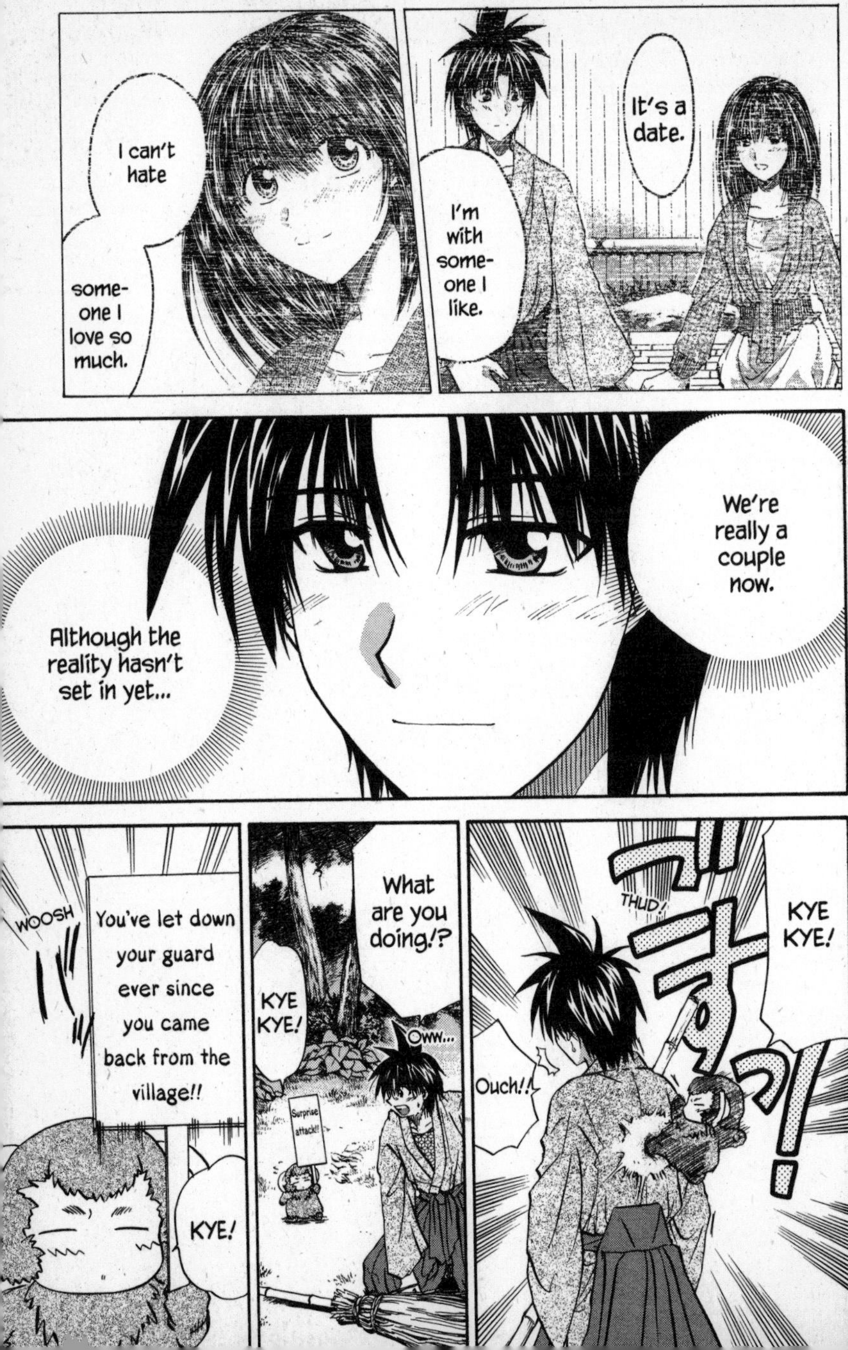
It's a date.
I'm with someone I like.
I can't hate someone I love so much.
We're really a couple now.
Although the reality hasn't set in yet...
KYE KYE!
THUD!
ずっ!
Ouch!!
What are you doing!?
OWW...
KYE KYE!
Surprise attack!!
WOOSH
You've let down your guard ever since you came back from the village!!
KYE!

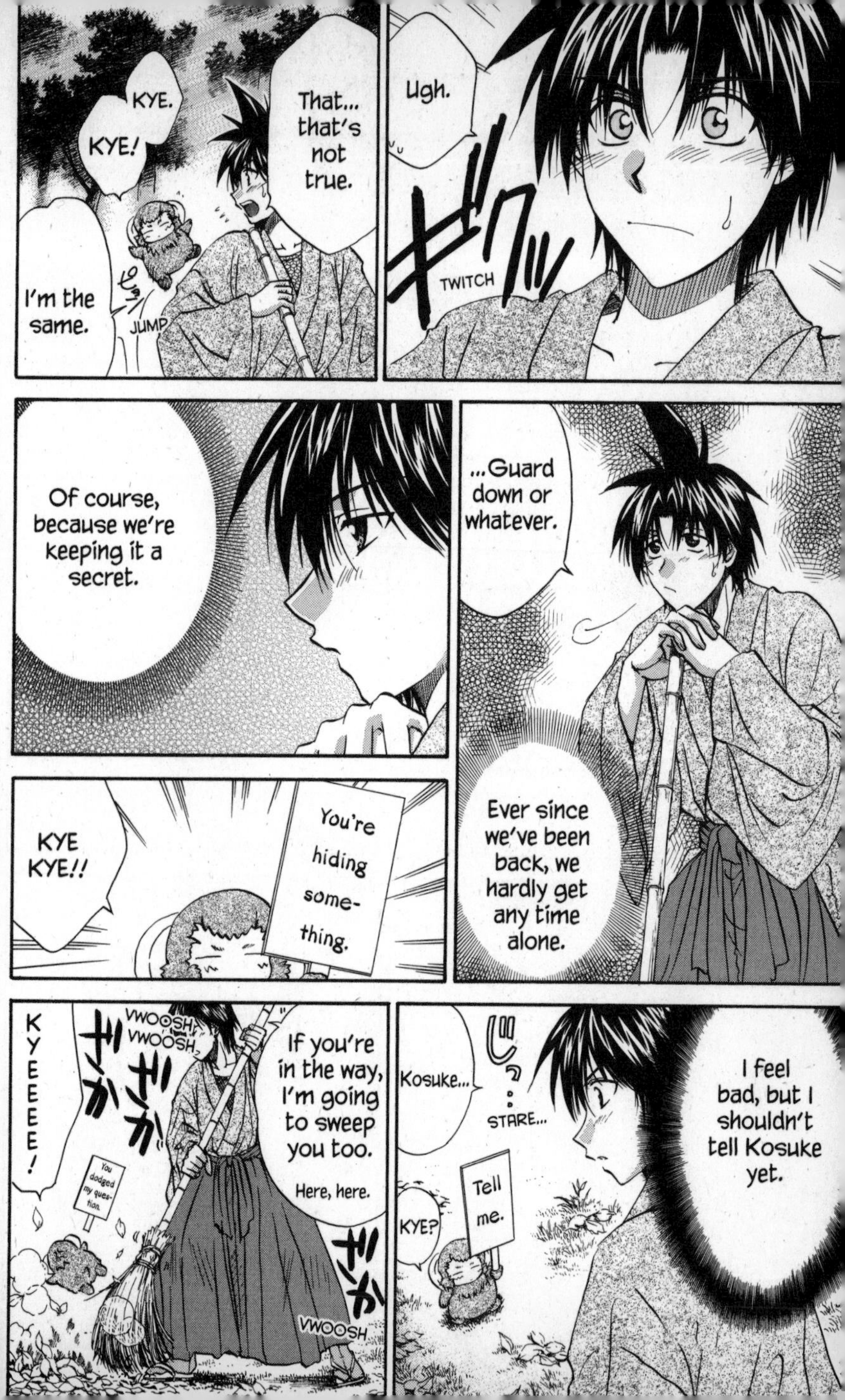

Ugh.
TWITCH
That... that's not true.
KYE.
KYE!
I'm the same.
JUMP
...Guard down or whatever.
Ever since we've been back, we hardly get any time alone.
Of course, because we're keeping it a secret.
You're hiding some-thing.
KYE KYE!!
I feel bad, but I shouldn't tell Kosuke yet.
Kosuke...
STARE...
Tell me.
KYE?
If you're in the way, I'm going to sweep you too.
Here, here.
VWOOSH VWOOSH
KYEEEEE!
You dodged my ques-tion.
VWOOSH

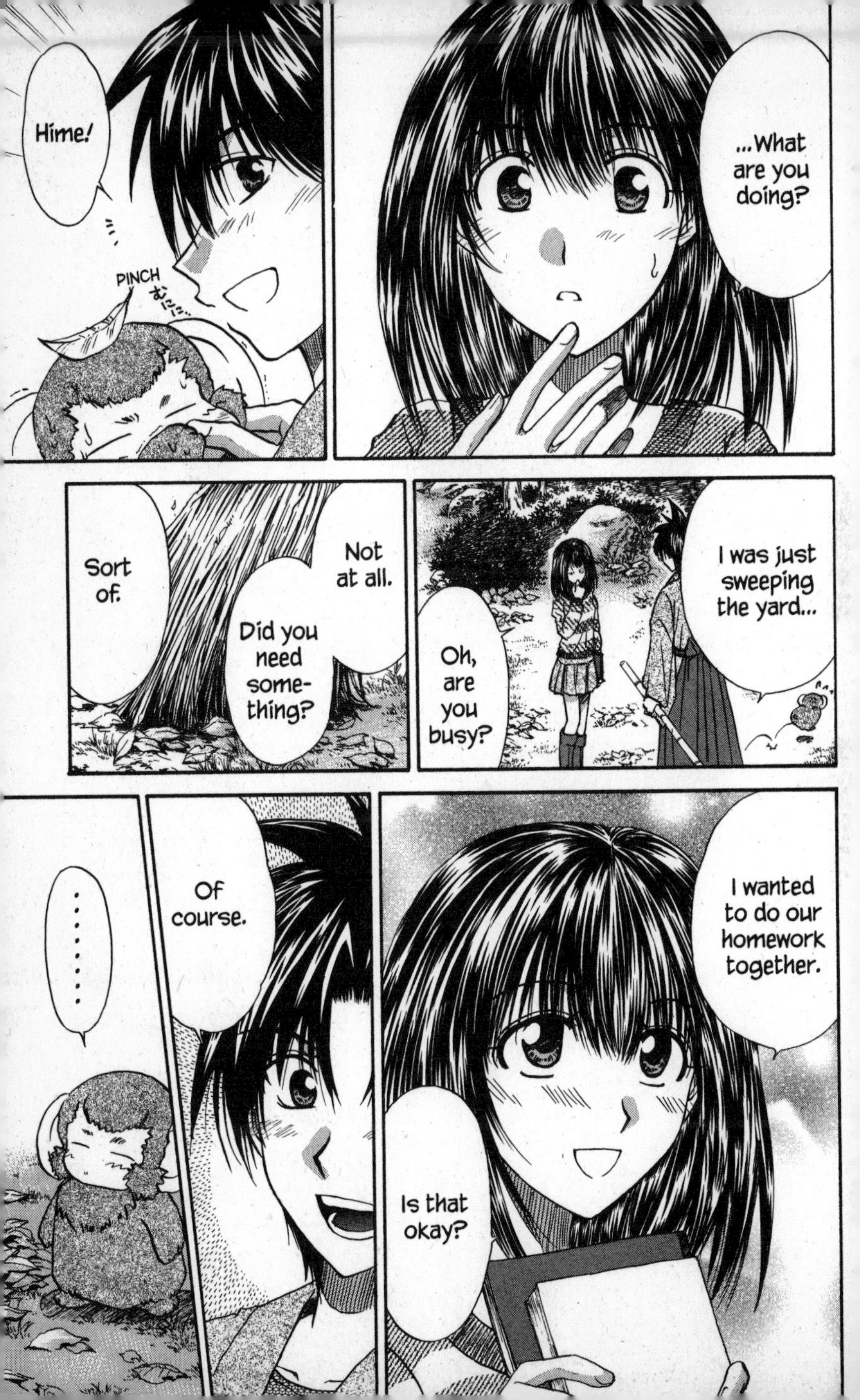
...What are you doing?
Hime!
PINCH
むにに..
I was just sweeping the yard...
Oh, are you busy?
Not at all.
Did you need some-thing?
Sort of.
I wanted to do our homework together.
Is that okay?
Of course.
....

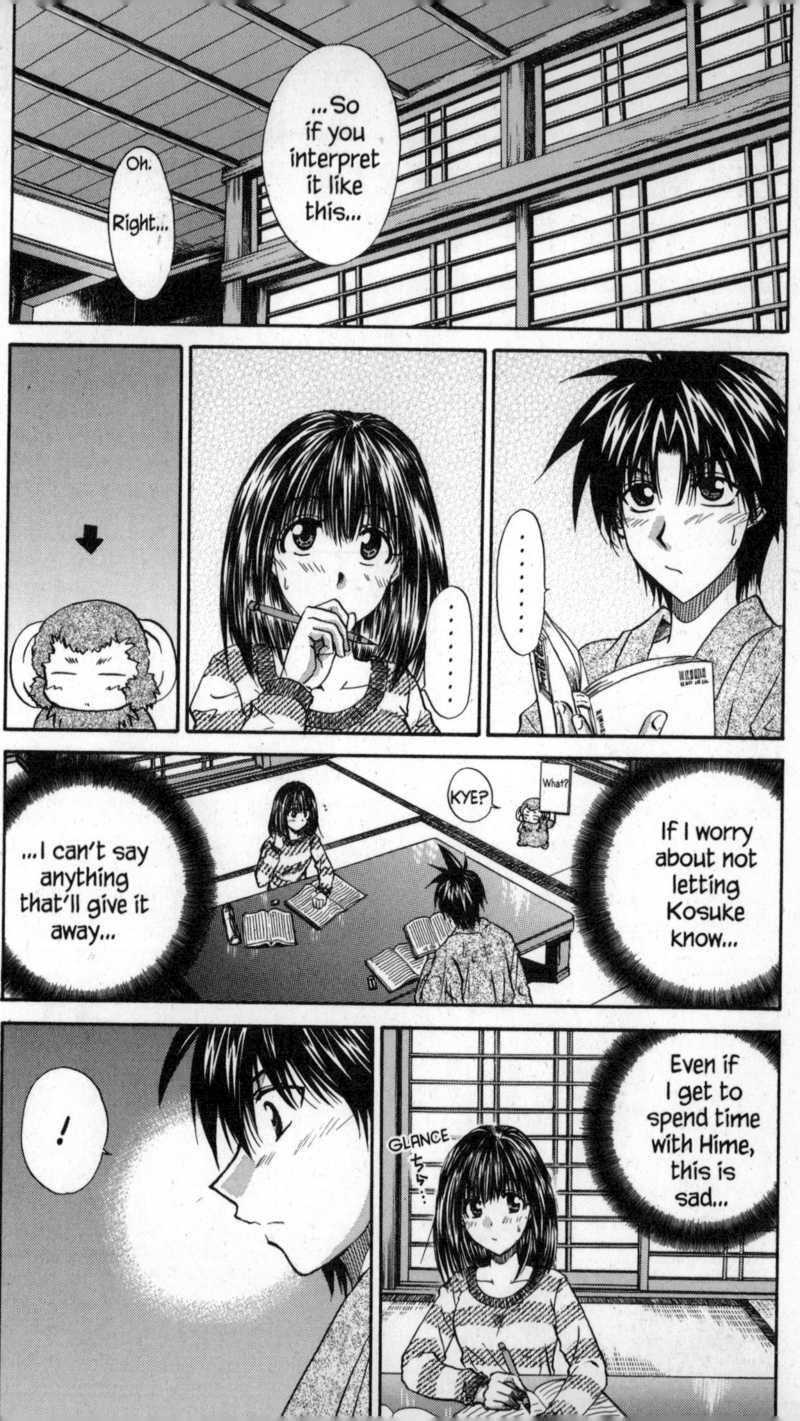
...So if you interpret it like this...
Oh. Right...
......
......
If I worry about not letting Kosuke know...
What?
KYE?
...I can't say anything that'll give it away...
Even if I get to spend time with Hime, this is sad...
GLANCE
!

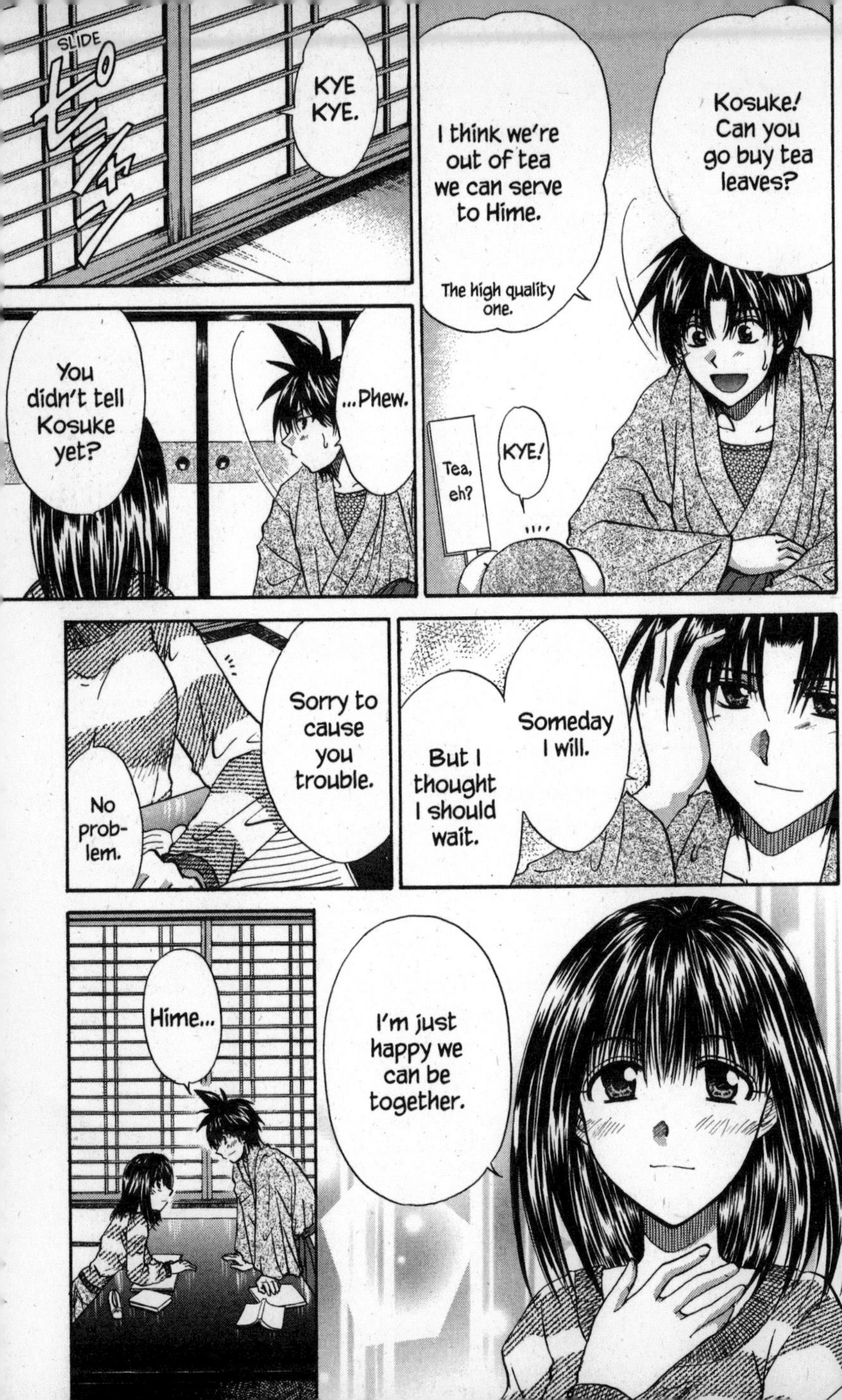
Kosuke! Can you go buy tea leaves?
I think we're out of tea we can serve to Hime.
The high quality one.
KYE!
Tea, eh?
SLIDE
KYE KYE.
...Phew.
You didn't tell Kosuke yet?
Someday I will.
But I thought I should wait.
Sorry to cause you trouble.
No prob-lem.
I'm just happy we can be together.
Hime...

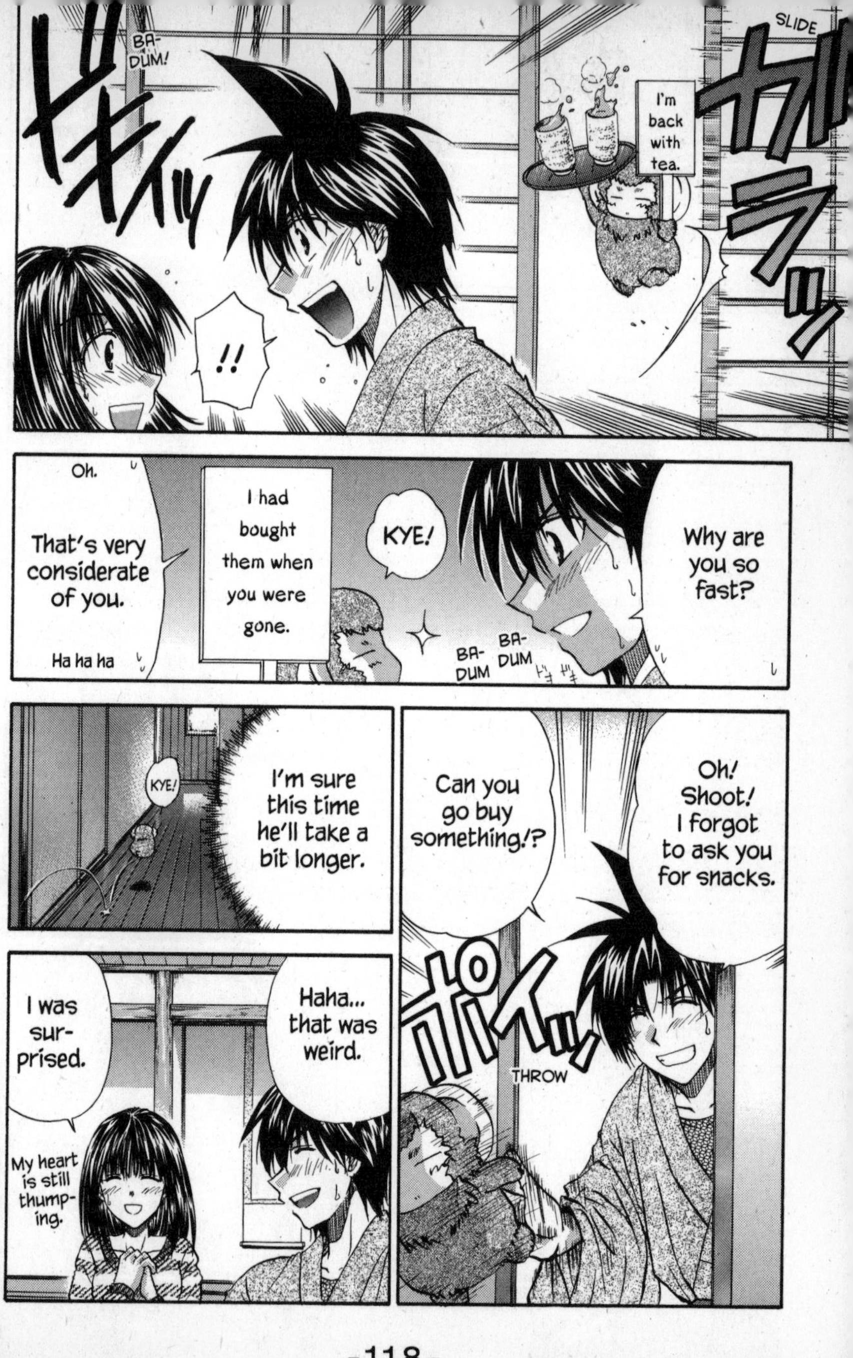
SLIDE
I'm back with tea.
BA-DUM!
!!
Why are you so fast?
BA-DUM
BA-DUM
KYE!
I had bought them when you were gone.
Oh.
That's very considerate of you.
Ha ha ha
Oh! Shoot! I forgot to ask you for snacks.
Can you go buy something!?
THROW
I'm sure this time he'll take a bit longer.
KYE!
Haha... that was weird.
I was sur-prised.
My heart is still thump-ing.

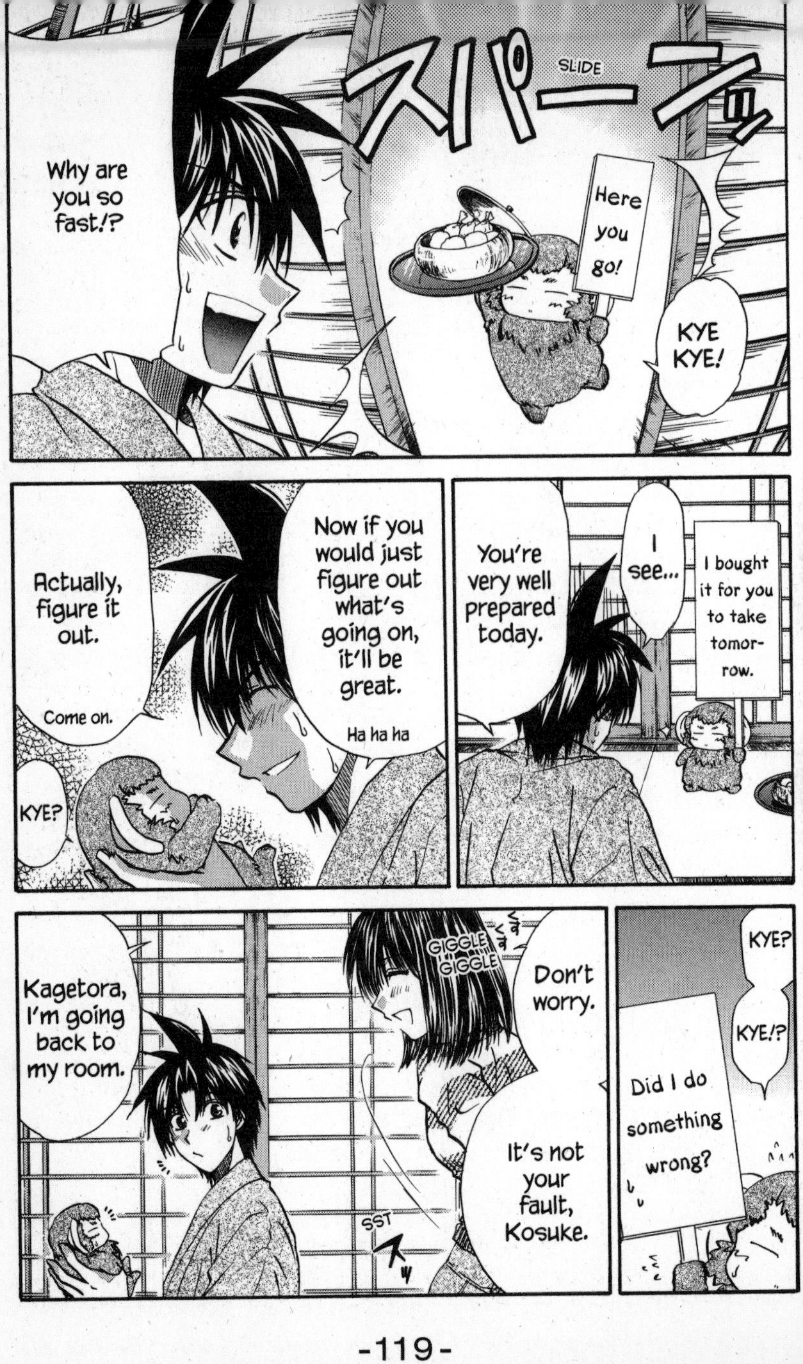
SLIDE
Here you go!
KYE KYE!
Why are you so fast!?
I bought it for you to take tomorrow.
I see...
You're very well prepared today.
Now if you would just figure out what's going on, it'll be great.
Ha ha ha
Actually, figure it out.
Come on.
KYE?
KYE?
KYE!?
Did I do something wrong?
GIGGLE GIGGLE
Don't worry.
It's not your fault, Kosuke.
Kagetora, I'm going back to my room.
SST

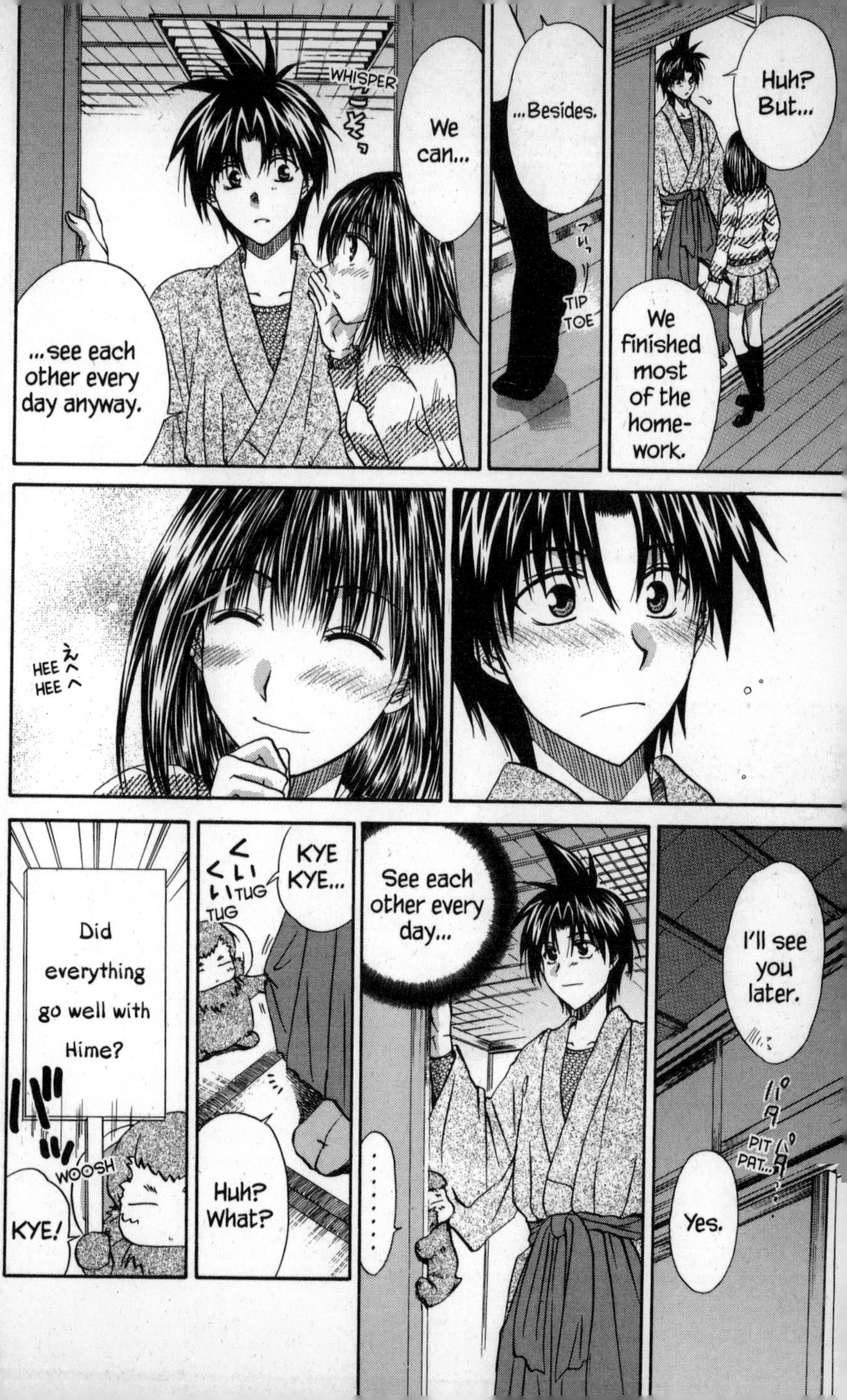
Huh? But...
We finished most of the home-work.
...Besides.
TIP TOE
We can...
WHISPER
...see each other every day anyway.
HEE HEE
I'll see you later.
PIT PAT...
Yes.
See each other every day...
......
KYE KYE...
TUG TUG
Huh? What?
Did everything go well with Hime?
WOOSH
KYE!

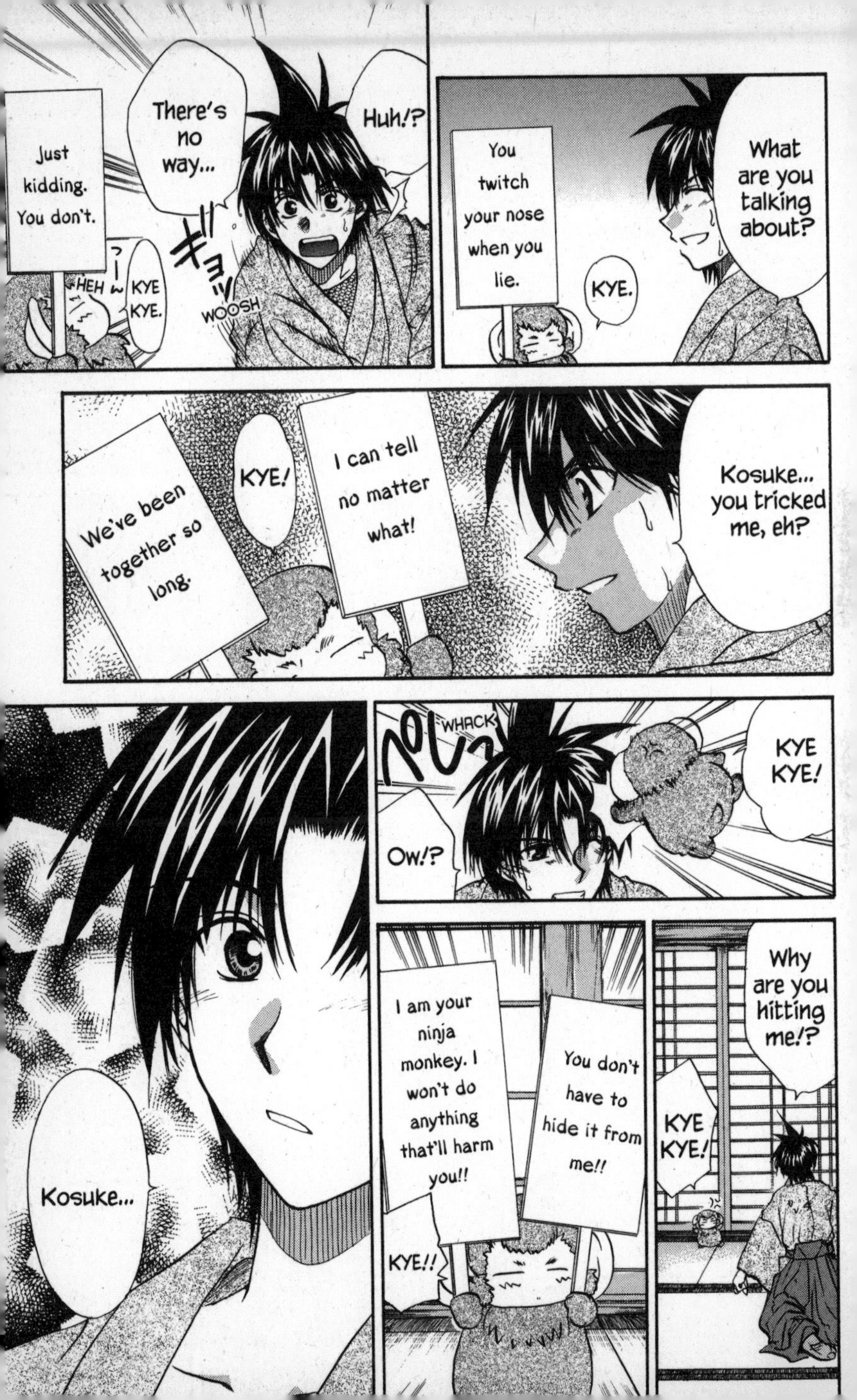
What are you talking about?
You twitch your nose when you lie.
KYE.
Huh!?
There's no way...
ギョッ
WOOSH
Just kidding. You don't.
KYE KYE.
HEH
Kosuke... you tricked me, eh?
I can tell no matter what!
KYE!
We've been together so long.
KYE KYE!
WHACK
Ow!?
Why are you hitting me!?
KYE KYE!
You don't have to hide it from me!!
I am your ninja monkey. I won't do anything that'll harm you!!
KYE!!
Kosuke...

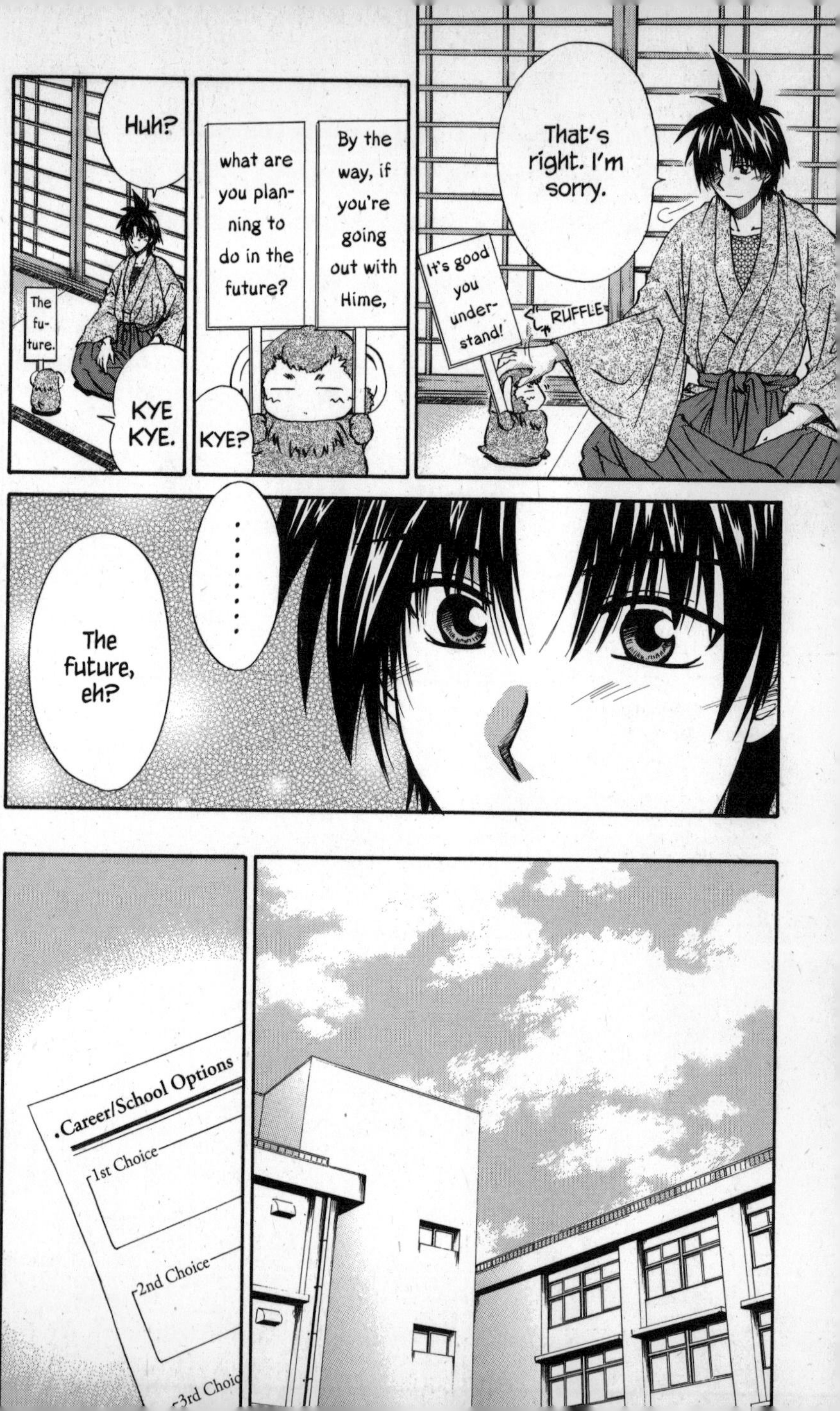
That's right. I'm sorry.
It's good you understand!
RUFFLE
By the way, if you're going out with Hime,
what are you plan-ning to do in the future?
KYE?
Huh?
KYE KYE.
The fu-ture.
....
The future, eh?
Career/School Options
1st Choice
2nd Choice
3rd Choic

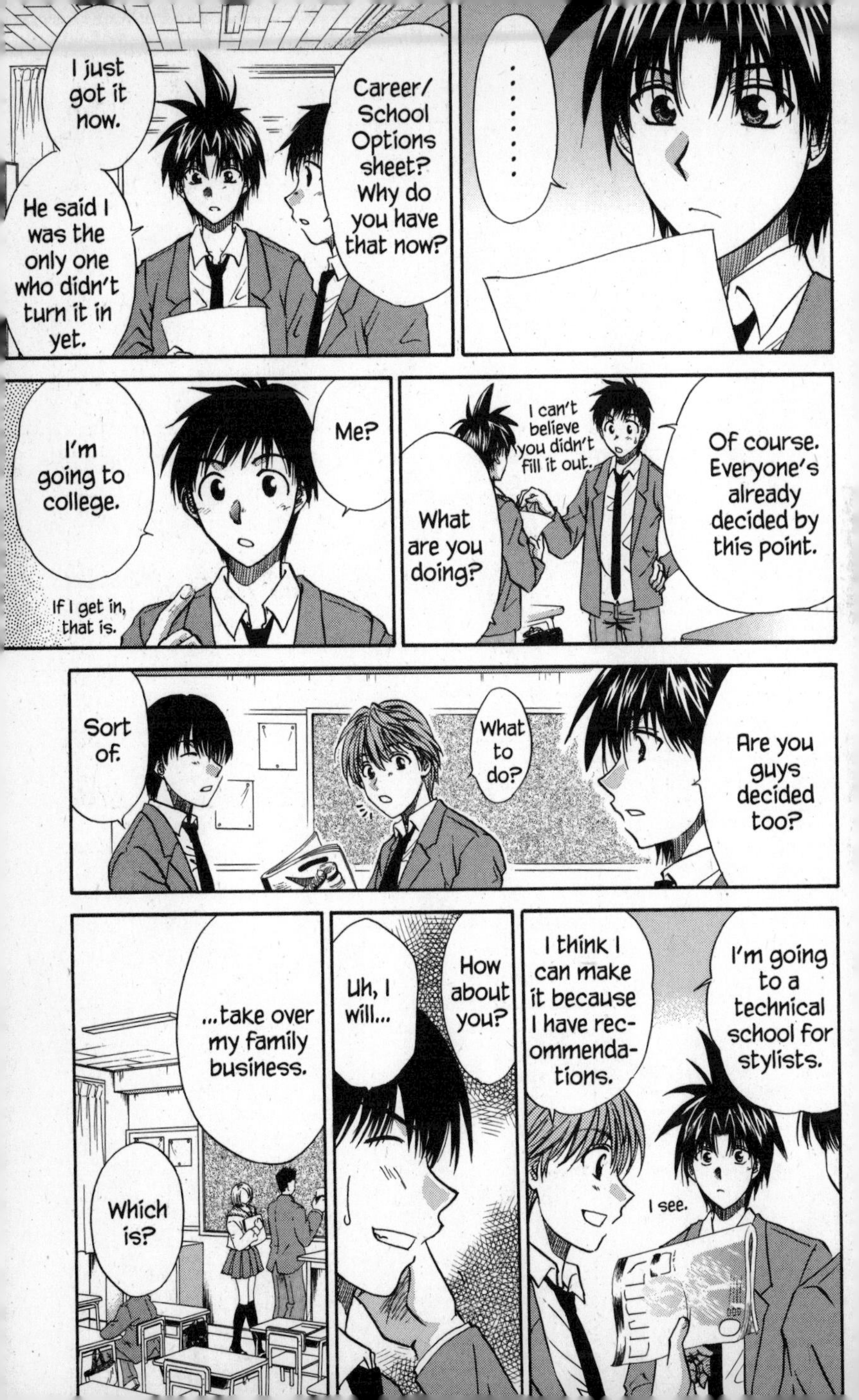
……
Career/ School Options sheet? Why do you have that now?
I just got it now.
He said I was the only one who didn't turn it in yet.
Of course. Everyone's already decided by this point.
I can't believe you didn't fill it out.
What are you doing?
Me?
I'm going to college.
If I get in, that is.
Are you guys decided too?
What to do?
Sort of.
I'm going to a technical school for stylists.
I think I can make it because I have rec-ommenda-tions.
I see.
How about you?
Uh, I will...
...take over my family business.
Which is?

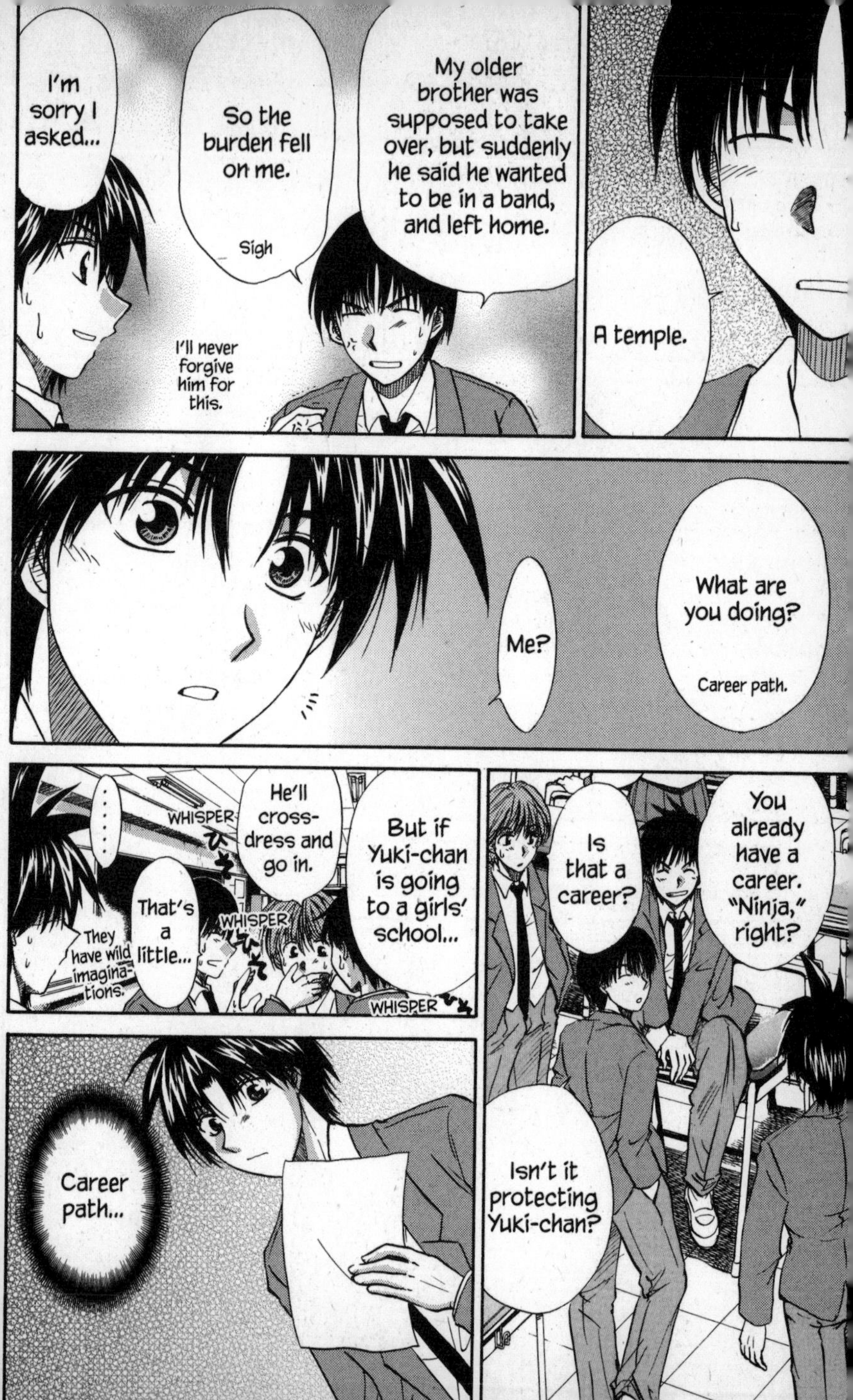
A temple.
My older brother was supposed to take over, but suddenly he said he wanted to be in a band, and left home.
So the burden fell on me.
Sigh
I'm sorry I asked...
I'll never forgive him for this.
What are you doing?
Career path.
Me?
You already have a career. "Ninja," right?
Is that a career?
Isn't it protecting Yuki-chan?
But if Yuki-chan is going to a girls' school...
He'll cross-dress and go in.
WHISPER
......
WHISPER
That's a little...
They have wild imaginations.
WHISPER
Career path...

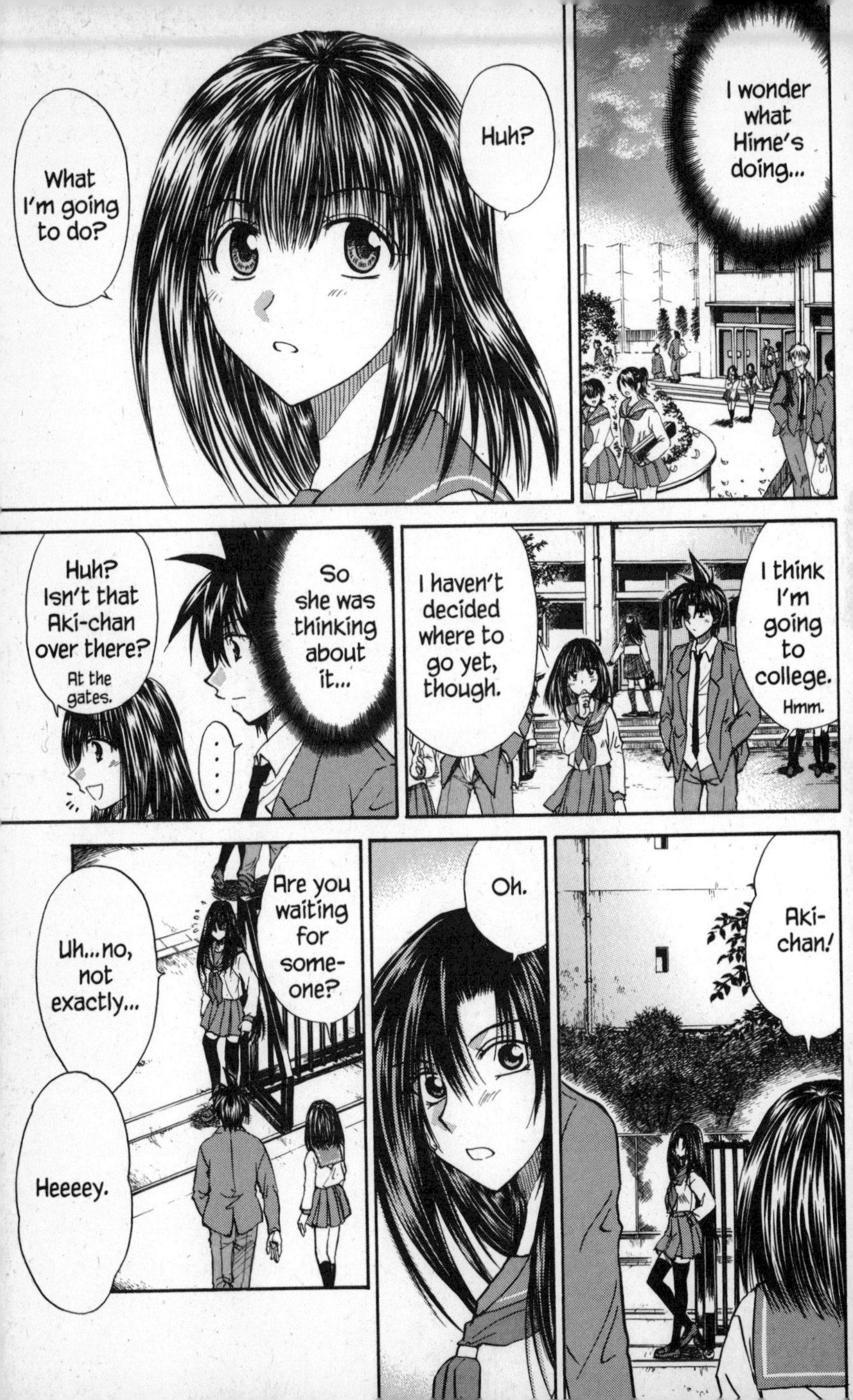

I wonder what Hime's doing...
Huh?
What I'm going to do?
I think I'm going to college.
Hmm.
I haven't decided where to go yet, though.
So she was thinking about it...
Huh? Isn't that Aki-chan over there?
At the gates.
....
Aki-chan!
Oh.
Are you waiting for some-one?
Uh...no, not exactly...
Heeeey.

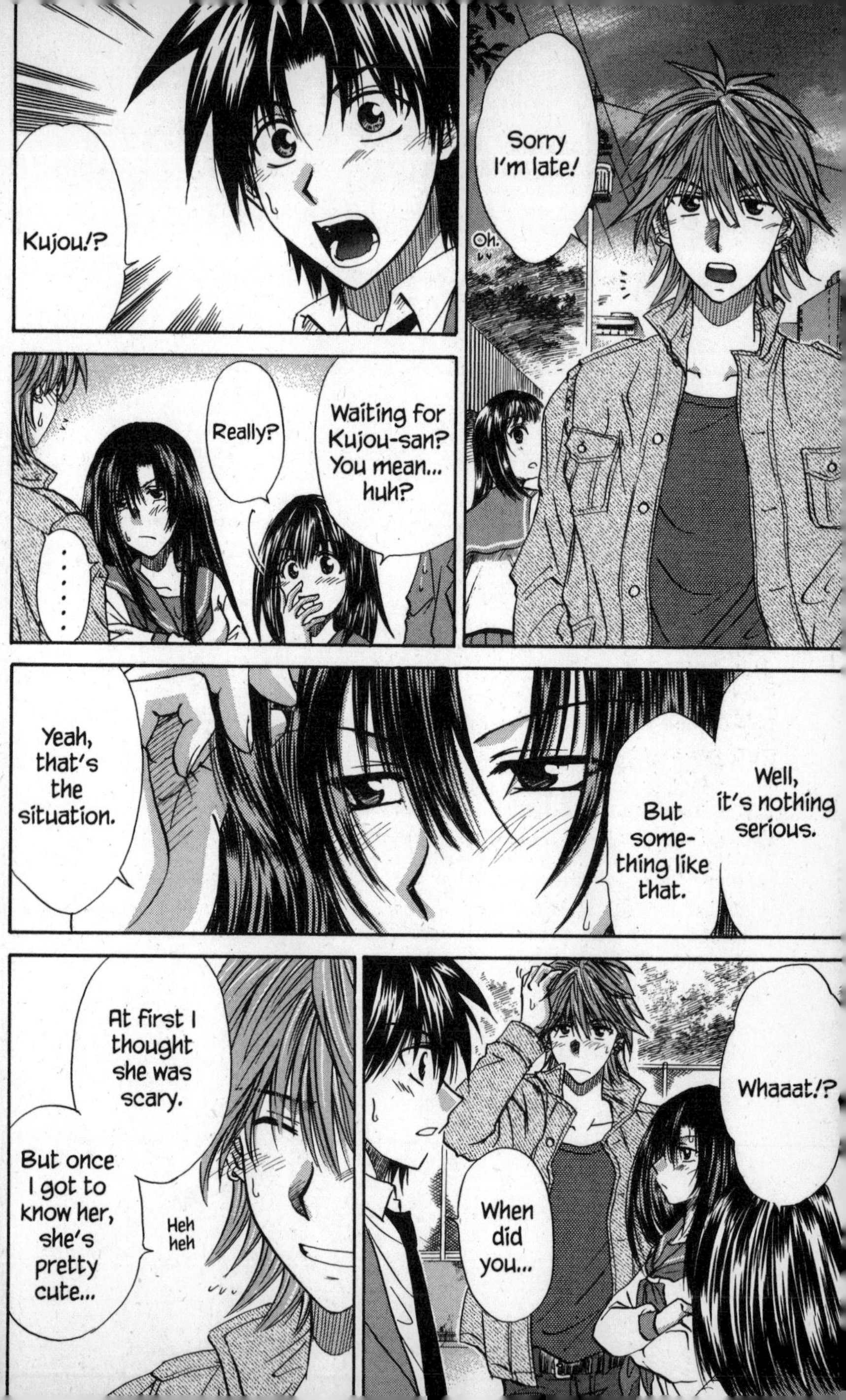
Sorry I'm late!
Oh.
Kujou!?
Waiting for Kujou-san? You mean... huh?
Really?
......
Well, it's nothing serious.
But something like that.
Yeah, that's the situation.
Whaaat!?
When did you...
At first I thought she was scary.
But once I got to know her, she's pretty cute...
Heh heh

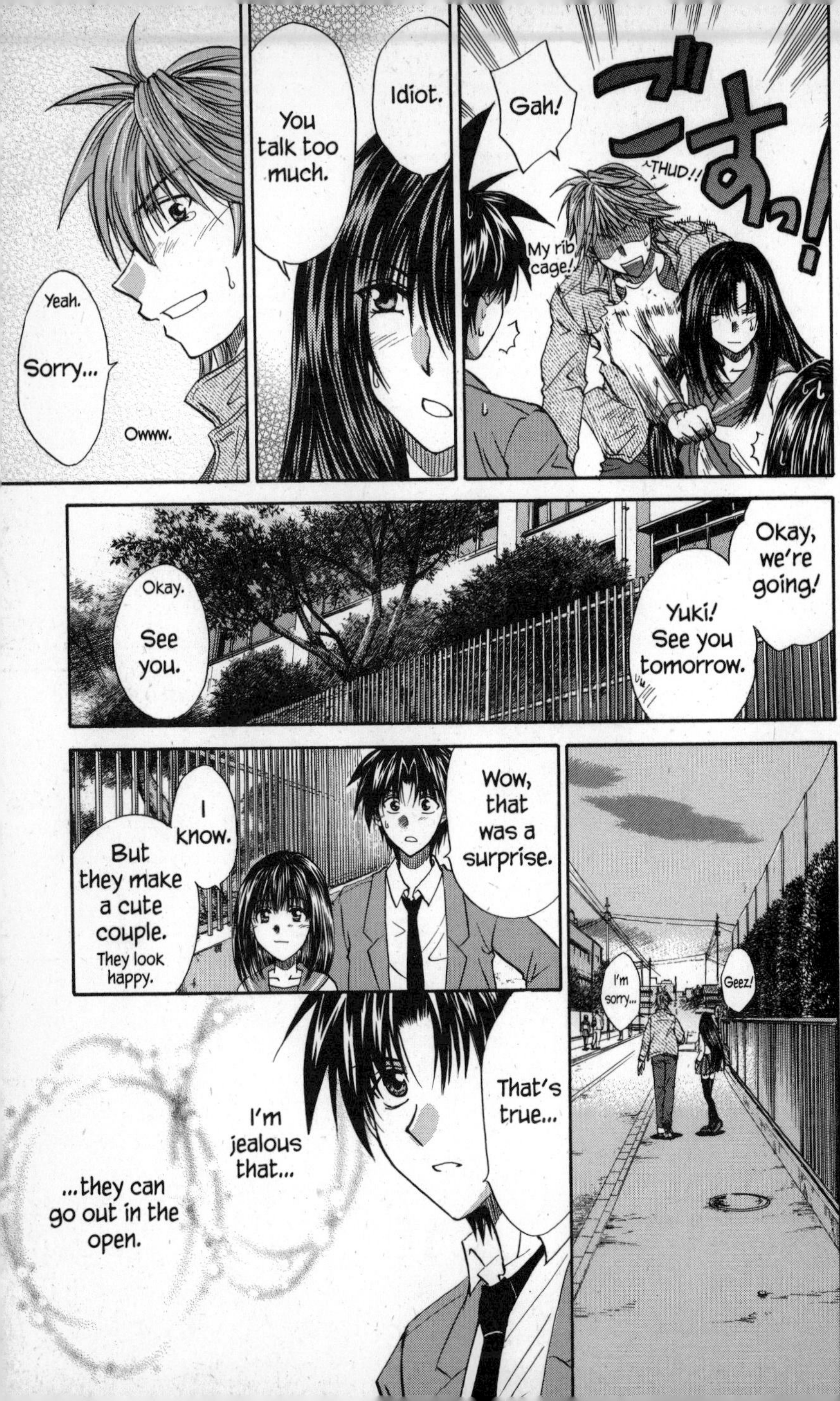
ごすっ!
THUD!!
Gah!
My rib cage!
Idiot.
You talk too much.
Yeah.
Sorry...
Owww.
Okay, we're going!
Yuki! See you tomorrow.
Okay.
See you.
Geez!
I'm sorry...
Wow, that was a surprise.
I know.
But they make a cute couple.
They look happy.
That's true...
I'm jealous that...
...they can go out in the open.

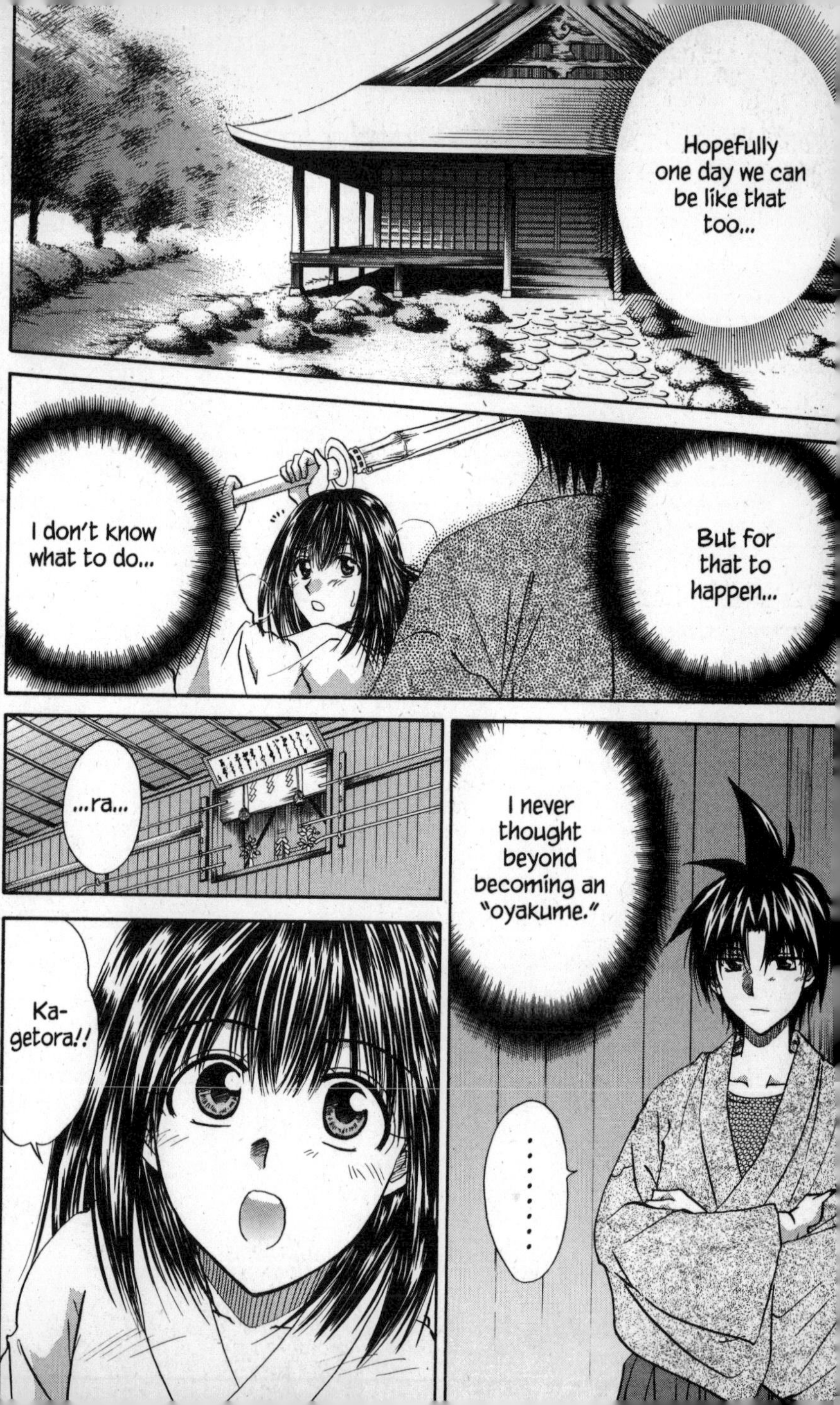
Hopefully one day we can be like that too...
But for that to happen...
I don't know what to do...
I never thought beyond becoming an "oyakume."
....
...ra...
Ka-getora!!

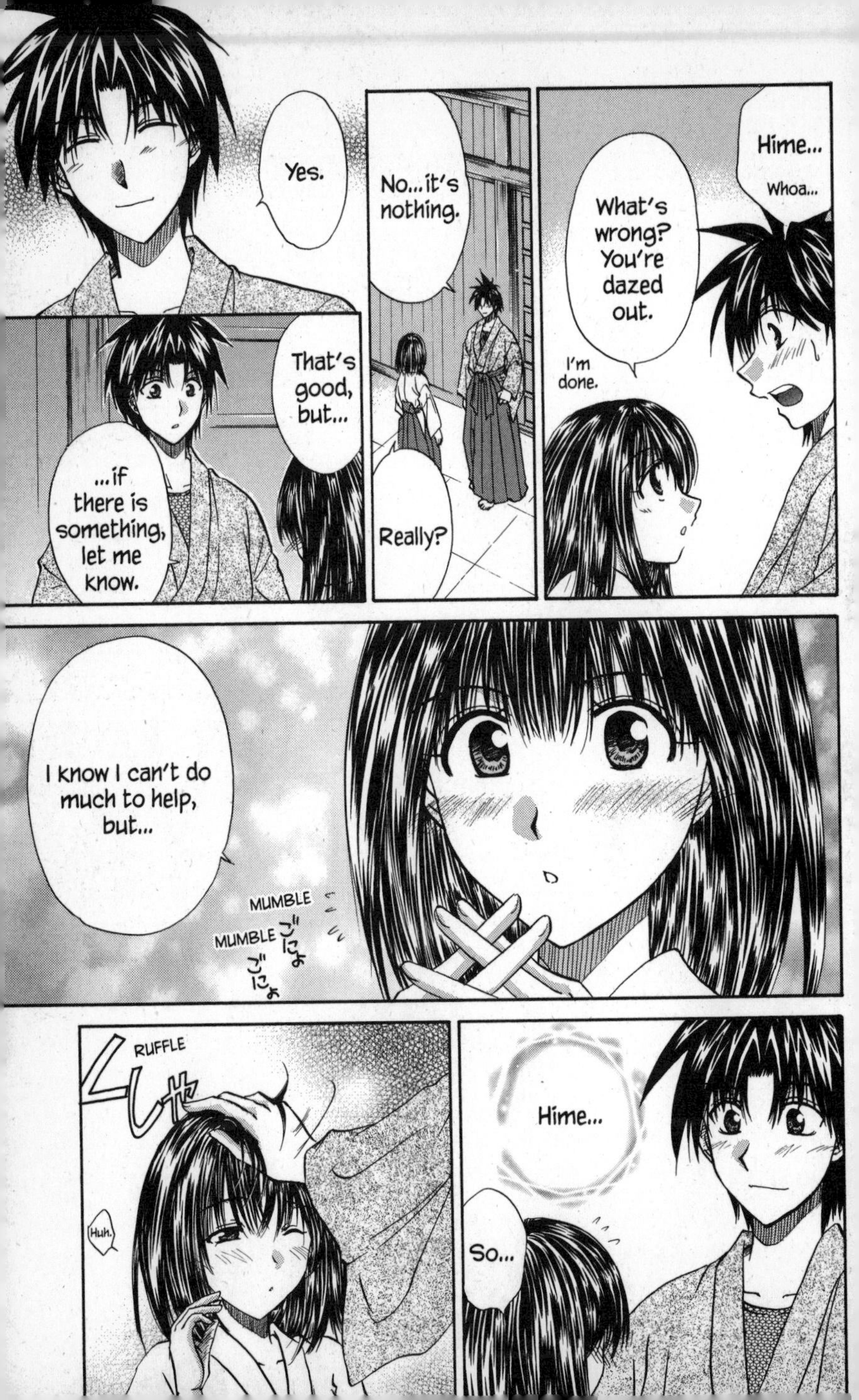
Hime...
Whoa...
What's wrong? You're dazed out.
I'm done.
No... it's nothing.
Really?
Yes.
That's good, but...
...if there is something, let me know.
I know I can't do much to help, but...
MUMBLE
MUMBLE
ごにょごにょ
Hime...
So...
RUFFLE
くしゃ
Huh.

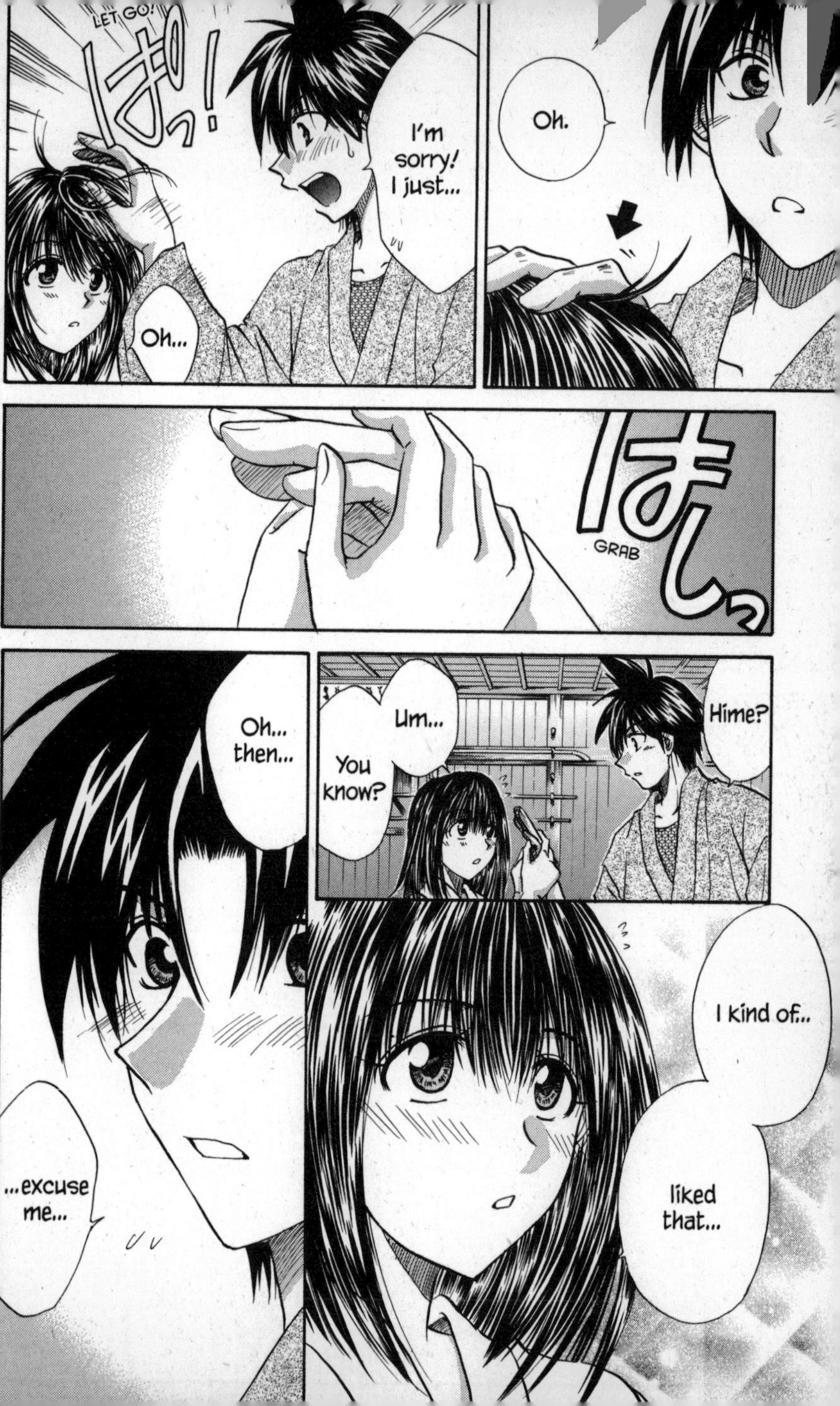
Oh.
ぱっ!
LET GO!
I'm sorry! I just...
Oh...
はしっ
GRAB
Hime?
Um...
You know?
I kind of...
liked that...
Oh... then...
...excuse me...

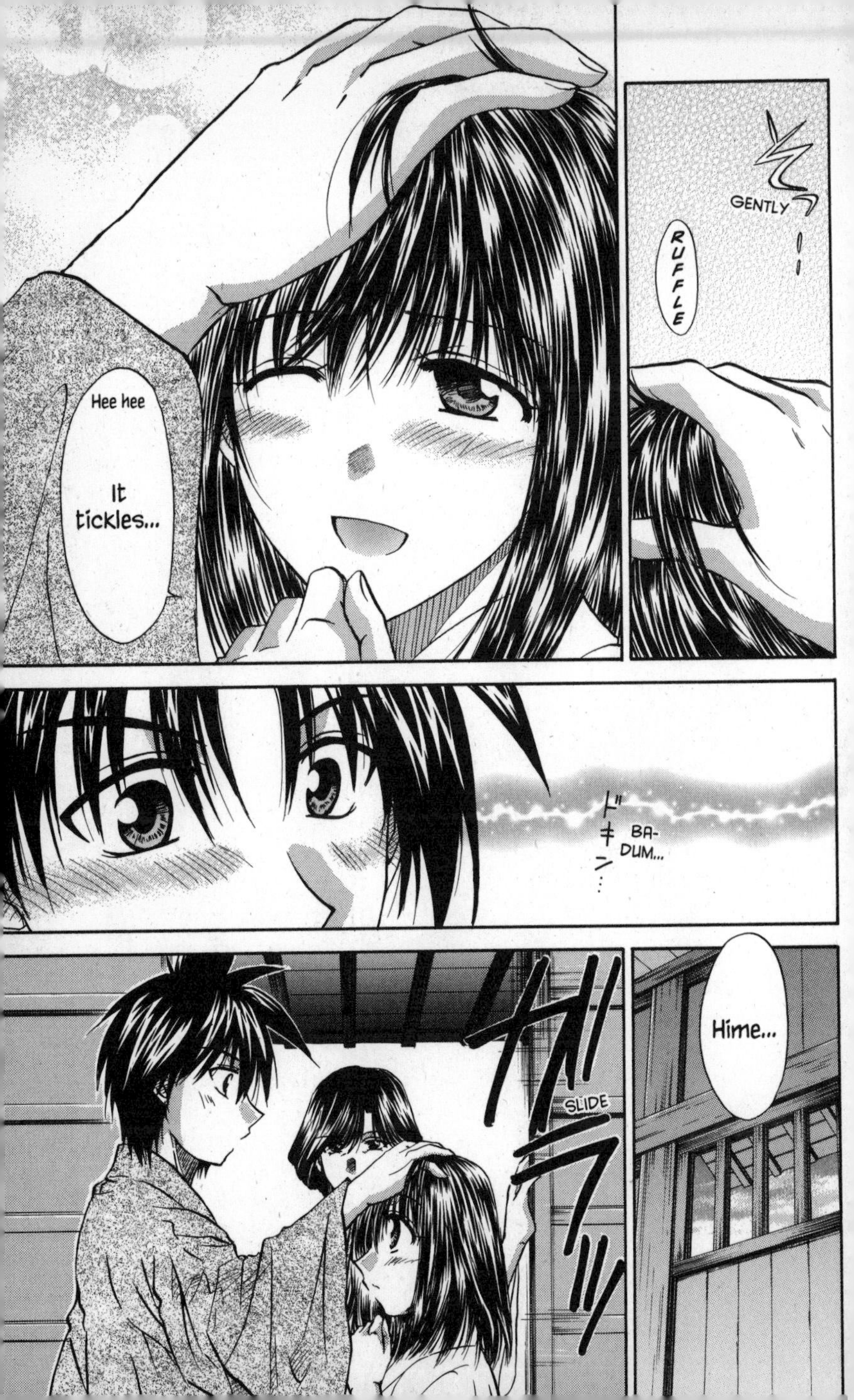
GENTLY
RUFFLE
Hee hee
It tickles...
BA-DUM...
Hime...
SLIDE

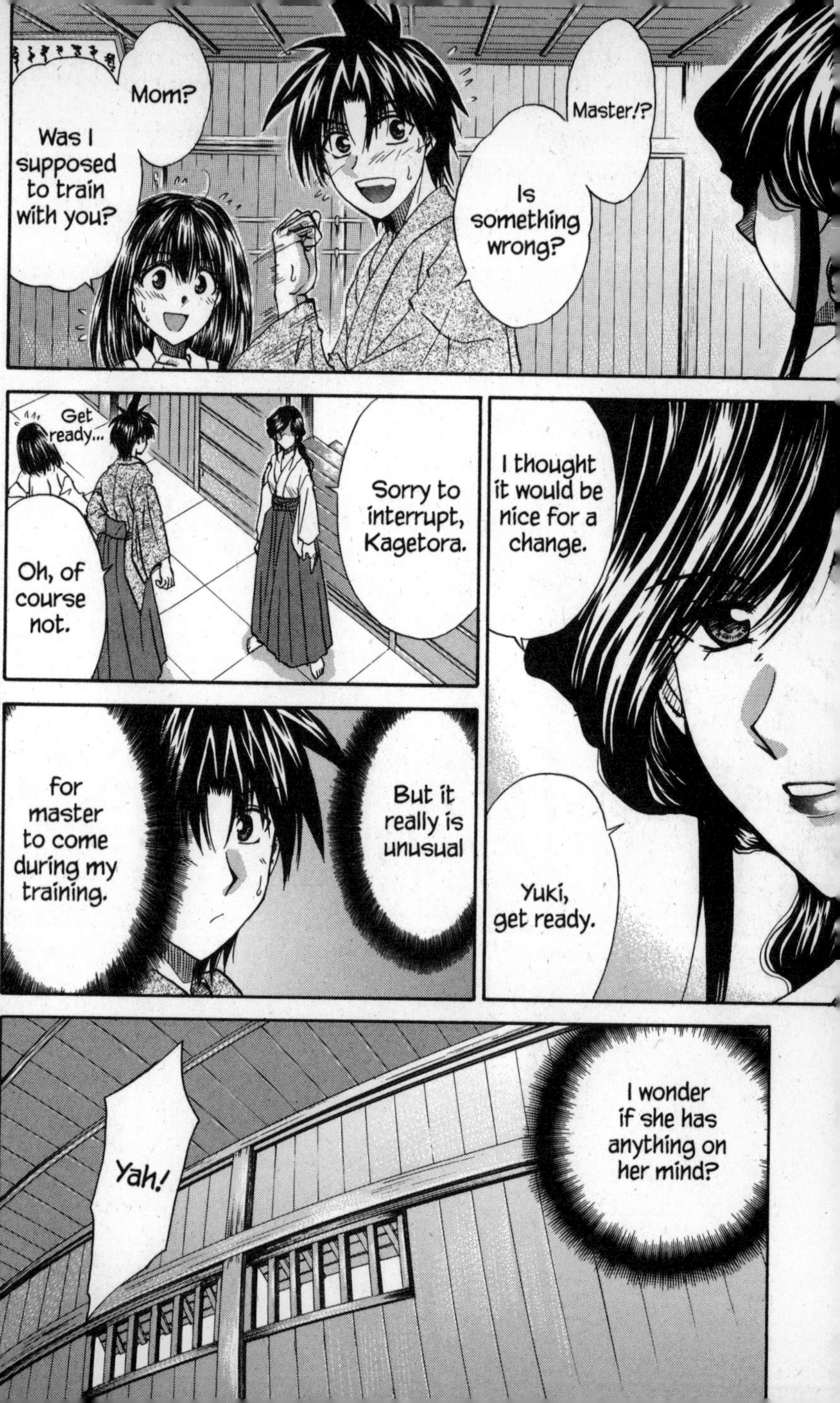
Master!?
Is something wrong?
Mom?
Was I supposed to train with you?
I thought it would be nice for a change.
Yuki, get ready.
Sorry to interrupt, Kagetora.
Get ready...
Oh, of course not.
But it really is unusual
for master to come during my training.
I wonder if she has anything on her mind?
Yah!

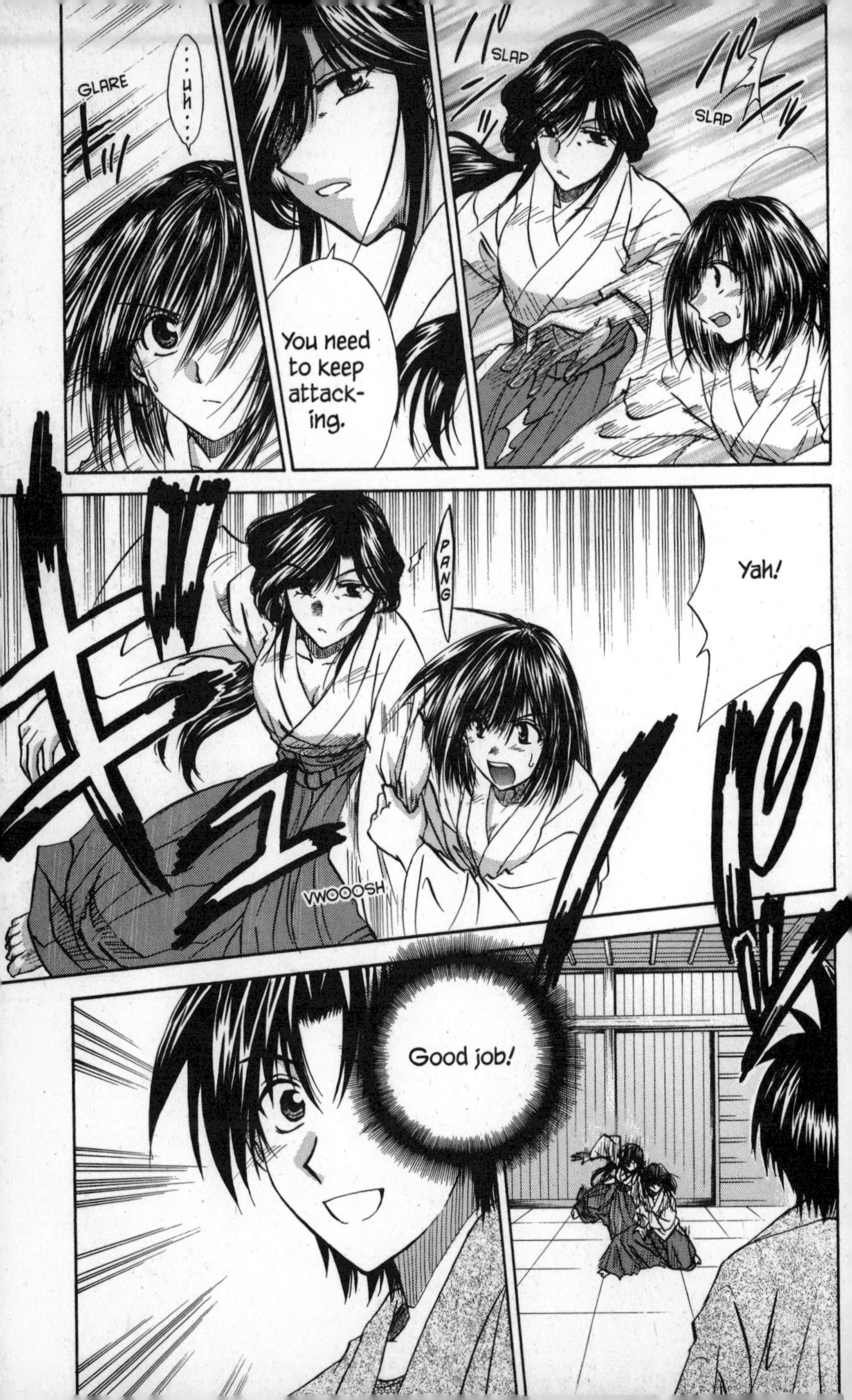
SLAP
SLAP
You need to keep attack-ing.
GLARE
...uh...
Yah!
PANG
VWOOOSH
Good job!

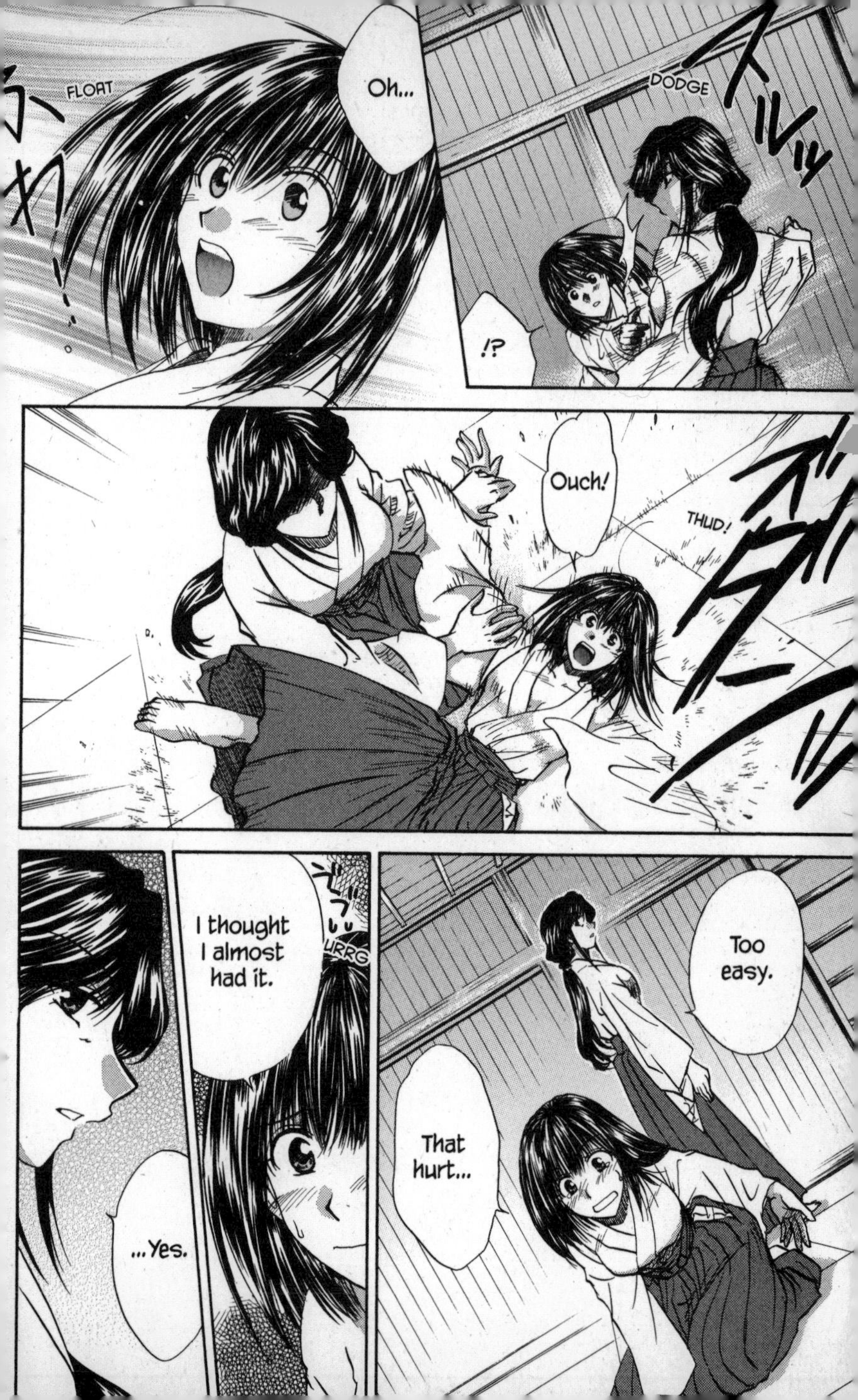
DODGE
!?
Oh...
FLOAT
Ouch!
THUD!
Too easy.
That hurt...
I thought I almost had it.
URRG
...Yes.

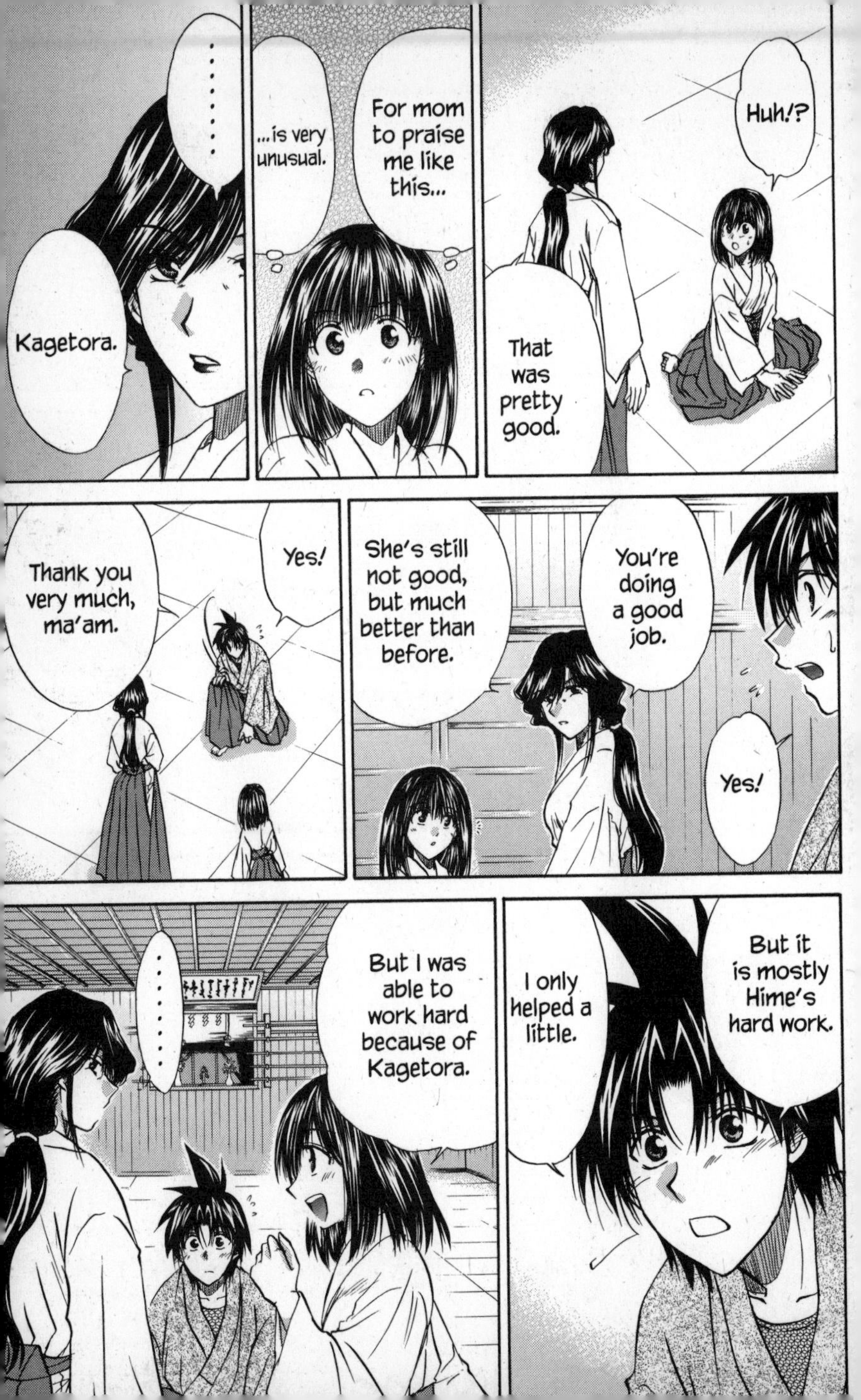

Huh!?
That was pretty good.
For mom to praise me like this...
...is very unusual.
......
Kagetora.
You're doing a good job.
She's still not good, but much better than before.
Yes!
Yes!
Thank you very much, ma'am.
But it is mostly Hime's hard work.
I only helped a little.
But I was able to work hard because of Kagetora.
......

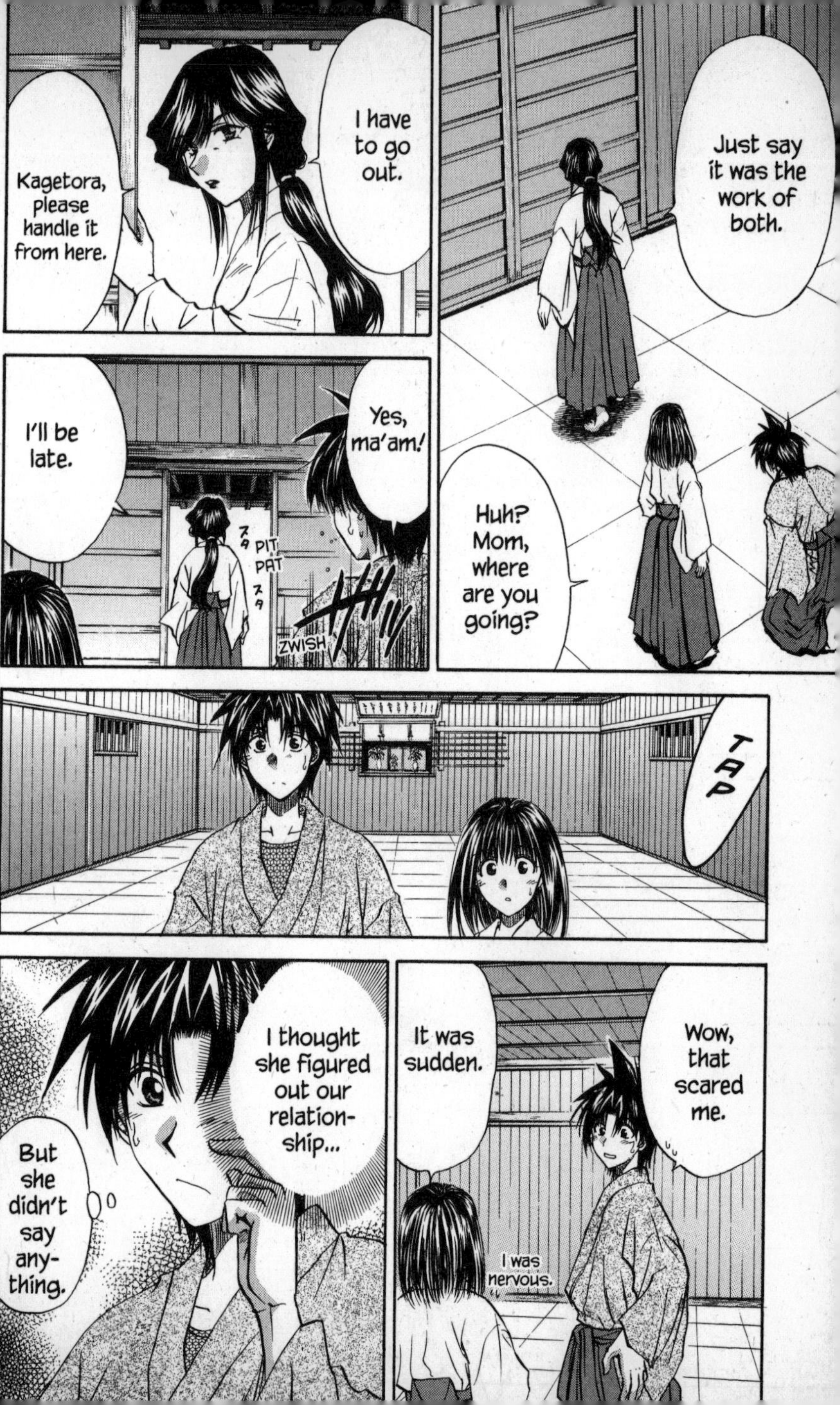
Just say it was the work of both.
Huh? Mom, where are you going?
I have to go out.
Kagetora, please handle it from here.
Yes, ma'am!
I'll be late.
PIT PAT
ZWISH
TAP
Wow, that scared me.
It was sudden.
I was nervous.
I thought she figured out our relationship...
But she didn't say anything.

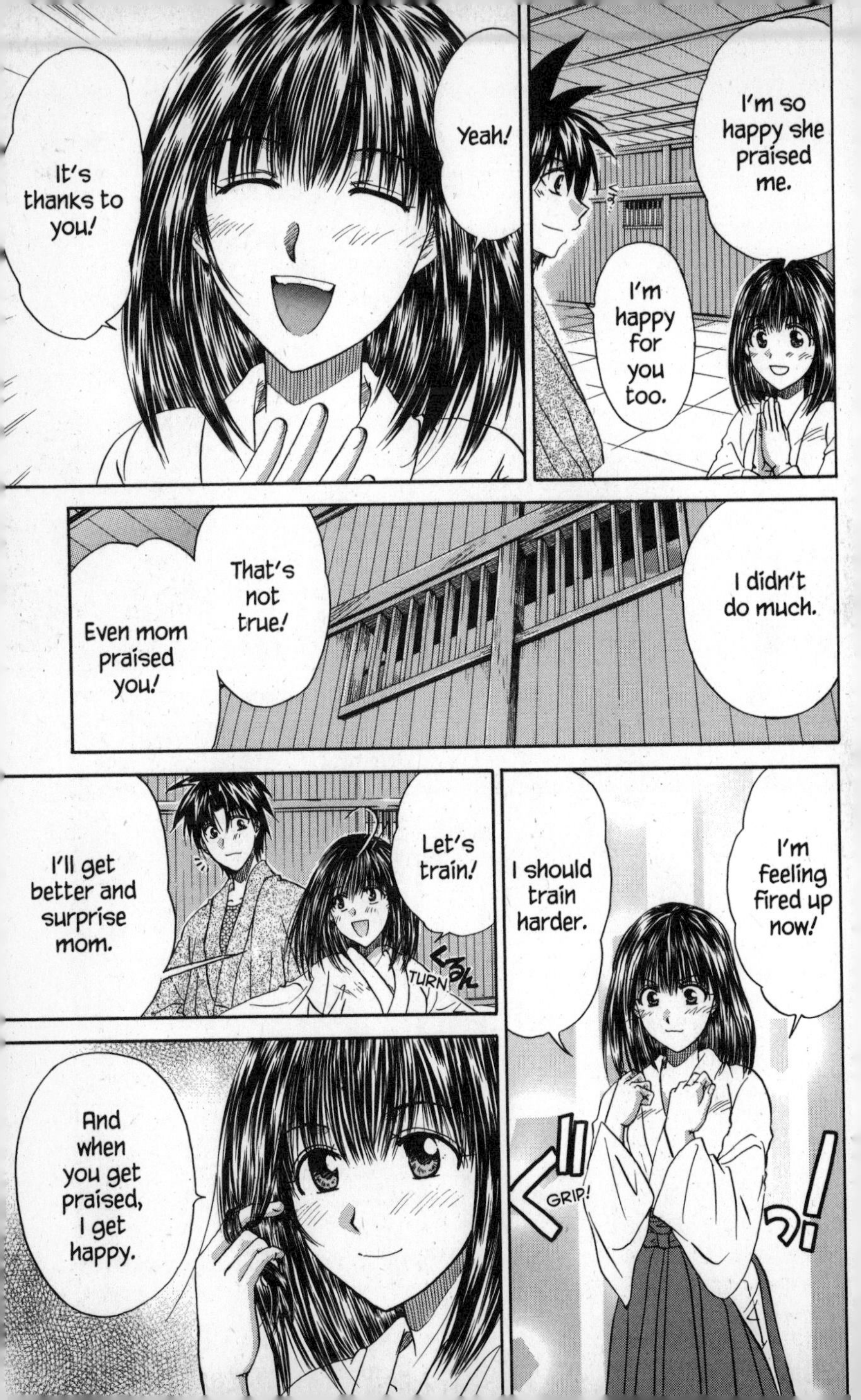
I'm so happy she praised me.
I'm happy for you too.
Yeah!
It's thanks to you!
I didn't do much.
That's not true!
Even mom praised you!
I'm feeling fired up now!
I should train harder.
GRIP!
Let's train!
TURN
I'll get better and surprise mom.
And when you get praised, I get happy.

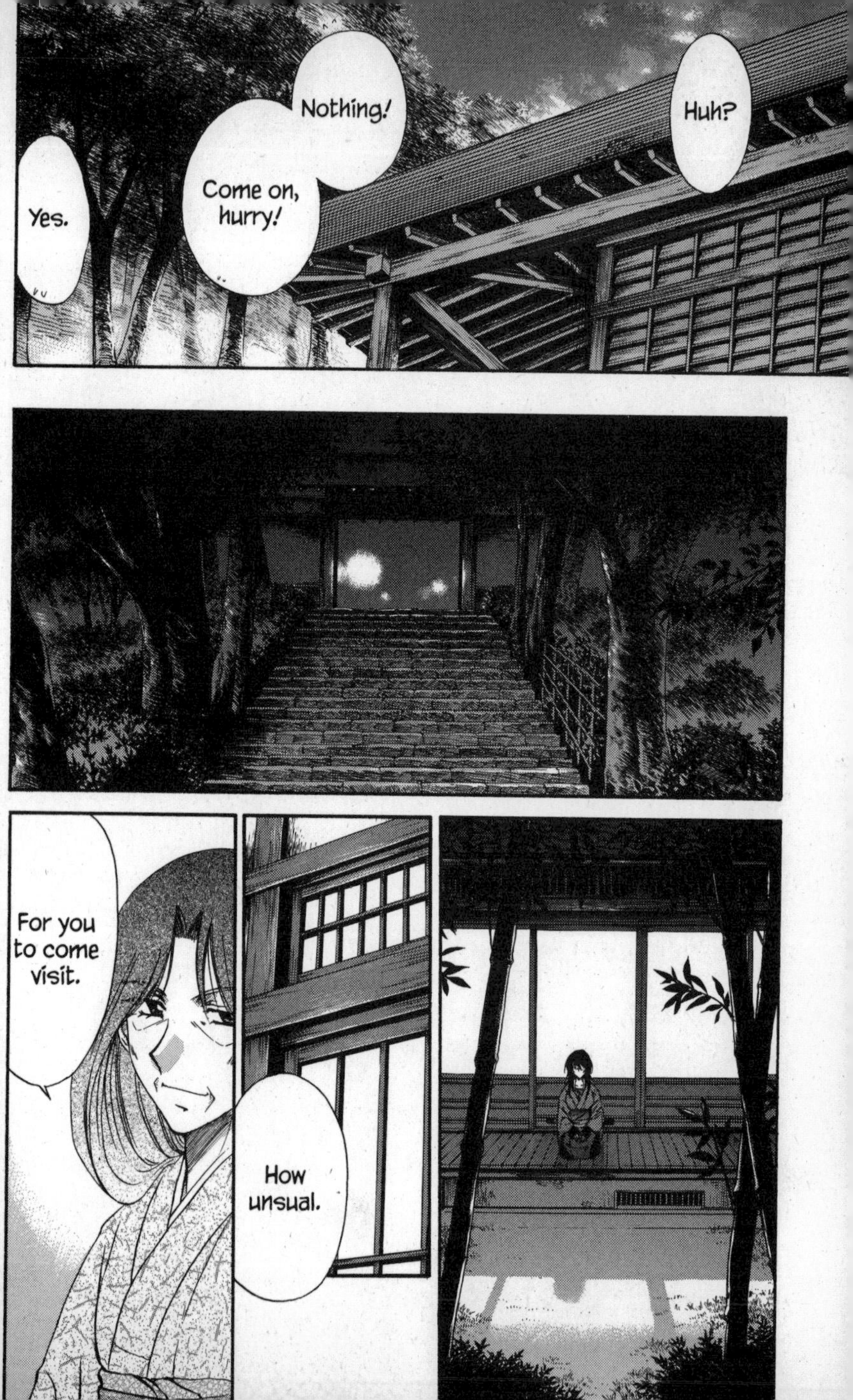
Huh?
Nothing!
Come on, hurry!
Yes.
How unsual.
For you to come visit.

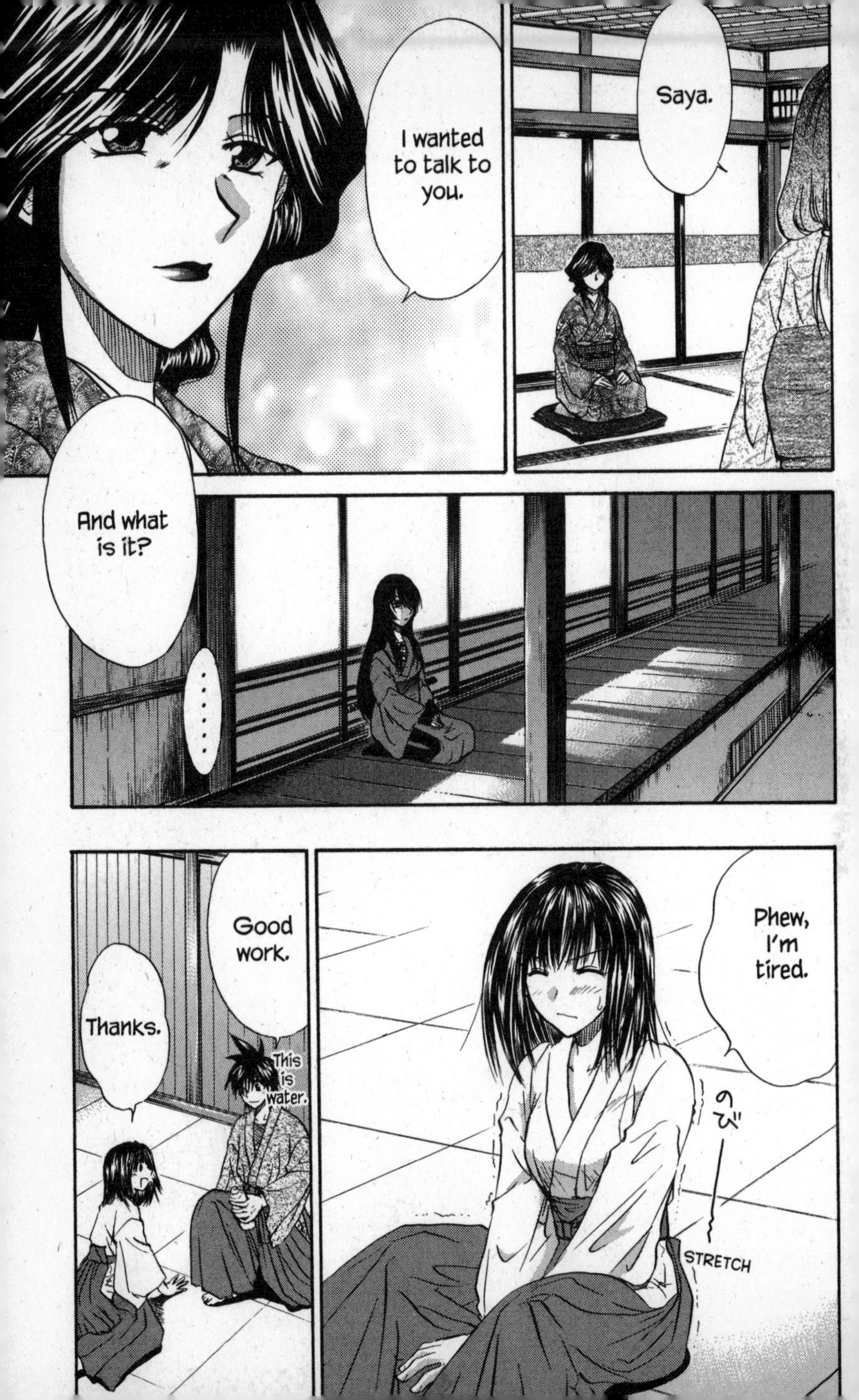

Saya.
I wanted to talk to you.
And what is it?
......
Phew, I'm tired.
のびー
STRETCH
Good work.
Thanks.
This is water.

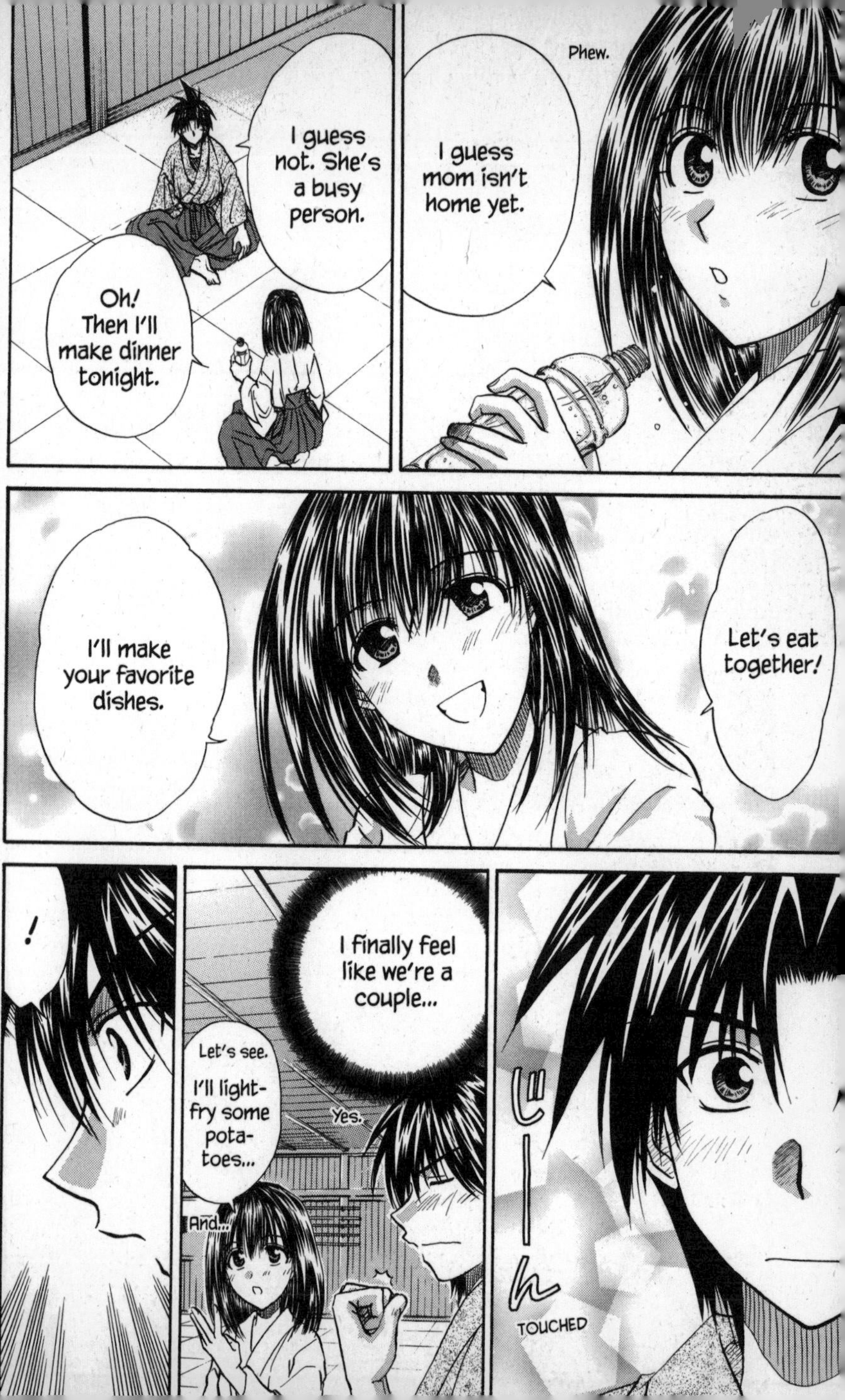
Phew.
I guess mom isn't home yet.
I guess not. She's a busy person.
Oh! Then I'll make dinner tonight.
Let's eat together!
I'll make your favorite dishes.
じーん
TOUCHED
I finally feel like we're a couple...
Yes.
Let's see. I'll light-fry some pota-toes...
And...
!

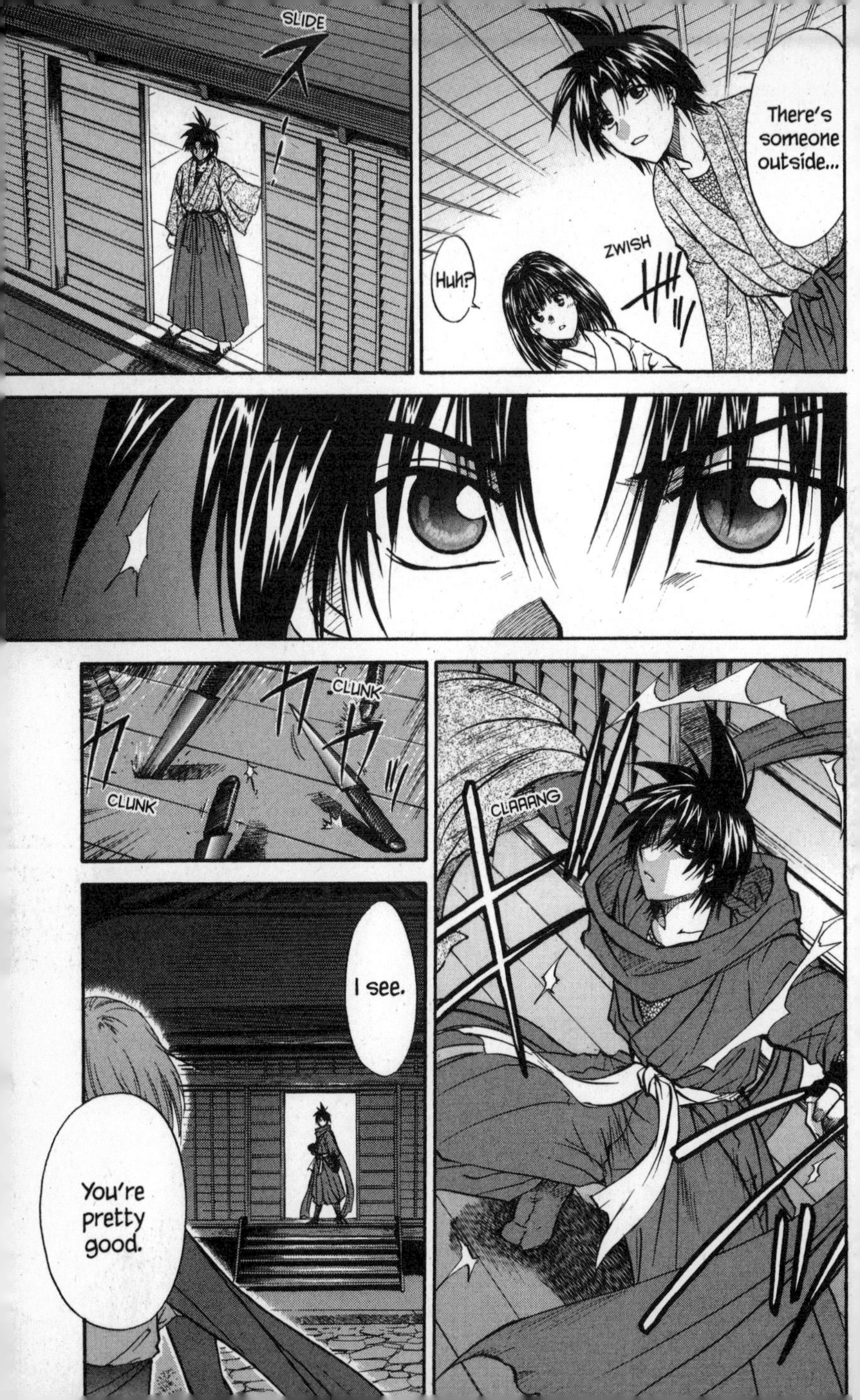
There's someone outside...
ZWISH
Huh?
SLIDE
CLAAANG
CLUNK
CLUNK
I see.
You're pretty good.

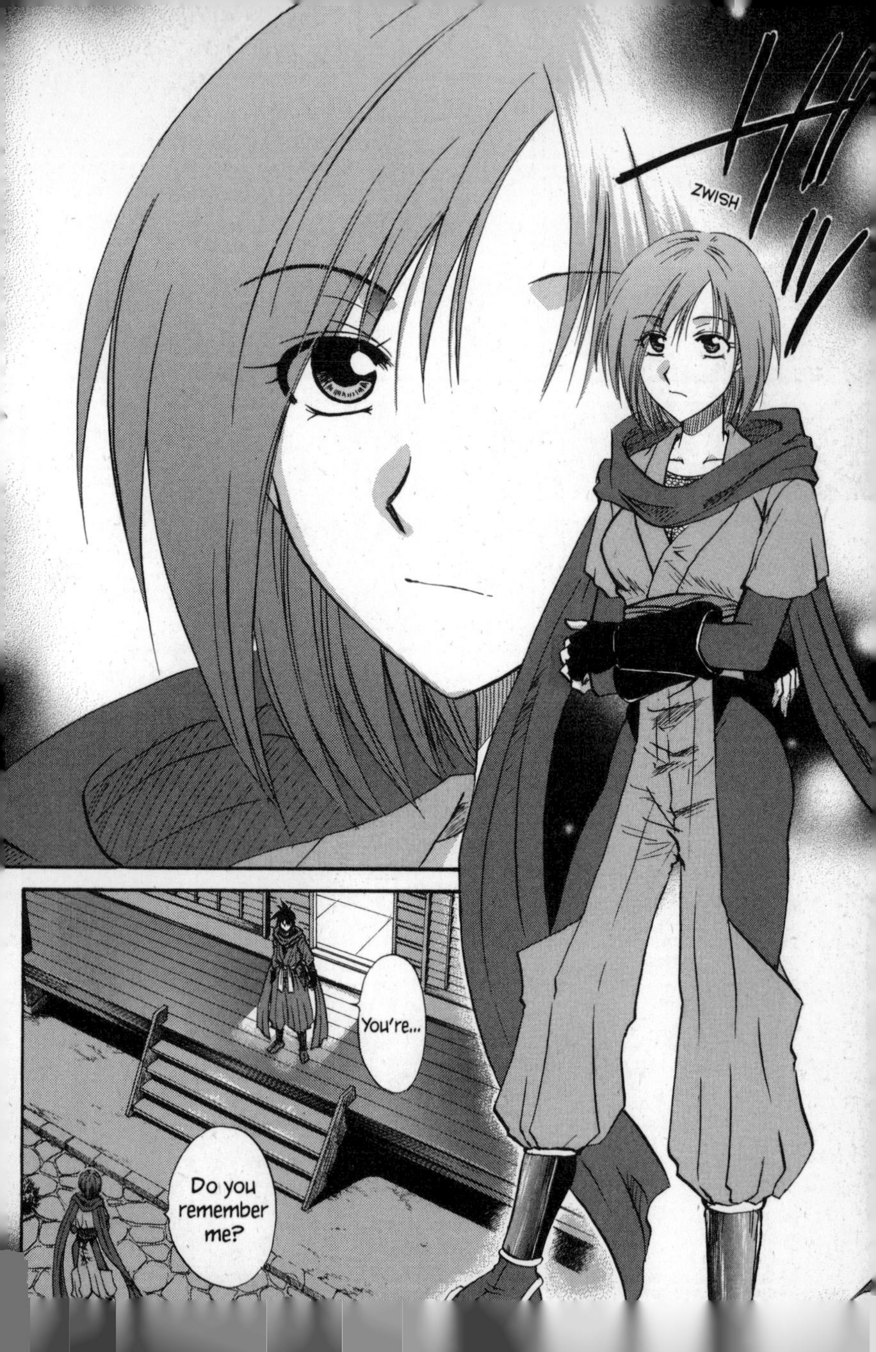
ZWISH
You're...
Do you remember me?

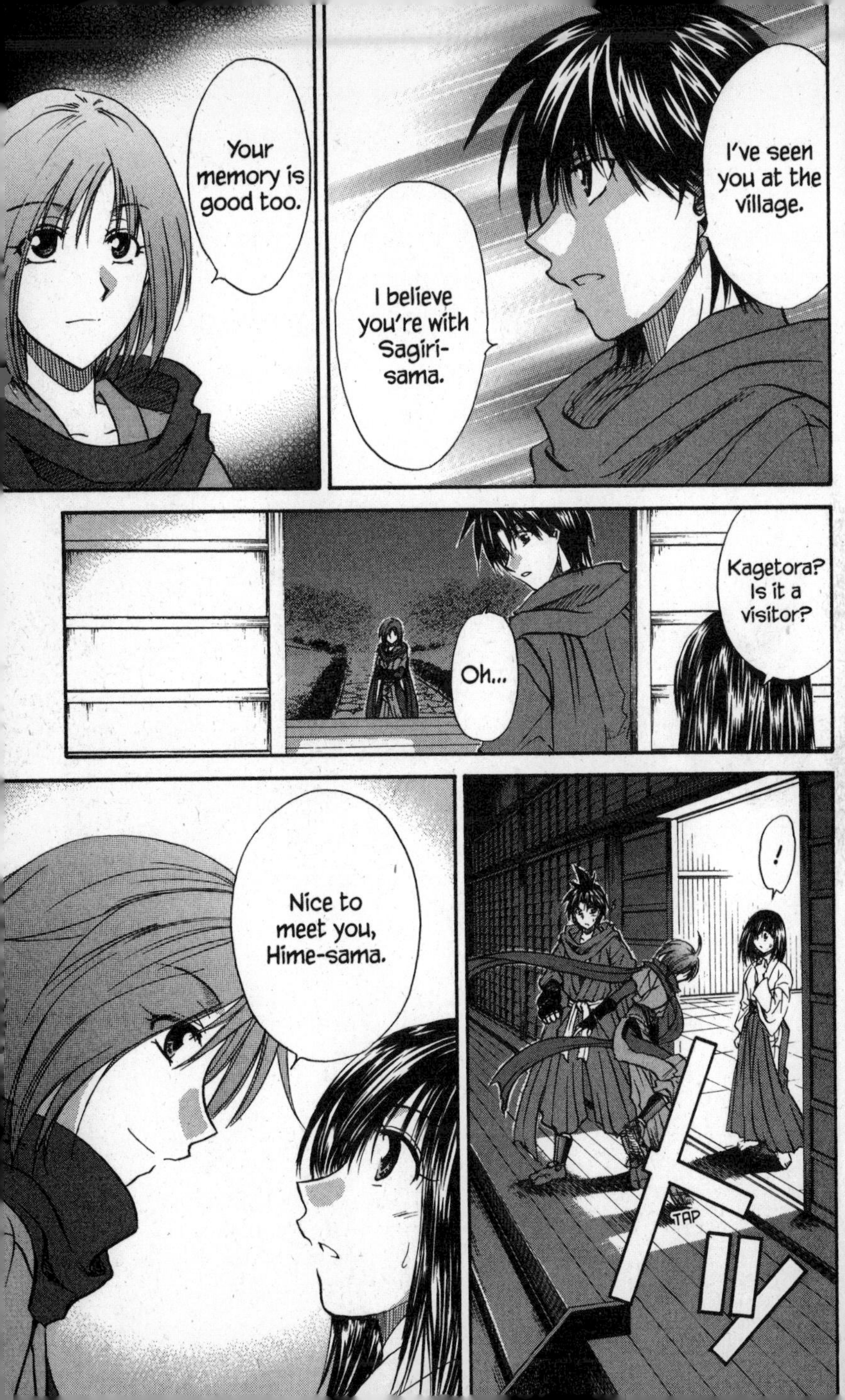
I've seen you at the village.
I believe you're with Sagiri-sama.
Your memory is good too.
Kagetora? Is it a visitor?
Oh...
!
TAP
Nice to meet you, Hime-sama.

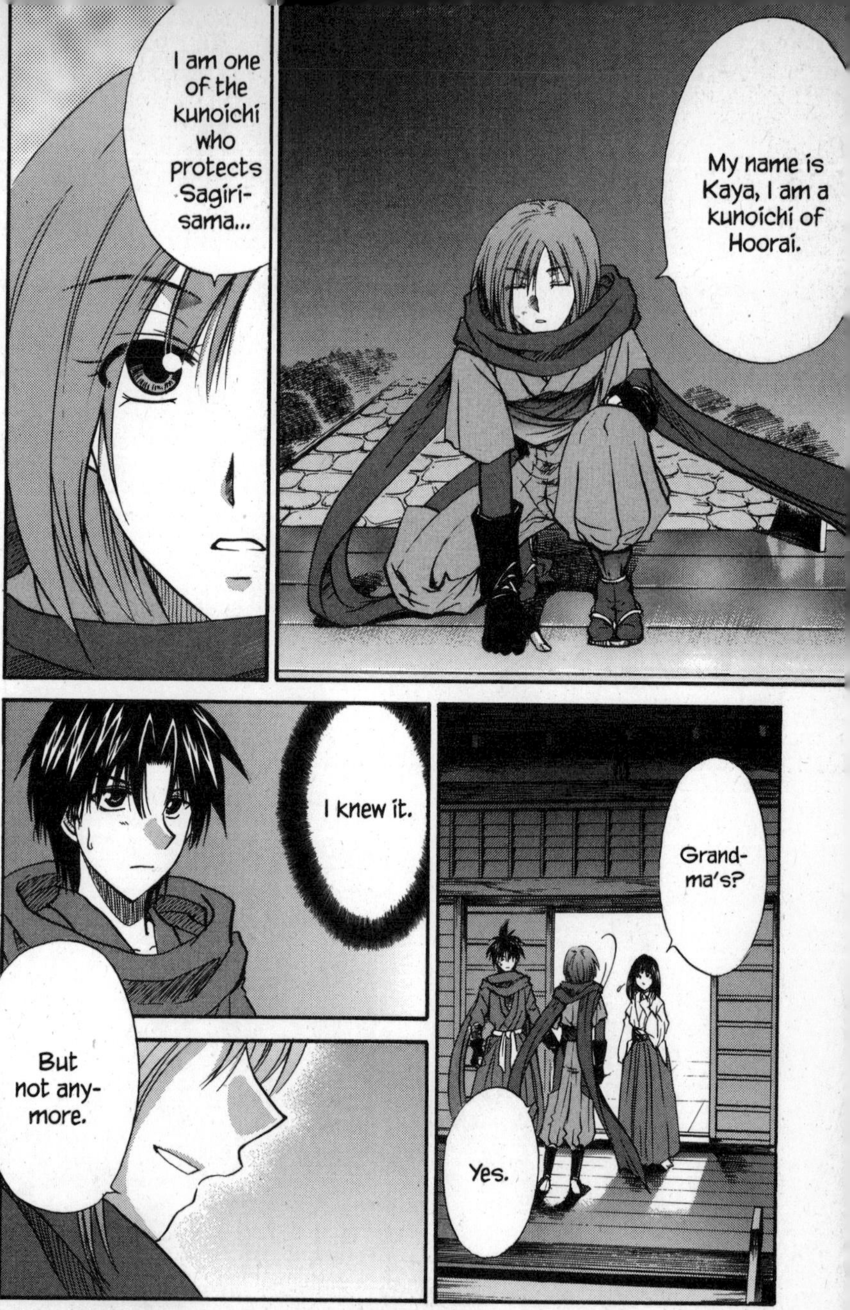
My name is Kaya, I am a kunoichi of Hoorai.
I am one of the kunoichi who protects Sagiri-sama...
Grand-ma's?
Yes.
I knew it.
But not anymore.

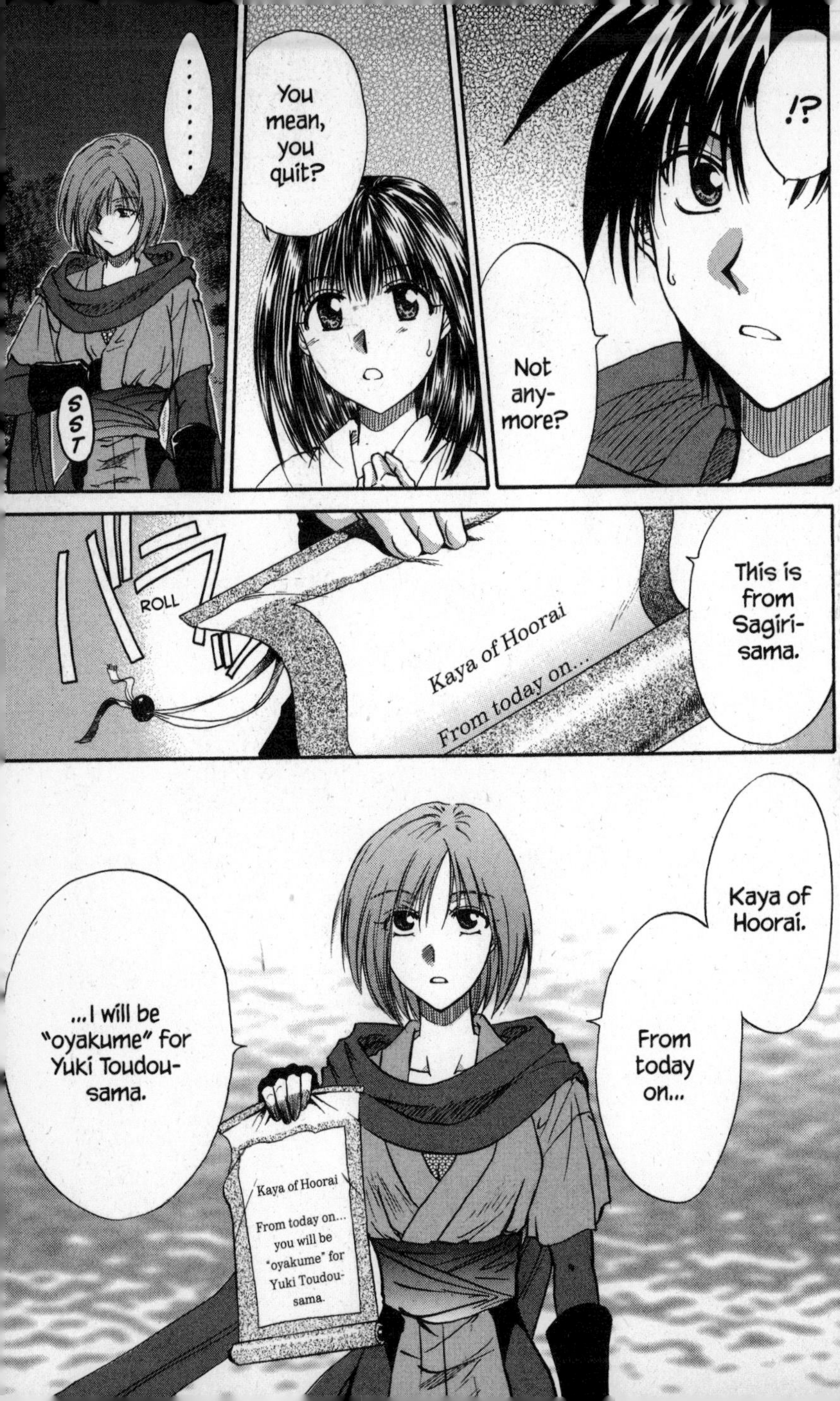
!?
Not any-more?
You mean, you quit?
......
SST
This is from Sagiri-sama.
Kaya of Hoorai
From today on...
ROLL
Kaya of Hoorai.
From today on...
...I will be "oyakume" for Yuki Toudou-sama.
Kaya of Hoorai
From today on... you will be "oyakume" for Yuki Toudou-sama.

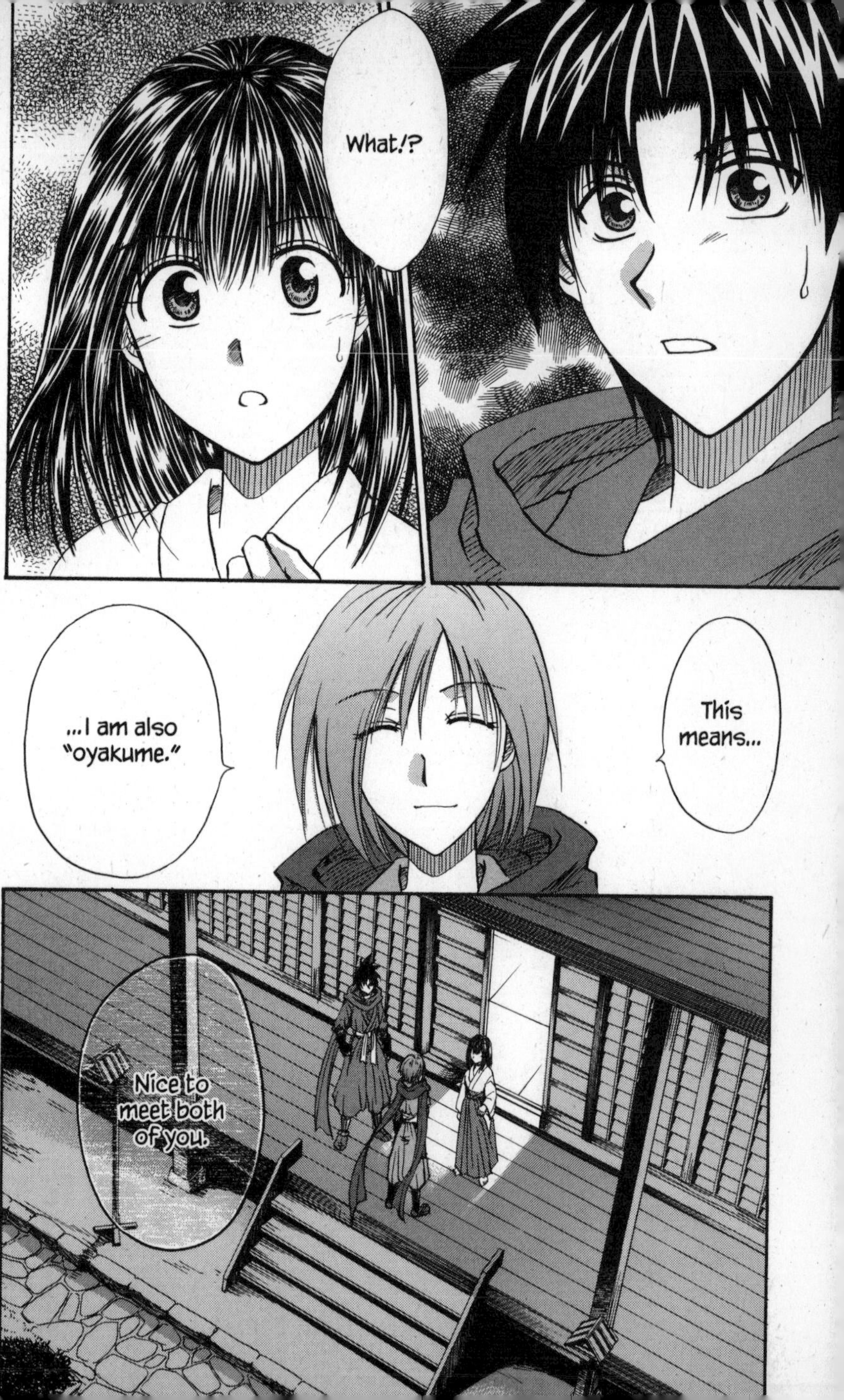
What!?
This means...
...I am also "oyakume."
Nice to meet both of you.

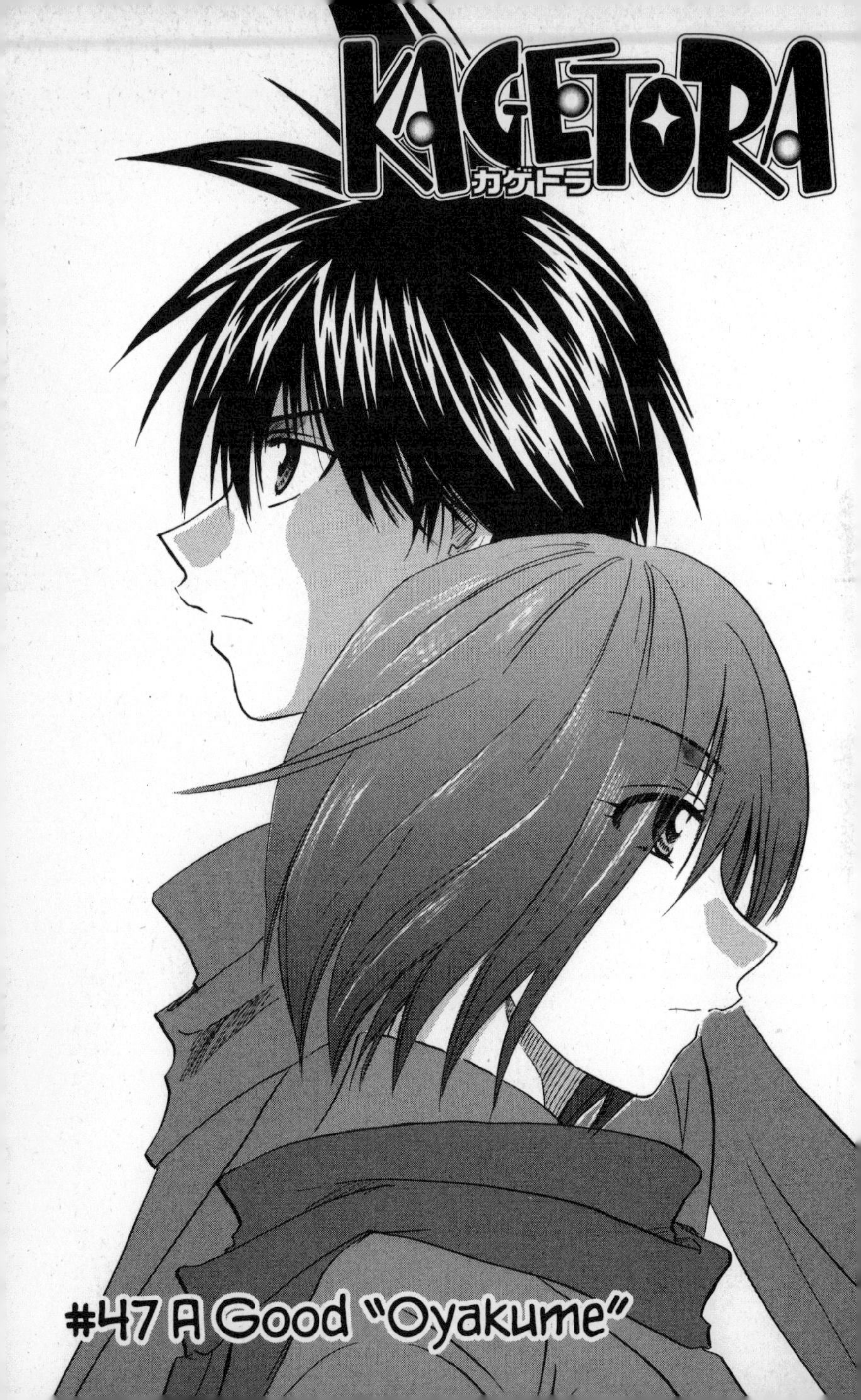
KAGETORA
カゲトラ
#47 A Good "Oyakume"

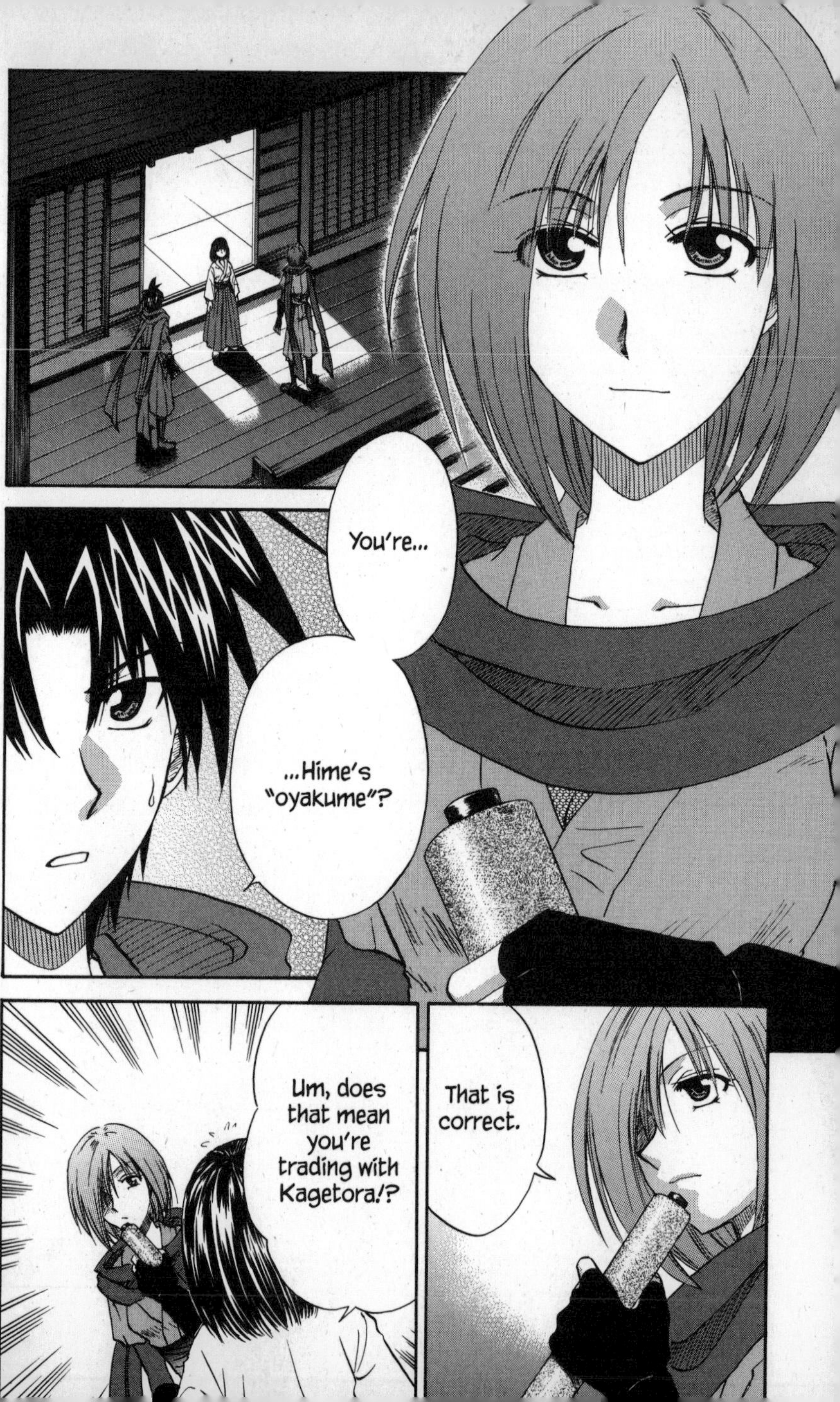
You're...
...Hime's "oyakume"?
That is correct.
Um, does that mean you're trading with Kagetora!?

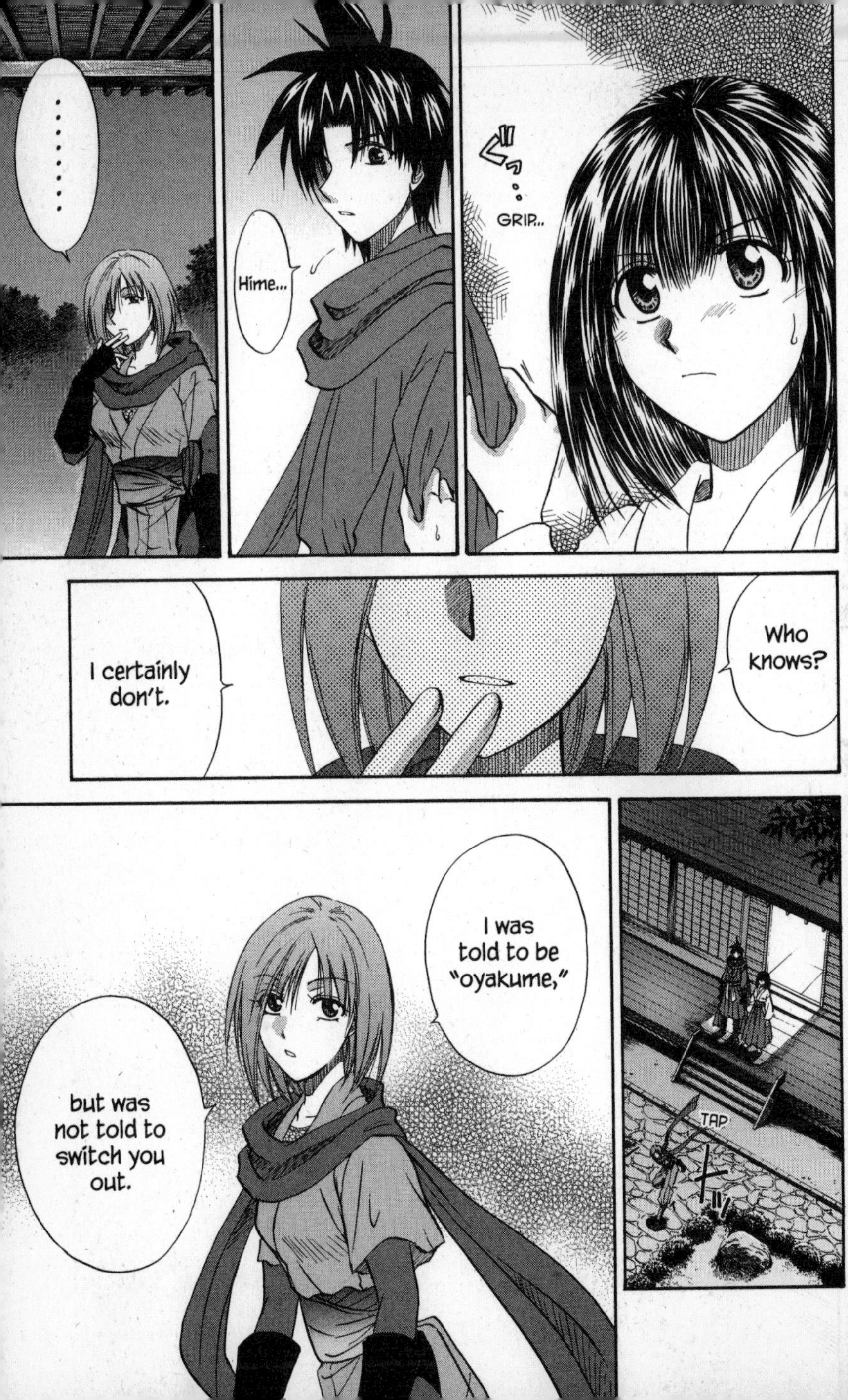
GRIP...
Hime...
......
Who knows?
I certainly don't.
TAP
I was told to be "oyakume,"
but was not told to switch you out.

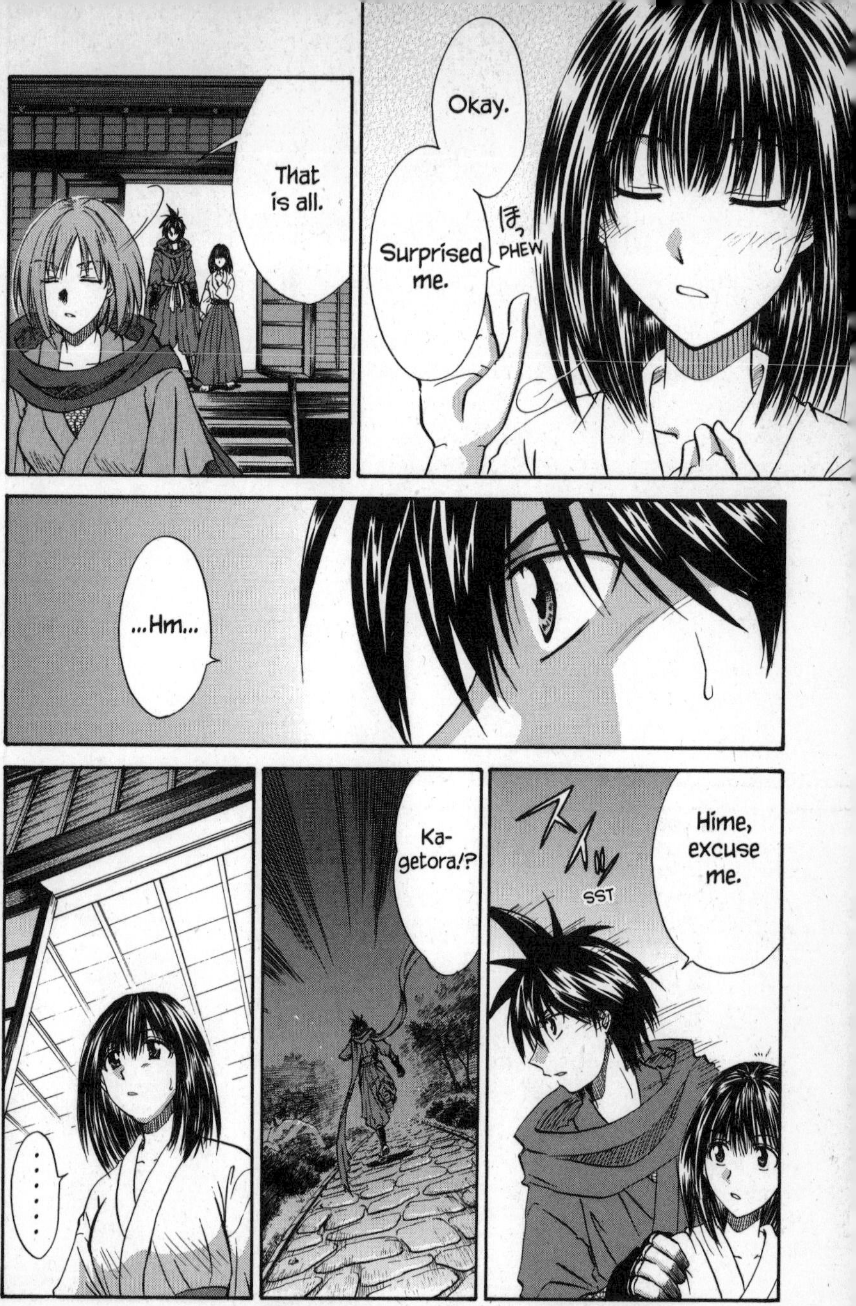
Okay.
ほっ
PHEW
Surprised me.
That is all.
...Hm...
Hime, excuse me.
スッ
SST
Ka-getora!?
......

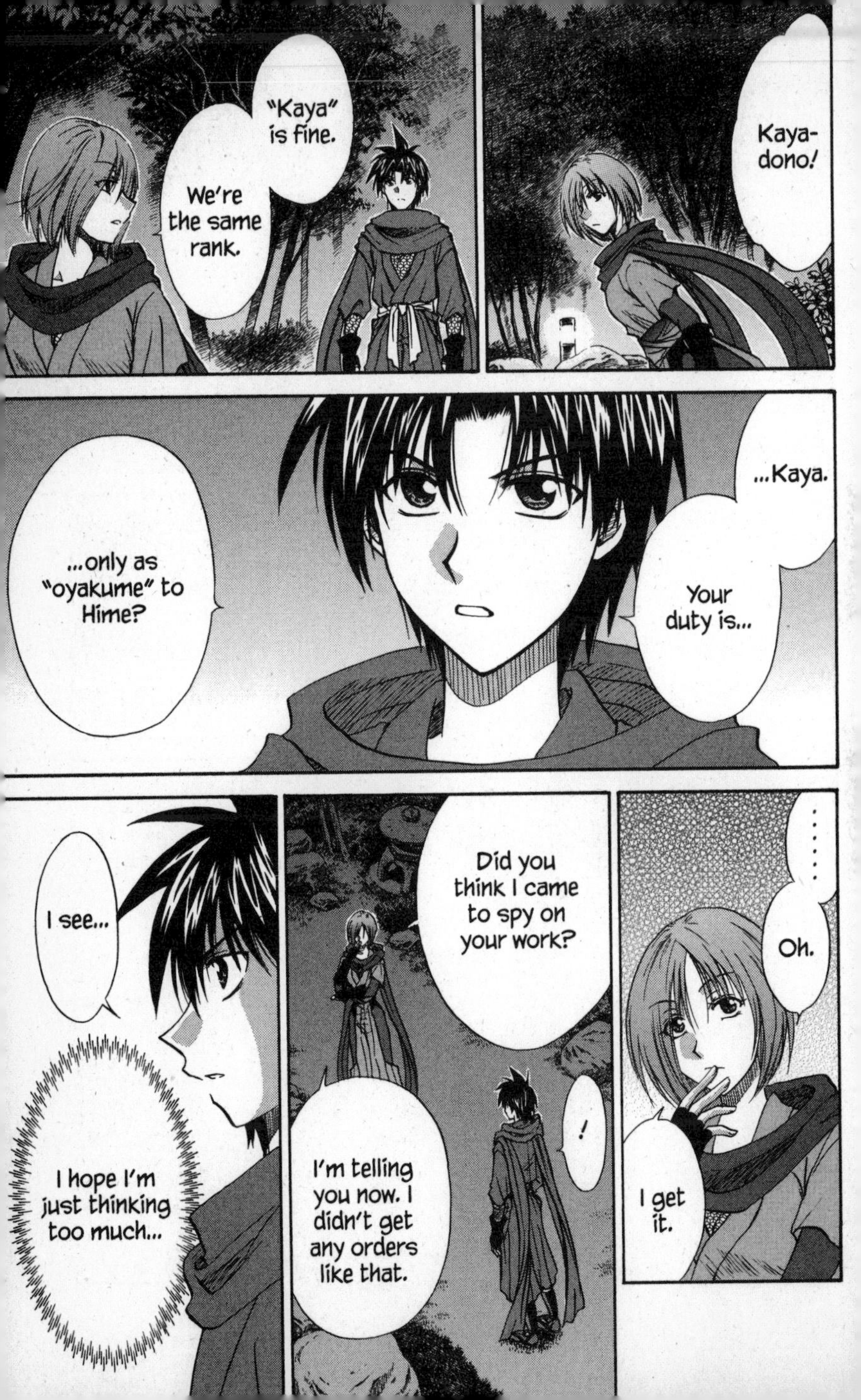
Kaya-dono!
"Kaya" is fine.
We're the same rank.
...Kaya.
Your duty is...
...only as "oyakume" to Hime?
......
Oh.
I get it.
Did you think I came to spy on your work?
!
I'm telling you now. I didn't get any orders like that.
I see...
I hope I'm just thinking too much...

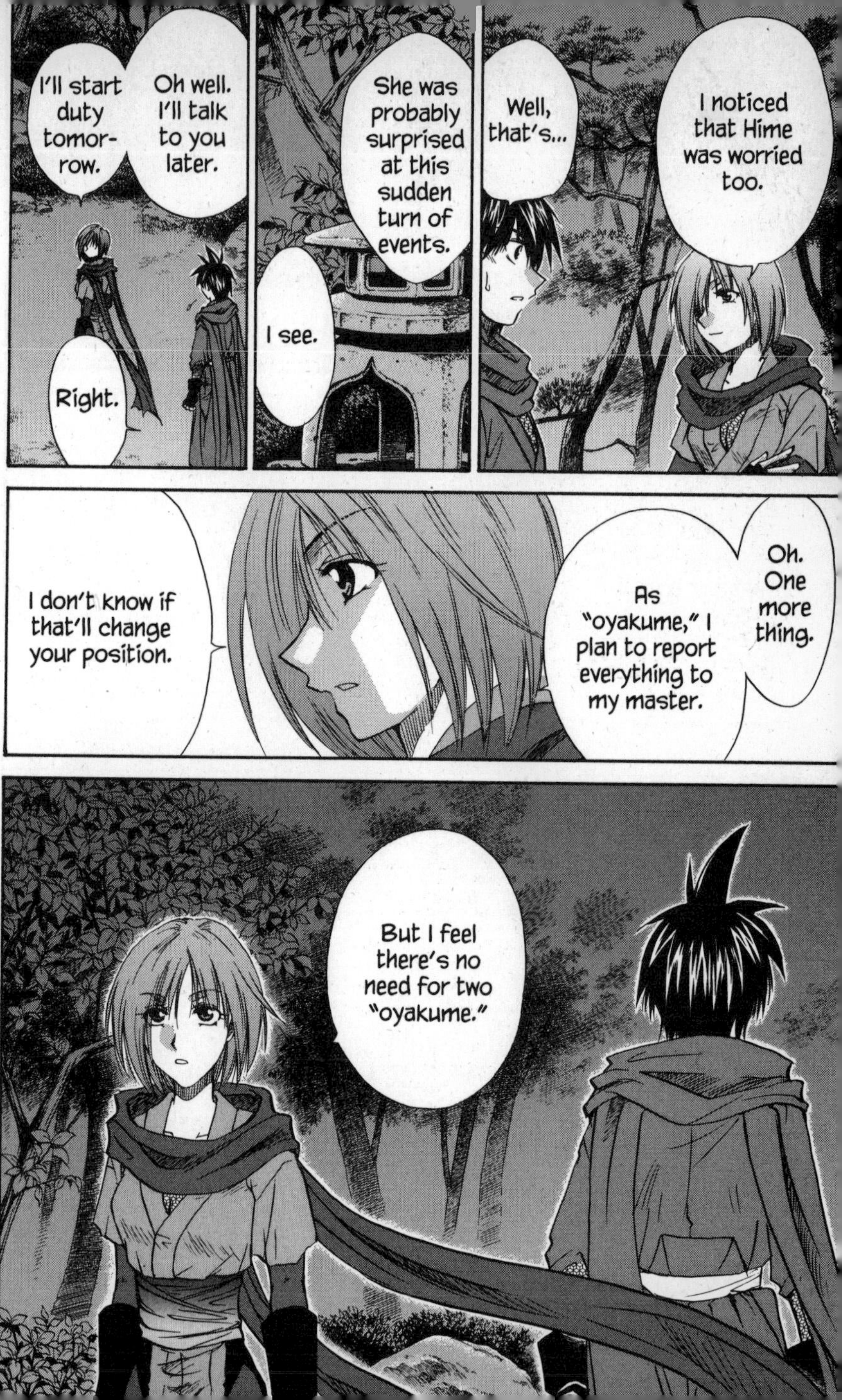
I noticed that Hime was worried too.
Well, that's...
She was probably surprised at this sudden turn of events.
I see.
Oh well. I'll talk to you later.
I'll start duty tomorrow.
Right.
Oh. One more thing.
As "oyakume," I plan to report everything to my master.
I don't know if that'll change your position.
But I feel there's no need for two "oyakume."

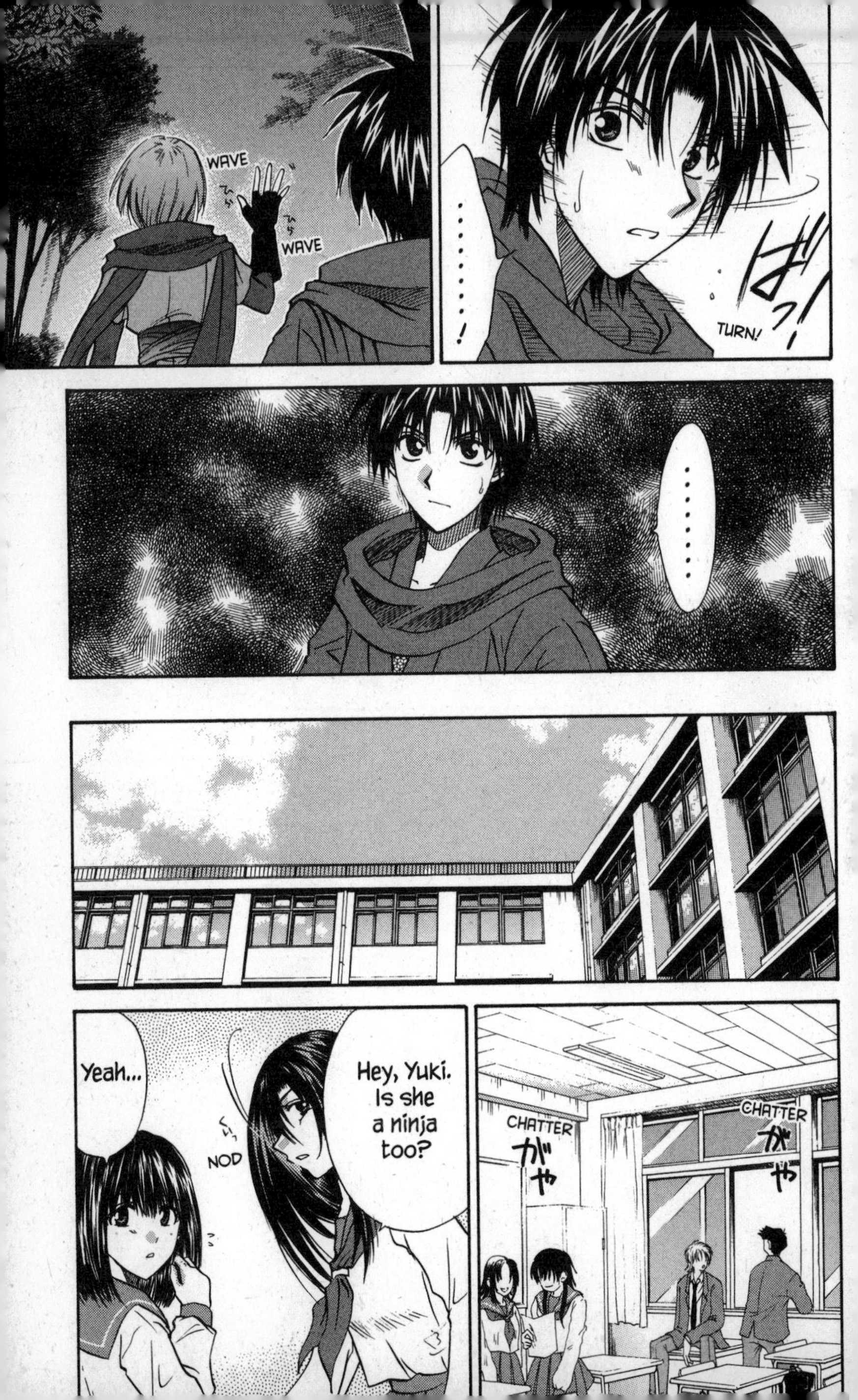

......!
ばっ
TURN!
WAVE
ひら
ひら
WAVE
......
CHATTER
がや
CHATTER
がや
Hey, Yuki. Is she a ninja too?
NOD
Yeah...

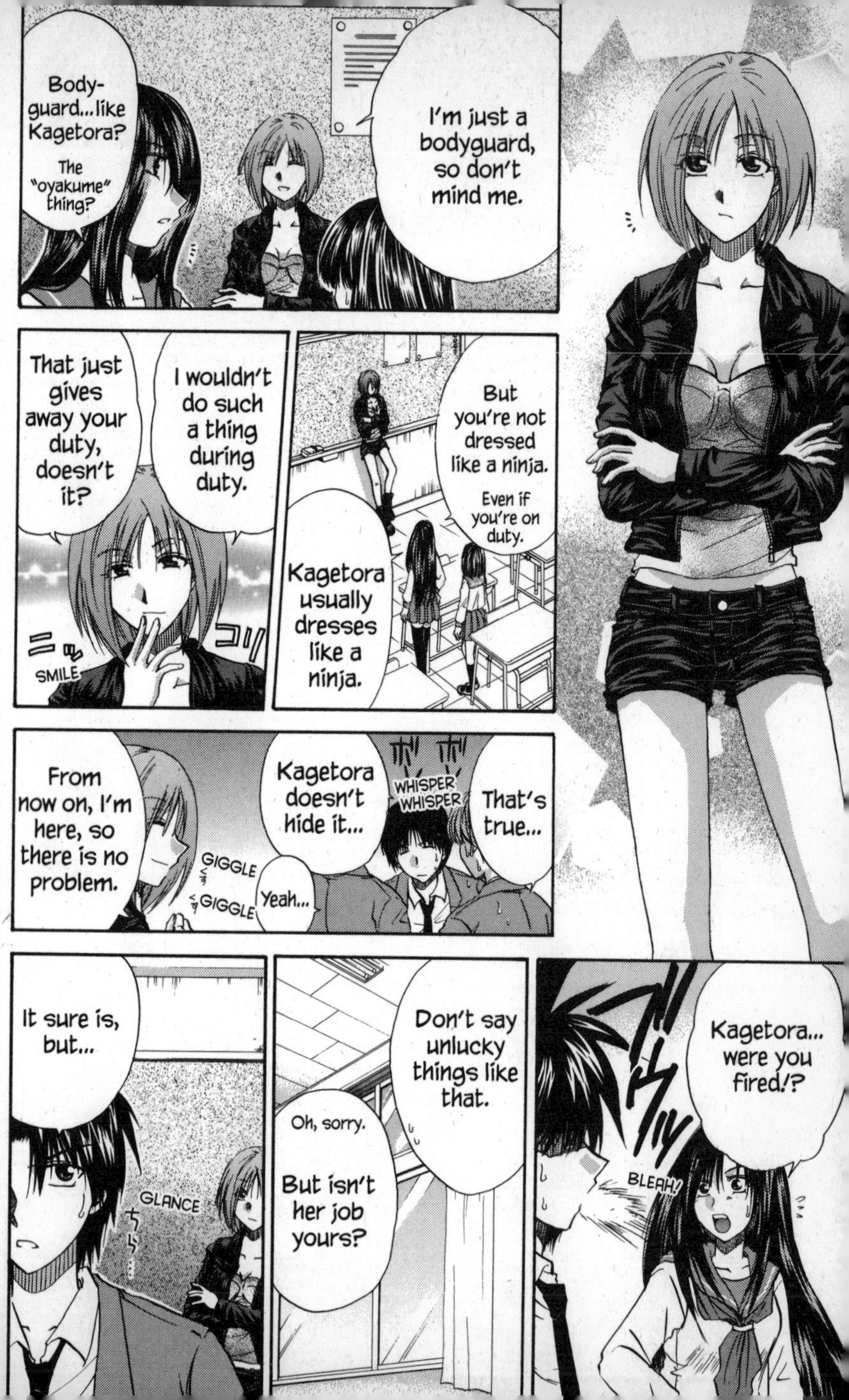
I'm just a bodyguard, so don't mind me.
Body-guard...like Kagetora?
The "oyakume" thing?
But you're not dressed like a ninja.
Even if you're on duty.
Kagetora usually dresses like a ninja.
I wouldn't do such a thing during duty.
That just gives away your duty, doesn't it?
SMILE
That's true...
WHISPER WHISPER
Kagetora doesn't hide it...
Yeah...
GIGGLE GIGGLE
From now on, I'm here, so there is no problem.
Kagetora... were you fired!?
BLEAH!
Don't say unlucky things like that.
Oh, sorry.
But isn't her job yours?
It sure is, but...
GLANCE

All Contra Costa County Libraries will be
closed on April 1st, and May 13th, 27th,
and 28th. Items may be renewed online at
ccclib.org, or by calling 1-800-984-4636,
menu option 1. Book drops will be open.
In addition, the Orinda Library will be closed fc
minor renovations March 2nd -March 14th, an
reopening on Thursday, March 15th.
Please visit ccclib.org or contact library staff
for more details about the Orinda closure.

Item Number: 31901052636026

GHEE LEONARD

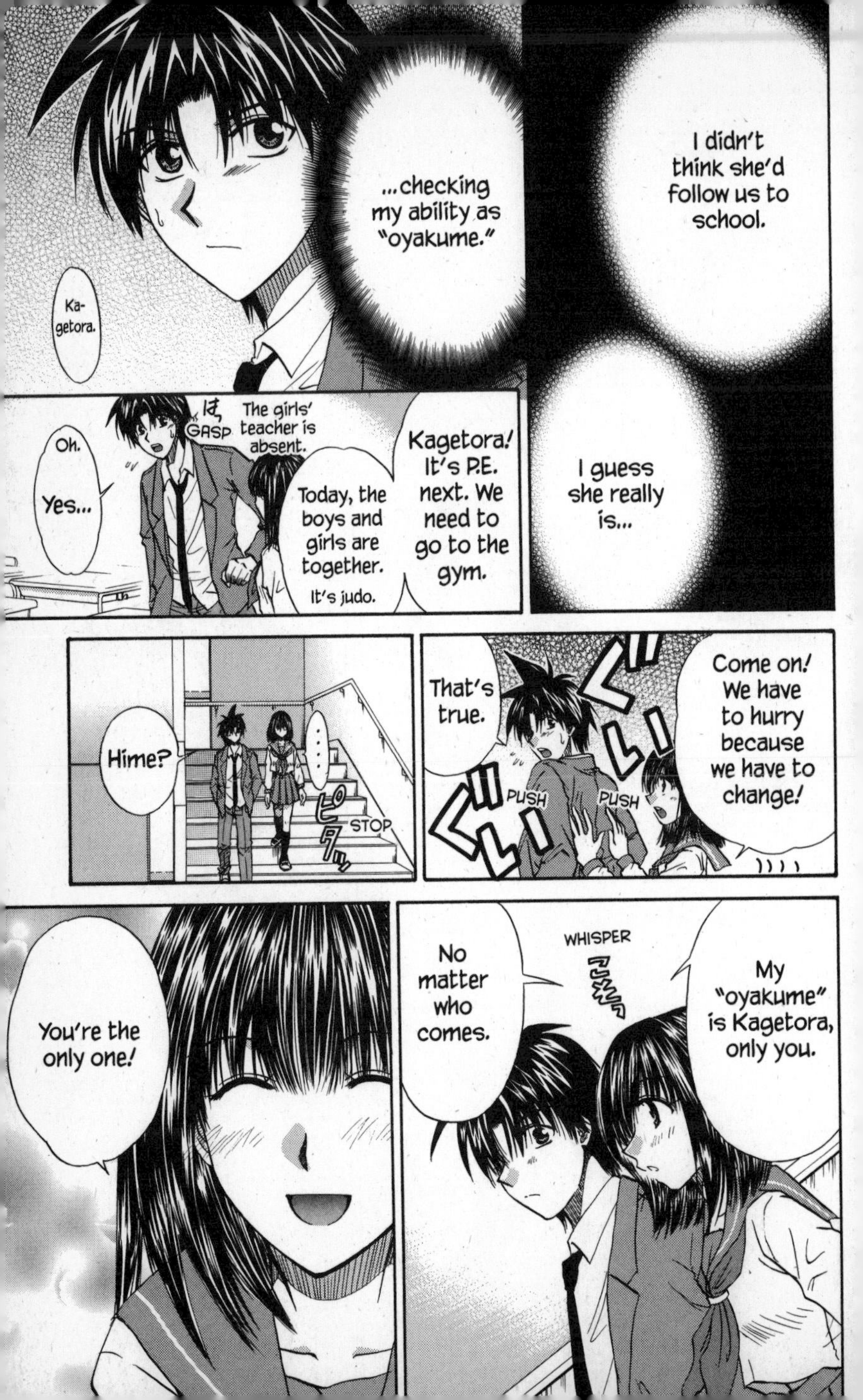

I didn't think she'd follow us to school.
I guess she really is...
...checking my ability as "oyakume."
Ka-getora.
Kagetora! It's P.E. next. We need to go to the gym.
Today, the boys and girls are together.
It's judo.
The girls' teacher is absent.
GASP
Oh.
Yes...
Come on! We have to hurry because we have to change!
PUSH
PUSH
That's true.
....
STOP
Hime?
My "oyakume" is Kagetora, only you.
WHISPER
No matter who comes.
You're the only one!

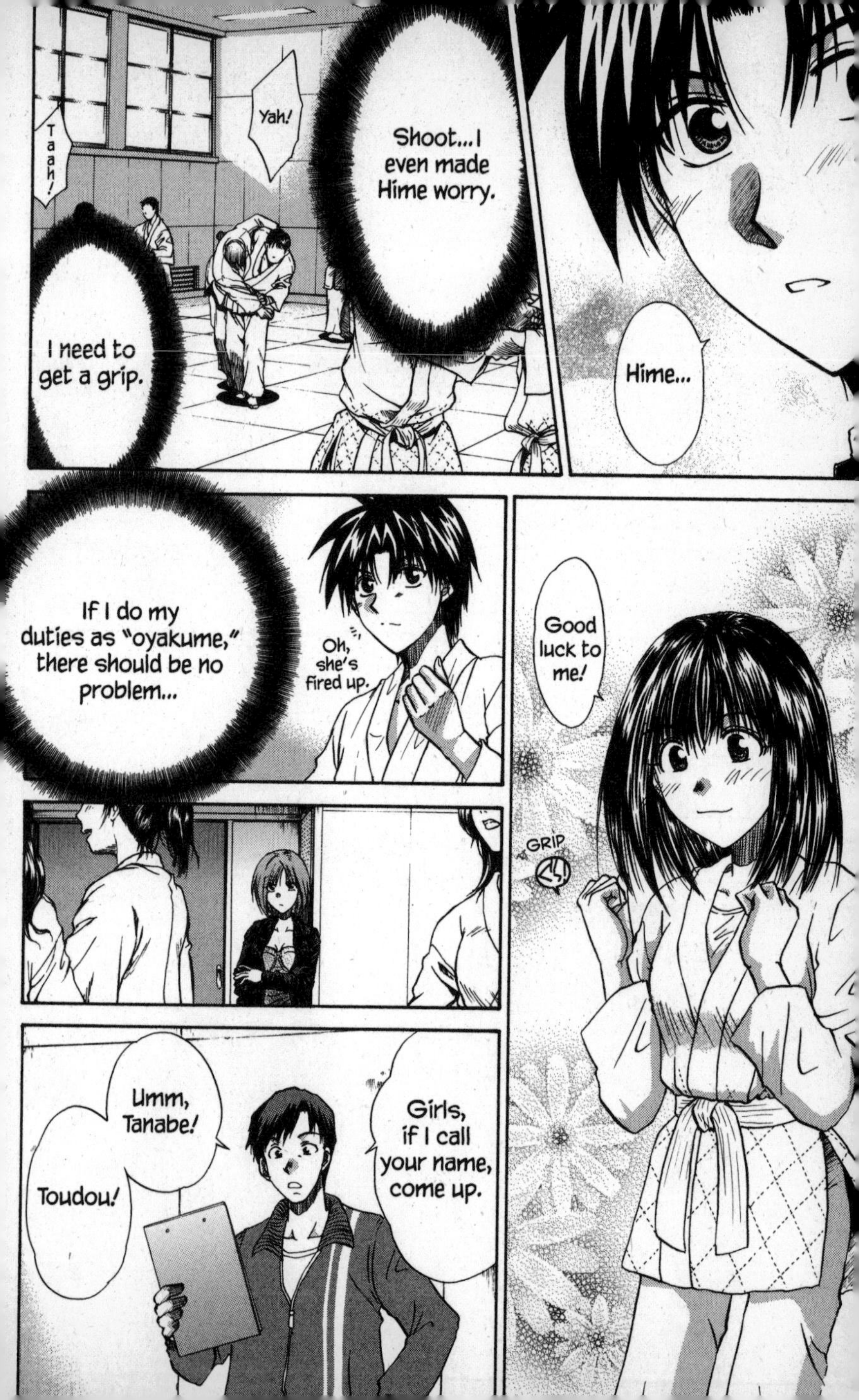
Hime...
Shoot...I even made Hime worry.
Yah!
Taah!
I need to get a grip.
Good luck to me!
GRIP
Oh, she's fired up.
If I do my duties as "oyakume," there should be no problem...
Girls, if I call your name, come up.
Umm, Tanabe!
Toudou!

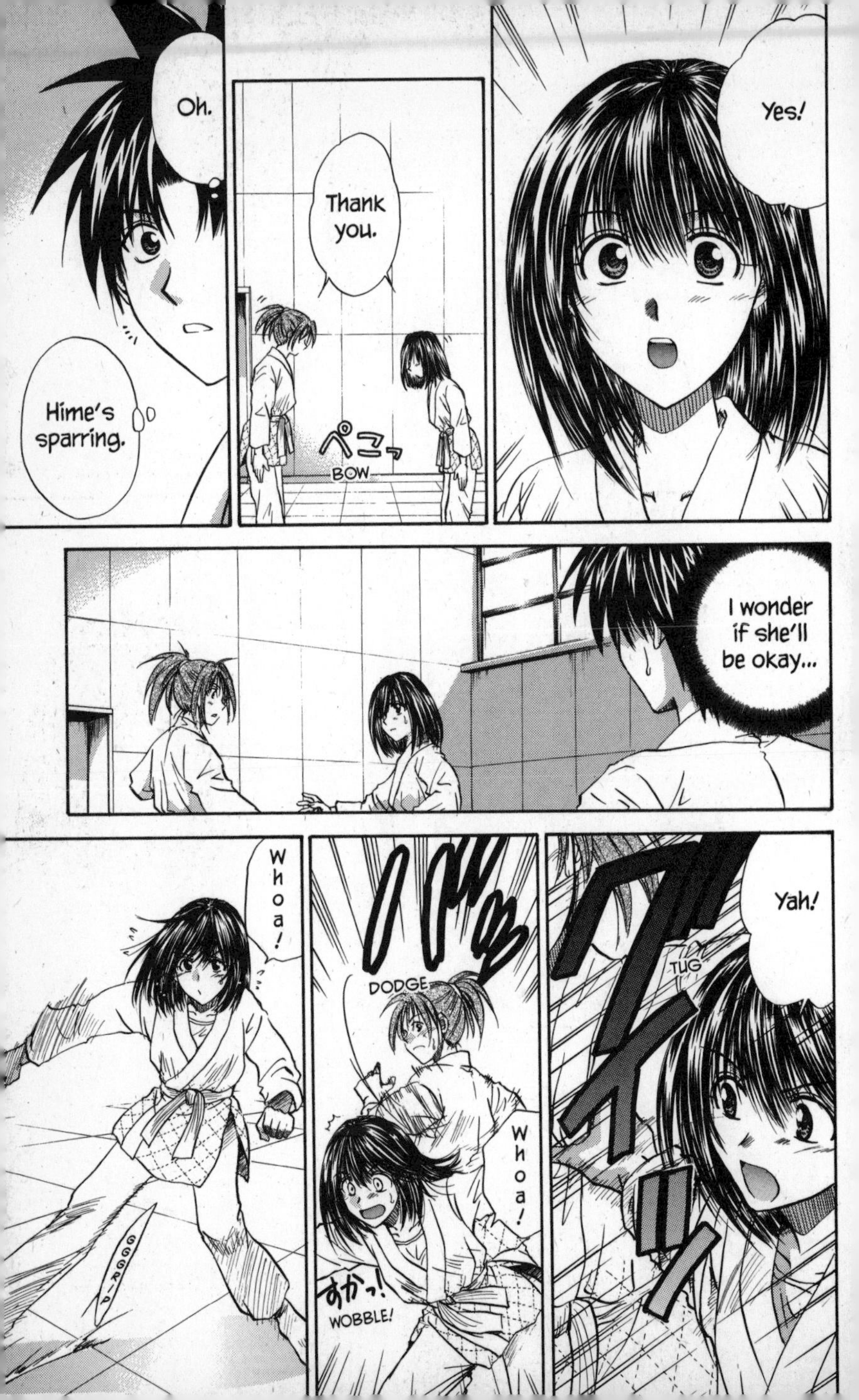
Yes!
Thank you.
ペコッ
BOW
Oh.
Hime's sparring.
I wonder if she'll be okay...
Yah!
TUG
DODGE
Whoa!
すかっ!
WOBBLE!
Whoa!
GGGRIP

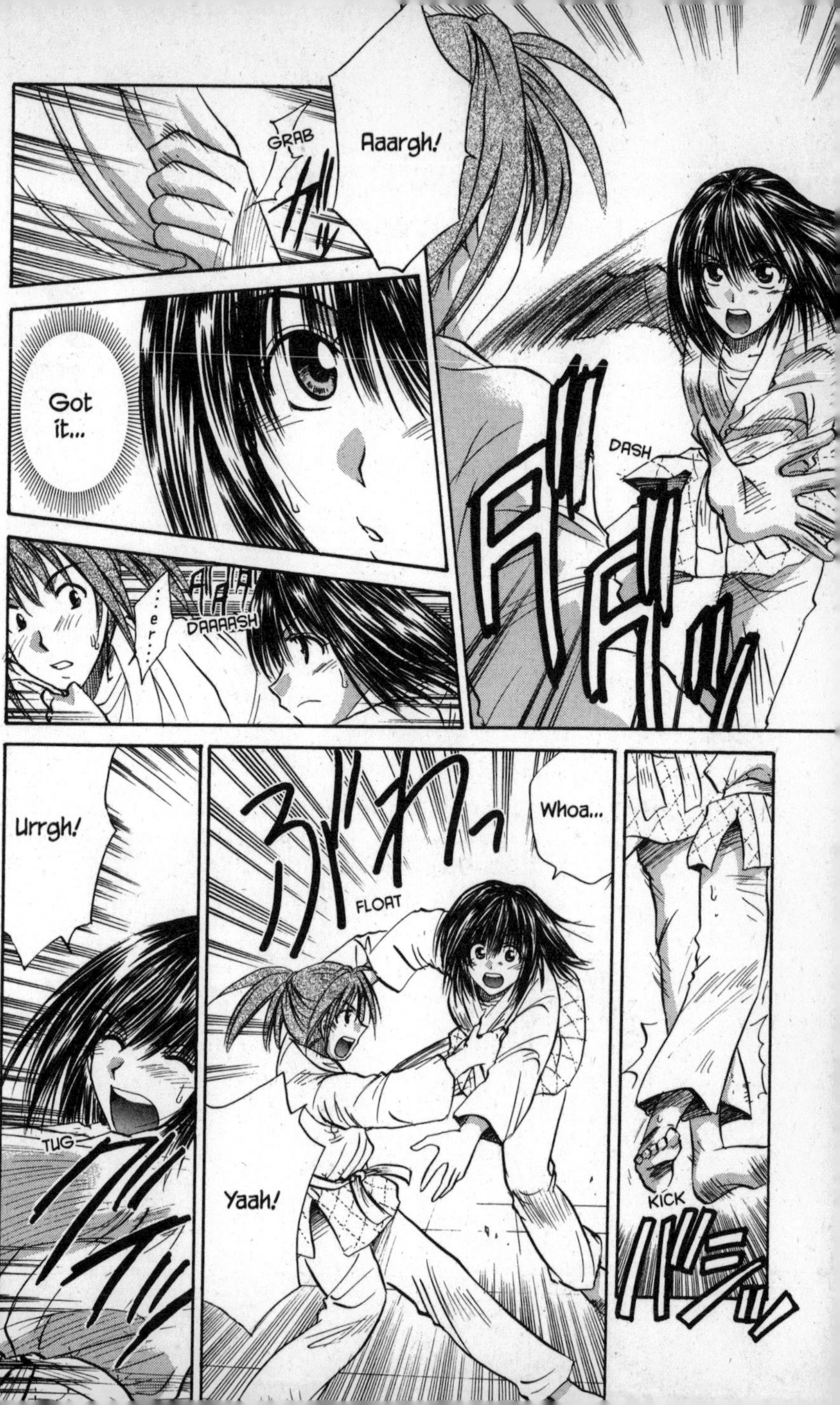
DASH
Aaargh!
GRAB
Got it...
...er...
DAAAASH
KICK
Whoa...
FLOAT
Yaah!
Urrgh!
TUG

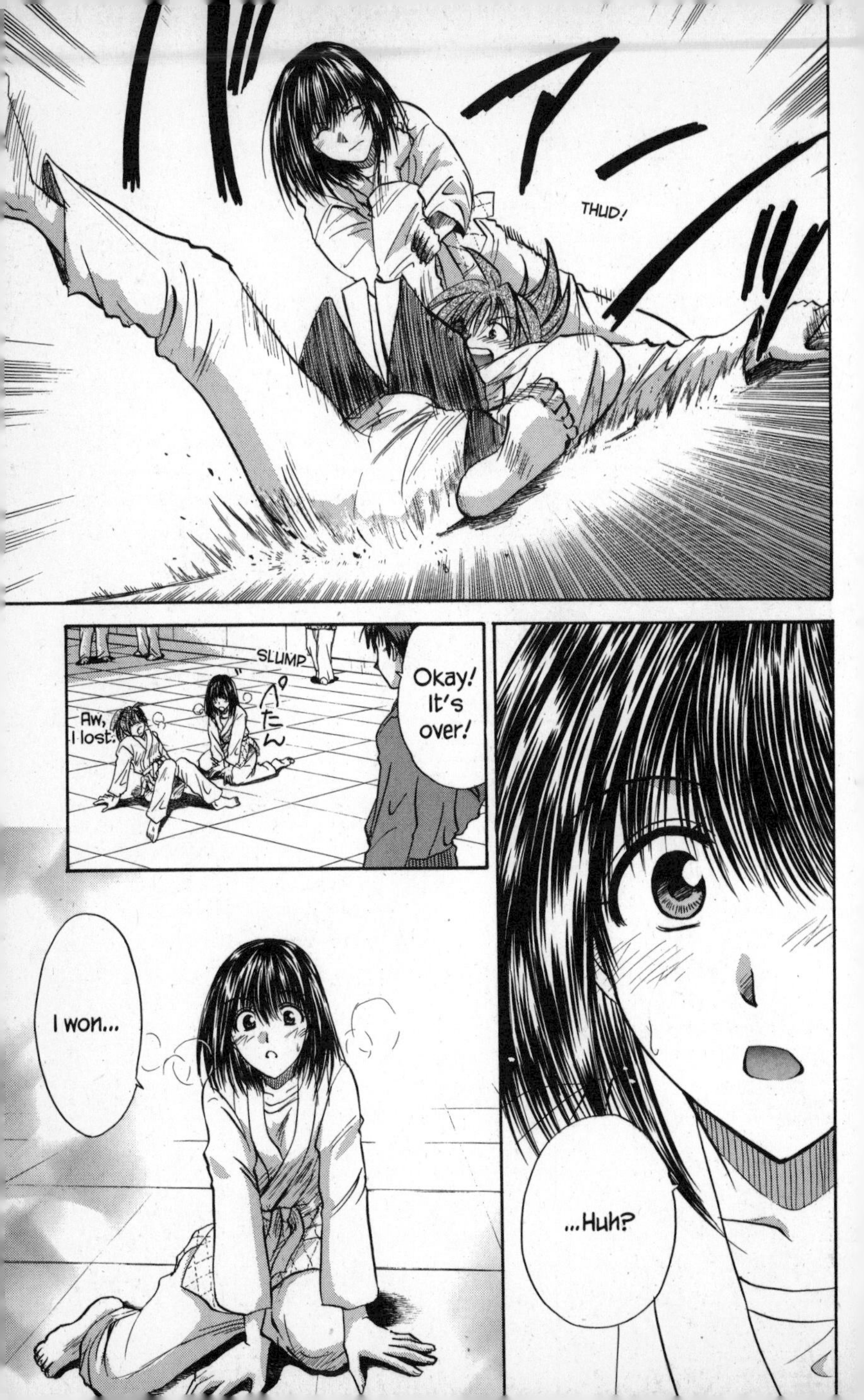
THUD!
...Huh?
Okay! It's over!
SLUMP
Aw, I lost.
I won...

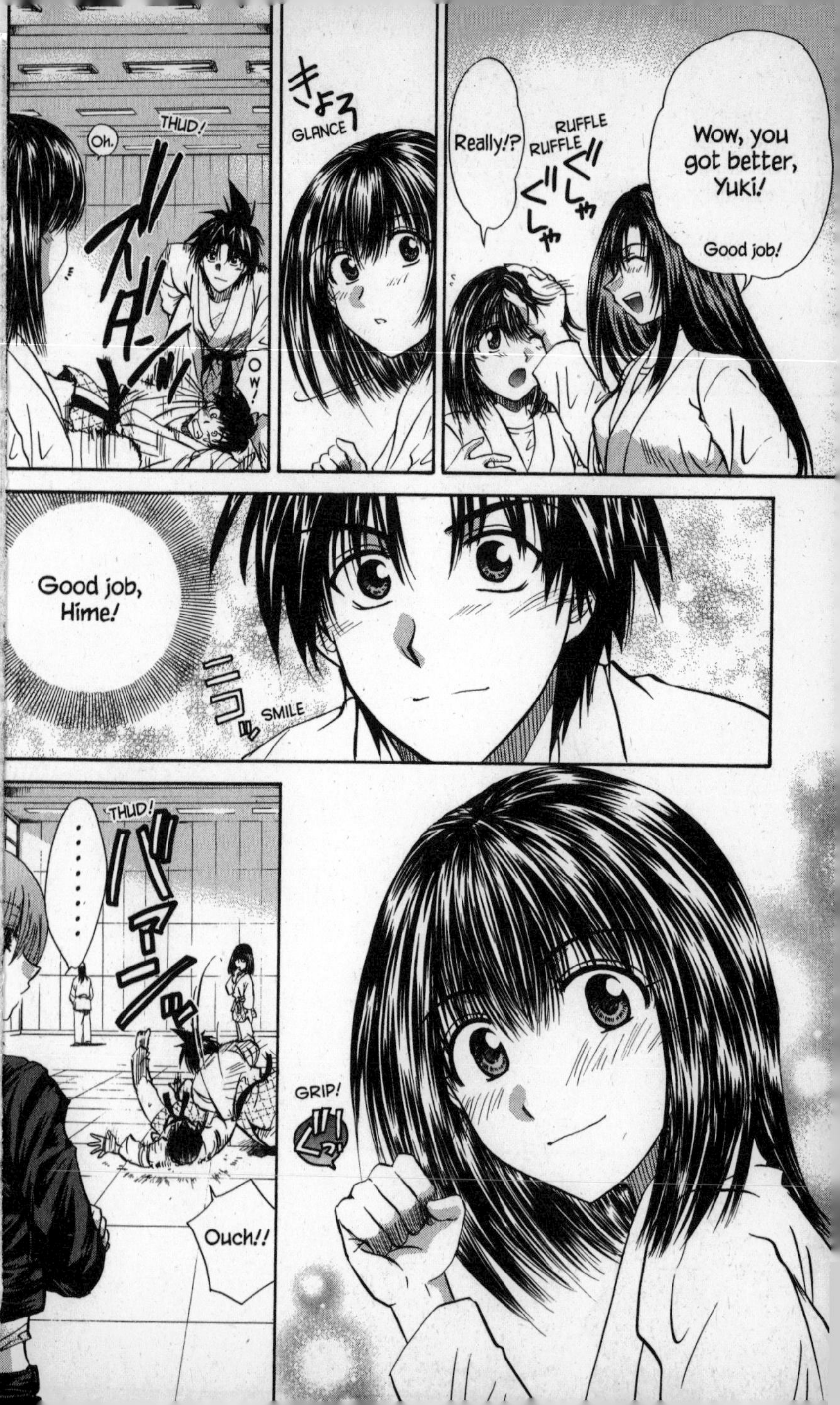
Wow, you got better, Yuki!
Good job!
RUFFLE RUFFLE
ぐしゃぐしゃ
Really!?
きょろ
GLANCE
THUD!
Oh.
OW!
Good job, Hime!
ニコッ
SMILE
GRIP!
THUD!
. . . .
Ouch!!

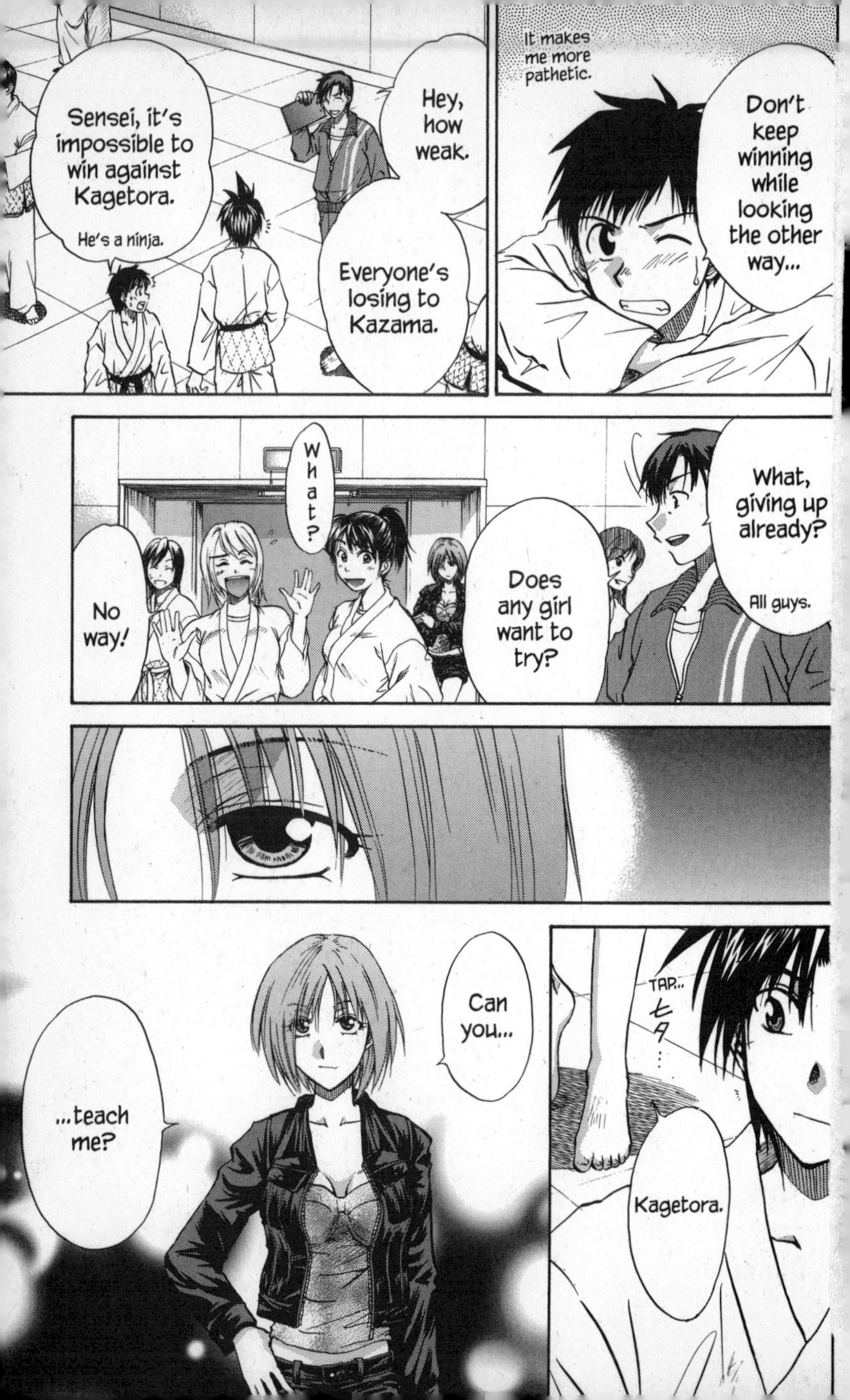
Don't keep winning while looking the other way...
It makes me more pathetic.
Hey, how weak.
Everyone's losing to Kazama.
Sensei, it's impossible to win against Kagetora.
He's a ninja.
What, giving up already?
All guys.
Does any girl want to try?
What?
No way!
TAP... ヒタ...
Kagetora.
Can you...
...teach me?

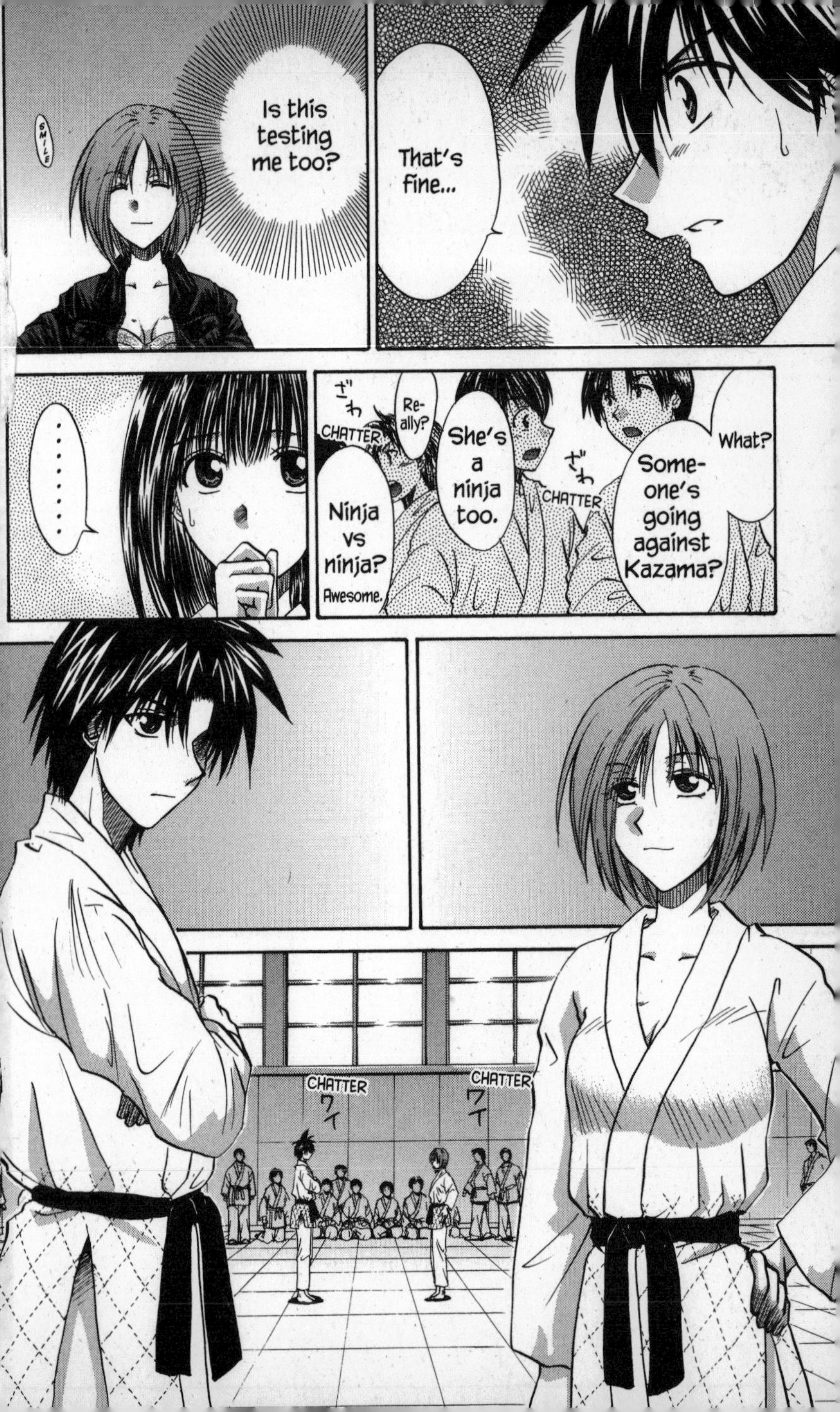
That's fine...
SMILE
Is this testing me too?
What?
Some-one's going against Kazama?
ざわ CHATTER
She's a ninja too.
Re-ally?
ざわ CHATTER
Ninja vs ninja?
Awesome.
....
CHATTER ワイ
CHATTER ワイ

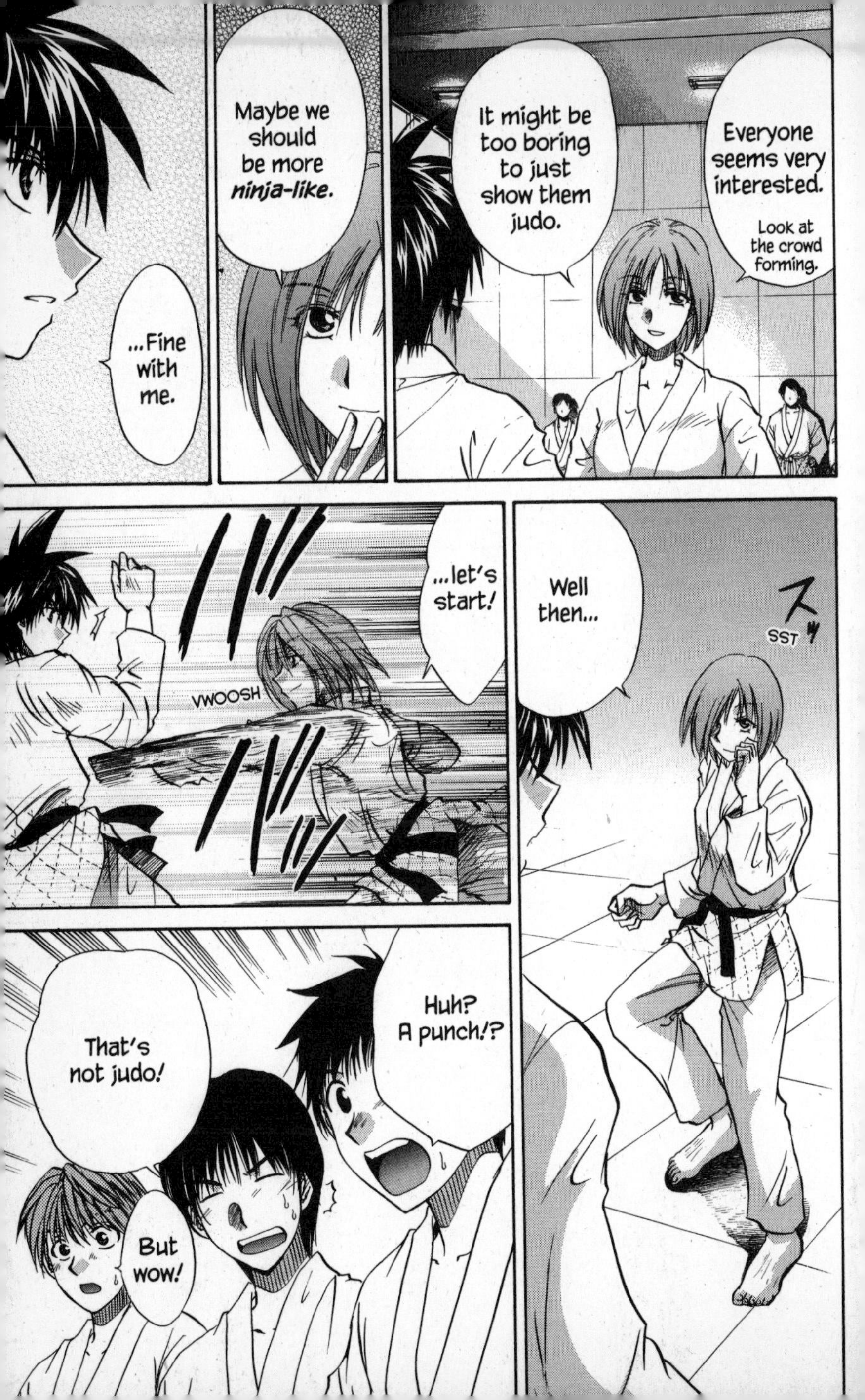
Everyone seems very interested.
Look at the crowd forming.
It might be too boring to just show them judo.
Maybe we should be more *ninja-like.*
...Fine with me.
スッ
SST
Well then...
...let's start!
VWOOSH
Huh? A punch!?
That's not judo!
But wow!

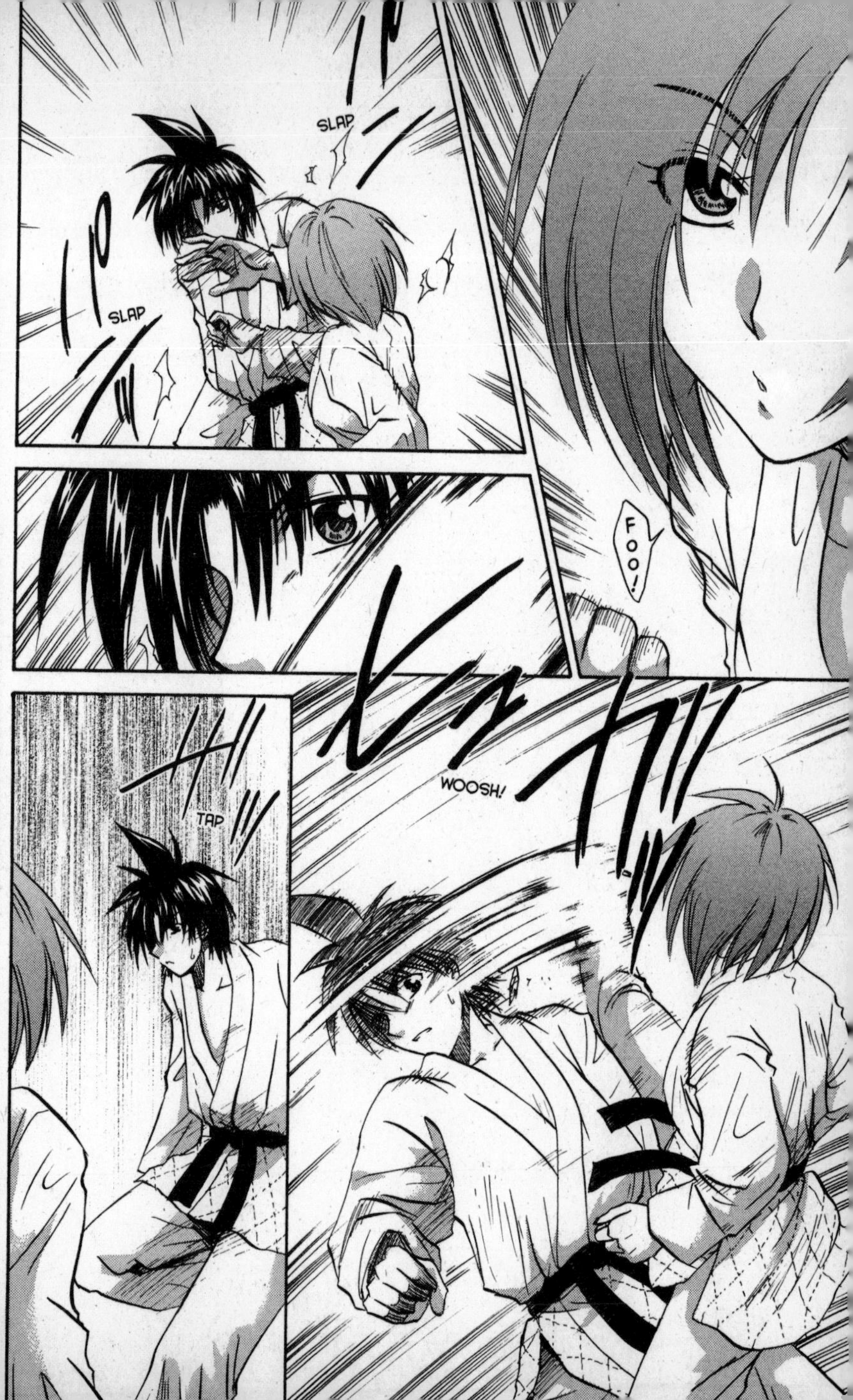
FOO!
SLAP
SLAP
WOOSH!
TAP

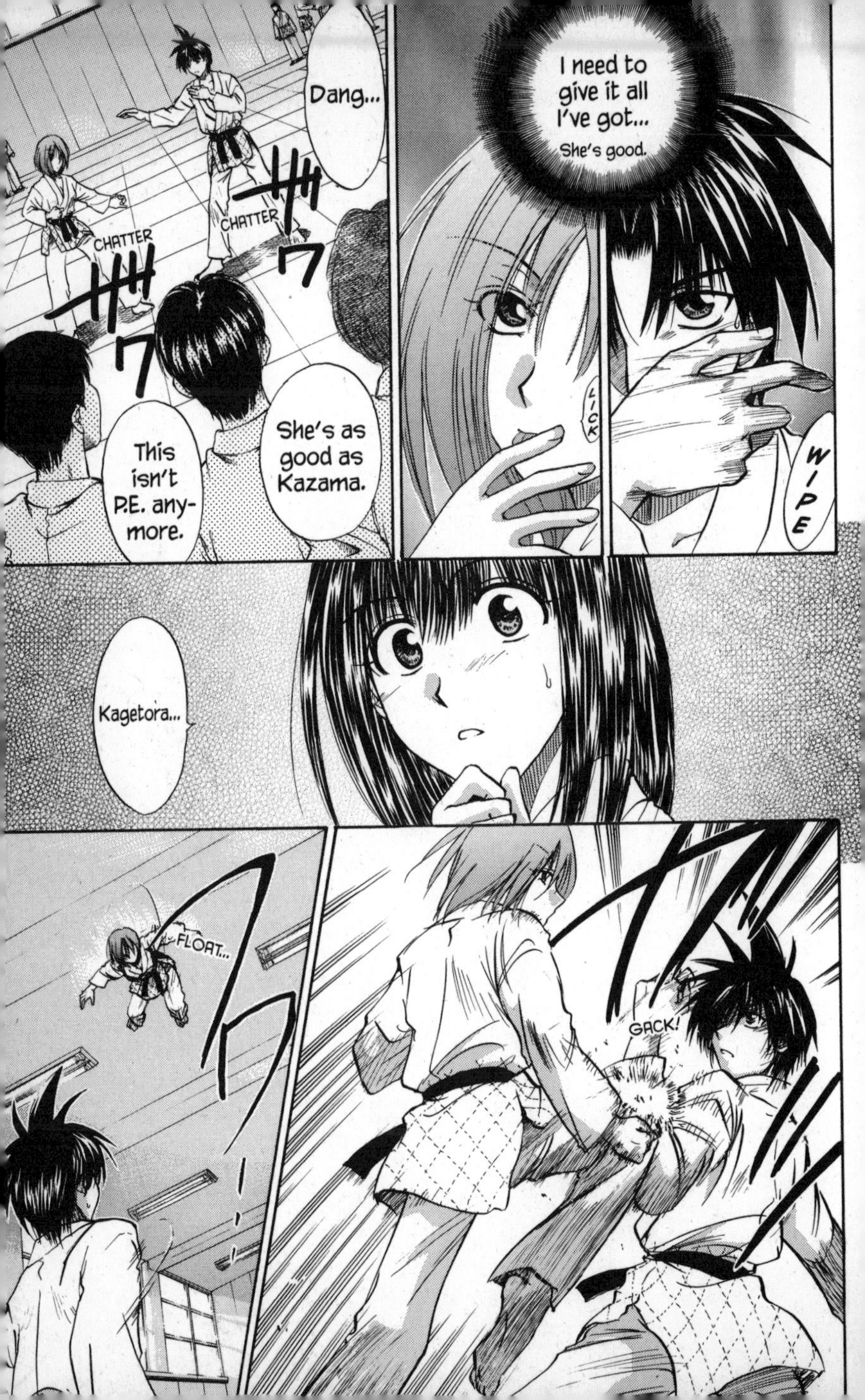

I need to give it all I've got...
She's good.
WIPE
LICK
Dang...
CHATTER
CHATTER
She's as good as Kazama.
This isn't P.E. any-more.
Kagetora...
GACK!
FLOAT...

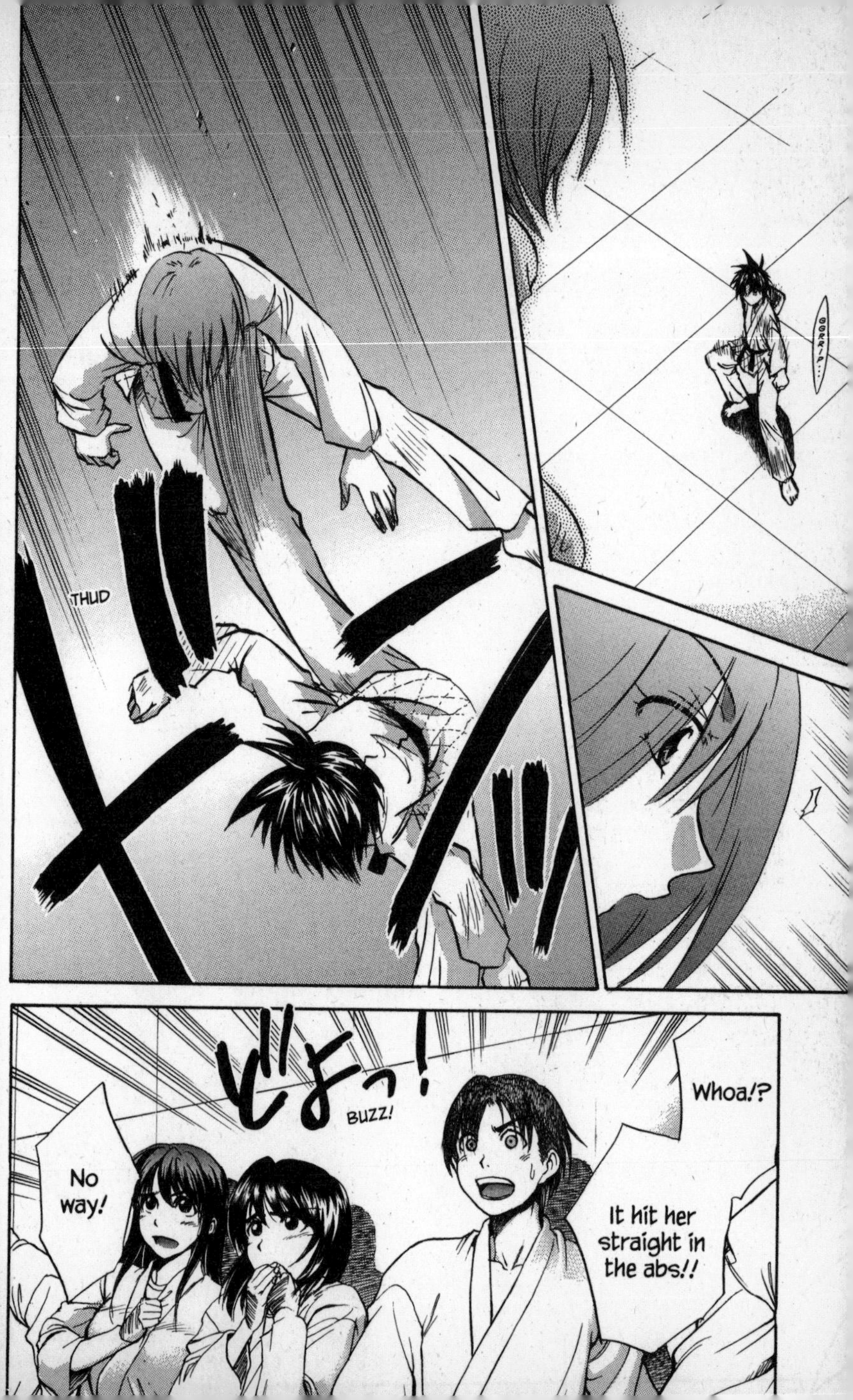
GGRRIP...
THUD
Whoa!?
どよっ!
BUZZ!
It hit her straight in the abs!!
No way!

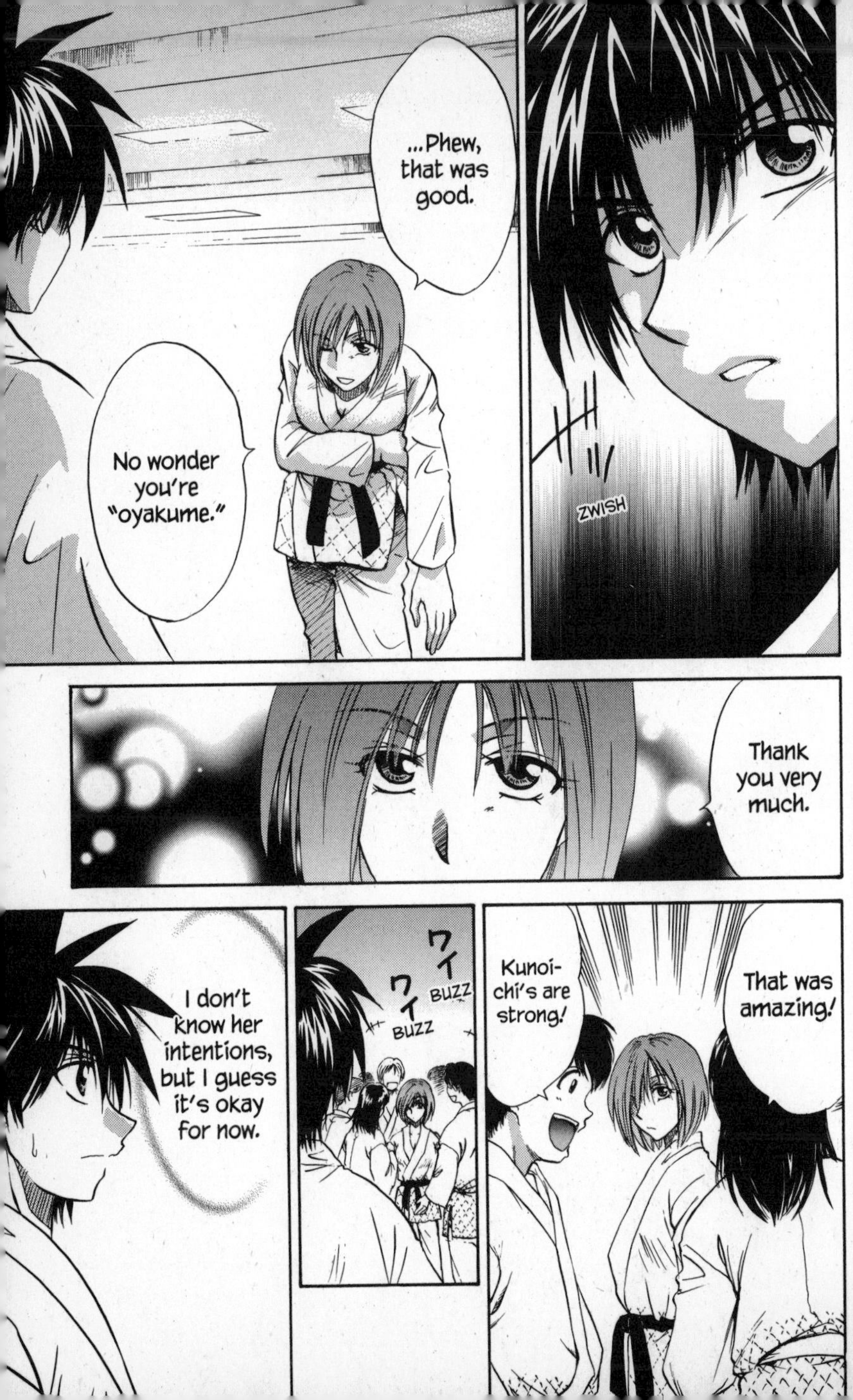
ZWISH
...Phew, that was good.
No wonder you're "oyakume."
Thank you very much.
That was amazing!
Kunoi-chi's are strong!
ワイ BUZZ
ワイ BUZZ
I don't know her intentions, but I guess it's okay for now.

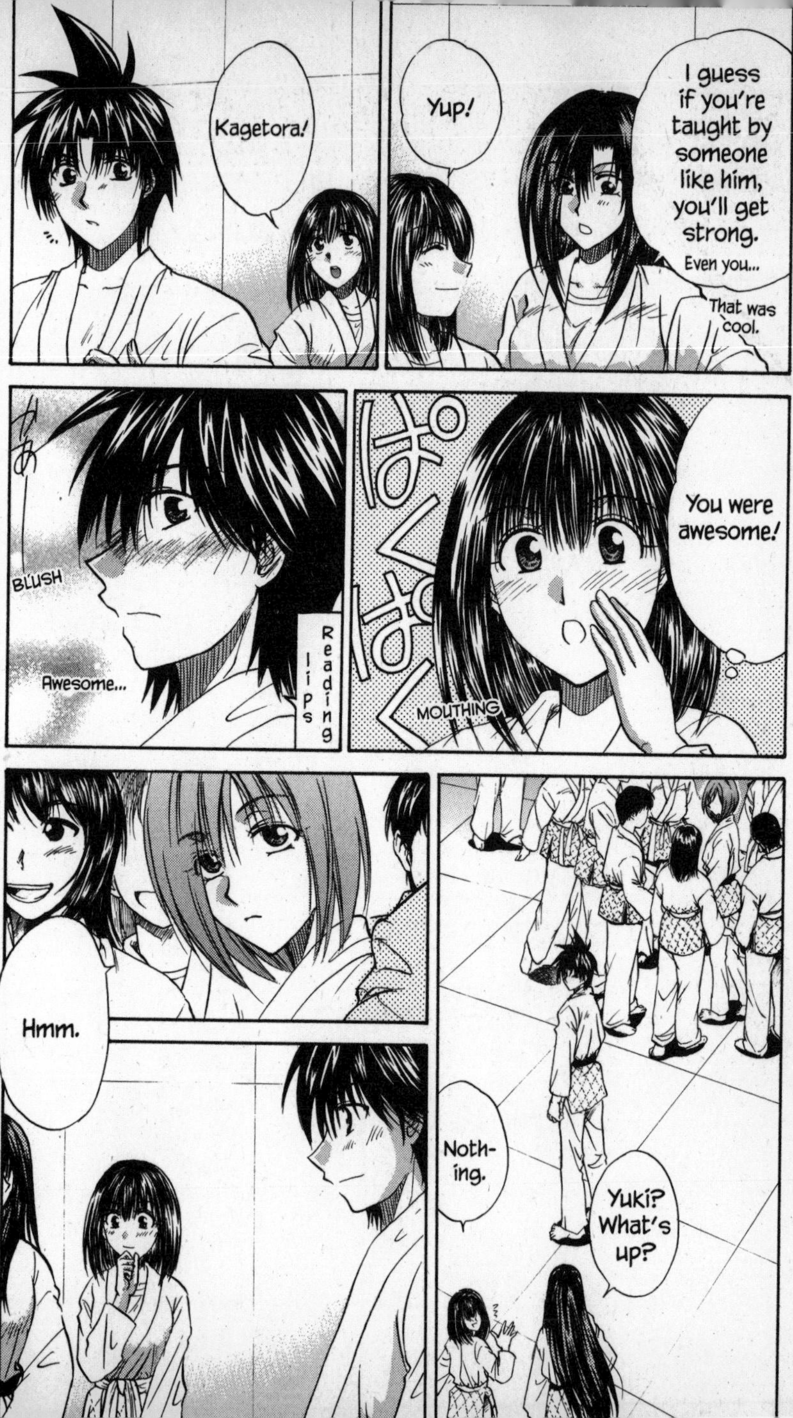
I guess if you're taught by someone like him, you'll get strong.
Even you...
That was cool.
Yup!
Kagetora!
You were awesome!
ぱくぱく
MOUTHING
Reading lips
かぁー
BLUSH
Awesome...
Yuki? What's up?
Hmm.
Noth-ing.

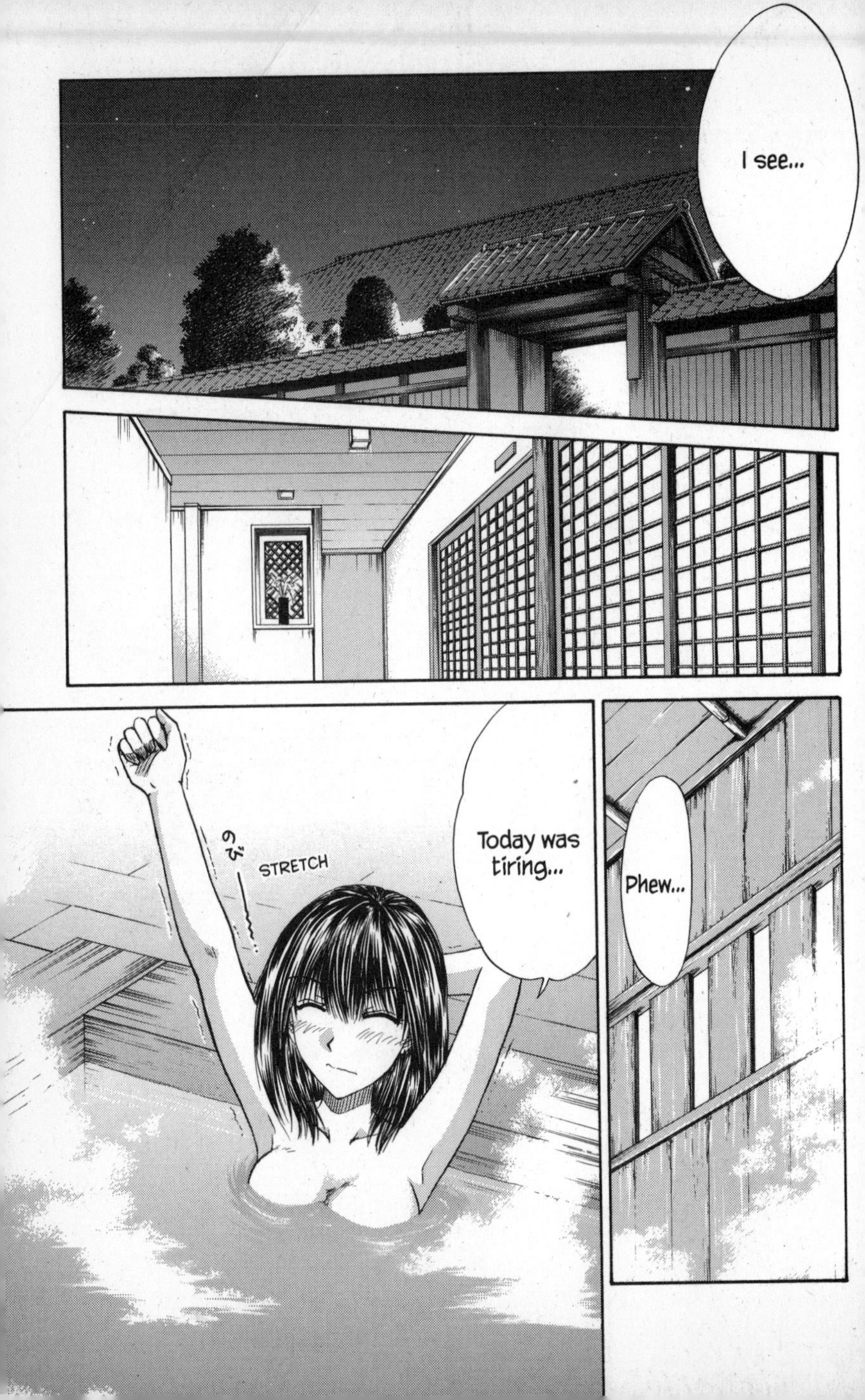
I see...
Phew...
Today was tiring...
のび
STRETCH

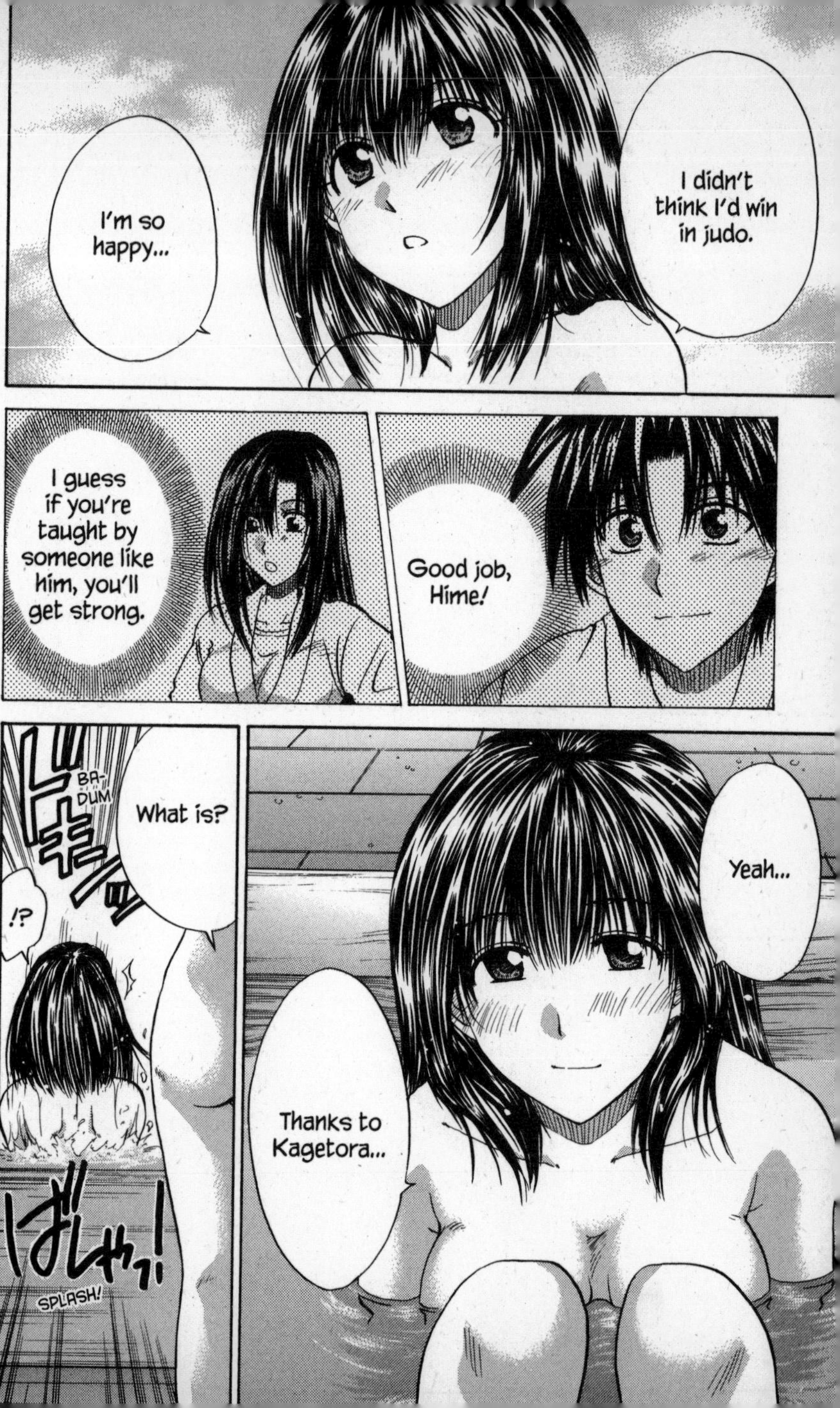
I didn't think I'd win in judo.
I'm so happy...
Good job, Hime!
I guess if you're taught by someone like him, you'll get strong.
Yeah...
Thanks to Kagetora...
What is?
BA-DUM
!?
SPLASH!

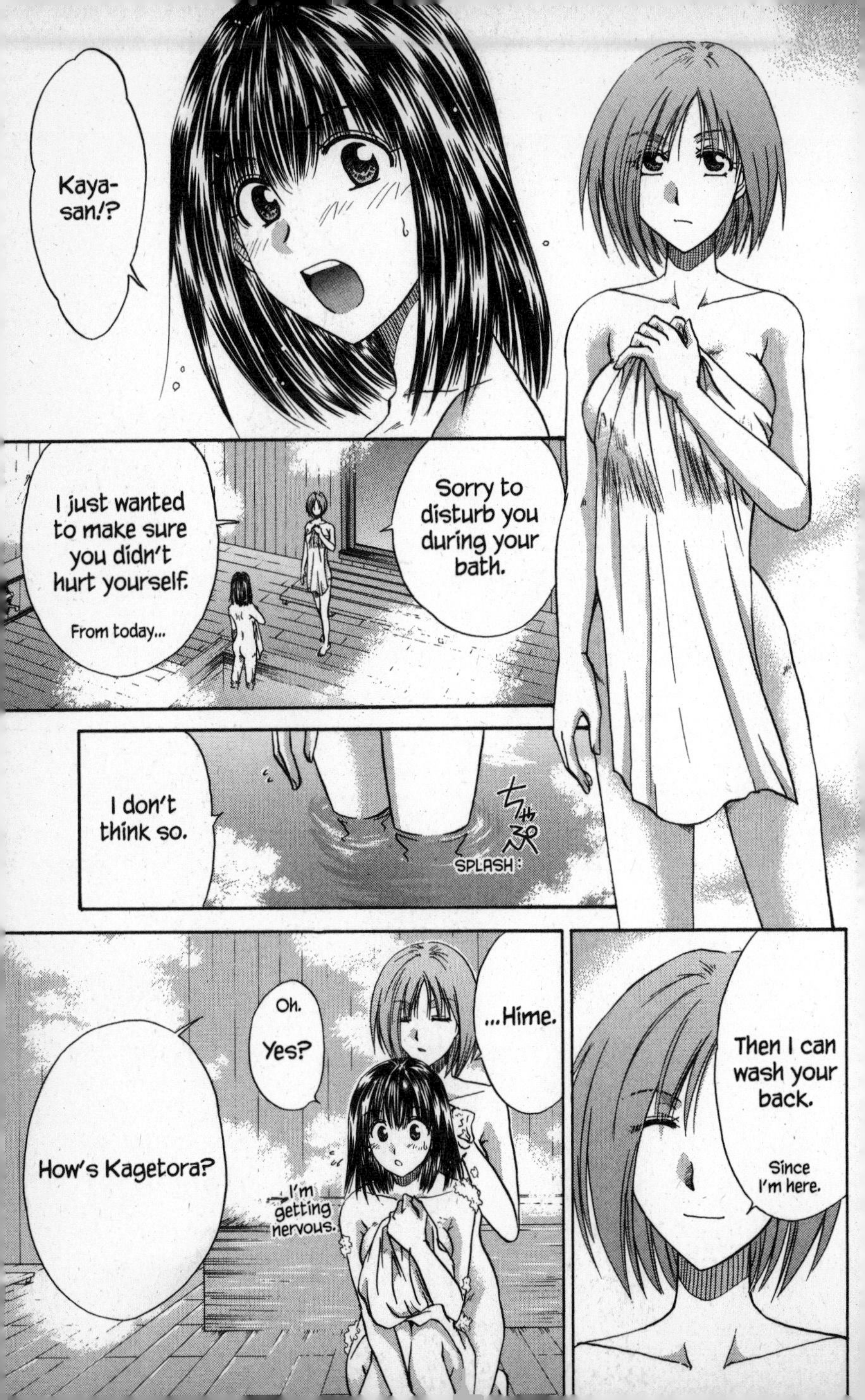
Kaya-san!?
Sorry to disturb you during your bath.
I just wanted to make sure you didn't hurt yourself.
From today...
I don't think so.
ちゃぷ
SPLASH
Then I can wash your back.
Since I'm here.
...Hime.
Oh.
Yes?
I'm getting nervous.
How's Kagetora?

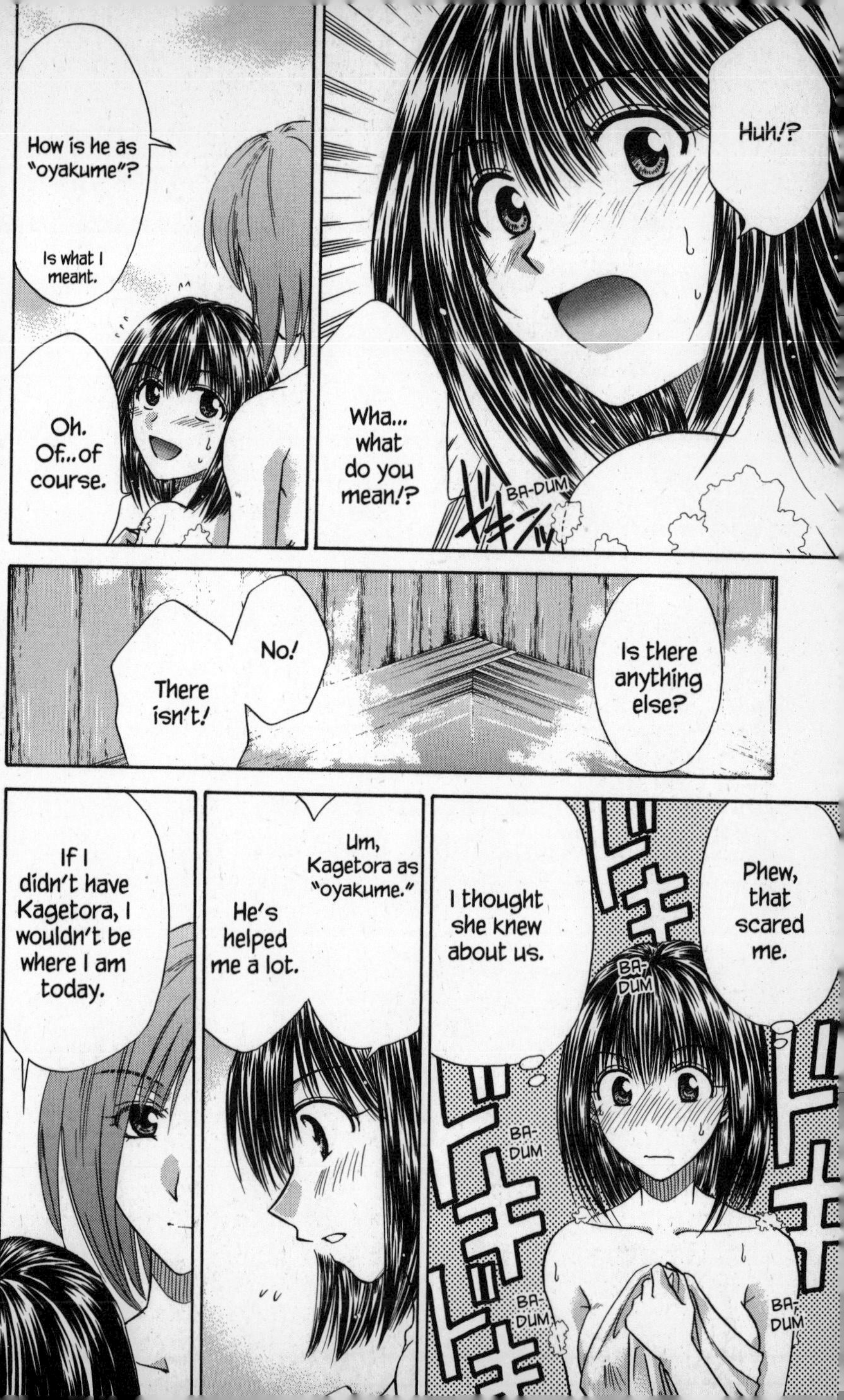
Huh!?
Wha... what do you mean!?
BA-DUM
How is he as "oyakume"?
Is what I meant.
Oh. Of...of course.
Is there anything else?
No!
There isn't!
Phew, that scared me.
I thought she knew about us.
BA-DUM
BA-DUM
BA-DUM
BA-DUM
Um, Kagetora as "oyakume."
He's helped me a lot.
If I didn't have Kagetora, I wouldn't be where I am today.

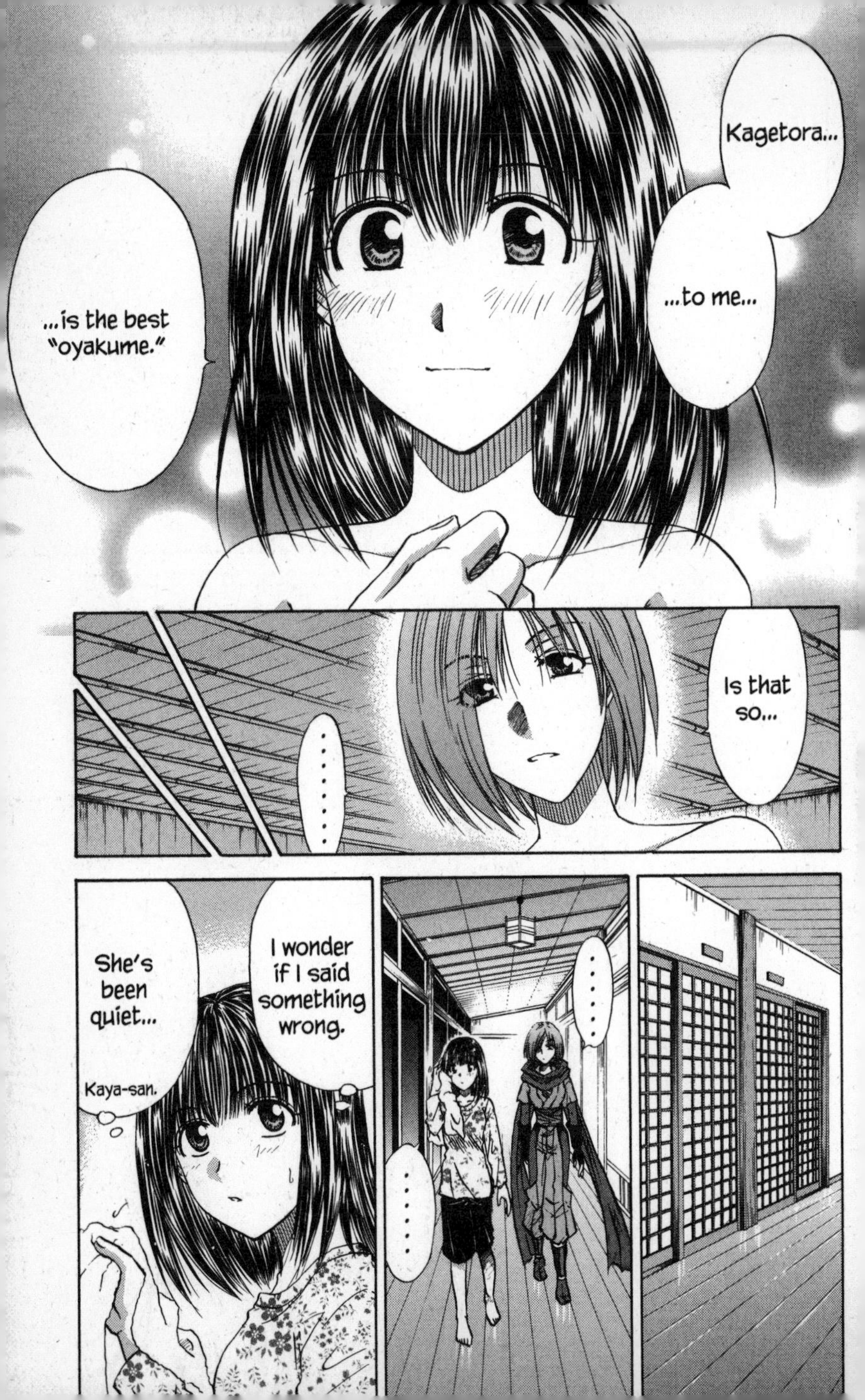
Kagetora...
...to me...
...is the best "oyakume."
Is that so...
......
......
......
I wonder if I said something wrong.
She's been quiet...
Kaya-san.

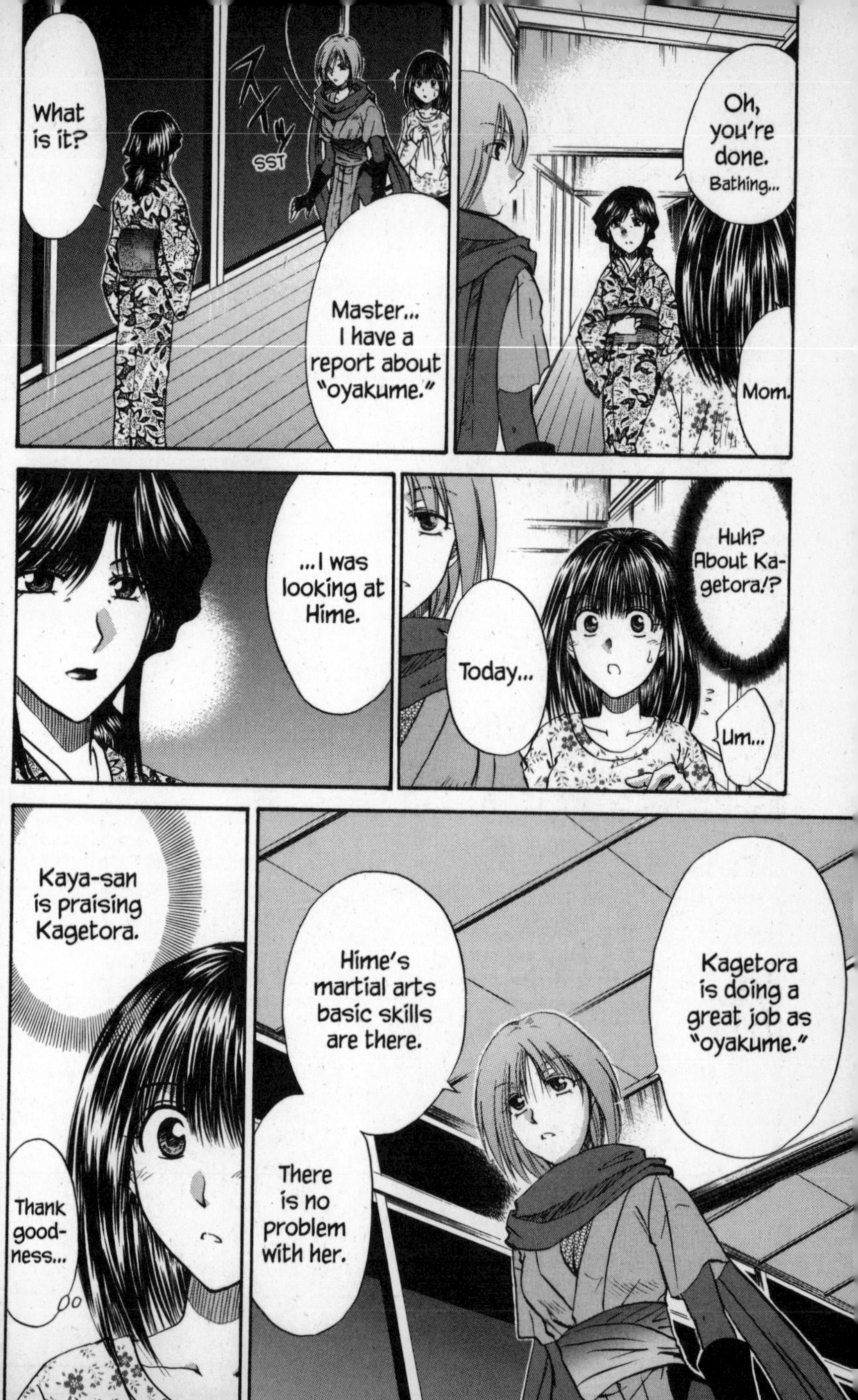
Oh, you're done. Bathing...
Mom.
SST
Master... I have a report about "oyakume."
What is it?
Huh? About Kagetora!?
Today...
Um...
...I was looking at Hime.
Kagetora is doing a great job as "oyakume."
Hime's martial arts basic skills are there.
There is no problem with her.
Kaya-san is praising Kagetora.
Thank goodness...

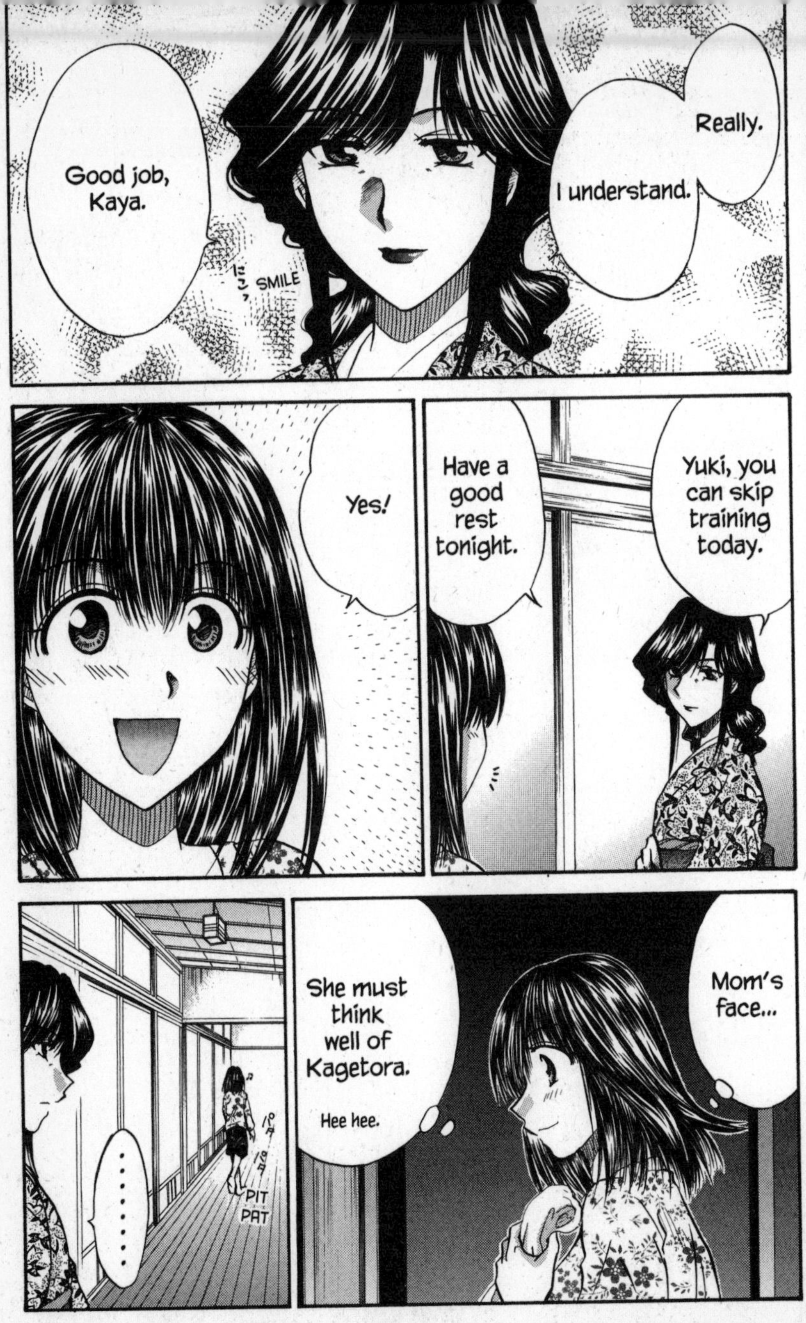
Really.
I understand.
Good job, Kaya.
SMILE
Yuki, you can skip training today.
Have a good rest tonight.
Yes!
Mom's face...
She must think well of Kagetora.
Hee hee.
PIT PAT
......

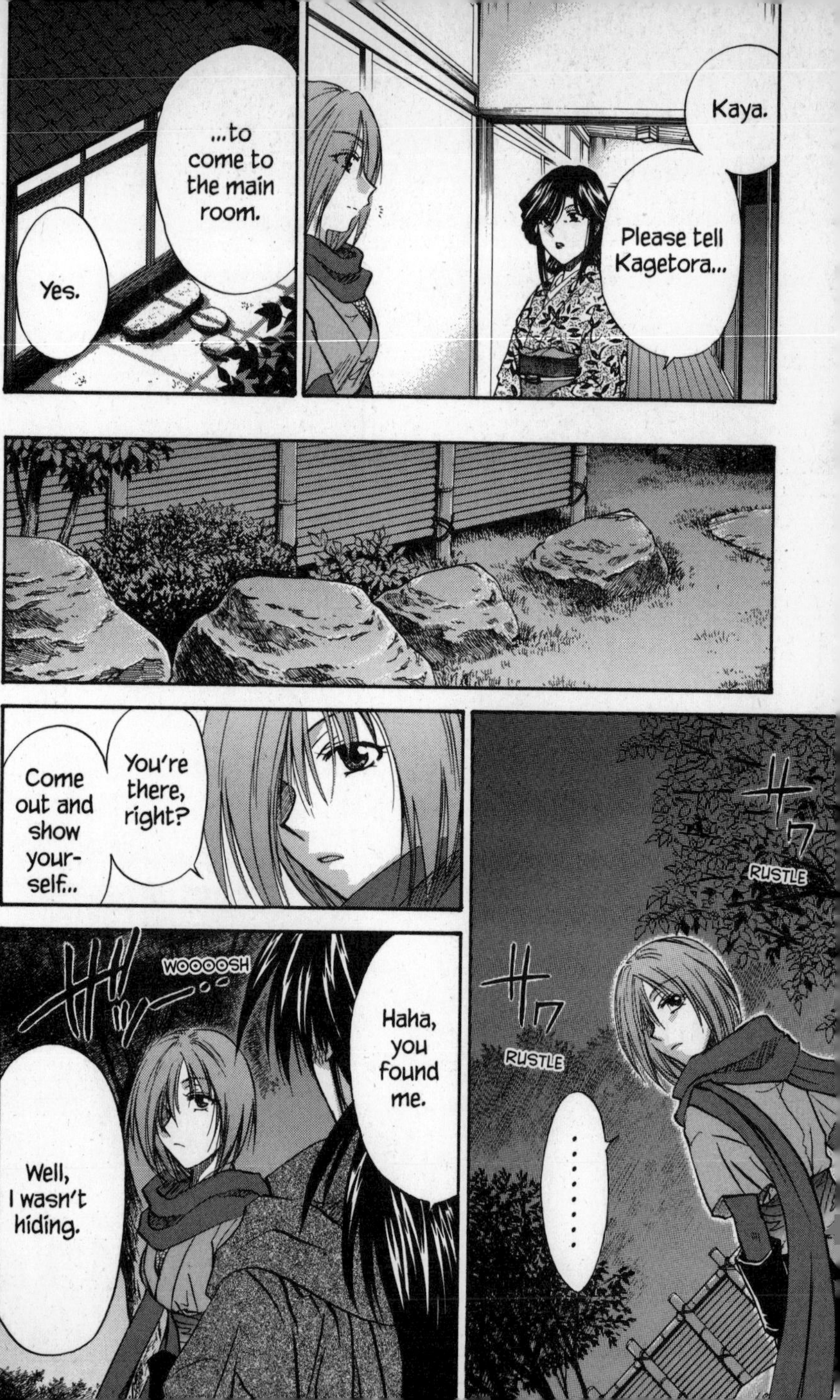
Kaya.
Please tell Kagetora...
...to come to the main room.
Yes.
RUSTLE
RUSTLE
......
You're there, right?
Come out and show your-self...
WOOOOSH
Haha, you found me.
Well, I wasn't hiding.

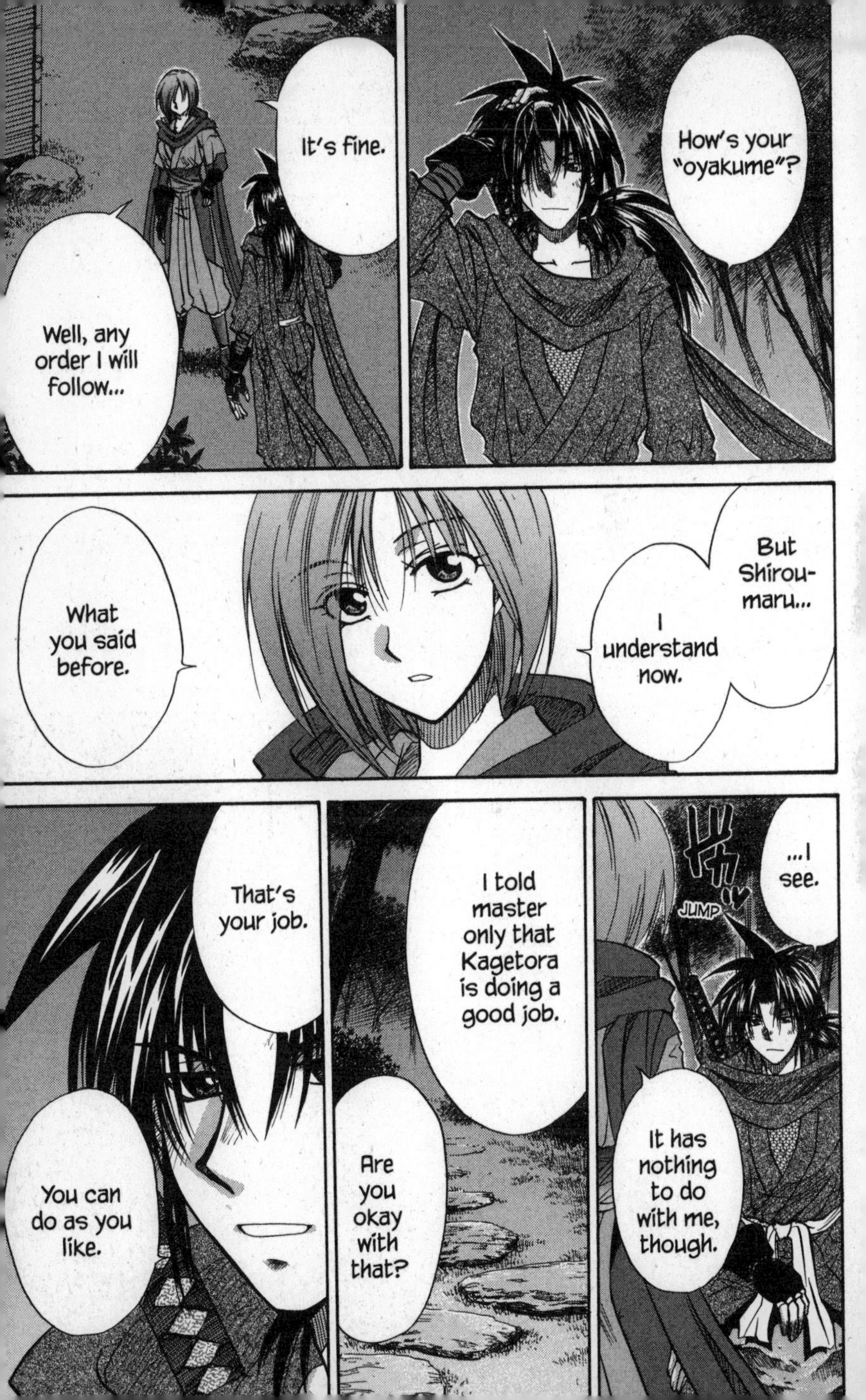
How's your "oyakume"?
It's fine.
Well, any order I will follow...
But Shirou-maru...
I understand now.
What you said before.
...I see.
JUMP
It has nothing to do with me, though.
I told master only that Kagetora is doing a good job.
Are you okay with that?
That's your job.
You can do as you like.

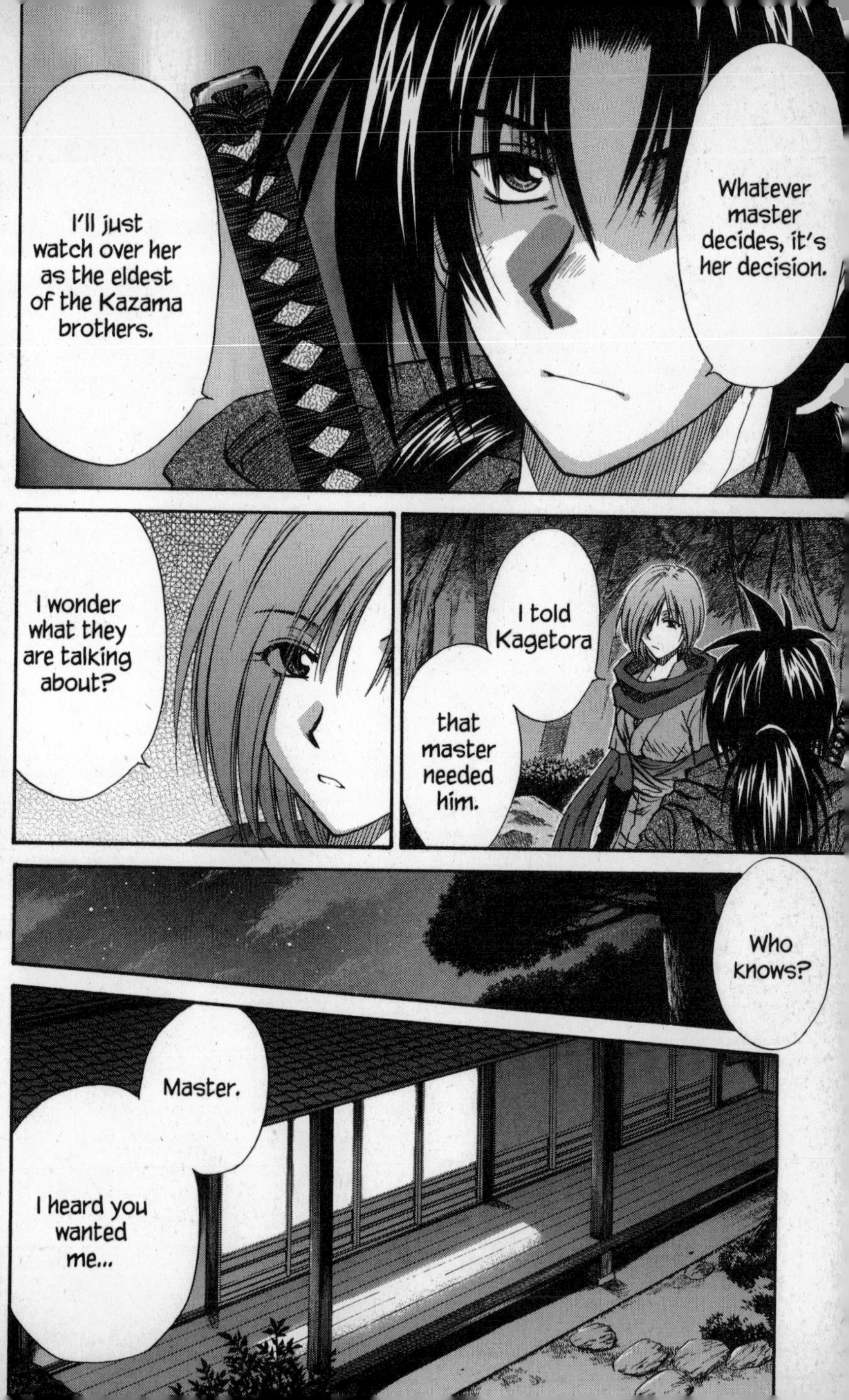
Whatever master decides, it's her decision.
I'll just watch over her as the eldest of the Kazama brothers.
I told Kagetora
that master needed him.
I wonder what they are talking about?
Who knows?
Master.
I heard you wanted me...

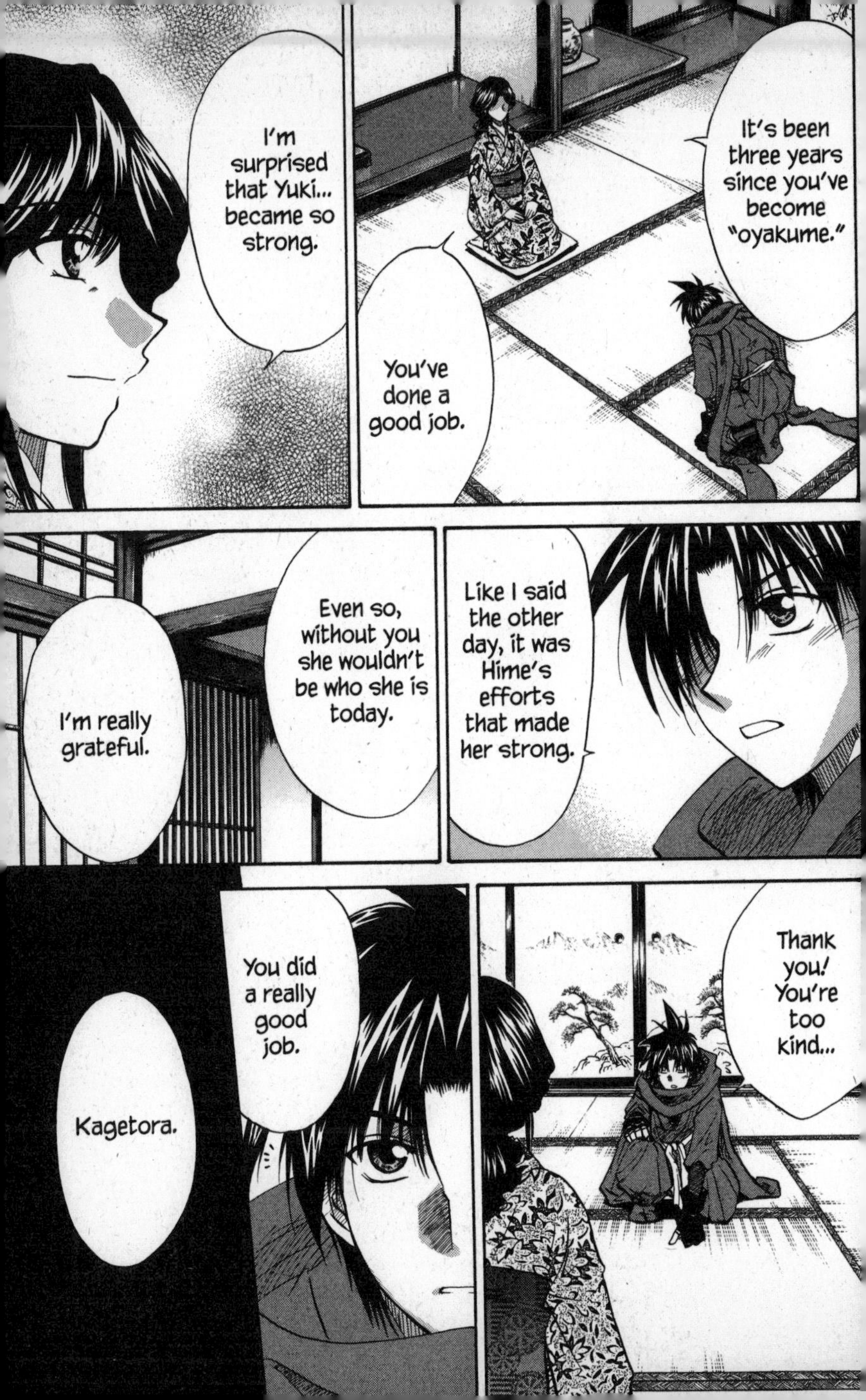
It's been three years since you've become "oyakume."
You've done a good job.
I'm surprised that Yuki... became so strong.
Like I said the other day, it was Hime's efforts that made her strong.
Even so, without you she wouldn't be who she is today.
I'm really grateful.
Thank you! You're too kind...
You did a really good job.
Kagetora.

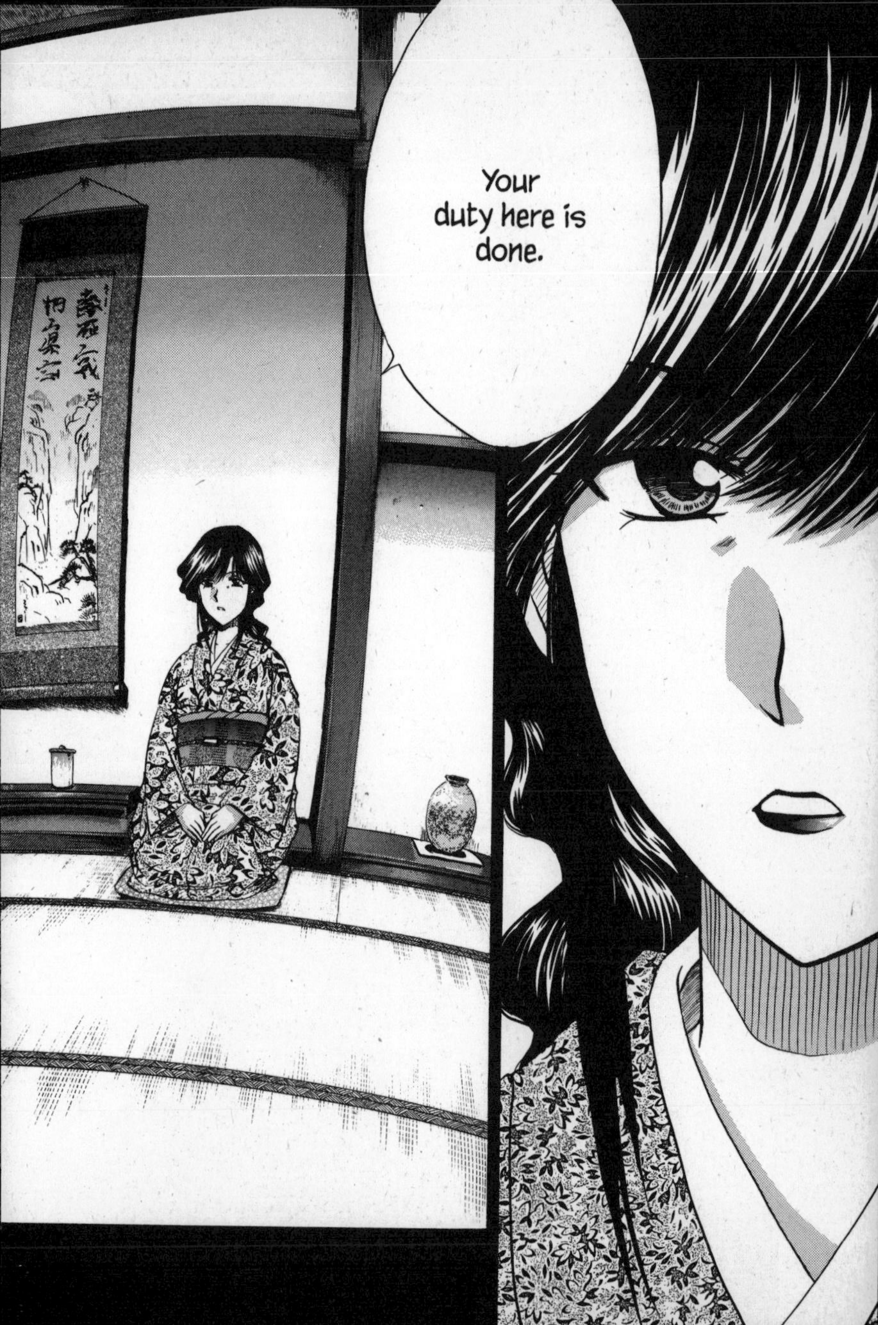
Your duty here is done.

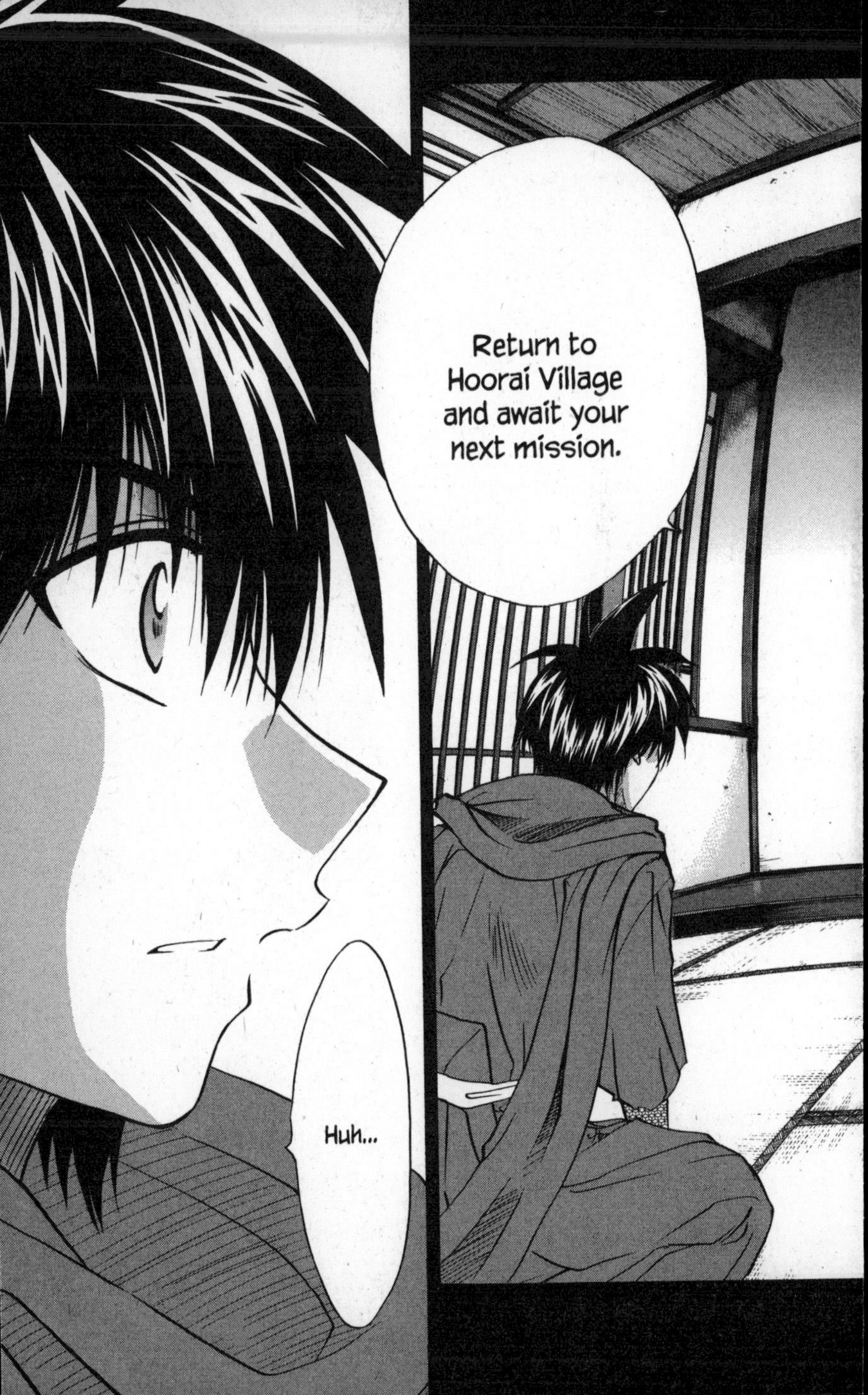
Return to Hoorai Village and await your next mission.
Huh...

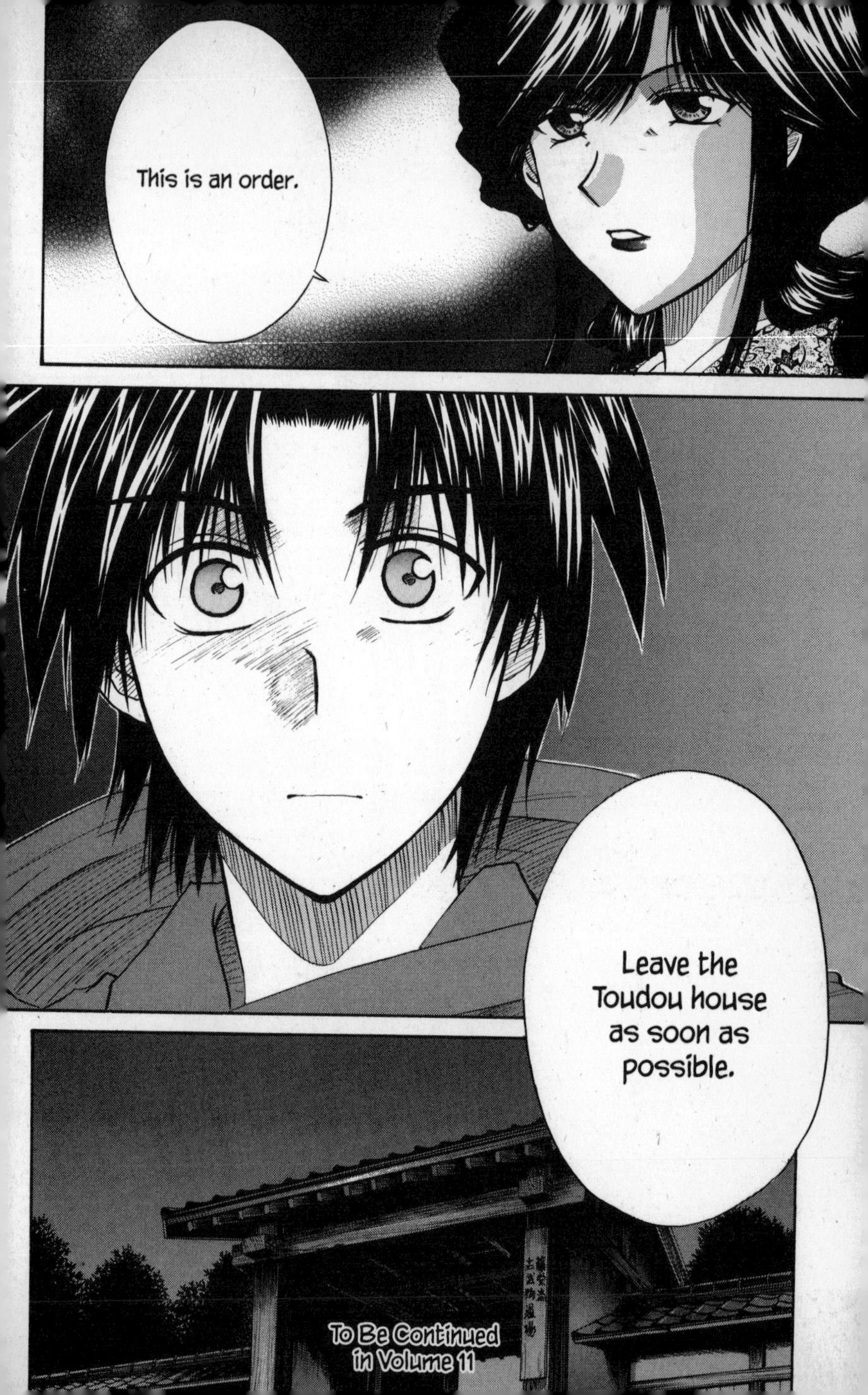
This is an order.
Leave the Toudou house as soon as possible.
To Be Continued in Volume 11

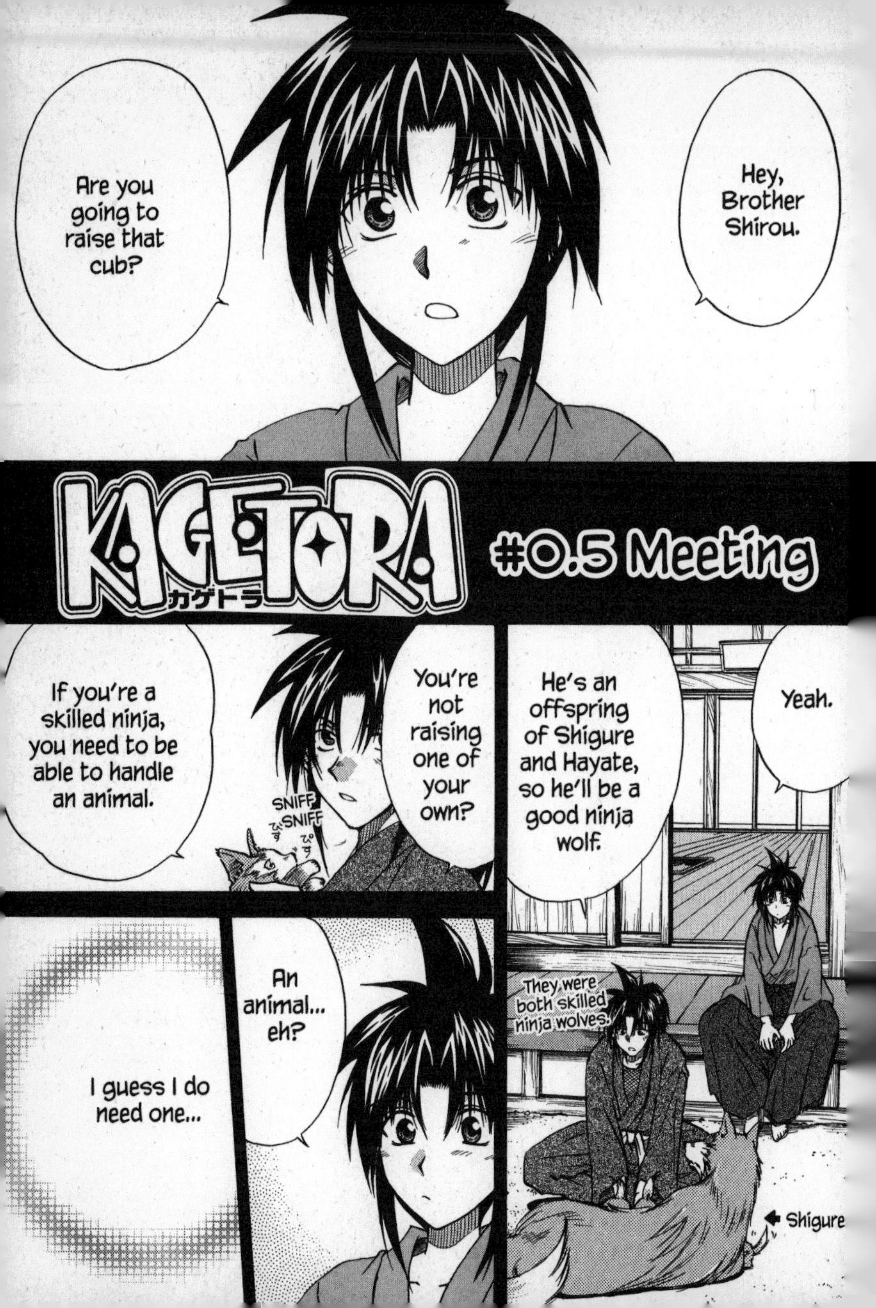
Hey, Brother Shirou.
Are you going to raise that cub?
KAGETORA
カゲトラ
#0.5 Meeting
Yeah.
He's an offspring of Shigure and Hayate, so he'll be a good ninja wolf.
They were both skilled ninja wolves.
Shigure
You're not raising one of your own?
If you're a skilled ninja, you need to be able to handle an animal.
SNIFF SNIFF
ぴすぴす
An animal... eh?
I guess I do need one...

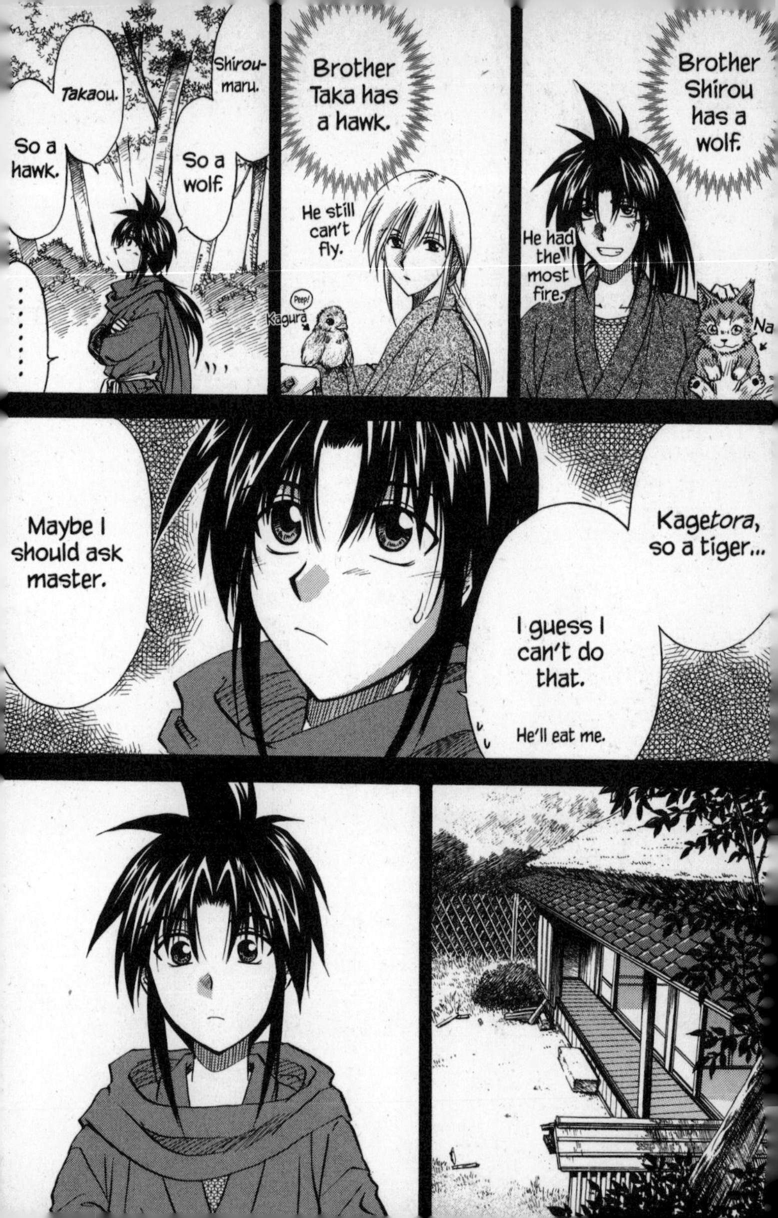
Brother Shirou has a wolf.
He had the most fire.
Na
Brother Taka has a hawk.
He still can't fly.
Peep!
Kagura
Shirou-maru.
Takaou.
So a wolf.
So a hawk.
......
Kagetora, so a tiger...
I guess I can't do that.
He'll eat me.
Maybe I should ask master.

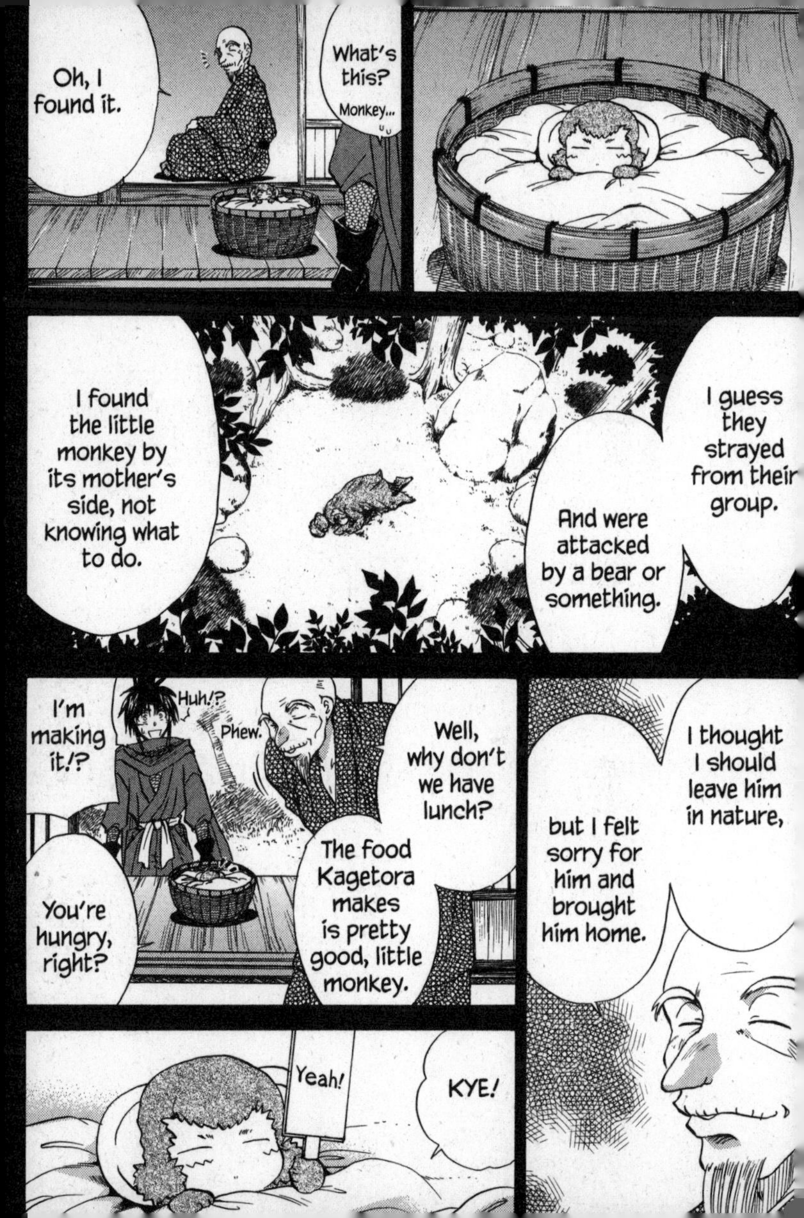
What's this?
Monkey...
Oh, I found it.
I guess they strayed from their group.
And were attacked by a bear or something.
I found the little monkey by its mother's side, not knowing what to do.
I thought I should leave him in nature,
but I felt sorry for him and brought him home.
Well, why don't we have lunch?
The food Kagetora makes is pretty good, little monkey.
Phew.
Huh!?
I'm making it!?
You're hungry, right?
KYE!
Yeah!

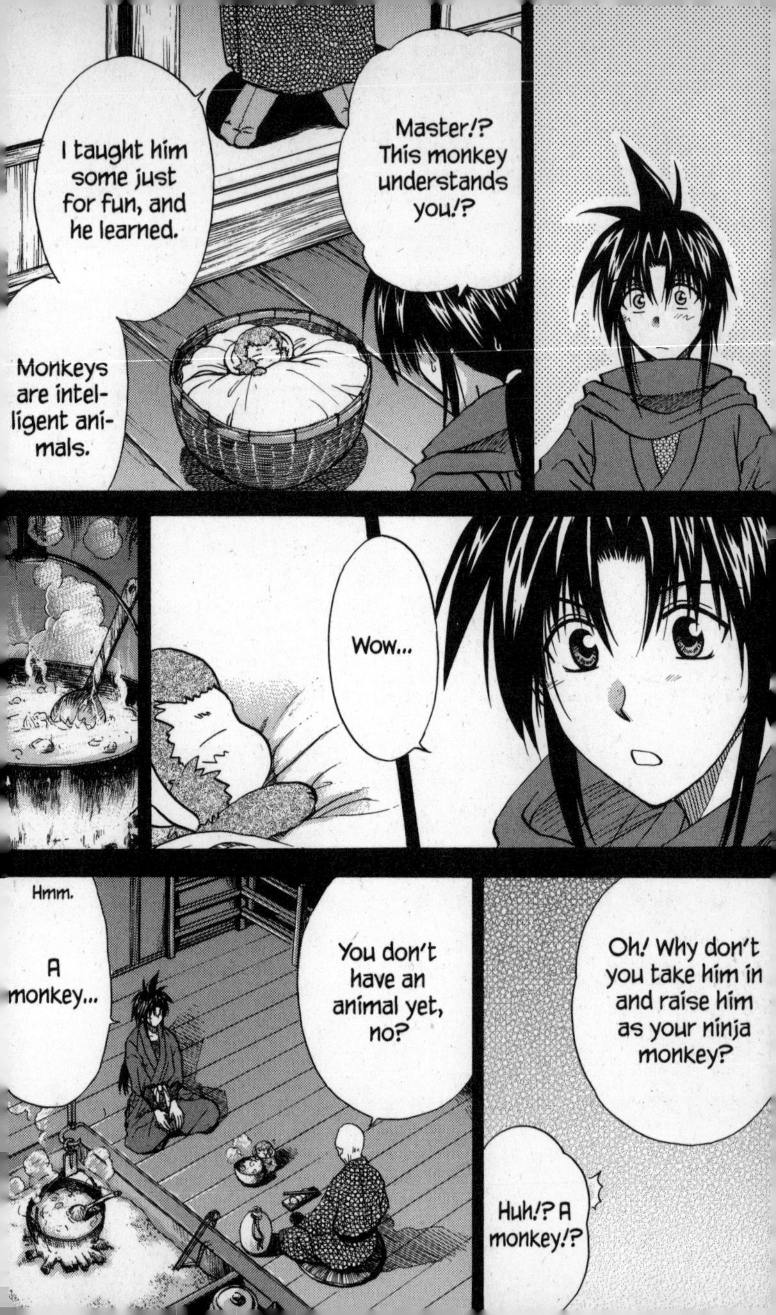
Master!? This monkey understands you!?
I taught him some just for fun, and he learned.
Monkeys are intel-ligent ani-mals.
Wow...
Oh! Why don't you take him in and raise him as your ninja monkey?
Huh!? A monkey!?
You don't have an animal yet, no?
Hmm.
A monkey...

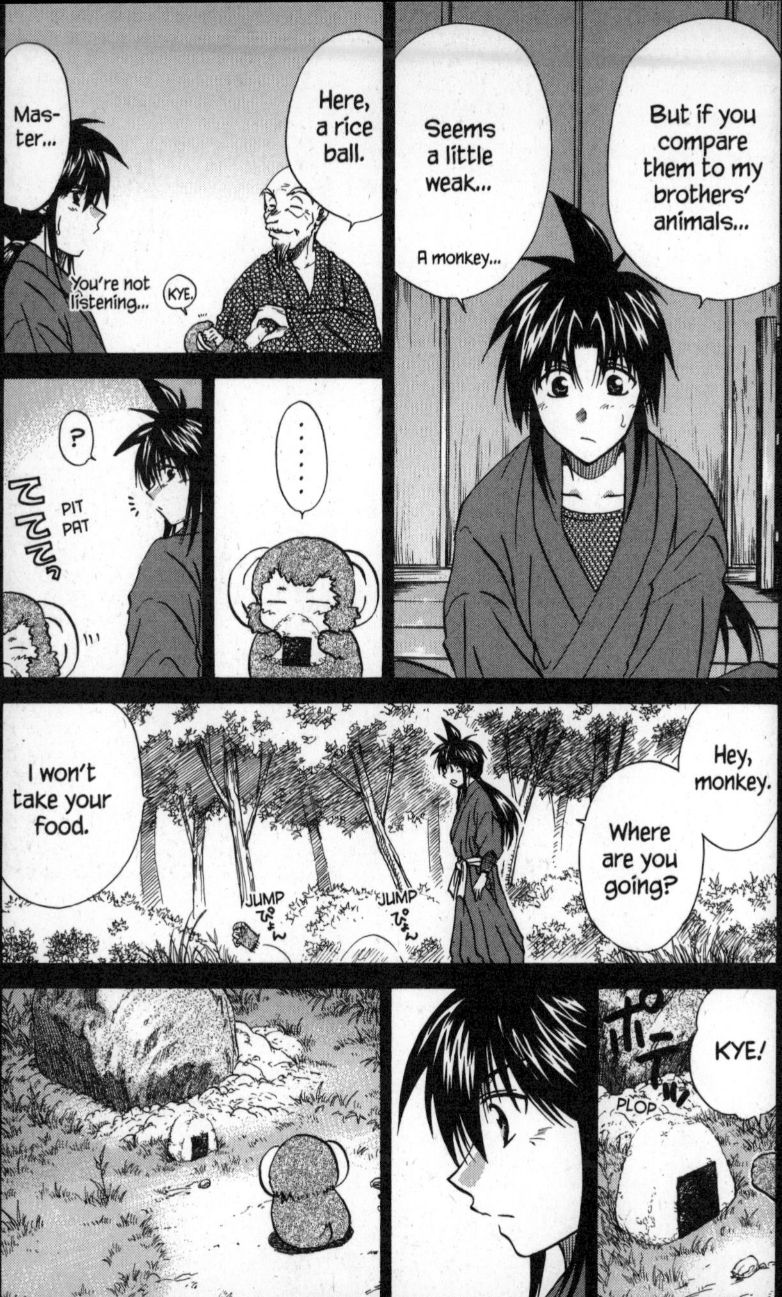
But if you compare them to my brothers' animals...
Seems a little weak...
A monkey...
Here, a rice ball.
Mas-ter...
KYE.
You're not listening...
......
?
PIT PAT
Hey, monkey.
Where are you going?
I won't take your food.
JUMP ぴょん
JUMP ぴょん
KYE!
PLOP

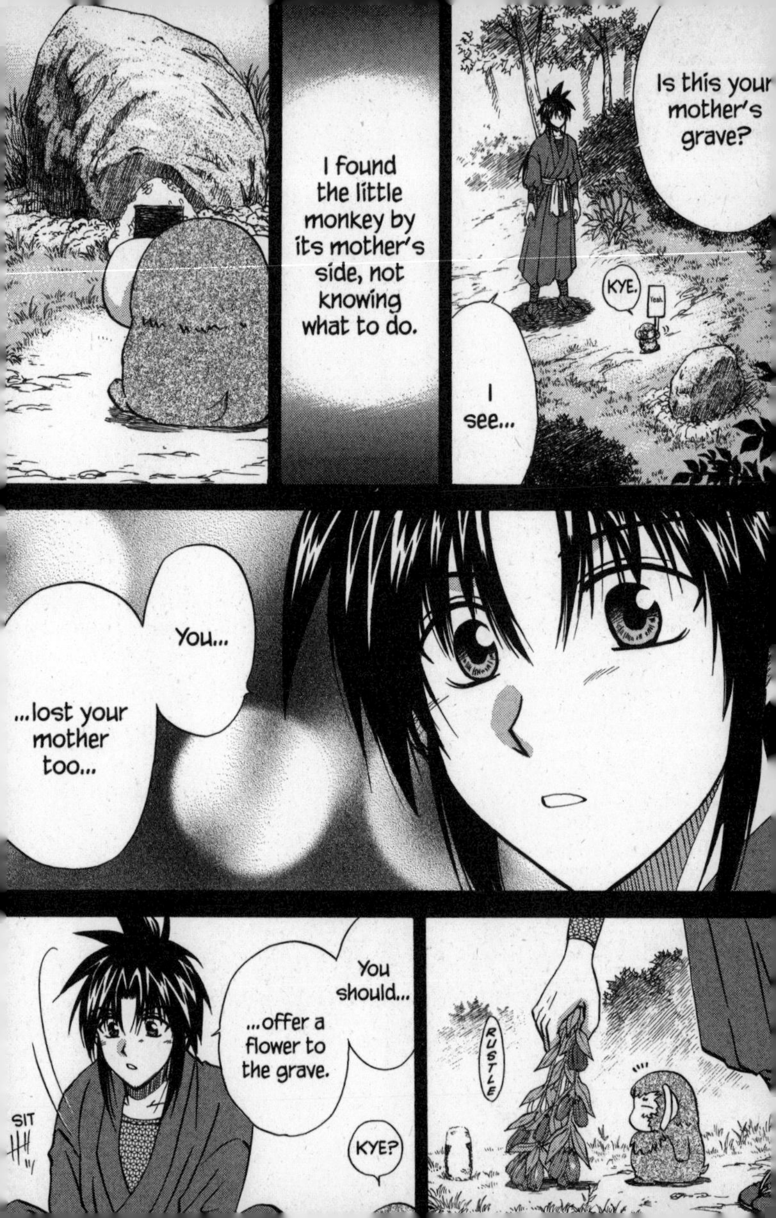
Is this your mother's grave?
KYE.
Yeah
I see...
I found the little monkey by its mother's side, not knowing what to do.
You...
...lost your mother too...
RUSTLE
You should...
...offer a flower to the grave.
KYE?
SIT

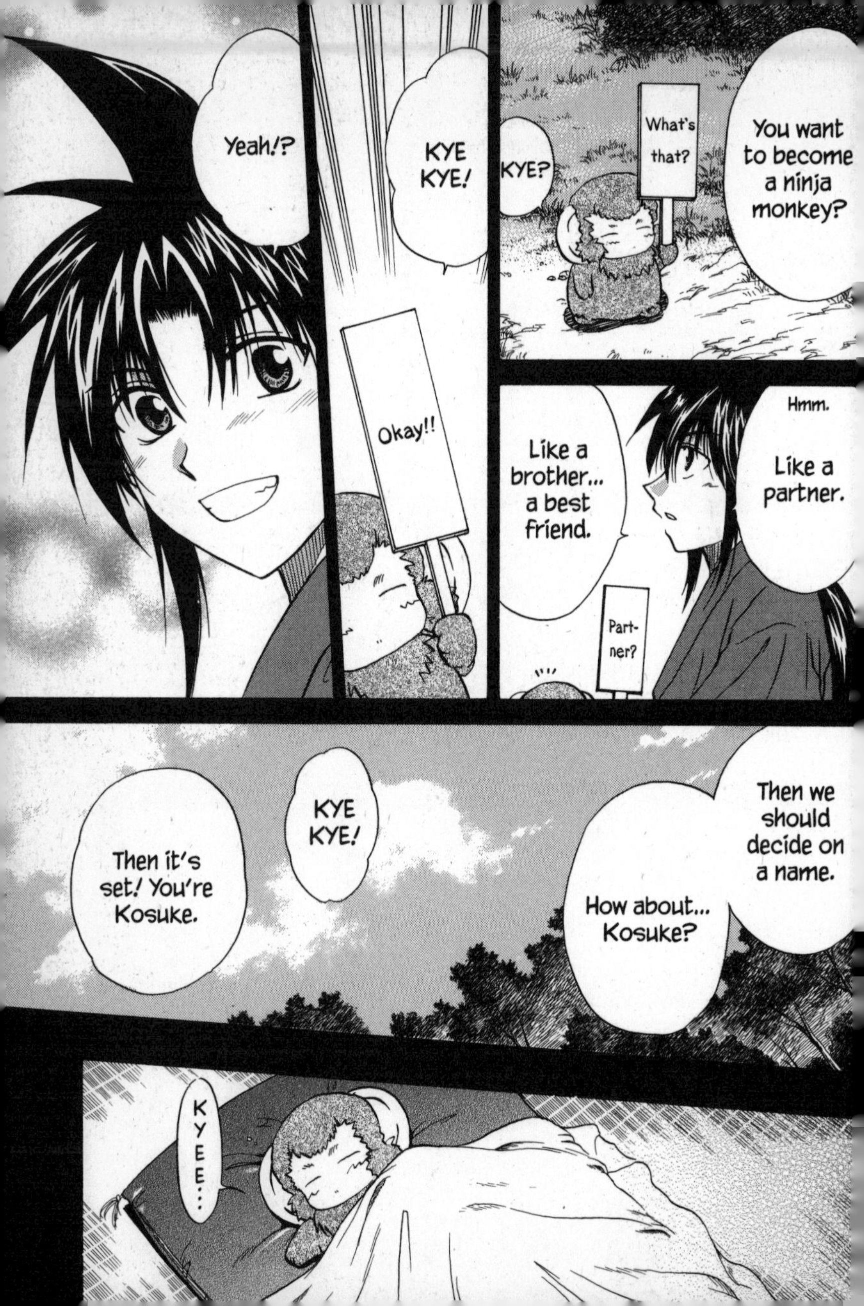
You want to become a ninja monkey?
What's that?
KYE?
Hmm.
Like a partner.
Like a brother... a best friend.
Partner?
KYE KYE!
Okay!!
Yeah!?
Then we should decide on a name.
How about... Kosuke?
KYE KYE!
Then it's set! You're Kosuke.
KYEE...

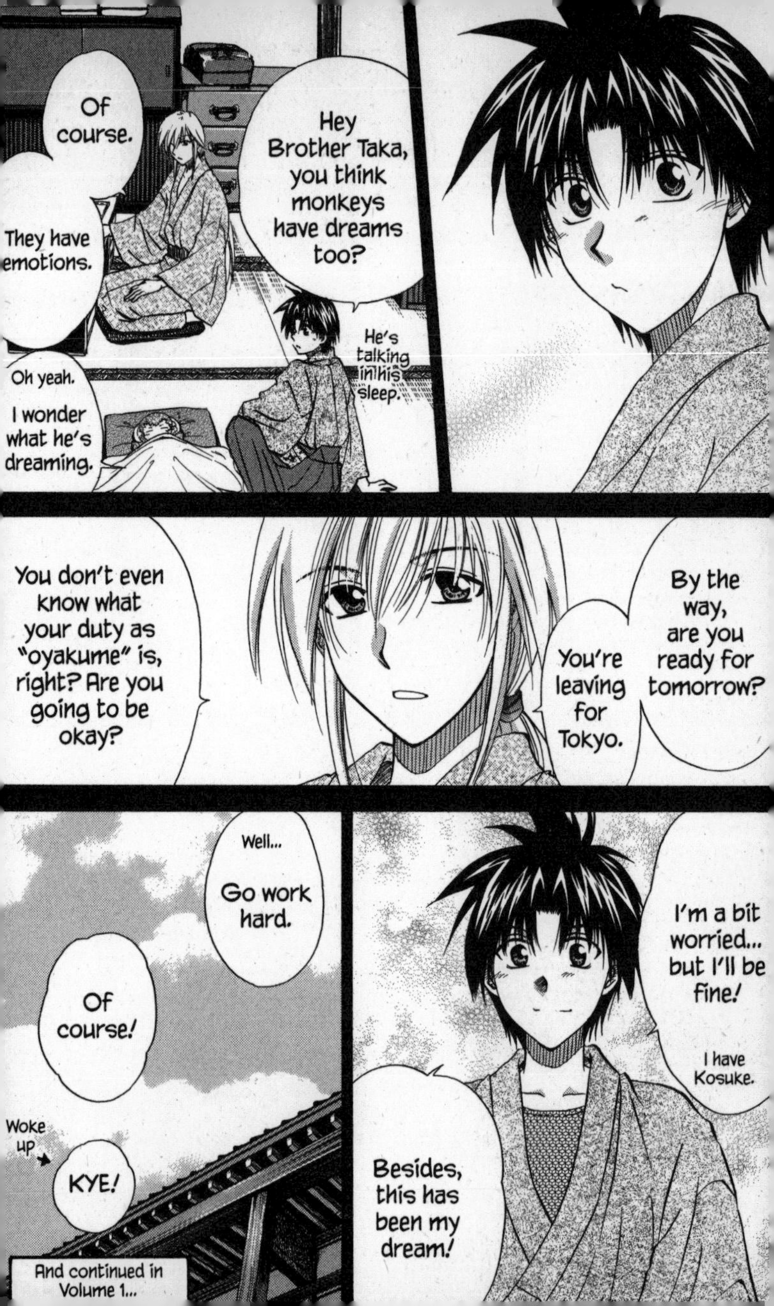
Hey Brother Taka, you think monkeys have dreams too?
Of course.
They have emotions.
He's talking in his sleep.
Oh yeah.
I wonder what he's dreaming.
By the way, are you ready for tomorrow?
You're leaving for Tokyo.
You don't even know what your duty as "oyakume" is, right? Are you going to be okay?
I'm a bit worried... but I'll be fine!
I have Kosuke.
Besides, this has been my dream!
Well...
Go work hard.
Of course!
Woke up
KYE!
And continued in Volume 1...

Bonus and Afterword Page

This is Segami. Yay, 2 digits!! (laugh) I finally got to Volume 10! Only a little bit more until the ending. Everyone, please hang on until the end...

About Ninjas, Part 10

I recently found a "chain sickle" at a shop! Of course I bought it immediately (laugh). But for safety reasons, it doesn't cut. When I was looking at it in the store, a lady came to talk to me.

Lady: "What is that?"
Me: "It's a chain sickle."
Lady: "Oh my...you're like a demon girl."
Me: "Huh..."

Demon girl? Was she talking about me?
The lady left, smiling...
A demon...really... Well, I guess a demon *girl* is better than a demon *hag*... But it's unusual to have a stranger call you a demon.
Well, I guess it was an interesting experience?
Well! This year I will hope to be a demon for work! I have to look on the bright side! (→ good thing) Oh...I also bought a Fortune Cat. ♡
It has a cute face. ☆

About Traveling

Whenever I have time, I go on a short trip! But lately... I feel my strength isn't keeping up with me. My travel mate is always worried about me. This isn't good!

In order to play, I need strength and endurance!! But I have no time to go to the gym!! (cry) ...So for now I try to get sleep before I take a trip.

...So that at least I don't fall dead asleep in a ferry...(sweat)

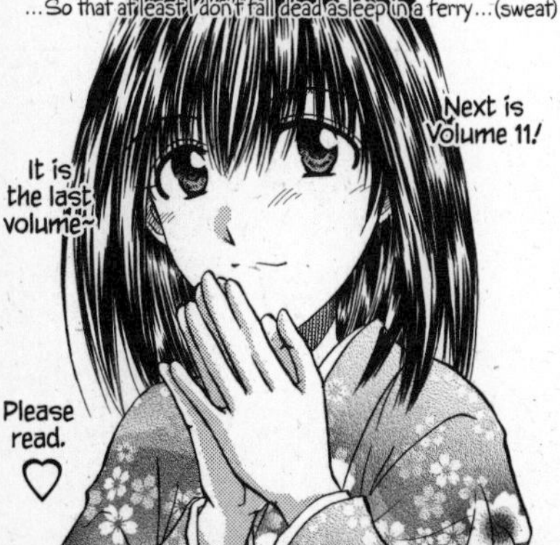

Next is Volume 11!
It is the last volume~
Please read. ♡

Lately

My editor, Morita-san, has moved to a different division. I've known him for ten years, and I'm really sad... To show my appreciation, I will continue to work hard! Thank you very much!!

Lately, part 2

I got into sort of an accident... At a train station, my foot got caught in the space between the train and the platform. A stranger pushed my feet (→ accidentally) and I was surprised but...the people around me were surprised even more (laugh).

Anyway, I was able to get it out fast, so they didn't have to stop operations, but I still have a bruise on my leg... These accidents are bound to happen, but I hope they don't happen to me anymore.

Thank you

Thank you for all of the letters!! There are so many regulars!! (laugh)

When this book comes out, I hope to have responded to all of them (I hope). I'm sorry it takes so long!

I'll continue to work hard, so please stay with me.

Special Thanks!

Assistants: Tanaka-kun Oshima-chan Takasou-san
Editor: Mr Morita Mr Yonemura
Comics Editor: Houdo-san
And all of the readers!!

瀬上あきら
Akira Segami

About the Author

Akira Segami's first manga was published by Shogakukan in 1996. He went on to do a few other small projects, including two short stories entitled "Kagetora" in 2001 and 2002. The character proved to be popular with fans, so Segami began his first ongoing series, Kagetora, with Kodansha in 2003. The series continues to run today.

Translation Notes

Japanese is a tricky language for most Westerners, and translation is often more art than science. For your edification and reading pleasure, here are notes on some of the places where we could have gone in a different direction with our translation of the work, or where a Japanese cultural reference is used.

Butsuma, page 59
A *butsuma* is a room in Japanese households where the Buddhist altar is set up. It is a location where family members or visitors can go to give their respects to the deceased.

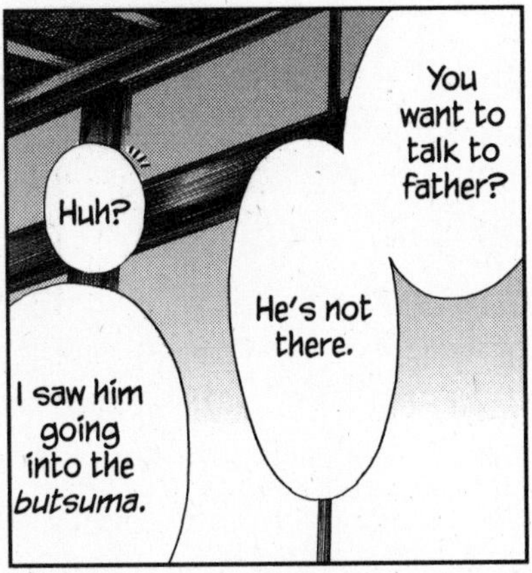
You want to talk to father?
Huh?
He's not there.
I saw him going into the *butsuma*.

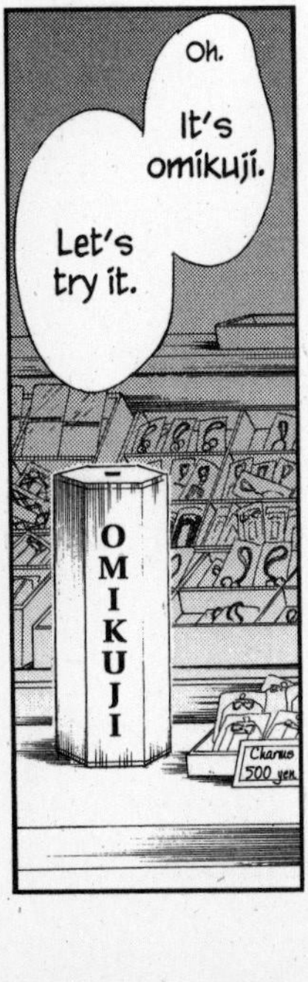
Oh.
It's omikuji.
Let's try it.
OMIKUJI
Charms 500 yen

Omikuji, page 98
Omikuji are fortunes written on thin strips of paper. They are sold at temples and shrines. Japanese people will usually buy one on New Year's Day to see what kind of fortune they will have for the year. First you shake a container with bamboo sticks. One will come out of the hole in the container, which will have a number on it. You take a slip of paper from one of the drawers with your number. *Omikuji* fortunes range from good to bad in six to seven levels.

CLUNK...
かたん…

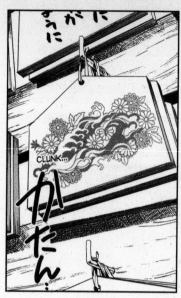

***Ema*, page 102**

At a shrine, there are wooden plates called *ema,* and visitors write their wishes on them. They then leave them at the shrine in the hope that their wishes come true. Most people wish for good health, success in business, passing entrance exams, love, or wealth.

Career/School Options, page 122

In Japanese high schools, they make you fill out a paper to indicate what you want to do after you graduate. Then your teacher will talk to you about what you need to achieve those goals. It is like guidance counseling.

.Career/School Options
1st Choice
2nd Choice
3rd Choic

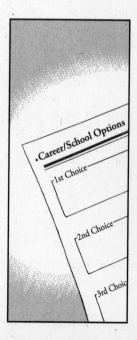

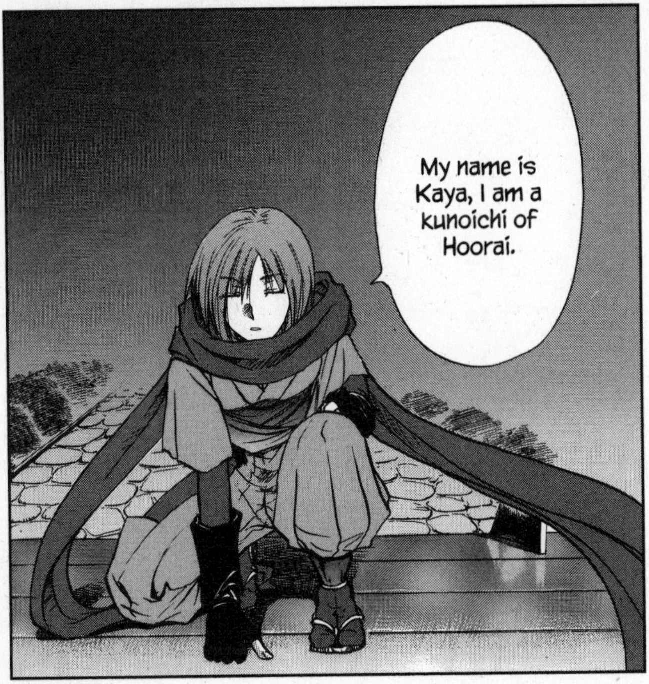
My name is Kaya, I am a kunoichi of Hoorai.

***Kunoichi*, page 144**

A *kunoichi* is a female ninja. They were given psychological skills to seduce men who had political power. They were mainly hired to collect information, often disguising themselves as dancers, geisha, and prostitutes.

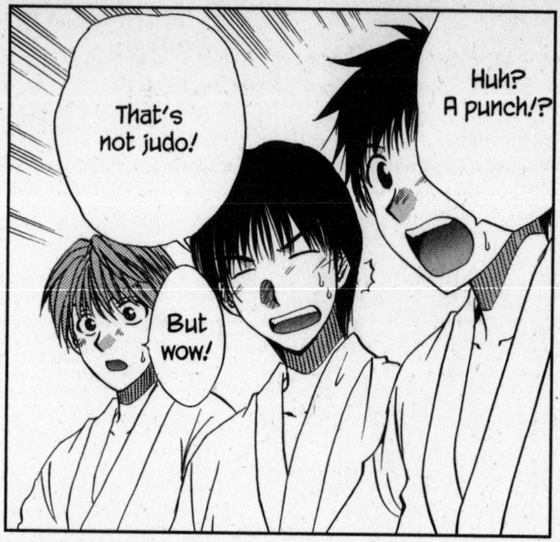
Huh? A punch!?
That's not judo!
But wow!

Kaya's moves, page 163

Ono here is surprised because Kaya tried to hit Kagetora. This is a karate move and not a judo move. In judo, you would try to grab your opponent rather than hitting them.

Kazama Brother names, page 184

The "rou" in Shiroumaru is the kanji for wolf. The "taka" in Takaou is the kanji for hawk. And "tora" in Kagetora is the kanji for tiger. It's not mentioned anywhere in the manga what animal their father Tenshu carries, but we assume it's an eagle, for the "shu" in Tenshu is the kanji for eagle.

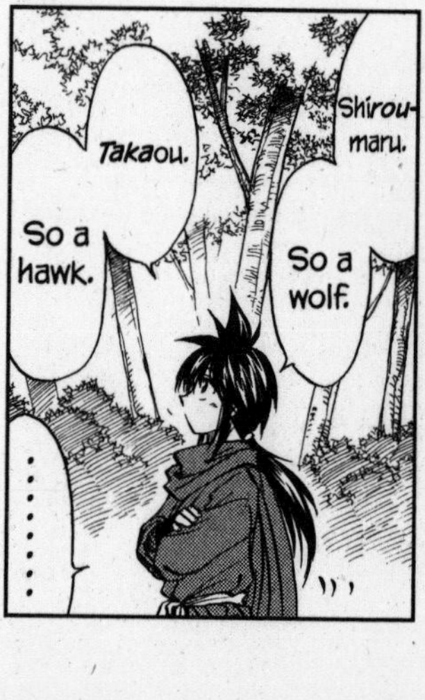
Shirou-maru.
Takaou.
So a wolf.
So a hawk.

Preview of Kagetora, Volume 11
(the last volume!)

We're pleased to present you a preview from Kagetora, Volume 11. Please check our website (www.delreymanga.com) to see when this volume will be available in English. For now you'll have to make do with Japanese!

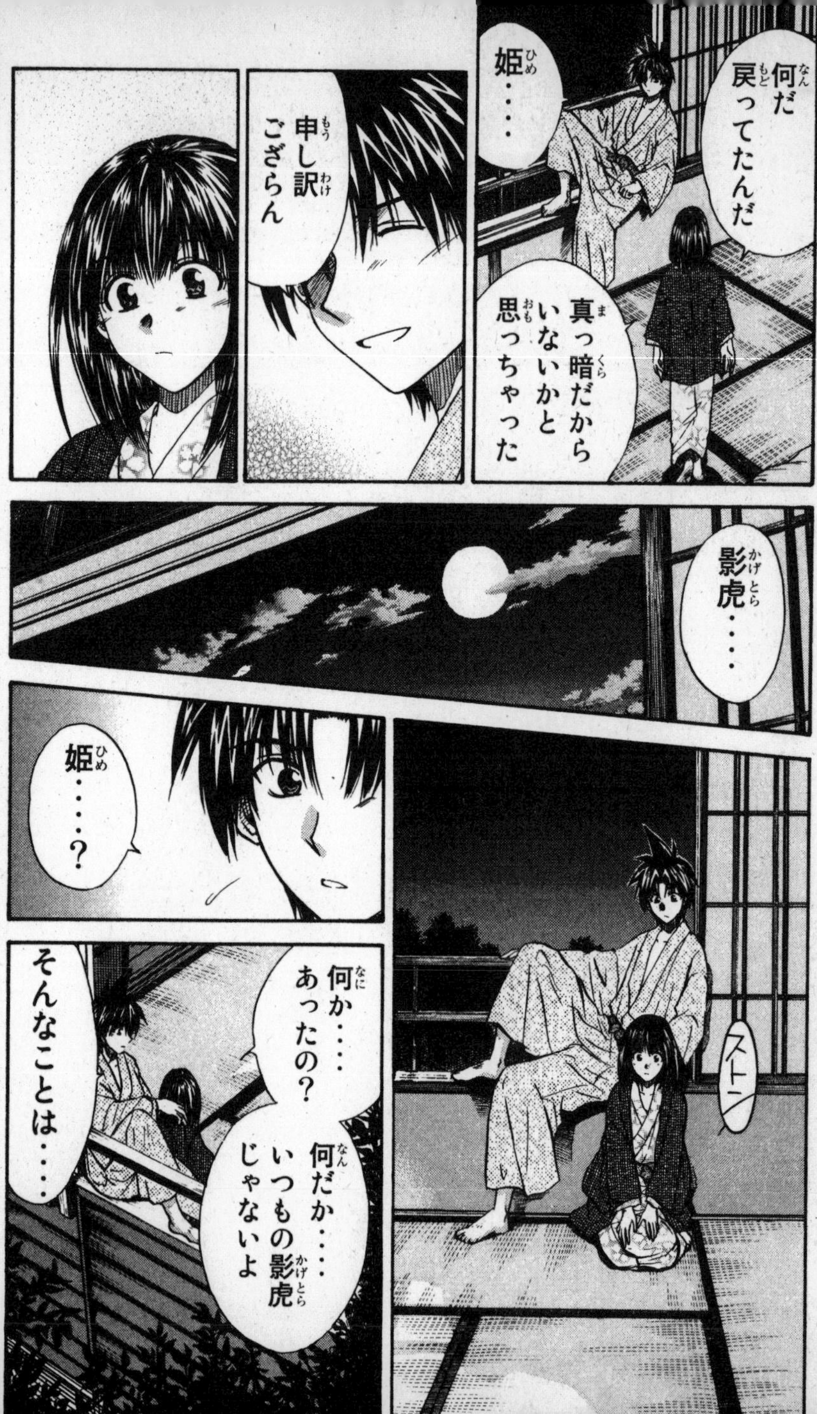

何だ戻ってたんだ
姫……
真っ暗だからいないかと思っちゃった
申し訳ござらん
影虎……
ストン
姫……？
何か……あったの？
何だか……いつもの影虎じゃないよ
そんなことは……

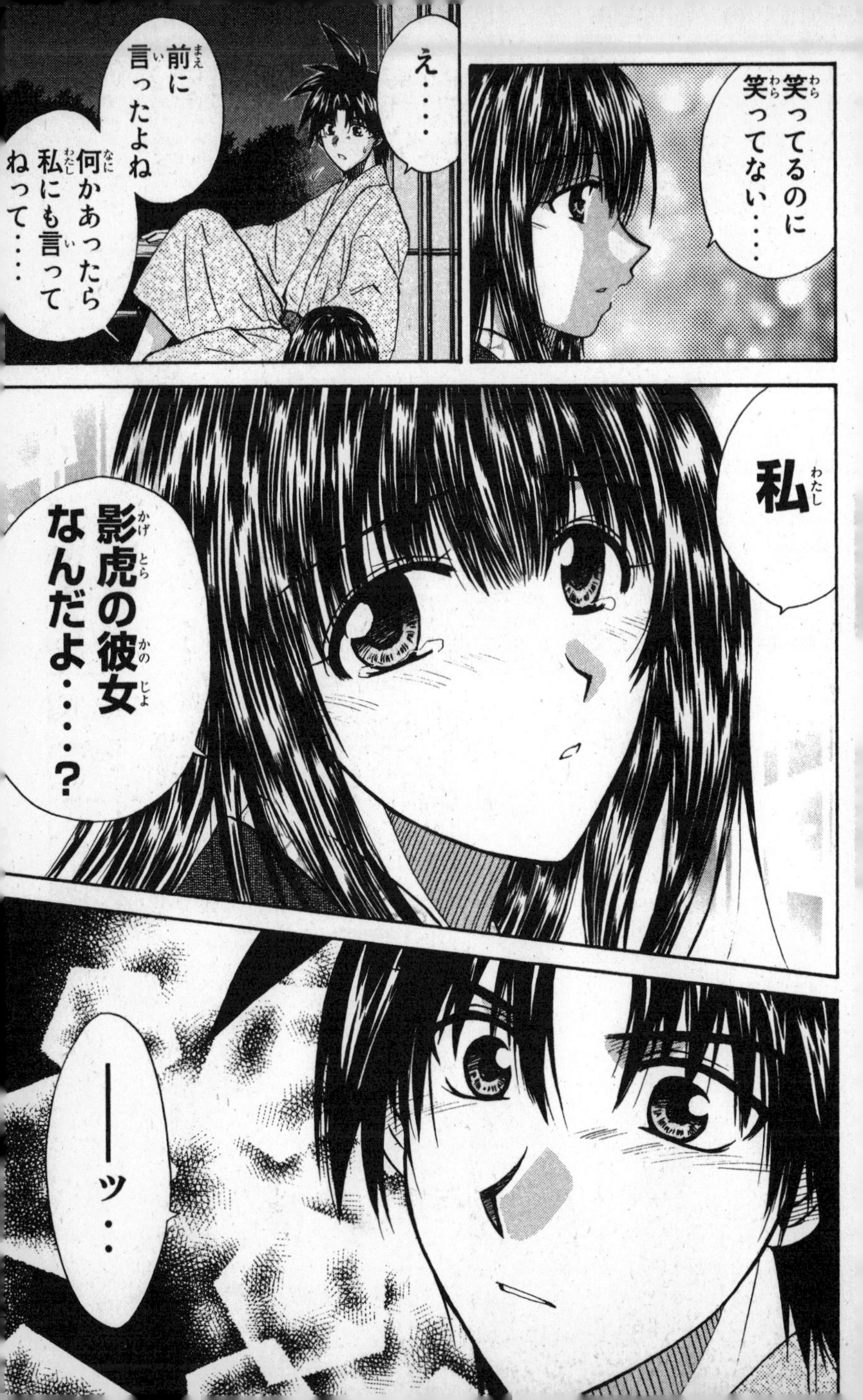
笑ってるのに笑ってない・・・・
え・・・・
前に言ったよね何かあったら私にも言ってねって・・・・
私
影虎の彼女なんだよ・・・?
ーーッ・・

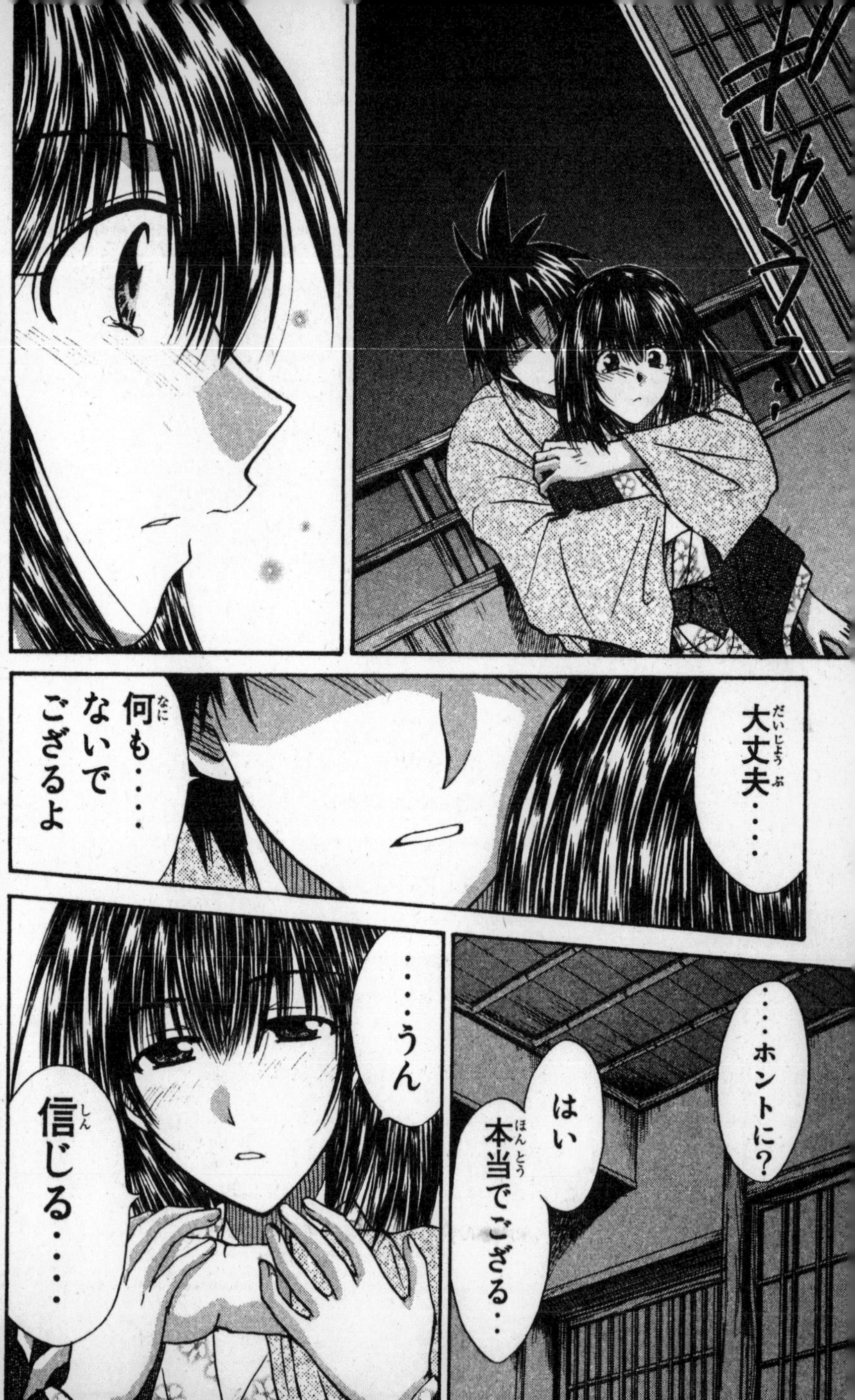
大丈夫……
何も……ないでござるよ
……ホントに？
はい
本当でござる……
……うん
信じる……

TOMARE!

[STOP!]

You are going the wrong way!

Manga is a completely different
type of reading experience.

To start at the *beginning*, go to the *end*!

That's right! Authentic manga is read the traditional Japanese way—from right to left. Exactly the *opposite* of how American books are r̶e̶a̶d̶. ̶I̶t̶'̶s̶ ̶e̶a̶s̶y̶ ̶t̶o̶ ̶f̶o̶l̶l̶o̶w̶.̶ ̶J̶u̶s̶t̶ ̶g̶o̶ ̶t̶o̶ the other end of the book, a̶n̶d̶ read each page—and each panel—from right side to left side, starting at the top right. Now you're experiencing manga as it was meant to be.

3 1901 05263 6026